International Labor Standards

The Expert Group on Development Issues (the EGDI) was formed by the Swedish government in 1995. The group consists of a number of international experts in development-related academic areas along with Swedish policy makers. The group initiates projects of importance to the development debate. More information about the EGDI may be found on the website: *www.egdi.gov.se*

International Labor Standards

History, Theory, and Policy Options

Edited by

Kaushik Basu
Henrik Horn
Lisa Román
Judith Shapiro

350 Main Street, Malden, MA 02148-5018, USA
108 Cowley Road, Oxford OX4 1JF, UK
550 Swanston Street, Carlton, Victoria 3053, Australia
Kurfürstendamm 57, 10707 Berlin, Germany

First published 2003 by Blackwell Publishing Ltd

Library of Congress Cataloging-in-Publication Data

International labor standards : history, theory, and policy options / Edited by Kaushik Basu,
Henrik Horn, Lisa Román, and Judith Shapiro.
    p. pm
    Papers based on a conference held in Stockholm in August 2001.
    Includes bibliographical references and index.
    ISBN 1-4051-0555-0 (hbk : alk. paper) – ISBN 1-4051-0556-9 (pbk : alk. paper)
       1. Labor policy – Congresses.   2. Labor – Standards – Congresses.   3. Labor laws
    and legislation, International – Congresses.   I. Basu, Kaushik.
HD7795 .I554 2003
331.12′02′18–dc21   2002006147

A catalogue record for this title is available from the British Library.

Set in 10/12pt Bell
by Graphicraft Limited, Hong Kong
Printed and bound in the United Kingdom
by MPG Books Ltd, Bodmin, Cornwall

For further information on
Blackwell Publishing, visit our website:
http://www.blackwellpublishing.com

Contents

Tables and Figures

Tables

Figures

Acronyms

BGMEA	Bangladesh Garment Manufacturers Association
FFE	Food for Education
GDP	Gross Domestic Product
IFPRI	International Food Policy Research Institute
ILO	International Labor Organization
IPEC	International Program on the Elimination of Child Labor
LFP	Labor Force Participation
NGO	Non-Government Organization
PETI	Brazilian Child Labor Eradication Program
PROGRESA	Program for Education, Health, and Nutrition
UNESCO	United Nations Educational, Scientific, and Cultural Organization
UNICEF	United Nations International Children's Emergency Fund
USDOL	United States Department of Labor
WTO	World Trade Organization

Contributors

Drusilla Brown is Associate Professor of Economics at Tufts University, Medford, Massachussets, USA.

Alan V. Deardorff is Professor of Economics and Public Policy at the University of Michigan, Ann Arbor, Michigan, USA

Tore Ellingsen is Professor of Economics at the Stockholm School of Economics, Sweden.

Stanley Engerman is Professor of Economics and Professor of History at the University of Rochester, New York, USA

Jane Humphries is Reader in Economic History at All Souls College, Oxford University, United Kingdom

Alan B. Krueger is Professor of Economics and Public Affairs at Princeton University, New Jersey, USA.

Luis-Felipe López Calva is Assistant Professor at El Colegio de Mexico, Mexico City, Mexico.

Petros C. Mavroidis is Professor of Law at the University of Neuchatel, Switzerland

Karl-Ove Moene is Professor at the Department of Economics at the University of Oslo, Norway.

Nirvrkar Singh is Professor of Economics at the University of California, Santa Cruz, USA

T. N. Srinivasan is Professor of Economics at Yale University, New Haven, Connecticut, USA

Robert W. Staiger is Professor of Economics at the University of Wisconsin, Madison, USA

Robert Stern is Professor of Economics and Public Affairs (emeritus) at the University of Michigan, Ann Arbor, USA

Michael Wallerstein is Professor of Political Science at the Northwestern University, Chicago, Illinois, USA

L. Alan Winters is Professor of Economics and the University of Sussex, United Kingdom

PART I
Introduction

Introduction

Kaushik Basu, Henrik Horn,
Lisa Román, and Judith Shapiro

The call for "international labor standards" has been one of the more controversial proposals in contemporary global policy debates. These proposals have varied greatly in their intended coverage. Often they build on some notion of "core labor standards," which include the prohibition of forced labor, the prohibition of discrimination in employment, the right to freedom of association, the right to bargain collectively, and the prohibition of exploitative child labor. But these proposals often also include more ambitious goals.

Few would dispute the need for at least some government legislation in the area of labor standards. Indeed, virtually all civil societies have legislated to assure workers certain minimal rights and to prevent or dissuade certain kinds of activities, such as ones involving exposure to excessive hazards or ones involving child labor. But though at an abstract level all would agree that these are aims that should be upheld, debate and controversy become the rule as soon as we get into specifics. What constitutes "forced" labor? When can child work be described as "exploitative?" How should these standards be assured? What each society considers to be a minimal standard, to be upheld by the state, also in practice varies a great deal. In addition, in poor countries, even agreed-upon standards are poorly enforced.

The controversial aspect of the proposals for international labor standards is largely the idea that they should be *internationally* agreed and enforced. In practice, this is likely to imply that poorer countries will be induced to set higher standards than what they would have chosen unilaterally, and presumably also that there would be some type of sanctions, should they violate these standards. Such an outcome can obviously be given very different interpretations. On the one hand, it is often argued that it would help the poorer countries out of a "Prisoners' Dilemma" type of situation, where the competition among poor countries for export markets leads to too low standards, and where there is need for some external help in breaking out of an undesirable situation.

Pitted against this view, however, are those who argue that these proposals will actually hurt the poor. In addition, it is argued that not only will such standards hurt poor countries if implemented, but that the proposals are partly intended to serve protectionist interests in import-competing sectors in developed countries, at the expense of these societies at large. According to this view, it has been easy for two sets of people, to share the same platform, to appear behind the same banner of concern and genuine commitment, but with very different agendas – one group concerned about the condition of workers the world over, and the other inspired by its perception of its own, narrow self-interest.

Recognizing that the debate had reached an unproductive impasse, this book grew out of a project, which sought, above all, to move the debate forward. To do this we had first to acknowledge the fact that the issues at stake are complicated, not only in their political aspects, but also from an economist's point of view – interventions made with the best of intentions may have desirable effects, but may also harm those they were meant to protect. Given the importance of the issues at stake, any policy decisions should be based on a thorough understanding of their likely effects. The purpose of this book is to contribute to such an understanding, by addressing four central questions:

1. What can we learn from economic history? – How did the labor standards movement evolve in the past, both domestically and internationally?
2. What do contemporary economic theories tell us about the possible impact of international labor standards?
3. So much has been written about child labor – but what solid empirical evidence do economists have about its incidence, causes, and effects?
4. Finally, what kinds of global institutions do we have, or need, to enforce any agreement on labor standards? In particular, what should be the role of the ILO and the WTO?

This book seeks to answer these questions by putting together between the covers of a single book what the best research in these areas can offer us. In each of the four main parts of the book (each one devoted to the four questions just laid out above), the first chapter is the main paper that was commissioned on the subject, and the two following papers are the comments of the two conference discussants, inspired by the main paper.

The history of labor standards is developed by Stanley Engerman of Rochester University, and commented on by Jane Humphries of All Souls College, Oxford University, and Karl-Ove Moene and Michael Wallerstein of the University of Oslo. Theories of international labor standards are presented by Nirvikar Singh, University of California, Santa Cruz. Comments are made by T. N. Srinivasan, Yale University and Tore Ellingsen, Stockholm School of Economics. An account of child labor issues is given by Drusilla Brown, Tufts University, and Alan Deardorff and Robert Stern of Michigan University. Alan Krueger, Princeton University, and Luis-Felipe López-Calva, of El Colegio de Mexico, discuss this aspect of labor standards. Finally, a proposal for a way to handle the international organization and enforcement of labor standards is given by Robert Staiger, University of Wisconsin. This contribution is discussed by Alan Winters, University of Sussex, and Petros Mavroidis, University of Neuchatel.

The book has grown out of a conference that we organized in Stockholm on August 23 and 24, 2001. The conference was sponsored by the Ministry for Foreign Affairs, Government of Sweden, and organized under the auspices of the Expert Group on Development Issues (EGDI), a government-funded but independent group of international experts with the mandate to initiate projects of relevance to the development debate. Our first thanks go to Gun-Britt Andersson, State Secretary, Ministry for Foreign Affairs, and Chairperson of the EGDI, for her keen interest in the project, deep intellectual commitment to the subject, and the good sense to leave it to us, as editors, to decide what to include and how to deal with the subject matter. Those hoping to learn about the official position of the Swedish Government on this sensitive subject will have to look elsewhere. The EGDI was conceived of and founded by Mats Karlsson, then State Secretary at the Ministry for Foreign Affairs. Though he was not involved by the time the International Labor Standards project was started, we want to record our appreciation of Mats' effort and commitment to policy-significant research, which led to the setting up of the EGDI.

In organizing the conference, we wanted to get some of the best researchers available not only to write the papers but also to discuss and comment on them. We all took away a great deal from the diverse comments and criticisms that the various participants made. These have, of course, influenced the revising of the papers that the authors undertook after the conference, but will also figure in a separate paper that Gote Hansson, Lund University, is preparing for the EGDI and which will, among other things, sum up the discussion from the floor and in the final round table session. We would here like to extend our particular gratitude to the invited participants whose comments are not published in this volume: Sarah Bachman, Asia/Pacific Research Center, Stanford University, Richard Blackhurst, Graduate Institute of International Studies in Geneva, and formerly with the WTO, Gösta Edgren, former ambassador to the Vietnam and formerly with the ILO, Ulf Edström, the International Secretariat of the Swedish Trade Union Confederation (LO), Lotta Fogde, State Secretary for International Trade, Policy and Strategic Export Control, Swedish Ministry for Foreign Affairs, Francis Maupain, the ILO, Geneva, Pradeep Mehta, Consumer Unity Trust Society, India, Ebrahim Patel, South African Clothing and Textiles Workers Union, South Africa, G. Rajasekaran, Malaysian Trade Union Congress, Malaysia, and Kari Tapiola, the ILO, Geneva. In addition we are most thankful to active and valuable contributions by the other participants at the seminar in August.

International labor standards is a subject where policy and research need to stand very close to each other. Our aim and hope, as editors, is that this book will be useful not only to students of trade, development, international relations and labor economics, but also to policy makers in government and in international organizations.

PART II
The Evolution of Labor Standards

Chapter 1

The History and Political Economy of International Labor Standards

Stanley L. Engerman

Introduction

Laws regulating the relations between masters and servants, or employers and employees as they latter became, have a long history in the European world, influencing wage rates, hours of work, and working conditions. In the fourteenth century, for example, the British imposed laws after the Black Death setting maximum wages as well as constraints on migration and settlement.[1] Legal rules set the terms for the rights and customary responsibilities of villains, while other legislation, such as the Poor Laws, influenced the treatment and behavior of the population, even when not specifically concerned with what we might today consider labor standards.[2] Laws as early as the sixteenth and seventeenth centuries regarding the treatment of slaves in the New World colonies of European nations often specified minimum consumption requirements, hours of work, and acceptable punishments.[3] Laws regarding transoceanic movement of people, initially of slaves from Africa, which specified conditions of shipment and treatment, later were also designed for indentured servants, and by the early nineteenth century these were more broadly applied, with somewhat different terms, to all free passengers.[4] The mercantilistic policies of European nations, often concerned with increasing population, provided for measures of public health and emigration restrictions, which impacted on the living and working conditions of the laboring classes.[5]

These, however, are not generally considered to have been concerned with labor standards as looked at today. Some, such as passenger regulations and public health measures, do not deal with the process of working. Most, however, are seen to have a different origin that those of the nineteenth and twentieth centuries. These early laws were generally imposed by the elites, in their own interests, and, although they may have provided some benefits to the non-elite, their primary intent was not to be benefits to the workers and others in the population. The later policies were intended to directly benefit the workers, whether these policies were advocated by the workers themselves or else by some reform groups within society. The modern story of labor standards generally starts in England in 1802, and is seen as an attempt to offset the social costs that accompanied the development of industrialization.[6] While there were argued-for benefits to factory owners, their main purpose was to protect members of the working class, or at least some of them, and there was frequent opposition by employers to such legislation and its enforcement.

Categories of Labor Standards

The present-day discussion of labor standards, both internal to a state or nation and international, involves a number of quite different aspects of the employer–employee relationship, and therefore there may be differences in the extent to which satisfaction of all desired ends can be achieved. We can divide the present-day aspects of labor standards most broadly into three categories. The most basic has been labor market conditions – wages (now minimum, not as earlier, maximum) and hours of work (maximum amount, as well as the specific hours of work, particularly night work). There has generally been a sharp distinction made among the different age and sex components of the labor force, with different provision for children, women, and adult males (See table 1.1 for a survey of European factory legislation.) Second, laws dictate acceptable working conditions for the factory – safety, sanitation, elimination of work hazards, and factory-floor arrangements, all intended to provide a healthy work environment. Third, laws specify the general range of arrangements permitted between labor and employer, including rules regarding rights of association, the formation and mainten- ance of labor unions, permanent bargaining rights, the conciliation and arbitration of disputes, terms of apprenticeship, and the more general terms of labor contracts (including laws such as the English Masters and Servants acts which regulated, among other things, hiring, firing, and quitting prac- tices). At times, however, there are trade-offs between ends, and there may also be some inconsistencies in achieving these goals. There may be differ- ences between the legislative imposition of specific terms and the establish- ing of rights of collective bargaining by unions to set the terms they desire. More frequently, in the past, was a perceived conflict between the coverage of government legislation and the rights of individuals to choose their own preferred contractual package.

The most general statement of core labor standards, presented by the ILO in 1999, includes:

- freedom of association and the effective recognition of the right to collective bargaining;
- the elimination of all forms of forced or compulsory labor;
- the effective abolition of child labor; and
- the elimination of discrimination in respect of employment occupation.

Note that these core standards make no direct statements about wages or hours.

In general, there are now some very basic terms of internationally agreed upon labor standards, reflecting both moral and economic beliefs. These include no slavery, serfdom, or other form of forced labor; no sales of goods produced by convict labor (certainly none to compete with free labor); free emigration and (unless it causes economic difficulties to residents) relatively few barriers to immigration; limited child labor so as to provide more education: and, in general, no discrimination on the basis of race, religion, gender, age, disability, political opinion, nationality, social origin, etc. unless these forms of discrimination or coercion might be considered to be either necessary or desired (as in wartime) or to recognize different needs of some specific groups.[7] More recently the concept of labor standards has expanded to explicitly include practices such as sexual harassment and related aspects of the workplace regime.

The Sources of Agitation for Improved Labor Standards

There have been several sources of agitation concerning labor standards, and the nature of the pressures for legislation have shifted over time. Even if different groups have the same professed aim, there can be grounds for skepticism as to what end is ultimately desired by any group. In general, the argument for imposing standards has been to protect certain individuals, who are, either legally or economically, too weak to be properly treated within the market economy, or else who lack the political voice to be able themselves to influence legislation. As laboring classes achieve more economic and political power, they might pursue enhanced labor standards via political and governmental actions rather than by the perceived-to-be more expensive method of piecemeal change via market and collective labor actions taken with individual firms or industries.

The modern push for improved laboring standards in England at the turn of the nineteenth century, at the same time as the expansion of the antislavery

Table 1.1a Factory laws of European countries

	France	Belgium	Holland
DATES OF EARLIEST FACTORY LEGISLATION. DATES OF LAWS IN FORCE.	1841. (1848, 12 hours' day regulation.) 1892. (Modifications from 1893 to 1898.)	1889. 1889. (With additions, 1892–1898.)	1815. (Sunday Rest.) 1874. 1889. (With additions, 1891–1898.)
TO WHAT PLACES THE LAWS APPLY.	*Factories, works, coal, and metalliferous mines, quarries, sheds, workshops, and all industrial establishments connected with them, whether public or private, lay or religious; state or charity workshops included. The Law does not apply to agricultural work and transport industries, nor to shops or bureaux. Domestic workshops are also excluded, but come under the inspector's authority if they deal with unhealthy trades or if power is used.	All steam-mills, factories, and works, industrial establishments private or public, educational (technical) or charitable; all mines (coal and metalliferous), quarries, yards, ports, stations, transport industries (sea or land); all brickfields and tile works not using power; all unhealthy trades, and all trades using power (steam or mechanical). Domestic workshops are excepted unless using power or dealing with unhealthy trades.	All factories and workshops, defined as places, open or shut, where articles are prepared for sale or use; and all industries, great or small. EXCEPTIONS: (1) Agriculture, horticulture, forestry, cattle raising, and the peat industry; (2) occupations in or for the trade of an employer with whom the worker lives, which are done outside the workshop, in so far as they belong to work usually done in the household or stables; (3) kitchens and pharmacies. Also barge and fishing industries, save as touching the age of admission of children; State, military, professional, and educational establishments and prisons.

		12.	12.
AGE OF ADMISSION OF CHILDREN.	13. (Or 12, if furnished with medical and educational certificates.)	12.	12.
DURATION OF WORKING-DAY.			
Children.	10 hours.† (For those under 16. Overtime usually forbidden.)	12 hours.§ (For those under 14.)	11 hours.‖ (For those under 14.)
Young Persons.	11 hours.† (And not more than 60 per week for those under 18. Overtime usually forbidden to both sexes under 18.)	12 hours.§ (For boys under 16 and girls under 21.) [Subsequent trade by trade legislation has in effect reduced the hours for all under 16 to an average of 10½.]	11 hours.‖ (For those under 16.)
Women.	11 hours.†		11 hours.‖

* The term "Factory" is translated throughout as a simple reproduction of the word used in the law. The meaning differs from country to country, but is not always defined in the law; for example, it is not defined in the German Industrial Code.
† Cut by a rest or rests amounting to 1 hour at least.
§ Cut by rests of a total of 1½ hours. In many industries the midday interval must be 1 hour at least. However short the working-day, a rest of ¼ hour after every 4 hours.
‖ Cut by a rest of at least 1 hour between 11 a.m. and 3 p.m.

Table 1.1b Factory laws of European countries

	Germany	Austria	Hungary
DATES OF EARLIEST FACTORY LEGISLATION.	1839 (Prussia). 1869 (North Germany), which 1870 extended to the Empire.	1787 (Forbad children under 9 to work in factories). 1842 (Factory age raised to 12).	1840.
DATES OF LAWS IN FORCE.	1891. (With additions up to 1897.)	1859. Modified by Laws 1883 (March) and 1885 (March), the latter limited the male adult working day. Latest changes in 1897.	1884. Is the main law called the Industrial Law. Additions in 1891 and 1893; with minor changes up to 1895.
TO WHAT PLACES THE LAWS APPLY.	Factories, mills, and workshops using power: underground quarries, mines, saltpits; smelting houses, timber and other building yards and dockyards; brick and tile kilns, mines and quarries, which are worked above ground and are not merely temporary. Domestic workshops are formally omitted. By an Imperial Decree of 1897 regulation is extended to ready-made clothing workshops—*save* where only members of the family are employed, or where the manufacture is only occasional. By Art. 154 the provisions may be extended by Imperial Decree with consent of the local authority to other industries.	Factories of the large and workshops of the small industries. A Factory is a place where articles are made or worked upon in a closed workshop employing more than 20 workmen; division of labour, use of machinery, an employer himself not working manually, may also bring the place under the Factory Law. Agricultural, fishing, transport (rail, steam and canal) industries are omitted, also earth-works and mines:* Domestic workshops, penitentiaries and charitable establishments are also exempt.	In principle to all industries and professions. No definition distinguishes factories and workshops; a factory is a place where a branch of work is done, or power or machinery is used. Express *exclusions* are agricultural, fishing, transport (rail, steam, canal) industries and mines; also State monopolies, domestic workshops, educational and reformatory institutes and prisons.

AGE OF ADMISSION OF CHILDREN.	13. (And not then unless primary education is complete.)	14. (In factories.) 12. (In other regular occupations.) From 12–14 must attend school for 12 hours a week in daytime, and may only be employed in easy work not injurious to health.	12. But may be admitted with educational certificate at 10 years old by permission of the industrial authority.
DURATION OF WORKING-DAY. *Children.*	6 hours. (For those under 14.)	8 hours.‡ (For those under 14, in workshops of the small industry.)	10 hours§ in small industries, 8 in large for those under 14. School hours are included.
Young Persons.	10 hours.* (For those under 16.) Young Persons to be allowed time to attend continuation schools until 18.	11 hours.‡ (For those under 16 in factories; and only in light non-injurious work.) Hours in workshops not limited after 14 years. Until 18 years must have time for night or secondary schools and also Sunday schools.	12 hours‡ in small industries, 10 in large for those under 16. School hours are included, and the young apprentice must attend the schools.
Women.	11 hours.* (For women over 16.) On Saturdays and Eves before Holidays 10 hours, and must leave work at 5.30 p.m. In certain cases of urgency or public interest women not having a household may work till 8.30 on Saturdays and Eves before Holidays.	11 hours.‡ (In Factories.)	No limitation. Rests in working day as below.‡

† For children, cut by a rest of at least ½ hour.
‡ Cut by rests of 1 hour and ½ hour in all industries for all workers without distinction of age or sex.
§ Cut by three rests, ½ hour before noon, 1 hour at noon, ½ hour afternoon.
* For young persons, cut by 3 rests of ⅓ hour, 1 hour, and ⅓ hour; for women, cut by a rest of 1 hour at mid-day or 1½ hours if they have a household to attend to.

Table 1.1c Factory laws of European countries

	Denmark	Sweden	Norway
DATES OF EARLIEST FACTORY LEGISLATION.	1873.	1881.	1892.
DATES OF LAWS NOW IN FORCE.	1873.	1881.	1892.
TO WHAT PLACES THE LAWS APPLY.	(With additions to 1891.) Factories and workshops, or places using factory processes, and which employ young persons under 18, whether the work be direct or accessory. Domestic workshops are not mentioned, but the Minister has power to decide doubtful cases.	(With changes to 1890.) Factories, manufactories, and other industries without further definition – save that in accordance with degrees of importance and nature of work, some industries are to be considered factories. [cf. Notes.] Domestic workshops are in effect excluded.	All industrial places occupying a number (great or small) of workmen at the same time and in a regular manner; all mines, foundries, metal works, and metal workshops in general. The Inspector is empowered to decide whether an establishment comes under the law.
AGE OF ADMISSION OF CHILDREN.	10. (And must have educational and medical certificates and must not be employed during school hours.)	12. (And must have educational and medical certificates. Up to 15 must attend school, certificated or not.)	12. (But must have a certificate of physical aptitude, and up to 14 must be free to attend school. The school-master may demand further time for schooling.)
DURATION OF WORKING-DAY.			
Children.	6 hours* in 24. (For those under 14.)	6 hours.† (In factories for those under 14.) [Not regulated in other industries.]	6 hours.†‡ (For those under 14.)

Young Persons.	10 hours* in 24. (For those under 18.)	10 hours.† (In factories for those under 18.) [Not regulated in other industries.]	10 hours.‡ (For those under 18.) From 12–18 years must rest after 4½ hours' work at latest.
Women.			
CONCESSIONS AS TO DURATION OF WORK.			
Young Persons.	Overtime is permitted to those of 14–18 years in exceptional industries (as when the work depends on the season or atmospheric condition) by the Minister of the Interior. Children may never be employed beyond or out of the legal hours.	Concessions are permitted exceptionally and only for 4 weeks a year, and the hours must not be in those constituting night-work.	In case of accident overtime is allowed without application to the authorities for 2 days only; if further leave is wanted can be had from the Inspector merely. With proper authority overtime is permitted at certain times of the year in seasonal trades. Overtime of ½ an hour is allowed to young persons of 14–18 in certain easy industries by authority, but hours may not exceed 60 per week.
Women.			

* Children: Cut by a rest of ½ hour; if employed before 11 a.m. must leave work at 1 p.m. Young persons: Cut by 2 hours rests; 1½ hours before 3 p.m., and ½ hour before 6 p.m. [In places other than factories rests are ordered but the amount is not stated.]

† Children: Cut by a rest of ½ hour. Young persons: Cut by rests of 2 hours, 1½ before 3 p.m.

‡ Children and young persons: Cut by a rest of ½ hour morning and afternoon. Young persons have additional rest of 1 hour after dinner when the duration of work exceeds 8 hours.

Table 1.1d Factory laws of European countries

	Russia	Italy	Spain
DATES OF EARLIEST FACTORY LEGISLATION.	1719. (For serf-labour in State factories.) 1816. (Same legislation extended to private mines.) 1882. (First law for general application.)	1886.	1873.
DATES OF LAWS NOW IN FORCE.	1882–1894. (Women and children.) 1897. (Male labour.)	1886. (New Bill for the Protection of Miners, 1897, now before the Government.) [See below.]	1873.
TO WHAT PLACES THE LAWS APPLY.	To all manufactories, industrial establishments, mines, smelting works, gold and platinum workings, railway workshops and workshops which, though not using power, employ over 16 persons. All industrial works and establishments belonging to the "Cabinet" of the Czar and to the Department of "Appanages," the Crown and Government administrations. State, military and naval establishments are not under the new law, but have special rules. EXEMPTIONS: Workshops employing less than 16 and domestic workshops. Ministers are charged to decide doubtful cases, and may extend the application of the law to certain workshops or categories of workshops.	Factories and workshops where power is used or workshops where 10 workers are employed; also mines and quarries. Building and agricultural works are exempt, also domestic workshops and shops.	Industrial establishments, factories, workshops, foundries and mines.

	12.	10.
AGE OF ADMISSION OF CHILDREN.	(But if not possessing a certificate of education, must attend school for 18 hours a week up to 15 years of age.)	9, and in underground work, 10 years. All under 15 must have a medical certificate, and an employer wishing to employ a child below 15 must make a declaration before the authority. [Cf. Notes.] [A Bill is before Parliament proposing to raise the age for mines and quarries to 14 underground and 12 above ground.]
DURATION OF WORKING-DAY.		
Children.	8 hours in 24 for those under 15. Must not work more than 4 hours without rest.† In certain industries may work for 6 consecutive hours, but then the working-day must be 6 hours only.	8 hours‡ for those 9–12 years old.
Young Persons.	Not regulated after 15 years of age, save for boys coming under the new law for male labour. [Cf. Men.]	5 hours for boys of 10–13 years, and for girls of 10–14 years. Education for 3 hours a day is compulsory up to these ages in State schools. 8 hours for boys of 13–15 years, and for girls of 14–17 years.
Women.		
CONCESSIONS AS TO DURATION OR WORKING-DAY.		
Young Persons.	In cases where 18 hours a day in 2 shifts of 9 hours are worked, children under 15 may work 9 hours in shifts of 4½ cut by a rest.	
Women.		

Finland has a Factory Law of its own; the principal enactments are given in the Notes.

† The Prefect of St. Petersburg issued an order in 1897 extending this rule to young people of 12 to 15 employed in dressmaking, military, or tailoring establishments.

‡ Cut by a rest of 1 hour when the duration of work is over 6 hours.

Table 1.1e Factory laws of European countries

	Portugal	Switzerland (Federal.)	St. Gall. (Cantonal.)
DATES OF EARLIEST FACTORY LEGISLATION.	1891.	The earliest legislation took place in different cantons at different dates.	1893.
DATES OF PRESENT LAWS.	1891.	1877. (With special decrees from 1891–1898.)	
TO WHAT PLACES THE LAWS APPLY.	Mines and quarries, docks and shipping yards, factories and workshops of all kinds; also State workshops and those of administrative corporations, professional and charitable institutions. Exceptions are small mills and workshops not employing steam-power and where dangerous trades are not practised, which are established in the home of the worker, and are executed by himself and family or pupils, and where the number employed does not exceed 5.	Any industrial establishment where a more or less considerable number of workmen are employed regularly in a closed place away from home. Domestic workshops and small industries are excepted, *save when dealing with unhealthy trades*, also mines. The Federal Council, in agreement with the Cantonal Departments, has the power to decide what small places shall be brought under the Law. The Decree of June 1891 brought under the Law: (1) Places using power and employing more than 5 persons, or any persons under 18, or which present dangers to life and health. (2) Any places employing more than 10 persons, though not having any of the features just mentioned. (3) Places employing less than 6 persons and presenting special dangers to life and health, or those occupying less than 11 but which are of the type of factories.	*St. Gall extends the protection to all places where girls under 18 are employed; to places where women are employed outside their homes when in a greater number than 2 together, in hotels or cafes, in commercial offices or for wages in agriculture.* *The protection is extended to the small industries employing girls and women, particularly those of "the fashions."*

	12.	14.
AGE OF ADMISSION OF CHILDREN.	(But where possessing educational and medical certificates may be admitted by authority to easy work only, at 10 years old.)	
DURATION OF WORKING-DAY.		
Children.	6 hours† in 24 for those under 10. Primary instruction is compulsory up to 12 years for 2 hours daily at least, and work must be specially interrupted for the purpose.	11 hours‡ for those of 14–16 years; but this must *include* time for instruction, and the instruction must not be sacrificed to the work. 10 hours Saturdays and Eves of Holidays.
	10 hours in 24 for boys of 12–16 years and girls of 12–21 years.	
Young Persons.		11 hours* for those of 16–18 years. Saturdays and Eves of Holidays 10.
Women.		11 hours.* (Saturdays and Eves of Holidays 10.)
CONCESSIONS AS TO DURATION OF WORK.		
Young Persons.		Concessions may be allowed in a passing manner where there is a cause, such as stop page of the motor force. But they must not cause night-work to those 14–18.
Women.		Concessions as above. But not so as to cause night-work.
		Concessions allowed to unmarried women over 18 in a few accessory trades. [*Cf.* Notes.]
		In shops 10 hours and 9 on Saturday.

† Cut by a rest after 4 hours' work of 1 hour under 12 years; the same rest after 5 hours' work for boys under 16 and girls under 21.

‡ Cut by a rest for all workers of at least 1 hour at noon.

Source: Emma Brooke (1898) *A Tabulation of the Factory Laws of European Countries*, London: Grant Richards.

* Cut by a rest for all workers of at least 1 hour at noon. Women with households may have half an hour longer at noon if the rest is less than one hour and a half.

movement, seemed to come primarily from individuals regarded as middle-class reformers and agitators, although there were some more conservative Parliamentary voices involved (including Sir Robert Peel). (For a listing of some of the major changes in English legislation in the nineteenth century, see table 1.2.) They often related their concerns to the problems of national economic growth as well as to individual economic betterment. They advocated measures, such as education and public health, arguing that they would benefit not only the individuals directly concerned but also society as a whole. Workers and unions advocated further reforms as they became more powerful, in part as a result of their strength due to nineteenth-century legislation permitting the formation and exercise of some forms of collective power by unions. In addition to advocating improved standards for their own direct benefits, there were attempts by unions and other groups to help others, or so they claimed. These, however appropriately sounding when advocated, might seek to limit the opportunities of those other workers by setting too high a cost for employers. Alternatively, they might be intended to generate similar benefits, such as lowered hours of work similar to those of children or women, to those individuals not legislatively protected, benefits, whether because of the nature of the production process or of some egalitarian norm. Factory owners might seek legislation regulating labor standards as a means of attracting labor in times of labor scarcity or as a means of enforcing standards upon those other producers who might otherwise benefit from having lower standards. There will generally be some redistributive impact from any labor standards since it is doubtful that, given differences in labor-market conditions by location, industry, labor force composition, etc., legislated labor standards will be neutral in their effects. Thus the introduction of labor standards will generate changes in relative employments, incomes, and profits throughout the economy, whether intended or not.

Governments might be considered as a separate factor introducing its own desired policies, particularly as bureaucracies develop. The governing groups may see the implementation of labor standards as a way to avoid or mitigate political stability although governments will often be the battleground among different seekers of policy implementations, each seeking to achieve preferred ends. And since governments can regulate the nature and amount of imports, labor standards can be used as part of national trade policy. A twentieth-century source of agitation has been the rise of international agencies seeking agreement on and enforcement of internationally accepted labor standards. This has meant the imposition of standards of international morality (similar in intent to the interests of the antislavery and aborigine society movements) as well as of standards of living upon other, generally less-developed nations, who are less than eager to accept such standards in their own self-interest. The international imposition of labor standards on nations not willing to accept such provisions has become an issue of contemporary political importance, even when it can be argued that the standards were initially imposed on these countries.

Morals and Economics: Long-standing Arguments

The most general arguments for labor standards have included both moral (at times religious, at times secular and humanitarian) and economic components. The basic moral and religious reasons have been to aid the poor and those without voice in society, policies that might have the further impact of helping to promote economic growth. In terms of economics, the arguments have been to correct some form of market failure and to have the economy become more efficient. Arguments for market failures are either that there are some externalities in the form of social benefits from a healthier and more productive society or else that there are difficulties generated by unequal bargaining power that can be adjusted by state action. The social benefits from the enforcement of labor standards include public health, population growth, education, economic growth, and political stability, each of which, it has been argued, requires some form of legislative intervention.[8] The private benefits to those directly influenced will include better health, more opportunities for education permitted by fewer working hours, and an opportunity to become more productive workers, thus earning higher incomes.

An early, inclusive, argument for imposing standards on child labor in Lancashire cotton factories, by a Dr Percival in 1796 (reprinted in Bland et al., 1933, pp. 495–6), spells out many of the now quite familiar standard arguments:

> It has already been stated that the objects of the present institution are to prevent the generation of diseases; to obviate the spreading of them by contagion; and to shorten the duration of those which exist, by affording the necessary aids and comforts to the sick. In the prosecution of this interesting undertaking, the Board have had their attention particularly directed to the large cotton factories established in the town and neighborhood of Manchester; and they feel it a duty incumbent on them to lay before the public the result of their inquiries:
>
> 1. It appears that the children and others who work in the large factories are peculiarly disposed to be affected by the contagion of fever, and that when such infection is received, it is rapidly propagated, not only amongst those who are crowded together in the same apartments, but in the families and neighborhoods to which they belong.
> 2. The large factories are generally injurious to the constitution of those employed in them, even where no particular diseases prevail, from the

Table 1.2 Development of legal minimum age for employment, and normal maximum working day for children in the United Kingdom

(a) Legal minimum age

Factory and workshops acts		Mines acts		Miscellaneous		
Textile Factories	Non-Textile Factories and Workshops	Coal Mines*	Metalliferous Mines	Chimney Sweepers	Agric. Gangs (Eng. & Wales only)	Publican Entertainments
1802. *Nil.* 1819. Cotton mills, **9**. 1833. All textile factories (with exceptions for silk), **9**; full time, 13. 1844. All textile factories, **8**; full time, 13. 1861. Lace factories, **8**; full time, 13.	1845. Print works, **8**; full time, 13. 1860. Bleach and dye works, **8**; full time, 13. 1864. Earthenware (except bricks), match, percussion caps and cartridges, paper staining, fustian cutting factories, **8**; full time, 13.	1842. Below ground, Boys, **10**; Girls and Women prohibited. 1860. Below ground, Boys aged 10–11 only to be employed either with educational certificate, or if attending school three hours on two days a week.		1788. **8**. 1834. **10**. 1840. **16**; in climbing chimneys, 21.		

Table 1.2 cont'd

(a) Legal minimum age

Factory and workshops acts		Mines acts		Chimney Sweepers	Miscellaneous	
Textile Factories	Non-Textile Factories and Workshops	Coal Mines*	Metalliferous Mines		Agric. Gangs (Eng. & Wales only)	Publican Entertainments
	1867. All non-textile factories and workshops, **8**; full time, 13.				1867. **8**.	
		1872. Below ground, Boys, **12**, except in thin seams in mines, where 10, full time, 12. Above ground, Boys and Girls, 10, full time, 12.	1872. Below ground, Boys, **12**. Above ground, no regulation.		1873. **10**.	
1874. Textile factories (including lace), **10**; full time, 14, or 13 with educational certificate.						
1878. All factories and workshops, **10**: full time, 14, or 13 with educational certificate.						
		1887. Below ground, Boys **12** (no exceptions). Above ground, Boys and Girls, 12; full time, 13.				1889. **7**.
1891. **11**; full time, 14, or 13 with educational certificate.						
		1900. Below ground, **13**.	1900. Below ground, **13**.			
1901. **12**; full time, 14, or 13 with educational certificate.						1903. **10**.
		1911. Below ground, **14**. Above ground, 13 (Boys and Girls).				

Cont'd

Table 1.2 cont'd

(a) Legal minimum age

Employment acts		Education Acts (School Attendance Provisions.)			
		England & Wales.		Scotland.	Ireland.
Street Trading†	General Employment	Minimum Age for Employment	Bye-law-making Powers re School Attendance	Minimum Age for Employment. Exemption provisions	Minimum Age for Employment. Exemption provisions
			1870. School Boards (where in existence) empowered, but not obliged, to make bye-laws covering children 5–13.	1872. Duty of parents and employers to provide education for all children aged 5–13. Educational certificate granted by H. M. Inspector alone exempts from this duty.	

Table 1.2 cont'd

(a) Legal minimum age

Employment acts		Education Acts (School Attendance Provisions.)			
Street Trading†	General Employment	England & Wales. Minimum Age for Employment	England & Wales. Bye-law-making Powers re School Attendance	Scotland. Minimum Age for Emloyment. Exemption provisions	Ireland. Minimum Age for Employment. Exemption provisions
		1876. **10.**	1876. School Attendance Committees created in all areas without School Boards, and given similar bye-law-making powers, except that in rural parishes such powers only to be exercised on requisition of parish. 1880. Enactment of bye-laws made compulsory on all Local Education Authorities. Education Department given power to make bye-laws in default of the Local Authority. 1900. Higher age limit of children subject to bye-laws extended from 13 to 14.	1878. **10.** Educational certificates required for employment for all children under 14, unless employed half-time under Factory or Mines Act.	
1889. **10.**		1893. **11.**			1892. In municipa boroughs and town and townships unde Commissioners, employment of children under **11** forbidden, except in setting or planting of potatoes, hay-making or harvesting educational certificate required for employment of children age 11–14, except where allowed by Factor Act. Commissioners of Education empowere to extend provisions to suburbs. 1898. Same provisions applied to Count Council areas.
1894. **11.**		1899. **12;** cept that in rural areas Education Authority may allow partial exemption at 11, if total exemption not allowed till 13.		1901. **12.** Up to 14 educational certificate required. School Boards given complete discretion with regard to granting or withholding such certificates.1908. School Boards empowered to compel young persons aged 14–17 to attend continuation classes during the normal hours of employment, as regulated by Act of Parliament.	
1903. Local Authorities empowered to raise minimum age up to 16.	1903. Local Authorities empowered to fix minimum age up to 14.				

* Since 1872 the Coal Mines Acts, as distinct from the Metalliferous Mines Acts, have covered ironstone mines.

† From 1899–1903 Local Acts in several town empowered the municipal authorities to fix a higher minimum age than 11.

‡ In 1894, by the Quarries Act, the provisions of the Metalliferous Mines Act with regard to the Employment of Children were extended so as to cover children employed in quarries over 20 feet deep.

Cont'd

Table 1.2 cont'd
(b) Normal maximum working day

Textile Factories.

Date of Acts	Children employed as Young Persons			Children employed under part-time systems			
				Morning and afternoon sets		Alternate day system	
	Normal maximum working days	Sats	Working week	Normal maximum working day	Working week	Normal maximum working day	Working week
1802, 1819	12	12	72	–	–	–	–
1825, 1831	12	9	69	–	–	–	–
1833	12	9	69	8	48	–	–
1844	12	9	69	7	42	10	30
1847	10	8	58	7	42	10	30
1850	10½	7½	60	7	41½	10	30
1874, 1878	10	6½	56½	6½	34 and 32½ in alternate weeks.	10	30 and 26½ in alternate weeks.
1901	10	5½	55½	6½	33 and 32½ in alternate weeks.	10	30 and 26½ in alternate weeks.
Non-Textile Factories and Workshops.							
1845 to 1867†	10½	7½	60	7	41½	10	30 and 27½ in alternate weeks.
1878, 1901	10½	7½	60	6½	34 and 32½ in alternate weeks.	10	30 and 27½ in alternate weeks.

Source: Keeling, Frederick (1914) Child Labour in the United Kingdom, London: P. S. King & Son.

close confinement which is enjoined, from the debilitating effects of hot or impure air, and from the want of the active exercises which nature points out as essential in childhood and youth, to invigorate the system, and to fit our species for the employments and for the duties of manhood.

3. The untimely labour of the night, and the protracted labour of the day, with respect to children, not only tends to diminish future expectations as the general sum of life and industry, by imparing the strength and destroying the vital stamina of the rising generation, but it too often gives encouragement to idleness, extravagance and profligacy in the parents, who, contrary to the order of nature, subsist by the oppression of their offspring.

4. It appears that the children employed in factories are generally debarred from all opportunities of education, and from moral or religious instruction.

5. From the excellent regulation which subsist in several cotton factories, it appears that many of these evils may, in a considerable degree, be obviated; we are therefore warranted by experience, and are assured we shall have the support of the liberal proprietors of these factories, in proposing an application for Parliamentary aid (if other methods appear not likely to effect the purpose), to establish a general system of laws for the wise, humane, and equal government of all such works.

While his wording may sometimes be awkward, Dr Percival's advocacy does indicate that the basic arguments for intervention have long been familiar. The introduction and extension of standards depends more on shifts in political power, effective rhetoric, changing attitudes regarding the role of men, new empirical data, or the attempt to apply standards to a broader group of nations, rather than upon the introduction of new justifications or new claims for what the policies will achieve.

The initial concerns when introducing labor standards were with children and women, who were not considered to be agents capable of deciding for themselves, were lacking in political rights, had limited controls over money, and were generally not union members able to bargain in a unit. This exclusion of adult males did not mean that these adult males, not directly benefiting from legislation, could not obtain benefits from the laws; whether because the costs of legislation would drive women and children from work, or because production arrangements regarding the time-pattern of work were such that similar gains regarding hours and conditions would accrue to adult males. Adult males were regarded as individuals with sufficient rights and ability to make decisions for themselves and, being able to take adequate care of themselves, they did not warrant legislative protection.

This early concern with benefiting children and reducing their labor, based on arguments of the need for better health and more education, did reflect a shift from preceding centuries, where the interest seemed more in having children work at early ages to learn discipline and production skills, and thus to become productive members of society at a relatively early age.[9]

The work, at that time, however, was primarily rural and agricultural, not the urban workhouses and industrial work that came with the Industrial Revolution.

The early arguments against labor standards, even for women and children, similarly anticipate most current claims. The basic concerns were the impact of higher costs (due, often, to fewer hours worked for the same total pay) on profits and thus on employment levels, particularly in regard to international trade, the nature of the probable alternatives available to those losing jobs, which may have meant a lowering of their living and working standards, and also the placing of those protected in a weakened political and social position. In regards to extending standards to adult males, the basic objection throughout the nineteenth century was the philosophical belief in that form of individualism that advocated the importance of choices made by male adults, free to contract. Given that belief, attempts to regulate the behavior of adult males were considered unconstitutional as well as undesirable. Changing legislation regarding male labor required a change in society's underlying belief system.

A long-standing argument, found as early as 1788, if not earlier, was the difficulty of achieving broadly acceptable standards in a trading world of different nations.[10] It was considered important that those firms that accepted high standards did not suffer competitive losses in trade, either internally or internationally. This, indeed, has long-been the major barrier to the international acceptability of labor standards. There have been similar difficulties within nations, particularly where, as in the United States, Australia, Canada, and Switzerland, subfederal entities and not the centralized national government were responsible for labor legislation.[11] The attempts by international conferences and agencies to apply uniform standards has made the issue more acute. Basic questions even today are: can a common international standard be defined?; should there be differential standards for countries differentially situated (in terms, e.g., of climate, resources, income levels)?; are there varying trade-offs for different countries in regard to the various forms of standards that might be preferred (e.g., better working conditions vs. higher wages)?; and is there an appropriate degree of flexibility to be introduced over time, depending on changing income, factory size, or other factors?[12] Almost 200 years of discussion has left such questions still unresolved.

Control and Enforcement

The nature of controls and enforcement of labor standards has followed several stages over time, differing somewhat if the standards discussed were to be set nationally or internationally. National standards have been established by legislation or by administrative decree, with the particular political units passing the legislation responsible for establishing the terms of the standards and the methods for enforcement. In some cases, e.g., the United States and Switzerland, being federal governments, there were some national policies, but each state was responsible for its own set of policies, resulting in a lack of national uniformity. Over time, however, separate state policies have been supplemented by the provision of financial incentives or by legal requirements imposed by the national government for at least some minimal set of standards, applied to all political units.[13] To have any chance of being effective, international standards require bilateral or multilateral agreements or else acceptance of policies set by some form of international agency. The actual passage and enforcement of such international standards runs into the basic problem of claims of national sovereignty, limiting any attempt by an international agency to impose a standard on a country.[14] The politics of any agreement may be tied in with trade policy, with the labor standards now being applied only to imported goods, rather than goods domestically produced and consumed in either trading country. Such controls on trade have been quite a recent development, at least by historical standards, using tariffs and quotas to enforce labor standards. The United States tariff of 1890 and its subsequent tariff legislation prohibited the import of goods produced by convict labor.[15] This restriction, was, however, similar to that imposed in some states on the internal trade of commodities produced by convicts.[16]

Critical to enforcement of the labor standards has been the role of inspection of factory procedures, whether originated by the state, by the workers, or by the firms themselves.[17] The effectiveness of any policy obviously depends on the frequency of inspections and the enforcement provisions required by the state, and the funds allotted to them, as well as the nature of the activities covered. The range of potential penalties for violators is quite diverse, from simple adverse publicity to forced closing of firms, and can include consumer- or worker-organized boycotts, restrictions on international or interstate trade, taxes and fines, forced expenditures upon improvements, and the use of labeling for consumer information. Some types of enforcement might involve the payment of subsidies rather than penalties. Recently, for example, in Mexico, Brazil, and elsewhere there are programs that provide payment in cash to the family of a child who has withdrawn from the labor force in order to attend school, a policy that is now being widely discussed.

Patterns of Labor Standards Evolution

Before entering into the details of labor standards in modern times, a brief survey of some basic trends and patterns will be useful. There were only a few scattered cases of what we might call labor standards before the start of the nineteenth century, none in what would soon become the first major industrial powers. These include Russian regulations, in the early eighteenth century, regarding serf labor in factories. From the early nineteenth century, the number of countries with labor standards increased, although most standards were not introduced until the second-half of the nineteenth century and first years of the twentieth century. Their introduction begins with England, then elsewhere in Western Europe and British overseas offshoots, Eastern Europe, Latin America, and, lastly, in Africa and Asia. Patterns of economic growth, suffrage, and education followed a similar chronology to the development of labor standards, as has the power to bargain collectively. (See the information on international patterns of suffrage and education presented in tables 1.3 and 1.4.)[18]

Standards were first applied to children and women, with very few provisions regarding hours and wages applied to adult males until the twentieth century. Standards began, in general, with requirements of the minimum age at which children could work. Maximum hours for women and children were then introduced. Provisions prohibiting night work for women and children, and restrictions on various types of hazardous work, were among the other standards introduced in the nineteenth century. The first industry to be affected in Britain was the manufacturing of textiles, particularly cotton textiles – not surprising given that these were not only the largest industries during Britain's early industrialization, but also because textiles had the largest numbers and shares of women and children in its industrial labor force.[19] Mining was also singled out early, often leading to restrictions that meant female and child laborers were not permitted to work in mines, particularly underground. Other manufacturing industries were often included, but neither agricultural nor service sectors were generally covered until rather late.[20] The main controls of laboring conditions were applied to manufacturing and mining industries, thus to a relatively small proportion of the labor force in most times, and in most countries.

The movement towards expanding labor standards can be divided into three distinct, although overlapping in time, categories.[21] First, is the development of standards internal to a nation, with legislation and enforcement established by the sovereign nation. These were the first such policies to be introduced and, as will be clear, have been the most successful. In the nineteenth century, particularly in its second half, there were attempts to impose international standards as the outcome of a series of international conferences and agreements. International here, unlike in the post-World War II era, meant only the developed countries of Western Europe, countries that were geographically contiguous, with similar climates, and with levels of economic development that were somewhat similar, at least compared to those in the rest of the world. Although European nations then had colonies

Table 1.3 Ratio of students in school to population ages 5–19 and the proportion of the population voting for selected countries, 1895–1945

	c. 1895	c. 1920	c. 1945
Austria			
Schooling ratios[1]	0.45	0.52	0.58
suffrage[2]	7.9%	46.1%	46.9%
Belgium			
Schooling ratios	0.42	0.46	0.53
suffrage	20.1%	26.3%	28.9%
Denmark			
Schooling ratios	0.49	0.49	0.50
suffrage	9.9%	30.3%	50.8%
Finland			
Schooling ratios	0.12	0.29	0.53
suffrage	4.6%	27.3%	44.3%
France			
Schooling ratios	0.56	0.43	0.60
suffrage	19.4%	21.0%	49.3%
Germany			
Schooling ratios	0.54	0.53	0.55
suffrage	14.6%	45.6%	48.8%
Ireland			
Schooling ratios	0.32	0.54	0.53
suffrage	–	21.9%	41.1%
Italy			
Schooling ratios	0.27	0.36	0.47
suffrage	4.1%	16.2%	52.5%
Netherlands			
Schooling ratios	0.44	0.45	0.56
suffrage	5.1%	20.5%	49.5%
Norway			
Schooling ratios	0.48	0.50	0.52
suffrage	7.9%	32.1%	47.5%
Portugal			
Schooling ratios	0.14	0.17	0.26
suffrage	–	–	–
Spain			
Schooling ratios	–	0.27	0.34
suffrage	–	–	–
Sweden			
Schooling ratios	0.50	0.42	0.45
suffrage	2.8%	11.2%	46.4%
Switzerland			
Schooling ratios	0.53	0.54	0.49
suffrage	11.8%	19.2%	20.5%
United Kingdom			
Schooling ratios	0.45	0.51	0.66
suffrage	9.8%	30.4%	49.9%
Argentina			
Schooling ratios	0.21	0.41	0.44
suffrage	1.8%	10.9%	15.0%

Table 1.3 cont'd

	c. 1895	c. 1920	c. 1945
Bolivia			
Schooling ratios	0.07	–	0.18
suffrage	–	–	–
Brazil			
Schooling ratios	0.08	0.10	0.22
suffrage	2.2%	4.0%	5.7%
Chile			
Schooling ratios	0.16	0.37	0.40
suffrage	4.2%	4.4%	9.4%
Colombia			
Schooling ratios	–	0.20	0.21
suffrage	–	6.9%	11.1%
Costa Rica			
Schooling ratios	0.22	0.22	0.29
suffrage	–	10.6%	17.6%
Cuba			
Schooling ratios	–	0.31	0.37
suffrage	–	–	–
Mexico			
Schooling ratios	0.13	0.22	0.28
suffrage	5.4%	8.6%	11.8%
Peru			
Schooling ratios	–	–	0.31
suffrage	–	–	–
Uruguay			
Schooling ratios	0.13	0.36	–
suffrage	–	13.8%	–
Canada			
Schooling ratios	0.60	0.65	0.64
suffrage	17.9%	20.5%	41.1%
United States			
Schooling ratios	0.62	0.68	0.76
suffrage	18.4%	25.1%	37.8%

1. Schooling ratios were calculated by dividing the total number of students (regardless of age) by the population between the ages 5–19. When groups of population were different from this range (5–19) we assumed that there was the same number of people in each age group, and weighed the population figures so as to make them comparable. An example of this was Bolivia.

2. Suffrage is used here to represent the proportion of the population that votes in each country.

Sources: Engerman, Stanley, Elisa Mariscal, and Kenneth Sokoloff (2000, unpublished) "Schooling, Suffrage, and the Perspective of Inequality in the Americas, 1800–1945."

For the schooling data: B. R. Mitchell, *International Historical Statistics: The Americas 1750–1988, and International Historical Statistics: Europe 1750–1988.*

For the data on suffrage: Peter Flora et al. (1983) vol. 1, and, Dieter Nohlan, ed. *Enciclopedia Electoral Latinamericana y del Caribe.*

Table 1.4   International comparisons of laws relating to suffrage, and the extent of voting

	Year when secret ballot attained	Year when women gain the vote	Year of universal equal male suffrage	Proportion of population voting, c. 1900 (%)
Austria	1907	1919	1907	7.9
Belgium	1877	1948	1919	22.0
Denmark	1901	1918	1918	16.5
Finland	1907	1907	1907	4.6
France	1831	1945	1848	19.4
Germany	1848	1919	1872	15.5
Italy	1861	1946	1919	6.8
Netherlands	1849	1922	1918	12.0
Norway	1885	1909	1921	19.5
Sweden	1866	1921	1921	7.1
Switzerland	1872	1971	1848	22.3
United Kingdom	1872	1918	1948	16.2
Canada	1874	1917	1898[1]	17.9
United States	1849[2]	1920	1870[3]	18.4
Argentina	1912	1947	?	1.8[4]
Bolivia	?	?	1956	–
Brazil	1932	1932	1988	3.0
Chile	1833	1949	1970	4.2
Costa Rica	1925	1949	1913	–
Ecuador	1861	1929	1978	3.3
El Salvador	1950	1939	1950	–
Guatemala	1946[5]	1946	1965	–
Peru	1931	1955	1979	–
Uruguay	1918	1932	1918	–
Venezuela	1946	1945	1946[6]	–

1 By 1898, all but two Canadian provinces had instituted universal equal suffrage for males.

2 By the end of the 1840s, all states except for Illinois and Virginia had adopted the secret ballot.

3 Eighteen states, 7 southern and 11 non-southern, introduced literacy requirements between 1890 and 1926. These restrictions were directed primarily at Blacks and immigrants.

4 This figure is for the city of Buenos Aires, and likely overestimates the national figure.

5 Illiterate males do not obtain the secret ballot until 1956; females do not obtain it until 1965.

6 The 1858 Constitution declared universal direct male suffrage, but this provision was dropped in later constitutions. All restrictions on universal adult suffrage were ended in 1946, with the exception of different age restrictions for literate persons and illiterates.

Source: Engerman, Stanley, Elisa Mariscal and Kenneth Sokoloff (2000, unpublished) "Schooling, Suffrage, and the Persistence of Inequality in the Americas, 1800–1945."

throughout the world, colonial labor markets were generally excluded from separate treatment, and presumably "native labor" (including non-whites born in tropical areas) was considered to be outside the scope of the standards to be applied to the metropolis. With the establishment of the International Labor Organization, in 1919, as an offshoot of the League of Nations, and then later with the independence movements after World War II, the coverage of international standards was expanded to include all nations, developed as well as less developed, with worldwide coverage, including former colonies as well as independent nations. In addition to this worldwide agency there have been a number of regional organizations, adding to the complications of developing and implementing labor standards. This more inclusive coverage, geographically and economically, has meant an even broader set of difficulties than earlier, when the problem was narrowed to the developed nations of Western Europe, although little had been accomplished even then.

Early Examples of Legislation

Most historians of labor standards begin with the English Factory Act of 1802, introduced by Sir Robert Peel, more symbolic than substantive given that it applied only to pauper apprentices. It set their workday at twelve hours, forbade night work, and included provisions regarding education and religious instruction.[22] This had been preceded by even more minor forms of regulation in several countries, the English bill of 1788, setting a minimum age (eight) and other terms, for chimneysweeps;[23] a Russian Law of 1719, applied to serf laborers in factories,[24] and Austrian Laws in the 1780's regarding factory apprentices.[25]

Throughout the nineteenth century, England expanded the coverage and requirements of its Factory Acts, setting a minimum age (nine) for cotton mills in 1819, and extending this minimum to all textile factories in 1833. They then lowered the minimum age to eight in all textile factories in 1844, but raised it to ten in all textile factories in 1874 (following the setting of a minimum age of eight in all non-textile factories in 1867). The minimum of age ten was expanded to include all factories and workshops in 1878, raised to 11 in 1891, and to 12 in 1901. Women, and boys under ten, were excluded from work in coal mines in 1842. In addition, starting with 1833, educational provisions were introduced, requiring either part-time school attendance as part of the employment arrangement or else proof of educational achievement was required in order to obtain employment. The 1802 act, set maximum daily hours of work for apprentices. Starting with the act of 1819, standards to be applied to textile factories were set. Coverage was extended to non-textile factories starting in 1845 (see table 1.2).[26]

As the discussion in the previous paragraph indicates, once legislation had commenced, there were frequent changes and revisions made. These generally meant both coverage of more workers as well as improved standards for covered workers. With a few minor exceptions no systematic or dramatic reversals reducing coverage or making terms unfavorable to workers seem to have occurred in the defining of standards. By the end of the nineteenth century most European nations and the British overseas offshoots had a broad coverage of factory labor, for women and for children, although there were some important differences in the specifics of the standards, as well as differences in the minimum size of factories to be covered by the legislation (for information on US state legislation regarding child and female labor, see tables 1.5, 1.6, 1.7, 1.9, 1.10, and 1.11; table 1.8 details the nature of factory inspections).[27] In most cases, as with England there were frequent changes and adjustments made in these standards, almost always to improve them, so that similar arguments were continuously made as part of the political debate. Few nations, however, had provisions for adult males, France in 1848 was the first major exception, but many felt that men did not require help, and also they indirectly received the benefit of provisions aimed at women and children.[28]

The conventional dating of the start of the movement towards international standards is 1818, with the writings of Robert Owen (1818, pp. 16–27).[29] While sensitive to the need for international agreement to reduce the costs to any one country of unilaterally setting standards for itself, Owen did not propose any satisfactory mechanism to achieve this end. The Englishman Charles Hindley's 1833 proposal for international labor regulation contained arguments that were to be frequently repeated – a moral call for international application of standards to improve world welfare, and an understanding that nations with high standards can gain economically only if other nations are convinced to follow their lead.[30] Several French businessmen and social activists, including Daniel Legrand, Jérôme Adolphe Blanqui, and Louis Rene Villerme, advocated international agreements on standards, but it was not until the second half of the nineteenth century that conferences and bilateral agreements were achieved within Europe. Conferences were arranged by individual countries, but were generally of limited success, from the Brussels Congress of Benevolent Societies in 1856 and the similar Congress of Frankfurt in 1857, through the more extensive Conference of Berlin of 1890 (with 14 European nations in attendance), and the meetings in Berne in 1905 and 1906 (with 15 and 14 countries, respectively).[31]

The major achievements agreed upon by bilateral agreements and conferences before World War I were limitations of night work for children and women, and prohibitions on the import or sale of matches made with white phosphorous, although these policies were implemented by only some of the nations, while others had introduced these provisions before any international

Table 1.5 (a) State compulsory education and child labor laws in 1879–80, and (b) State maximum hours' laws affecting women in 1879–80

(a)

State	Education law			Child labor law		
	Year	Ages	Requirement	Year	Max. hours	Ages
California	1874	8–14	16 weeks	–	–	–
Connecticut	1872	8–14	in sess.	1857	10/58	< 15
Indiana	–	–	–	1867	10	< 16
Kansas	1874	8–14	12 weeks	–	–	–
Maine	1875	8–15	16 weeks	1848	10	< 18
Maryland	–	–	–	1876	10	< 16
Massachusetts	1852	8–14	20 weeks	1842	10/60	< 18
Michigan	1871	8–14	4 months	–	–	–
New Hampshire	1871	6–15	12 weeks	1846	10	< 14
New Jersey	1875	7–16	20 weeks	1851	10/60	< 21
New York	1874	8–14	14 weeks	–	–	–
Ohio	1877	8–16	20 weeks	1852	10	< 14
Pennsylvania	–	–	–	1848	10/60	< 21
Rhode Island	1854	7–15	3 months	1853	11	< 15
Vermont	1867	8–14	20 weeks	1868	10	< 15
Washington	1871	8–18	3 months	–	–	–
Wisconsin	1879	7–15	12 weeks	1853	10	< 14

(b)

State	Year passed	Per day	Max. hours per week	Enforcement	Contracting out allowed?
California*[a]	1853	10	–	none	Yes
Connecticut*[a]	1855	10	–	none	Yes
Dakota	1863	10	–	$10–100	Yes
Florida*[a]	1874	10	–	none	Yes
Georgia[b]	1853	daylight	–	$100	Yes
Illinois*[a]	1867	8	–	none	Yes
Maine*[a]	1848	10	–	$0–100	Yes
Massachusetts	1874	10	60	$0–50	No
Minnesota	1858	10	–	$10–100	Yes
Missouri*[a]	1867	8	–	none	Yes
New Hampshire*	1847	10	–	none	Yes
New Jersey*[a]	1851	10	–	none	Yes
New York*[a]	1853	10	–	none	Yes
Ohio[c]	1852	10	–	$5–50	Yes
Pennsylvania*	1848	10	60	none	Yes
Rhode Island	1853	10	–	$20	Yes
Wisconsin	1867	8	–	$5–50	Yes

* Made no distinction between men and women.
[a] The law established the length of the "legal day."
[b] Applied to white labor only.
[c] Repealed 1879 effective January 1, 1880.
Source: Atack, Jeremy and Fred Bateman (1991, unpublished) "Who Did Protective Legislation Protect? Evidence from 1880."

agreement. Other important sources of pressure for international standards were the International Workingman's Association Congresses, a socialist organization, after 1864, and the more traditional trade unions, which began meeting after 1883.[32] These organizations were important for their advocacy, but this lacked political power within nations, so they had only a limited legislative impact.

The next major stage came with the formation of the International Labor Organization (ILO) in 1919, under the auspices of the League of Nations.[33] Beginning with 44 members in 1919, at present its membership includes 174 nations. The range of labor issues discussed and for which policy improvements were sought resembles that of the pre-ILO era, although there were some shifts in emphasis over time towards more political and social goals regarding human rights, which were previously believed to be outside the scope of concern with labor standards. This reflects, in part, the proclaimed broadened world interest in economic growth and political freedom in other nations, particularly the less-developed nations. The increased international concern with the distribution of welfare has meant a greater interest in all aspects of labor standards. There has also been an acceptance of an expansion in the methods used by nations to encourage the adoption of labor standards by other nations, but on a unilateral basis. In particular, the tying together of labor standards with international trade and tariff policies, has led to significant political debate over the linking of issues which had not been contemplated earlier.[34]

The Types of Legislation

The introduction of labor standards of all types throughout Europe was a product of the nineteenth century, particularly the second half, and preceded their introduction in Africa, Asia, and South America by at least one half-century. Precision in dating of legislation and effective impact is complex, given the different aspects of labor standards, the variations in the specific terms of legislation on these different aspects, and the differences in the extent to which these terms were enforced. In centralized states a uniform date for national legislation is possible, but for federal states such as the United States, Switzerland, Canada, and Australia, where subfederal units often made the decisions, there were a range of years for the introduction of legislation. Nevertheless, since once some set of standards was introduced other provisions frequently followed within some reasonable time, some understanding of the political and social timing of change is possible.

Regulation of economic activities by states and by national governments was not unknown before the legislation of labor standards. Most nations had already imposed restrictions on the transatlantic movement of passengers

Table 1.6 Labor-hour laws in all occupations for men, women, or minors in all States and Territories, November 1, 1899

State	General labor day in the absence of contract (except agricultural and domestic)	Labor day in State or public labor, municipal contractors, etc	Compulsory labor day for all women in factories (but special contracts for overtime permitted in States so[1] noted)	Compulsory labor day for women under 21 in factories (for women over 21 see previous column)
N. H.	10 hrs.		10 hrs. a day, 60 per week.	10 hrs. a day, 60 per week.
Mass		8 or 9 hrs.	10 hrs. a day, 58 per week.	10 hrs. a day, 58 per week.
Me	10 hrs.		10 hrs. a day, 60 per week.[1]	Under 18, 10 hrs., 60 per week.
Vt				
R. I.			10 hrs. a day, 60 per week.	10 hrs. a day, 60 per week.
Conn	8 hrs.	8 hrs.	do	do
N. Y.	do		do	do
N. J.			10 hrs. a day, 55 per week.	10 hrs. a day, 55 per week.
Pa	8 hrs.	8 hrs.	12 hrs. a day, 60 per week.	12 hrs. a day, 60 per week.
Ohio				Under 18, 10 hrs., 55 per week.
Ind	8 hrs.	8 hrs.		Under 18, 10 hrs., 60 per week.
Ill	do			
Mich	10 hrs.			Under 16, 10 hrs., 60 per week.
Wis	8 hours (mfg).		8 hrs., a day[1]	10 hrs. a day, 60 per week.
				8 hrs. a day[1]
Iowa				
Minn	10 hrs.			10 hrs. a day, 60 per week;[1] under 16, 10 hrs. a day.[1]
Kans		8 hrs.		

Table 1.6 cont'd

State	General labor day in the absence of contract (except agricultural and domestic)	Labor day in State or public labor, municipal contractors, etc	Compulsory labor day for all women in factories (but special contracts for overtime permitted in States so[1] noted)	Compulsory labor day for women under 21 in factories (for women over 21 see previous column)
Nebr	10 hrs.		10 hrs. a day, 60 per week.	10 hrs. a day, 60 per week.
Cal	8 hrs.	8 hrs.[3]		Under 18, 10 hrs., 60 per week.
Colo		8 hrs.		
Wash		do		
N. Dak		8 hrs.[3]	10 hrs. a day[1]	Under 18, 10 hrs.[1]
S. Dak			do	do
Idaho				
Mont		8 hrs.[3]		
Wyo		do		
Utah			10 hrs. a day	Under 18, 10 hrs.[1]
Okla			10 hrs. a day[5]	Under 16, 10 hrs., 60 per week.
Md		8 hrs. in Baltimore		
Va			10 hrs. a day, 60 per week.	10 hrs. a day, 60 per week.
W. Va				
Mo	8 hrs.			
Tenn				
Ark				
S. C.				
Ga	Sunrise to sunset.		11 hrs. a day, 60 per week.	Sunrise to sunset.
Ala			do	
Fla	10 hrs.			
La		9 hrs.		
Tex		8 hrs.	10 hrs. a day, 60 per week.	10 hrs. a day, 60 per week.
D. C.				

Cont'd

Table 1.6 cont'd

State	Compulsory labor day for male minors in factories	Age at which labor of children in factories is prohibited	Compulsory labor of women and minors in stores or mercantile establishments	Labor hours in mines	Labor prohibited in mines
N. H.	Under 18, 10 hrs. a day, 60 per week.	10			
Mass	Under 18, 10 hrs. 58 per week.	14	Minors under 18, 60 hrs. per week.		
Me	Under 16, 10 hrs. 60 per week.	12			
Vt	Under 15, 10 hrs. 60 per week.	10			
R. I.	Under 16, 10 hrs. 60 per week.	12	No children under 12.		
Conn	do	14	Same laws as in factories.		
N. Y.	Under 18, 10 hrs. 60 per week.	14	Males under 16, females under 21, 60 hrs. per week, etc.		
N. J.	Under 18, 10 hrs. 55 per week.	14 for girls, 12 for boys.			Children under 12.
Pa	Under 21, 12 hrs. 60 per week.	13	Same laws as in factories.		All women and children under 14.
Ohio	Under 18, 10 hrs. 55 per week.	13	do		Children under 15.
Ind	Under 16, 10 hrs. 60 per week.	14	do		All women in coal mines and children under 14; children under 12 in other mines.
Ill	do	14			
Mich	Under 18, 10 hrs. 60 per week.	14	do		
Wis	Under 18, 8 hrs. a day.[1]	14[2] or 12 where more than 3 are employed.			
Iowa					Boys under 12.
Minn	Under 21, 10 hrs. 60 per week;[1] under 16, 10 hrs. a day.[1]	14	Same laws as in factories, but children under 14 may be employed in vacations.		Children under 14.
Kans					Children under 12 or 16 who can not read, etc.
Nebr		12, not more than 4 mos.; 10, absolutely.	Same laws as in factories.		Under 12, not more than 4 mos.; 10 absolutely.
Cal		10	do	8 hrs.[4]	
Colo	Under 18, 10 hrs. 60 per week.	14			Children under 12 in any; all women in coal mines or children under 14 or 16, etc.

Table 1.6 cont'd

State	Compulsory labor day for male minors in factories	Age at which labor of children in factories is prohibited	Compulsory labor of women and minors in stores or mercantile establishments	Labor hours in mines	Labor prohibited in mines
Wash					All women in coal mines and children under 14.
N. Dak	Under 18, 10 hrs.[1]				Children under 14.
S. Dak	do.[1]				Children under 14.[3]
Idaho					Children under 14.
Mont					All women and children under 14.[3]
Wyo				8 hrs.[3]	Do.
Utah				8 hrs.	
Okla	Under 18, 10 hrs.[1]				
Md	Under 16, 10 hrs., 60 per week.	12	In Baltimore, same law as in factories.		
Va		12			
W. Va	Under 14, 10 hrs., 60 per week.	12			All women in coal mines and children under 12.
Mo		14		8 hrs. in certain mines.	
Tenn		12			Children under 12.
Ark					All women and children under 14.
S. C.					
Ga	Sunrise to sunset.				
Ala					
Fla					
La	Under 18, 10 hrs., 60 per week.	14 for girls, 12 for boys.			Children under 10 and all women.
Tex					
D. C.					

[Oreg., Nev, Mont, Ky., N. C., Ala, Miss., N. M, and Ariz. have no legislation whatever on the subject.]

[1] If such labor is compulsory only.
[2] Except upon permit of the judge, etc.
[3] Provided by the constitution of such State.
[4] Law annulled as unconstitutional.
[5] In certain kinds of factories.

Source: US Congress, House of Representatives (1900) *Report of the Industrial Commission on Labor Legislation*, vol. 5 of the Commission's reports, Washington, DC: Government Printing Office.

Table 1.7 Women and child labor laws in the United States, 1910

States	Minimum Age Limit			Educational Provisions (a)		Hours (jj)			Night work prohibited
	Factories	Stores	Mines	Illiterate Children Can not be Employed Under (b)	Certificates of School Attendance (c) Required Under	Male "Young Persons"	Female "Young Persons"	Women	
Alabama	10 (d)	–	12	–	–	12, 66w. (kk)	12, 66w. (kk)	–	Under 13
Arkansas	10 (d)	–	14	14 (e) (f)	14	14, 10d. 60w.	14, 10d. 60w.	–	Under 14
California	12	12	–	–	–	18, 9d. 54w. (r)	18, 9d. 54w. (r)	–	–
Colorado	14	–	14	16 (g)	14 (h)	16, 8d. (ll)	16, 8d. (ll)	–	–
Connecticut	14	14	–	16	14 (h)	16, 10d. (r)	16, 10d. (r)	10d. (r)	–
Delaware	–	–	–	–	–	–	–	–	–
Florida (i)	–	–	–	–	–	–	–	–	–
Georgia	–	–	–	–	–	21, Sunrise to sunset (mm)	21, Sunrise to sunset (mm)	–	–
Idaho	–	–	14	–	–	–	–	–	–
Illinois	14	14	14	16	14	16, 8d. 48w. (nn)	16, 8d. 48w. (nn)	–	Under 16 (nn)
Indiana	14	14	14	16 (j) (k)	–	16, 10d. 60w. (k)	16, 10d. 60w. (k)	–	Females
Iowa	–	–	12	–	–	–	–	–	–
Kansas	–	–	12	16 (g)	16 (g)	–	–	–	–
Kentucky	14 (l)	–	14	16 (g)	–	–	–	–	–
Louisiana	12 (m)	–	–	–	14 (e)	18, 10d. 60w. (oo)	18, 10d. 60w. (oo)	10d. 60w. (oo)	–
Maine	12	–	–	–	15 (n)	16, 10d. 60w. (n)	16, 10d. 60w. (n)	10d. 60w. (n) (rr)	–
Maryland	14 (o) (l)	–	12	16 (p) (q)	–	16, 10d. (pp)	16, 10d. (pp)	–	–
Massachusetts	14	14	–	16 (r)	14	18, 10d. 58w. (r)	18, 10d. 58w. (r)	10d. 58w. (r)	Women and minors (qq)
Michigan	14	14	–	16 (s)	–	{ 14, 5d. (nn) 18, 10d. 60w. (ss)	16, 9d. (nn) 21, 10d. 60w. (ss)	–	Under 16 (n)
Minnesota	14	14 (j)	14	16 (l)	14 (l)	16, 10d. 60w. (nn)	16, 10d. 60w. (nn)	10d. 60w. (nn) (rr)	Under 16 (nn)
Mississippi (t)	–	–	–	–	–	–	–	–	–
Missouri	14	–	12	14 (g)	–	–	–	–	Under 16 (tt)
Montana	–	–	14	16	14	8d. (nn)	8d. (nn)	8d. (nn)	–
Nebraska	10 (u)	10 (u)	10 (u)	–	14 (v)	–	10d. 60w.	10d. 60w.	–
Nevada	–	10 (u)	10 (u)	–	–	–	–	–	–
New H'mpshire	12	14 (j)	–	16 (w)	14	18, 10d. 60w. (n)	18, 10d. 60w. (n)	10d. 60w. (n)	–

Table 1.7 cont'd

	Minimum Age Limit			Educational Provisions (a)		Hours (jj)			Night work prohibited
States	Factories	Stores	Mines	Illiterate Children Can not be Employed Under (b)	Certificates of School Attendance (c) Required Under	Male "Young Persons"	Female "Young Persons"	Women	
New Jersey	14	–	14	–	15	18, 10d. 55w.	18, 10d. 55w.	10d. 55w.	Under 18 (e) (tt)
New York (x)	14	12 (y)	–	16	16	16, 9d.; 16, 10d. 60w.	16, 9d.; 18, 10d. 60w.	10d. 60w.	Under 18 and women (qq)
North Carolina	12 (z)	–	12 (aa)	–	–	16, 9d. 54w. (uu)	16, 9d. 54w. (uu)	21, 10d. 60w. (uu)	Under 16 (uu)
North Dakota	12	–	12	–	14	18, 66w.	18, 66w.	–	–
Ohio	14	14	14	16	14 (bb)	14, 10d. (vv)	14, 10d. (vv)	10d. (vv)	g. 18, b. 16 (nn)
Oregon	14	14	14	16	14	18, 10d. 55w. (r)	18, 10d. 55w. (r)	–	Under 16 (nn)
Pennsylvania	13	13	14 (cc)	16 (k)	13 (k)	16, 10d. (nn)	16, 10d. (nn)	–	Under 18 (tt)
Rhode Island	12	12	–	–	13	21, 12d. 60w. (ww)	21, 12d. 60w. (ww)	12d. 60w. (ww)	–
South Carolina	11 (dd) (l)	–	11 (dd)	–	11 (dd)	16, 10d. 58w. (n)	16, 10d. 58w. (n)	10d. 58w. (n)	Under 12 (xx)
South Dakota	–	–	14	–	14 (ee)	–	–	–	–
Tennessee	14	–	14	–	–	14, 10d. (vv)	14, 10d. (vv)	10d. (vv)	–
Texas	12	–	16	14 (ff) (l)	–	–	–	–	Under 14 (yy)
Utah	10	10	14	–	–	–	–	–	–
Vermont	12	–	–	14	15 (e)	8d. (nn)	8d. (nn)	8d. (nn)	–
Virginia	–	–	12	–	–	15, 10d. (n)	15, 10d. (n)	–	Under 14 (n) (g)
Washington	12 (gg)	12 (gg)	12 (hh)	16 (r) (ii)	15 (r) (ii)	14, 10d.	14, 10d.	10d.	Under 16 (tt)
West Virginia	12	–	12	–	–	–	10d.	10d.	–
Wisconsin	14	12 (y)	14	–	14	18, 8d. 48w. (zz); 16, 10d. (nn)	18, 8d. 48w. (zz); 16, 10d. (nn)	8d. (rr)	Under 16 (nn)
Wyoming	–	–	14	–	–	–	–	–	–

(a). In all occupations unless otherwise indicated.
(b). Employment is usually permitted if child attends night school.
(c). Attendance either before or during employment, must usually be during previous year.
(d). Under 12 only in cases of extreme poverty.
(e). In manufacturing establishments.
(f). 16 in mines.
(g). In mines.
(h). 16 if illiterate.
(i). Under 15 may not be employed more than 60 days without consent of legal guardian.
(j). Except in vacation.

Cont'd

Table 1.7 cont'd

(k). In any manufacturing or mercantile establishment, laundry, renovating works, bakery, printing office, mine or quarry.

(l). Except in cases of extreme poverty.

(m). 14 for girls.

(n). In manufacturing and mechanical establishments.

(o). Except 20 counties and canning industries.

(p). Applies only to Baltimore and Allegheny County.

(q). 14 in mines.

(r). In manufacturing, mechanical and mercantile establishments.

(s). In any manufacturing establishment, hotel or store.

(t). Boys under 21 and girls under 18 may not be employed without consent of legal guardian.

(u). Under 14 only if certificate of at least 20 weeks' school attendance during previous year is presented.

(v). In manufacturing, mechanical, industrial or mercantile establishments.

(w). 21 if illiterate.

(x). No boy under 10 or girl under 16 can sell newspapers in cities of the first class, i.e., New York City and Buffalo.

(y). 14 except in vacation.

(z). Except in oyster canning and packing manufactories.

(aa). Except where not more than 10 men are employed.

(bb). 15 in mines.

(cc). 14 about mines; 16 in mines.

(dd). After May 1, 1905, the age limit is to be 12 years. Any child who has attended school at least 4 months during the current school year and can read and write may be employed in textile establishments during June, July and August.

(ee). In manufacturing, mechanical, or mercantile establishments or mines.

(ff). In any manufacturing or other establishment using machinery.

(gg). 14 except in cases of extreme poverty.

(hh). 12 about mines; 14 in mines.

(ii). In telegraph or telephone offices.

(jj). In manufacturing establishments unless otherwise indicated.

(kk). The hours of children under 16 are limited to 48 per week if they are employed at night.

(ll). In any manufacturing establishment, store or mine, or any occupation deemed unhealthful or dangerous.

(mm). In manufacturing establishments other than cotton and woolen mills.

(nn). In all occupations.

(oo). In any factory, warehouse, workshop, telephone or telegraph office, clothing, dressmaking or millinery establishment, or in any place where the manufacture of any kind of goods is carried on, or where any goods are prepared for manufacture.

(pp). In any manufacturing business or factory in any part of the State or in any mercantile establishment in Baltimore.

(qq). Children under 14 in the street trades.

(rr). Contracts for overtime allowed.

(ss). In manufacturing establishments and stores employing more than 10 persons.

(tt). In bakeries.

(uu). In any mercantile establishment, business office, or telegraph office, restaurant, hotel, apartment house, or in the distribution or transmission of merchandise or messages.

(vv). Children under 18 and women can not be *compelled* to work more than these hours.

(ww). In any manufacturing establishment, mercantile industry, laundry, workshop, renovating works, or printing office.

(xx). In any factory, mine or textile manufactory.

(yy). If illiterate.

(zz). In tobacco factories; and shall not be *compelled* to work in manufacturing establishments.

Source: Adams, Thomas Sewall and Helen L. Sumner (1910) *Labor Problems: A Textbook*, New York: Macmillan.

Table 1.8 Duties of factory inspectors in the United States, various States, 1877–91

Factory inspectors' duties relate to	Mass. (1877)	N.J. (1883)	Ohio. (1884)	N.Y. (1886)	Conn. (1887)	Pa. (1889)	Ill. (1893)	R.I. (1894)	Me. (1887)	Mich. (1893)	Mo. (1891)	Wis. (1883)	Minn. (1887)	Penn. (1891)
Employment of children	*	*	*	*		*	*	*	*	*		*	*	
Employment of women	*	*				*	*	*	*	*		*	*	
Payment of wages	*	*	*	*		*			*					
Lunch hour, women and children	*	*		*		*				*				
Seats for females	*	*	*	*	*	*		*		*	*		*	
Separate toilet facilities for the two sexes	*	*		*	*			*		*	*		*	
Guarding machinery	*	*	*	*	*	*		*		*	*	*		
Cleaning machinery in motion by children and women	*	*		*	*	*		*		*	*			
Mechanical belt and gear shifters	*			*						*			*	
Communication with engineer's room	*											*		
Guarding vats containing molten metal or hot liquids		*	*	*										
Railing on stairways			*	*							*			
Regulation of dangerous or injurious occupations	*	*												
Use of explosive or inflammable material	*	*												
Exhaust fans for dust, etc.	*	*		*						*	*		*	
Safety appliances for elevators	*													

Cont'd

Table 1.8 cont'd

Factory inspectors' duties relate to	Mass. (1877)	N.J. (1883)	Ohio. (1884)	N.Y. (1886)	Conn. (1887)	Pa. (1889)	Ill. (1893)	R.I. (1894)	Me. (1887)	Mich. (1893)	Mo. (1891)	Wis. (1883)	Minn. (1887)	Tenn. (1891)
Guarding elevator and hoistway openings	*	*	*	*	*	*		*		*	*		*	
Fire escapes	*	*	*	*		*				*	*	*	*	
Doors to swing outward; to be unlocked	*	*	*	*										
Sanitary condition	*	*	*	*		*		*	*		*		*	
Ventilation	*	*	*	*	*	*		*			*			
Lighting		*	*											
Heating		*	*											
Overcrowding		*		*							*	*		
Lime washing or painting walls		*		*							*			
Reporting accidents	*		*	*		*		*			*		*	
Regulation of "sweating system"	*		*	*		*	*							
Inspection of mercantile establishments				*										
Inspection of mines		*												
Inspection of steam boilers	*										*			*
Inspection of school houses, theaters, etc.	*		*											
Regulation of bakeries		*									*		*	
Approval of plans for factories	*													

Source: Willoughby, W. F. (1897) The Inspection of Factories and Workshops in the United States, Bulletin of the Department of Labor no. 12 (September), Washington: Government Printing Office.

Table 1.9 Maximum-hours legislation and scheduled hours, by state women, 1909–1919, in the United States

	First Enforceable Law			Legislated Daily Hours in Manufacturing as of			Scheduled Hours in Manufacturing as of	
State	Date	Hours	Coverage	1909	1914	1919	1909	1919
Alabama[a]							10.2	9.4
Arizona	1913	10/56	S,L,T				9.5	8.9
Arkansas	1915[b]	9/54	M,S,L			9	9.9	9.5
California	1911	8/48	M,S,L,T		8	8	9.2	8.0
Colorado	1903	8/	M,S	8	8	8	9.7	8.6
Connecticut	1887	10/60	M,S	10	10	10	9.4	8.6
Delaware	1913	10/55	M,S,L,T		10	10	9.5	8.3
District of Columbia	1914	8/48	M,S,L,T		8	8	9.0	8.2
Florida							10.0	9.3
Georgia							9.4	8.9
Idaho	1913	9/	M,S,L,T		9	9	9.8	8.3
Illinois	1893[c]	8/48	M	10	10	10	9.4	8.3
Indiana							9.6	8.8
Iowa							9.6	8.8
Kansas	1917	9/54	S,L			8	9.7	8.6
Kentucky	1912	10/60	M,S,L,T		10	10	9.5	8.9
Louisiana	1886	10/60	M	10	10	10	10.2	9.3
Maine	1887[d]	10/	M	10	10	9	9.7	8.7
Maryland	1912	10/60	M,S,L		10	10	9.6	8.3
Massachusetts	1879[a]	10/60	M	10	10	9	9.4	8.1
Michigan	1885[f]	10/60	M	9	9	9	9.7	8.6
Minnesota	1895[g]	10/	M	10	9	9	9.5	8.6
Mississippi	1914	10/60	all		10	10	10.2	9.4
Missouri	1909	/54	M,S,L	/54	9	9	9.3	8.5
Montana	1913	9/	M,S,L,T		9	8	9.2	8.6
Nebraska	1899	10/60	M,S	10	9	9	9.6	8.8
Nevada	1917	8/56	M,S,L			8	9.3	8.5
New Hampshire	1887[h]	10/60	M	9.7	10.25	10.25	9.5	8.3
New Jersey	1892[i]	/55	M		10	10	9.4	8.2
New Mexico	1921[j]	8/56	M,L				9.7	9.1
New York	1886[k]	/60	M	10	9	9	9.3	8.3
North Carolina	1915	11/60	M			11	10.3	9.4
North Dakota	1919[l]	8.5/48	M,S,L,T			8.5	9.4	8.5
Ohio	1911[m]	10/54	M		10	9	9.5	8.6
Oklahoma	1915[n]	9/	M,S,L,T			9	9.6	8.9
Oregon	1903	10/	M,L	10	10	9	9.6	8.0
Pennsylvania	1897[o]	12/60	M,S,L	12	10	10	9.7	8.6
Rhode Island	1885	10/60	M	10	10	10	9.5	8.5
South Carolina	1907[p]	10/60	CW	10	10	10	10.0	9.5
South Dakota	1923[l]	/54	M				9.6	8.9

Table 1.9 cont'd

	First Enforceable Law			*Legislated Daily Hours in Manufacturing as of*			*Scheduled Hours in Manufacturing as of*	
State	*Date*	*Hours*	*Coverage*	*1909*	*1914*	*1919*	*1909*	*1919*
Tennessee	1908[q]	/62	M	/61	10.5	10.5	9.9	9.1
Texas	1913	10/54	M,S,T		10	9	9.9	8.9
Utah	1911	9/54	M,S,L,T	9	9	8	9.4	8.7
Vermont	1912	11/58	M		11	10.5	9.4	8.7
Virginia	1890	10/	M	10	10	10	9.9	8.8
Washington	1901	10/	M,S,L	10	8	8	9.7	7.8
West Virginia							9.7	8.8
Wisconsin	1911[r]	10/55	M,S,L,T		10	10	9.7	8.9
Wyoming	1915	10/56	M,S,L,T			10	10.3	9.4
Number of states with effective hours laws in manufacturing				20	33	40		
Mean scheduled hours								
Weighted by number of employees							9.5	8.5
Unweighted							9.6	8.7

[a] An 8-hour law (unenforceable) was passed in Alabama in 1887 and was repealed in 1894.
[b] Cotton textile firms were exempted.
[c] Declared unconstitutional in 1895; a 10-hour law was passed in 1909.
[d] Maine passed a 10-hour law (unenforceable) in 1848. The 1887 law allowed weekly hours to exceed 60 if workers received overtime pay.
[e] Massachusetts passed a 10-hour law in 1874 that is termed "unenforceable" in the source listed below, but Atack and Bateman (1988) note that at least one case was upheld in court under the law.
[f] The Michigan law was amended in 1893 to apply only to girls under 21 years old; the law again regulated the hours of all women in 1907.
[g] Minnesota passed a 10-hour law (unenforceable) in 1858.
[h] New Hampshire passed a 10-hour law (unenforceable) in 1847.
[i] New Jersey passed a 10-hour law for all workers in 1851, but it carried no fines or penalties. A /55 hour law (applying only in women) was passed in 1892, repealed in 1904, and later followed by a 10/60 hour law passed in 1912.
[j] The 1921 law also provided for a 9/56 maximum for sales workers, and a 8/48 maximum for telephone workers on day and 10/60 on night work.
[k] The law applied only to female workers under 21 years of age, but was extended to all women in 1899.
[l] A 10-hour law (unenforceable) for the Territory of Dakota was passed in 1863. South Dakota passed a law in 1913, but it allowed workers to contract for more than 10 hours a day.
[m] A 10-hour law (unenforceable) was passed in 1852 and was repealed in 1880.

Table 1.9 cont'd

[n] The Territory of Oklahoma passed a 10-hour law (unenforceable) in 1890, which was repealed in 1909.

[o] A 10/60-hour law (unenforceable) was passed in 1848 and applied to all workers in textile and paper factories in Pennsylvania.

[p] The law applied to all persons; a 12/60 law, passed in 1911, applied only to women.

[q] The Tennessee law was passed in 1907 but applied after January 1, 1908. The reduction to 60 hours per week took place by 1910.

[r] Wisconsin passed an 8-hour law (unenforceable) in 1867 that was repealed in 1913.

Notes: Hours; daily/weekly. Coverage: M = manufacturing; S = sales; L = laundries; T = telephone and telegraph; CW = cotton and woolen textiles. Many early laws (e.g., New Hampshire, 1847; Maine, 1848; Pennsylvania, 1848; Ohio, 1852; Minnesota, 1858) were unenforceable because they allowed workers to contract for more than the maximum number of hours. These laws stated that firms could not "compel" workers to labor over the maximum. Enforceable here also means that the law provided fines and/or jail sentences for violators, and that it was enforceable as a legal document. Legislated daily hours in manufacturing includes only enforceable legistation; weekly maximum is given when there was no daily maximum. For southern states, manufacturing can include only textiles. At one time or another, many states (e.g., Arkansas, California, Delaware, Idaho, Maryland, Minnesota, Nevada, New Jersey, New Mexico, New York, Oregon, and Washington) exempted canning in general or during certain months. Additional, but minor, restrictions applied in various states.

Scheduled hours refers to the average across all workers and is the weekly average divided by 6. See Goldin (1988a) for a discussion of the hours data.

Sources: U.S. Department of Labor, Women's Bureau, *Chronological Development of Labor Legislation for Women in the United States*, Bulletin No. 66-II (Washington, DC: Government Printing Office, 1932); U.S. Bureau of the Census, *Thirteenth Census 1910.* Vol. 8, *Manufactures 1909: General Report and Analysis* (Washington, DC: Government Printing Office, 1913b); U.S. Bureau of the Census, *Population 1920. Fourteenth Census of the United States, Census of Manufactures, 1919* (Washington, DC: Government Printing Office, 1928).

Source: Goldin, Claudia (1990) *Understanding the Gender Gap: An Economic History of American Women*, New York, Oxford University Press.

(including slaves), special provisions had been made for seamen and the military, as well as for workers in government-operated establishments, and apprenticeship was often controlled, but these were not the form of the labor standards which were to come later, affecting larger numbers of workers at their place of employment.[35] As discussed above, these began primarily with the introduction of legislation effecting the working hours of women and children (both the total number of working hours per day and the specific hours of work [night work]), as well as the minimum ages of employment for children in different occupations.

Table 1.10   (a) Minimum age of admission to industrial labor (1919), and (b) Duration of nightly recess for women

(a) Minimum age of admission to industrial labor

Class I: Minimum legal age of employment 15 years or more

Europe	America	Canada
	California (both sexes)	British Columbia (girls)
	Michigan (both sexes)	Mantitoba (girls)
	Nevada (16 for girls only)	
	Ohio (both sexes, 16 for girls)	*Australia*
	Texas (both sexes)	Victoria (girls)

Class II: Minimum legal age of employment at 14, or at 13 with special provision for completion of schooling

Europe	America	America (Cont.)	America (Cont.)
Austria	Alabama	Maine	South Dakota
Bosnia	Arizona	Maryland	Tennessee
Belgium	Arkansas	Massachusetts	Utah
Denmark	Colorado	Minnesota	Vermont
Germany	Connecticut	Missouri	Virginia
Great Britain	Delaware	Montana	Washington
Norway	District of	Nebraska	West Virginia
Serbia	Columbia	Nevada (boys)	Wisconsin
Sweden (girls)	Florida	New Hampshire	
Switzerland	Georgia	New Jersey	*Canada*
	Idaho	New York	British Columbia
Australasia	Illinois	North Dakota	Manitoba (boys)
New South Wales	Indiana	Oklahoma	New Brunswick
New Zealand	Iowa	Oregon	Nova Scotia
Queensland	Kansas	Pennsylvania	Ontario
Tasmania	Kentucky	Puerto Rico	Quebec
Victoria (boys)	Louisiana	Rhode Island	Saskatchewan
Western Austrialia			

Class III: Minimum legal age of employment 13 years

Europe	America	Africa
France	North Carolina	Algeria
Netherlands		
Sweden (boys)		

Class IV

Greece	South Carolina
Italy	
Luxemburg	*Latin America*
Portugal (by exception 10)	Buenos Aires
Russia	Mexico
Rumania	

Class V: Minimum legal age of employment 10 years or less

Europe	Latin America	Asia
Hungary	Argentina	East India (9 years)
Spain	Brazil (8 in textile factories)	
		Africa
		Egypt (9 years)

Table 1.10 cont'd

(b) Duration of nightly recess for women

Class I: Recess of 11 hours or more required by law

Nation	Previous to Berne Agreement	Since Berne Agreement
Austria	9 hours	11 hours
Belgium	no law	11 hours
France	8 hours	11 hours
Germany	9 hours	11 hours
Great Britain	12 hours	11 hours
Greece	no law	11 hours
Hungary	no law	11 hours
Italy	{ 8 (summer)	11 hours
	{ 10 (winter)	11 hours
Luxemburg	no law	11 hours
Netherlands	10 hours	11 hours
Portugal	no law	11 hours
Spain	no law	11 hours
Sweden	no law	11 hours
Switzerland	{ 9 (summer)	11 hours
	{ 10 (winter)	11 hours

Class II: Recess of less than 11 hours required by law

Nation	Previous to Berne Agreement	Since Berne Agreement
Bosnia	no law	9 hours
Bulgaria	no law	9 (summer)
		12 (winter)
Russia	8 hours (textile factories)	8 hours
Serbia	no law	9 (summer)
		10 (winter)

Class III: No legislation
Denmark, Finland and Rumania have not yet legislated on the subject.

Source: Shotwell, James T. (ed.) (1934) *The Origins of the International Labor Organization*, vol. 2, Documents, New York: Columbia University Press.

Table 1.11   Age of legal employment and maximum legal hours of labor of children employed in factories in the United States, January 1, 1913

States	Age below which			Maximum legal hours of labor per day	Night work prohibited between
	Employment is prohibited	Hours of labor are restricted	Night work is prohibited		
					p.m. a.m.
Alabama	12	14	16	60[1]	7 and 6
Arizona	14	16[2]	16[2]	8	7 and 7
Arkansas	14	14	14	10	7 and 6
California	15	18	18	9	10 and 5
Colorado	14	16	14	8	8 and 7
Connecticut	14	16	16	10	([3])
Delaware	14	16	16	9	6 and 7

Table 1.11 cont'd

	Age below which			Maximum legal hours of labor per day	Night work prohibited between
States	Employment is prohibited	Hours of labor are restricted	Night work is prohibited		
District of Columbia	14	16	16	8	7 and 6
Florida	12	12	12	9	9 and 6
Georgia	12	12	14	10	7 and 6
Idaho	14	16	16	9	9 and 6
Illinois	14	16	16	8	7 and 7
Indiana	14	16	16	8	6 and 7
Iowa	14	16	16	10[4]	9 and 6
Kansas	14	16	16	8	6 and 7
Kentucky	14	16[5]	16	10	7 and 7
Louisiana	14	18	16[2]	10	7 and 6
Maine	14	16[2]		10 (58)[1]	
Maryland	14	16	16	10	8 and 8
Massachusetts	14	18	21	10 (54)[1]	10[6] and 6
Michigan	14	18	16[2]	54[1]	6 and 6
Minnesota	14	16	16	8	7 and 7
Mississippi	12	16[2]	16[2]	8	7 and 6
Missouri	14	16	16[4]	8	7 and 7
Montana	16				
Nebraska	14	16	16	8	8 and 6
New Hampshire	14	16[2]	16[2]	11 (58)[1]	7 and 6.30
New Jersey	14	16	16	10 (55)[1]	6 and 6
New York	14	16	16	8	5 and 8
North Carolina	12	18	14	60[7]	8 and 5
North Dakota	14	16	16	8	7 and 7
Ohio	14	16[2]	16[2]	8	6 and 7
Oklahoma	14	16	16[2]	8	6 and 7
Oregon	14	16	16	10	6 and 7
Pennsylvania	14	16[2]	16[2]	10 (58)[1]	9 and 6
Rhode Island	14	16	16	10 (56)[1]	8 and 6
South Carolina	12	([8])	16	10	8 and 6
South Dakota	15	14		10	
Tennessee	14	16		60[1]	
Texas	15				
Utah	14	14[9]		54[1]	
Vermont	14	16	16		([10])
Virginia	14	14	14	10	6 and 7
Washington	14		16		8[11] and 5
West Virginia	14				
Wisconsin	14	16	16	8	6 and 7

[1] Per week.
[2] To 18 years for females.
[3] After 10 p. m.
[4] 9 hours if written consent of parent is obtained.
[5] To 21 years for females.
[6] 6 and 6 in textile factories.
[7] Per week; no more may be required.
[8] Law is general for cotton and woolen mills; no age limit.
[9] To 16 years for females.
[10] After 8 p. m.
[11] In bakeries.

Source: US Department of Labor, Bureau of Labor Statistics (1913) *Prohibition of Night Work of Young Persons*, Bulletin of the United States Bureau of Labor Statistics no. 117 (April), Washington, Government Printing Office.

It is difficult to adequately describe the full range of legislation, covering total hours of work, safety provisions, the number of consecutive hours to be worked, provisions for meal times, rights of association and union formation, etc. The precise range of issues covered earlier would not be surprising to those looking at similar legislation today. Their imposition a century ago, however, must have shocked many employers and employees at the time, as well as imposed problems for the relatively new set of bureaucrats charged with their enforcement. A brief summary cannot convey the nature of the legal changes made at any time, while the problems of enforcement makes determination of the impact of any legislation uncertain.

The United States Department of Health, Education, and Welfare, Social Security Administration, publishes a report summarizing the terms and dates of introduction for five basic welfare and standards programs.[36] To simplify the examination I prepared a breakdown of the date of the introduction of coverage under Work Injury. For 30 European countries, 12 had this provision before 1900, another ten added these in the first two decades of the twentieth century, five in the interwar period, and only three (Turkey, Cyprus, and Albania) after the start of World War II. For the 71 nations of Asia and Africa, there were none before 1910, and only three (Japan, Algiers, and South Africa) before 1920 (although there was earlier legislation of some form of labor standards in British India in 1881). In 36 cases the provision came between 1921 and 1940, and in 30 after World War II.[37] For Latin America, the provisions all came after 1910, with three (Haiti, Honduras, and Guatemala) after 1944. The British and French overseas offshoots (Canada, Australia, New Zealand, the United States, South America, and Algiers) all introduced coverage for work injury between 1902 and 1914, after legislation in many European nations, but before most of the other countries of the world. Thus for Europe and the British offshoots overseas, over three-quarters of the countries had work injury provisions before 1920, one-third by 1900. For the nations of Asia, Africa, and Latin America there were none with coverage before 1900, and only about 13 percent had legislation in place before 1920, all but one of these independent nations being in Latin America. Clearly the pattern of reforms of labor and welfare standards was originated and led by the nations of Europe, particularly England.

The first major discussion and implementation of factory legislation, as noted above, was that of the British in 1802, covering pauper apprentices, extended in 1819 to cover the minimum age required for employment in cotton mills (nine) and also the hours to be worked by those young workers under 16 in cotton mills. It was several decades, however, before other continental countries introduced their own significant factory acts, usually in reference to child labor: Germany 1839, Hungary 1840, France 1841, and Austria, 1842. There was then a further lag before more countries undertook such measures: Denmark 1873, Spain 1873, Holland 1874, Switzerland 1877,

Sweden 1881, Russia 1882, Italy 1886, Belgium 1889, Portugal 1891, and Norway 1892 see table 1.1. (For more on the Scandinavian history regarding labor standards, see Appendix 1.)[38] The two most populous provinces of Canada introduced child labor legislation in 1884 and 1885,[39] Australia and New Zealand did so in the 1870s, and 1880s,[40] the states of the US after 1836 (mainly those in New England at first, while national legislation was not successful until 1938),[41] India in 1881, Japan in 1911 (several decades after its laws requiring education), China in the 1920s, and Egypt in 1933.[42] The timing within Europe, and its offshoots, provides some guide to the timing of the expansion of industrialization, as well as an indication of the contemporaneous movement of ideas about morality and economic welfare across the continent.

Because of the number of states and their differences in political and economic structure, the dating for the US is more complex.[43] In general, legislation began in the years after 1836, with Massachusetts often leading the way. The eastern states generally introduced legislation regarding children and women in the second half of the nineteenth century, and then, in the first two decades of the twentieth century, most of the remaining states adopted these policies. Legislation at the federal level was attempted in these years, but these were often declared to be unconstitutional by the Supreme Court at the initial stage. By 1920 the basic program of labor and related standards was adopted, but with differences persisting among the states in regards to specific provisions. The debate at the state level within the US raised the important issue of interstate competition. The imposition of national standards with the Fair Labor Standards Act of 1938 was the source of an interregional debate on the issue of uniform national versus regional differentiated levels for minimum wages.[44] Although similar questions had long existed in Europe regarding international competition, the possibilities for national legislation could make an easier resolution of these federal issues in the United States than was possible for those cases dependent on international agreements.

In most of the cases of the introduction of labor legislation in different countries, similar sets of political issues often arose. First, almost all legislation regarding hours of work dealt only with women and children (a key early exception being France in 1848), since adult males were considered to be individuals with the power and capacity to freely choose and influence their working conditions. A noteworthy early-nineteenth-century case was that of the United States president, Martin Van Buren, in 1840, setting a ten-hour workday for those employed in federal government public works. This was broadened to an eight-hour workday for all federal workers in 1868.[45] Neither, however, had much effect on legislated male hours of work in the private sector. The concern with child labor was twofold. First, to reduce labor by young children that might weaken them physically, since it was argued, that without rules on child labor, Lancashire would (as quoted by Lord Ashley in 1844) "speedily become a province of pigmies," mentally, physically, and morally.[46] This would lower the productive capacity of society. Second, limits were needed because of the benefits of providing more time for schooling and education of the young. In many cases, laws regarding child labor included provisions for education of child workers, and, similarly, laws regarding education were framed with consideration of the issue of child labor.[47] Children were regarded as wards, of their parents or of others including the state, unable to make informed decisions on their own.

Women were also seen, for both different and related reasons, to be lacking in the power to make decisions. Their legal status limited their financial resources, and they seldom were members of unions that could bargain for terms. Also of importance in the political arena was the argument that as potential mothers and providers of childcare women were deserving of special treatment. Not all agreed with this position then (or now). The economist Nassau Senior claimed special treatment of adult women would mean that they were not being treated as being as capable as men, a position held by other classical economists, including John Stuart Mill, who believed that legislation linking women and children was "indefensible in principle and mischievous in practice."[48] In the one case where women were excluded from an occupation, by the Mining Act of 1842, Senior raised the issue of whether those women who were displaced from mining should be compensated.[49] This, interestingly, was one of the very few times where the issue of compensation to offset the impact of the introduction of labor standards was raised. In general the benefits resulting from standards were considered to be their own just reward. Senior provided several basic arguments against labor standards including philosophical argument against the government's imposing restraints on adult males, as well as the more practical economic one that high standards imposed by only one country would place it at a disadvantage in international trade.[50]

Few of these acts, anywhere, had special provisions for disabled or impaired workers. If these were to be provided with special benefits it would usually be given via coverage under some more general terms of legislation. Similarly, few had distinctions based upon race, ethnicity, or citizenship status, in the defining of labor standards, although such distinctions were often made for other political and social purposes. Interestingly exceptions include the legislation of the state of Georgia in 1853, with labor standards being applied only to white workers, and the Australian law of 1888 which specified that any industrial firm with a Chinese worker would be considered a covered factory, otherwise the requirement for coverage being at least four workers.[51] Except for the belated introduction of the prohibition on the import of goods produced by prison labor, by the United States and by the United Kingdom and its overseas offshoots between 1890 and 1913, there was in this period no direct ideological linking of foreign trade with any form of labor standards.[52]

Debates also persisted, then as now, on the motive for the advocating of standards imposed on (or for) certain groups in the labor force. Was it altruism, or were there some more selfish aims, that led men to advocate policies for women and children, such as restraints on hours of work. Was it a means of eliminating competition in the labor market or was it a way for men to "fight the battle from behind the women's petticoats," in order to obtain the same benefits for themselves. Nevertheless, as noted above, it took a long time in most nations before adult men were legislatively given the same standards as adult women.

In some countries, most particularly England, and several of the New England states in the United States, the introduction of standards was applied, at first, to cotton and other textile industries, not to the overall industrial sector. The explanation seems straightforward, since cotton textiles was a labor-intensive industry, was a large industrial sector, and had a higher proportion of women and children in its labor force than had other industries. Over time, however, there was an expansion to cover all manufacturing industries, although often with the requirement of a minimum size of factory employment before coverage was applicable. In England, for example, the major factory act of 1819 applied to cotton mills, changing over time to apply to all textiles firms using steam and water power (1833), all textile firms (1844), and all industries (1867). Those nations and states following in the introduction of labor standards did not usually distinguish textiles from other manufacturing industries, although there were separate restrictions applied to what were considered to be hazardous or dangerous industries.

The other sector that was sometimes singled out for the imposition of standards was mining, both because of the nature of the work, particularly underground, and because of the safety and health problems of explosions and ventilation. In 1842, England introduced prohibitions against female work underground, as well as restrictions against boys under ten from doing such work, whereas in textile industries the age limit was then nine. Similar distinctions regarding mining were later introduced in several European nations, as well as several states in the US, while others effectively introduced restrictions by classifying mining as a dangerous or unhealthy trade. In addition to these rules regarding labor in the coal-mining sector, some countries had early specific safety regulations in mining. Britain enacted safety rules after 1850 while, in the US, Pennsylvania introduced laws regulating coal mines in one county in 1869. These provisions were subsequently expanded, and by 1900 20 states had similar legislation, ten having introduced them in the 1880s.[53] Rules regarding mining safety preceded those for factory safety in most cases, but the lags were not long.

The federal government of the US had earlier introduced safety legislation, following some European legislation, including inspection for steamboats in 1838. This was made more effective in 1852, and several states in the South and Midwest has earlier imposed their own restrictions. The professed aim of the federal legislation was the protection of passengers, since it was argued that the employees could control their conditions, and did not require separate treatment. Only in 1871 was the protection of crew as well as passengers cited as a specific reason for safety standards on steamboats. State inspection of stationary steam boilers did not begin until 1867.[54]

Throughout the nineteenth century the main thrust of labor legislation was upon factories in manufacturing, mining, and later, sweatshops. At the end of the century, when increased immigration led to the development of sweatshops, these too, were the focus of legislation.[55] Limited coverage of agriculture and services (except for the occasional introduction of shop laws) was provided through the start of the twentieth century, even though these were quite obviously the largest sectors of employment in the national economy. Whether the absence of legislation regarding agricultural labor reflected the policies of landowners' control, a belief in the family farm (and an unwillingness to impose legislation interfering with families), the absence of the negative publicity that factories and mines, located in higher population density areas, had achieved, or the perceived difficulties in enforcing any such legislation across a broad geographic expanse, is debated, but few nations had labor standards applied to agricultural labor until the twentieth century.

The development of labor standards in Europe and in Britain's overseas offshoots came at a time of secularly high and rising incomes, the shift of labor from agriculture to manufacturing sectors and from rural to urban areas, some relative expansion of the suffrage in most countries, a widespread increase in educational levels and literacy, and the expansion of a widespread, legally acceptable, labor movement.[56] They were one part, widely diffused, of the changing economic and social patterns that came with modern industrialization, so that the labor standards as they then emerged were limited to a relatively small, geographically and in terms of world populations, part of the world. And while they were first applied to only a limited part of the labor force, women and children, it seemed politically inevitable that they would ultimately be extended in terms of labor-force coverage, industrial scope, and national concerns. Whatever may have been the specific economic condition of each nation, the spread of the basic ideology accompanying industrialization and economic growth meant that the adoption of labor standards, whether internally accepted or imposed from outside, was to become part of the new international system.

The Impact of Labor Standards

The impact of labor standards has been long debated by contemporaries, as well as by later historians and economists. Legislative debates in England and in the states of the US, as well as other countries, posed several questions, such as the impact of hours of work on the measured output per hour of each worker, the effect of introducing standards in one state or nation on its ability to compete with other areas, and the changes in labor-force employment of the groups presumably aided by labor standards.[57] That hours of work declined with economic growth is clear, but the relative importance of economic changes compared to imposed social norms or compulsory education remains debated. These debates were often inconclusive, or, as with recent studies, conflicting due to issues of economic and econometric specification.[58]

While the relationship between the legislation and changes in wages, hours, and labor-force participation may be uncertain, it seems clear that in the period after the introduction of labor standards there have been reductions in hours worked in affected sectors, increases in wages, reductions in child labor along with substantial increases in education and child literacy, and increases in female labor-force participation. Factories have become cleaner and safer, and the rate of industrial accidents has declined. Nevertheless, it has been argued these change were not due primarily to legislation but were the consequences of higher national income, with accompanying changing preferences regarding work time and work arrangements as income rose. In some cases, it has been argued that legislation imposed only such standards as those that had already been achieved, or that the actual standards meant only a very small change from what was already occurring, unlike the changes discussed today.[59] In some cases, the benefits were broadly diffused, helping individuals other than those who were covered by the legislation, and not giving those covered any differential benefits. Intra-industry diffusion was quite possible, given production relations, but the extent to which benefits aimed at only a limited part of the labor force provided gains to workers in other sectors is not obvious, nor, indeed, some would argue, it is not clear that even those for whom the benefits were intended were net gainers.

Early International Agreements

The discussions among European nations about international agreements for the introduction of labor standards began at almost the same time as the debates about domestic standards in England and other countries. The conventional story starts either with Owen in 1818 or Hindley in 1833, with various French, Swiss, and German advocates following soon thereafter. There were, as now, two basically interrelated arguments for the desirability of international conferences and agreement to provide for uniformity of provisions among European nations. There was the moral claim that the same benefits should be provided to individuals in all nations, as a basic human right. Then there was the understanding that uniformity across nations would be necessary to make it possible for any one nation to impose domestically based acceptable standards, given the fear that introducing standards in one country would result in a loss in its competitive position. Thus it is not surprising that the richer nations and states were among the first advocates of international agreement on labor standards. And, given widespread beliefs in free trade, the use of trade and tariff policy was not mentioned as a means to achieve desired ends.

There was one, however, important debate in the 1830s and 1840s that did examine the use of tariff policy to achieve appropriate labor standards internationally.[60] This concerned, not the industrializing nations, but less developed colonies in the Americas and elsewhere. In the debates on the British sugar duties, differential tariffs were proposed (and achieved for a limited time) on sugar produced by slave labor (in Cuba and Brazil) contrasted with sugar produced by free labor in the British colonies after slave emancipation, sugar produced in India by nominally free (albeit extremely poor) labor, and sugar produced elsewhere. These were, however, less of a direct attempt to change labor systems in slave societies (although that was clearly part of British policy), but were, rather, intended as a support for the British colonies to offset the cost of their shift from slave to free labor, with the lowered plantation labor force and higher sugar prices (relative to still-slave Cuba and Brazil) that resulted from slave emancipation. This was an unusual and short-lived case, and while the imposition of tariffs was widespread among European (and other) nations, their intention was presumably to serve not as a basis for the imposition of labor standards, as conventionally defined, upon other countries, but rather to reduce the production of foreign nations for sale in British markets. In the second half of the nineteenth century international conferences and bilateral agreements were only for the countries of Europe, countries with relatively small differences in climate, income, and culture, in comparison with those that existed in the twentieth century between Europe and the less-developed world. This meant that several of the later problems in establishing uniform international labor standards among countries with quite different incomes did not arise.

Although there was talk of international conferences on labor issues starting in the early decades of the nineteenth century, the first of the major proposed organized meetings to provide for setting international legislation on factories, was at the initiative of the government of Switzerland in 1881.

The negative reactions from both employers and laborers in the six countries approached to attend meant that this attempt was unsuccessful. Switzerland tried again, with a conference planned but not held in Berne in 1889, with four countries accepting invitations. In 1890, however, the Germans organized a conference in Berlin, with 14 states in attendance including "the twelve chief industrial states of Europe." The meeting lasted only ten days, and reached no policy conclusions. Clearly these nations were not yet ready for any actions across national borders. Among subsequent meetings were sessions in Brussels (12 European nations plus the United States) in 1897, with later conferences held under the auspices of the International Association for Labor Legislation. These included conferences in Paris in 1900, (7 countries, including the United States and Mexico) Basel in 1901 (7 nations) Cologne (12 nations) in 1902, and Berne in 1905 (15 nations), 1906 (14 nations), and 1913 (15 nations). The only successful agreements reached concerned "the prohibition of the manufacture, sale, and importation of matches containing white phosphorous," and limits on night work for women.[61] These restrictions were applied to the adopting nations and to their colonies. The outcomes of European conferences before the start of World War I, were, therefore, quite limited.

Between 1904 and 1915 there were more than 20 bilateral agreements on labor issues signed between European nations (in one case the United States was involved) with Italy, France, and Germany being the most frequent signatories (see table 1.12).[62] Prior to this, in the second half of the nineteenth century there had been several international labor agreements, usually concerning emigration of contract labor and Chinese migration, free and contract. The early-twentieth-century bilateral agreements covered many different types of labor issues, but in only one case (the French–Italian treaty of 1904) did it include a statement of intent to change laws controlling hours of work and the age of entry into the labor force in the country with lower standards, Italy, to reach the levels in force in France. The most frequent coverage related to equal treatment in regard to insurance compensation for accidents of the citizens of one country when working in another. Thus by World War I, despite a long interest and a growing labor union movement in most countries, the multilateral achievement of uniform standards among the developed nations of Europe was quite limited, as were the number of internal standards intended to improve the position of adult males. Enforcement procedures for internal, but even more for international, provisions, were generally weak and somewhat inconsequential.

Table 1.12 List of bilateral and plurilateral international agreements regarding labour questions

Date of signature	Parties	Agreement
26 June 1858	China–Great Britain	Treaty of peace, friendship and commerce (Art. 13 employment of Chinese)
25 July 1860	France–Great Britain	Convention relative to the emigration of labourers from India to the Colony of Réunion
24 Oct. 1860	China–Great Britain	Convention of friendship (Art. 5: coolie emigration)
1 July 1861	France–Great Britain	Convention relative to the emigration of labourers from India to the French Colonies
6 Oct. 1863	China–Netherlands	Treaty of friendship and commerce (Art. 5: employment of Chinese)
31 July/ 30 Nov. 1865	France–Great Britain	Protocol of Conference respecting the duration of the Convention of 1 July 1861 relative to the emigration of labourers from India
28 July 1868	China–United States	Additional articles to the treaty between the United States and China of 18 June 1868
8 Sept. 1870	Great Britain–Netherlands	Convention relative to the emigration of labourers from India to the Dutch Colony of Surinam
2 Nov. 1871	Great Britain–Netherlands	Protocol, Recruitment of free labourers (Guinea)
5 Nov. 1872	France–Great Britain	Declaration as to the annual time of emigration from India to the French Colonies west of the Cape of Good Hope
26 June 1874	China–Peru	Treaty of friendship, commerce and navigation (Art. VI: emigration)
17 Nov. 1877	China–Spain	Convention for regulating the emigration of Chinese subjects to Cuba
17 Nov. 1880	China–United States	Treaty concerning immigration of Chinese labourers into the United States and their residence therein
5 May 1882	Hawaii–Portugal	Provisional Convention concerning commerce, navigation and emigration (Art. 3: emigration)
31 May 1882	Belgium–France	Arrangements concerning savings funds
17 Mar. 1894	China–United States	Convention concerning Chinese immigration to the United States
29 May 1896	Great Britain–Liberia	Agreement respecting the engagement of labourers in Liberia and the Colony of Sierra Leone
4 Mar. 1897	Belgium–France	Convention relating to savings funds
14 Nov. 1899	Germany–Great Britain	Convention and Declaration for the settlement of the Samoan and other questions (West Africa, Zanzibar, etc.) (Art. 4: right of Germany to engage labourers in the Solomon Islands falling to Great Britain)
14 Dec. 1899	China–Mexico	Treaty of amity and commerce (Art. V: free emigration; Art. VI: contract labourers)

Cont'd

Table 1.12 cont'd

Date of signature	Parties	Agreement
18 Dec. 1901	Great Britain–Portugal	Agreement for a *modus vivendi* between the Transvaal and the Province of Mozambique: engagement of Native labourers
15 Apr. 1904	France–Italy	Labour treaty
13 May 1904	China–Great Britain	Convention concerning the employment of Chinese labour in British Colonies and Protectorates
13 July 1904	Italy–Switzerland	Treaty of commerce (Art. 17: equality of treatment in respect of workmen's insurance)
3 Dec. 1904	Germany–Italy	Treaty of commerce (Art. 4: equality of treatment in respect of workmen's insurance)
25 Jan. 1905	Austria–Germany	Commercial treaty with clauses providing for agreements relating to workmen's compensation and labour legislation in general (Art. 6: equality of treatment)
15 Apr. 1905	Belgium–Luxembourg	Convention relating to compensation for industrial accidents
2 Sept. 1905	Germany–Luxembourg	Treaty relating to compensation for industrial accidents
20 Jan. 1906	France–Italy	Arrangements relating to the transfers from ordinary savings funds of the two countries
21 Feb. 1906	Belgium–France	Treaty relating to compensation for injuries resulting from industrial accidents
27 Feb. 1906	France–Great Britain	Protocol respecting the New Hebrides (Arts. XXXI–LVI: recruitment of Native labourers)
8 May 1906	Germany–Sweden	Treaty of commerce
22 May 1906	Belgium–Luxembourg	Supplementary convention
9 June 1906	France–Italy	Agreement relating to compensation for injuries resulting from industrial accidents
27 June 1906	France–Luxembourg	Convention relating to compensation for injuries resulting from industrial accidents
20 Oct. 1906	France–Great Britain	Convention concerning the New Hebrides (Arts. XXXI–LVI: recruitment of Native labourers)
27 Aug. 1907	Germany–Netherlands	Treaty relating to accident insurance
1 Apr. 1909	Mozambique–Transvaal	Convention between the Governor of the Transvaal and the Portuguese Province of Mozambique (Part I: matters concerning Natives)
3 July 1909	France–Great Britain	Convention in regard to workmen's compensation for accidents
15 Apr. 1908/ 9 Aug. 1909	Great Britain–Sweden	Treaty relating to accident insurance
19 Sept. 1909	Hungary–Italy	Agreement respecting accident insurance
12 Mar. 1910	Belgium–France	Note in pursuance of the Convention of 21 Feb. 1906 respecting compensation for injuries resulting from industrial accidents
10 June 1910	France–Italy	Agreement relating to the protection of young persons of French nationality employed in Italy and of young persons of Italian nationality employed in France

Date	Countries	Subject
9 Aug. 1910	France–Italy	Arrangement respecting the application of the provisions contained in Art. I, b, of the Convention of 15 Apr. 1904, having in particular the object of enabling the citizens of the two countries working abroad to benefit from the social insurance laws
Nov. 1910	France–Great Britain	Arrangements respecting the application of Art. 5 of the Anglo–French Convention of 3 July 1909 in regard to compensation to workmen for accidents arising out of their employment
21 Feb. 1911	Japan–United States	Treaty and protocol respecting commerce and navigation (clause relating to limitation and control of emigration of labourers from Japan to the United States)
3 Apr. 1911	Great Britain–Japan	Treaty of commerce and navigation
2 May 1911	Germany–Sweden	Treaty of commerce and navigation (equality of treatment in respect of workmen's compensation)
9 Aug. 1911	Denmark–France	Treaty of arbitration (Art. II, No. 4: international protection of workers)
26 Jan. 1912		Draft for Spitzbergen Convention (Chapter X: Rules respecting workmen)
6 July 1912	Belgium–Germany	Convention in regard to insurance against industrial accidents
31 July 1912	Germany–Italy	Convention with respect to workmen's insurance
30 Nov. 1912/	Germany–Spain	Agreement concerning the reciprocal communication of notices of accidents to Spanish sailors on German ships and of German sailors on Spanish ships
12 Feb. 1913		
25 Feb. 1913	Italy–United States	Treaty amending the Treaty of Commerce and Navigation concluded 26 Feb. 1871 between the same high contracting parties (equality of rights for the purpose of compensation for injuries or for death caused by negligence or fault)
9 Aug. 1913	Belgium–Germany	Administrative regulations in connection with Art. 11 of the Convention with respect to accident insurance signed 6 July 1912
13 Oct. 1913	France–Switzerland	Agreement relating to pensions to be granted to members of the staff of the Swiss Federal Railways employed on French territory
22 May/	Liberia–Spain	Convention respecting the recruiting of labourers in the Republic of Liberia to work in the Colony of Fernando Po
12 June 1914		
30 May 1914	Germany–Netherlands	Treaty supplementary to the treaty signed on 27 Aug. 1907 respecting accident insurance
6 Aug. 1914	France–Great Britain	Protocol respecting the New Hebrides (Arts. 31–56: recruiting, engagement and employment of Native labourers)
21 May 1915	Germany–Italy	Arrangement respecting the reciprocal treatment of the subjects of the two States and of their property during the state of war (includes clause relating to social insurance)

Source: International Labor Office (1952) *The International Labor Code, 1951: vol. II: Appendices*, Geneva: ILO.

The International Labor Organization

The big breakthrough in the development of international standards came with the formation of the International Labor Organization in 1919. With some impetus from the American Federation of Labor in the United States and other national labor movements, the ILO was created as a part of the League of Nations. Later, after 1946, it was to become an agency of the United Nations. The initial membership included 44 nations, increasing to 54 in 1924, reaching 121 in 1969, and 174 today. Since membership was automatic with (or required by) membership in the League of Nations, or by invitation "to accede to the covenant," several major powers, including the United States and the Soviet Union did not become members until the 1930s. While most European nations were members, accounting for 36 percent (16) of the original membership (21) (or 48 percent, if the British overseas offshoots are included), there was also membership from Latin America (17 nations), Asia (5 nations), and Africa (1 nation). Nevertheless, the early power in the organization was with the European nations.

Clearly the sheer size of the membership would make agreements difficult, but a further problem arose because of the expansion of the organization beyond Europe, to include Asia, Africa, and Latin America. These nations had rather different income levels and economic structures than did the nations of Europe, so that an important issue of difference in labor standards emerged. Claims were made that because of geographic and climatic differences, differences in legal systems, and differences in social traditions, no uniform standards would be acceptable to all members. As Article 405 of the charter of the ILO specified, "the Conference shall have due regard to those countries in which climatic conditions, the imperfect developments of industrial organization, or other special circumstances make the industrial conditions substantially different, and shall suggest the modifications, if any, which it considers may be required to meet the case of such countries."[63] With this agreement in principal, however, the specifics of the appropriate adjustments remained unstated, and it was argued that in some cases introducing labor standards would require some modification from the basic standards, delays in their introduction, or the leaving of basic decisions to the individual countries themselves. In acknowledging the circumstances of "tropical countries," and of countries with low levels of development, the ILO included Japan, China, Persia, India, South Africa, Siam, and "tropical America," as nations to be provided special treatment.[64] Recognizing differences, the more developed nations nevertheless feared that they would be at a competitive disadvantage if they alone were held to high standards, and they were not anxious to provide waivers to the less-developed world.

Since its founding, and with the redefinition of aims at the Philadelphia Conference in 1944, the ILO has been concerned with a very broad range of labor policies, including not only economic but also political and social ends. One major goal has been the ending of slavery and all forms of forced labor (except military service, convict labor, forced labor in wartime, and forced labor as the response to natural disasters). Other goals include the right to freedom of association, the ability to organize and to bargain collectively, policies to avoid discrimination in employment "on grounds of race, color, sex, religion, political opinion, national extraction, or social origin," as well as the enforcement of policies to eliminate child labor and to provide "more and better jobs for women."[65] With such a broad agenda and with limited ability to offset national sovereignty, the ILO has had a somewhat mixed record of success on the imposition of basic labor standards, narrowly conceived. It is no doubt more successful in its function of providing information on labor issues, but information alone cannot solve these difficult problems. There were, of course, dramatic social and political changes in several nations, including Germany, Italy, Japan, the Soviet Union and South Africa. Germany, Italy, and Japan each left the ILO between 1935 and 1940, and Russia was expelled from 1940 to 1954, limiting the ILO's effectiveness in dealing with these particular problems of forced labor.

In its initial decade the ILO did achieve some success in having policies discussed, passed, and ratified by many nations, but in the absence of a strong enforcement mechanism many problems remained, including that of the failure to attract some of the major nations of the world as members. The ILO was less successful in the depression decade of the 1930's, since most nations were less interested in raising their own labor standards and, on moral grounds, those of other nations, than they were with implementing policies to reduce domestic unemployment. Moreover, the particular coerced labor policies of Germany, the Soviet, and Japan were not a central concern of the ILO, even before they ended their membership. The ILO did discuss such policies to reduce unemployment insurance, but these had little direct influence on policy in most nations. Similarly the period of World War II saw limited attention to issues of labor standards. Even the basic survival of the ILO was uncertain until its transition to become an agency of the United Nations in 1946.

After World War II the nature of the ILO's involvement in international labor standards shifted. With the postwar concern with underdeveloped nations, often the former colonies of European powers, and with attention to the problems of sustained economic growth and increased international welfare, the ILO has now cast more of its policies towards improvement in the less-developed nations. Concern with the improvement of working conditions for the impoverished in third-world countries replaced the past focus on organized labor in developed nations. The ILO also expanded the provision of technical aid throughout the world. A further change in economic events and beliefs made for a critical shift in policies for the enforcement of labor standards.[66] World trade expanded, but, unlike in the past, it was now considered appropriate to link trade with the acceptance of labor standards in trading partners, whether these had come about by agreements at conferences of trading nations (e.g., the World Trade Organization (WTO)) or by unilateral actions undertaken by one of the trading nations. There has been more pressure by consumers, labor unions, and governments to introduce measures that will force other, usually the less-developed nations, to improve labor conditions, whether for the good of the workers in the less-developed nations or those in the more-developed, remains the basis of the international struggle. This also means there are now at least two major international sources for attaining improved labor conditions, the ILO and also international trade organizations, such as the WTO.

Final Remarks

This chapter has intended to describe many of the similarities in past and present debates on labor standards. Debates on who should be covered – women, children, men – and in which industries, persist, as do issues of whether there should be different standards for different nations, or for different states within a federal nation. The mix of regulations regarding wages, hours, safety, working conditions, and the rights to form unions remains important. Would enhanced standards reduce the prospects for the advancement of less-developed nations, implying a trade-off, with benefits for the present generations of workers at the cost of economic improvement for future populations? How is individual and national welfare influenced by income, by leisure, and by favorable working conditions, and what should be the policymakers objectives when aiding the labor force? Should advocacy and enforcement be based upon domestic organizations, be done by trading partners, or by regional or international organizations created for this purpose? How can national sovereignty and international aims be reconciled? Are unilateral measures regulating international trade an acceptable means of dealing with the problems of low income in the less-developed nations? How much should rich countries be willing to pay, in grants and other forms of aid, to improve labor and living conditions in poorer countries? Progress has been made by labor, but whether this has been due to imposed standards, collective bargaining, or market forces, remains debated. It is clear, however, that, given the present day circumstances, debates on labor standards, both domestically and regarding other nations, will remain a basic institutional concern for a long time.

Appendix 1: Labor Standards in the Scandinavian Nations

The Scandinavian nations were not among the European Leaders in the introduction of labor standards, but they all had some legislation in place by the end of the nineteenth century. Their patterns followed that of most of the other European nations, with legislation applied first to children, covering industrial firms, and with no provisions regarding the much larger agricultural sector. Some earlier legislation did influence laborer conditions, such as the public health measures, for example that, regarding factory ventilation, passed by Norway in 1860, and the ending of restrictions on emigration from Sweden and Norway that were achieved in the 1850s. There were also laws regarding required education, which impacted on the labor of children and on certain aspects of women's work.

The first nation to regulate the age at which children could work in factories (over 10) as well as the number of hours children of different ages could work was Denmark in 1873. Ability to gain permission to do factory work was tied to the level of education achieved. Denmark did have one unusual law, requiring that young persons and children be kept, if possible, apart from adult male workers during both working hours and rest intervals. Only minor changes in laws were made before the start of the twentieth century, with further legislation tightening the rules in 1901 and 1913 reducing the maximum hours of work and raising the minimum age necessary for factory work. After some relatively minor and ineffective legislation including public health and safety regulations applied to factories, and an 1852 law prohibiting night work for those under 12, Sweden in 1881, passed legislation regarding the age of work in factories (must be over 12) and the length of the workday for children (the same as for Denmark), with a requirement that primary education be completed. No night work was allowed by children under 18 and by women. The final country to introduce legislation regarding labor standards was Norway, which, after several years of investigation, passed a law regulating child labor in 1892. Children under 12 could not work in industrial establishments, children under 18 had limits imposed on work hours, and night work by children was prohibited. Women were not to work for four weeks after confinement. Nevertheless, while there was legislation involving night work for women and prohibition on female work in mines, none of the Scandinavian nations had introduced laws regulating hours of adult female labor before the start of World War I.

Sweden, Norway, and Denmark attended all of the important European conferences on labor standards between 1890 and 1913, although they did not sign all the conventions passed at these meetings. Sweden was involved in only three pre-World War I bilateral agreements, and Denmark only one, none concerned with the specifics of labor standards. All three Scandinavian nations were, as members of the League of Nations, charter members of the ILO in 1919.

Acknowledgments

An earlier version of this chapter was presented at the EGDI seminar on International Labor Standards in Stockholm, August 2001, and I greatly benefited from the discussions by Jane Humphries, Kalle Moene, and the other seminar participants. I also wish to thank, for comments on various drafts of this paper, Kaushik Basu, Seymour Drescher, David Eltis, Bob Hepple, and Robert Steinfeld.

Notes

1. See, e.g., Minchinton (1972), and the earlier discussions of gilds and of statutes in Cunningham (1922, vol. I, pp. 336–53, 441–7, 506–25, and vol. II, pp. 35–52). On the role of the gilds and their regulations of working conditions, see Epstein (1991, pp. 562–79).
2. For a brief useful survey of Poor Law history, see Slack (1990).
3. See, for example, the laws of various European settling nations regarding slavery in Engerman et al. (2001), part 3.
4. For a summary of these, see Klein et al. (2001), and Engerman (2002).
5. See, e.g., the discussions in Heckscher (1935) and in Furniss (1965). In the first part of the nineteenth century several European nations had quite explicit restrictions on emigration with limited controls regarding immigration. Emigration restrictions in parts of Asia persisted through the end of the century. The frequent and extensive controls regarding immigration are primarily a product of the twentieth century. See Engerman, (2002).
6. For the English origins, see, in particular Hutchins and Harrison (1966), Thomas (1948), and Keeling (1914).
7. These are based upon various publications of, or, about, the International Labor Organization. The attempt to abolish slavery and coerced labor was a goal from the start of the ILO. For some of the key agreements on this, see Brownlie (1992). The ending of slavery in the colonies of the European nations and of serfdom in Europe in the nineteenth century may be regarded as the first major, worldwide change in labor standards, although nations of Asia and Africa lagged in making such changes, as they were also to do with other forms of labor standards. The distinctions drawn between different areas of the world would be a recurring issue. The particular nature of the successful movement to end the slave trade and slavery in the Americas (and the related ending of serfdom in nineteenth-century Europe) provides a cautionary lesson for movements to improve labor standards and end world poverty. From the effective

political start of the attack on American slavery in England it took about 100 years to end slavery in the colonies of the European powers, and another three-quarters of a century to end it elsewhere in the world. In almost all cases the abolition of slavery and serfdom was accomplished by compensating the owners, not the workers (Engerman, 1996). Another feature was the sense of disappointment that generally followed freedom, and the demand for further measures to accomplish the previously expected goals (Engerman, 2000).

8. At some times, however, population growth might not be considered an unmixed blessing for society.

9. See, e.g., the discussion of "Child Labour in America Before 1870," in Abbott (1910, pp. 327–51). See also Farnam (1938, pp. 253–4), and Furniss (1965, pp. 114–16). Alexander Hamilton's advocacy of a protective tariff in his *Report on Manufactures* (1791) included the point that "women and children are rendered more useful, and the latter more early useful," in protected manufacturing establishments. An issue debated later was to be the relative contribution to human capital formation obtained from work, on-the-job training, or from schooling of those outside the labor force. This type of legislation was presumably applied to all children, whether orphaned, living with parents, or living away from parents. It should be noted that English laws regarding apprentices go back to at least the sixteenth century.

10. The Swiss banker, J. Necker, in regard to the Sunday rest-day, claimed that this could only be protected if all countries had the same law. Otherwise the competitive position of the nations with that provision would worsen. Alcock (1971, p. 6). The same point was frequently made in debates over national legislation or, in federal nations, by state governments. For mentions of such discussions in the United States, where labor standards legislation was a state matter, see Farnam (1938, p. 264) (on the Massachusetts 10-hour day agitation in the 1840s) and Goodrich (1967, pp. 471–83), and Hartz (1948, pp. 200–4) (on child labor controversies in Pennsylvania in the 1830s). See also Mummery and Hobson (1956, pp. 213–15), on the relations and substitutions among restriction of hours legislation, tariffs, and controls over migration. For a recent excellent discussion of these issues, see Charnovitz (1987).

11. Even when there were attempts at nationwide legislation, competition among the states of the United States persisted. See Seltzer (1995) on the interstate conflicts concerning the appropriate minimum wage to be introduced in the Fair Labor Standards Act of 1938, where the ultimate imposition of the higher northern rate helped to retard southern development. Earlier, in 1900, the minority report of the US Industrial Commission argued that uniform national labor laws would be unfair, since there were differences in the length and the heat of the day, as well as other climatic differences. For some discussion on nineteenth-century Switzerland, see BLS Bulletin 26 (US Department of Labor, 1900a, pp. 136–77).

12. See, e.g., the discussion at the formation of the ILO in ILO (1923, pp. 52–3, 189–91, 299–301), as well was in Shotwell (1934, vol. II, pp. 180–1, 391–2, 404–5). For an extended discussion, see Ayusawa (1920, pp. 135–72). For a claim of differential standards for Belgium, required because of wartime destruction, see ILO (1923, p. 89).

13. In the first part of the twentieth century, several attempts in the United States at federal regulation of child labor were attempted, one by prohibition of shipping goods made by children, the other by a differential tax on goods produced by child labor. The United States Supreme Court declared both unconstitutional. See Brandeis in Commons (1935, pp. 437–50).

14. See the discussions of this point when the ILO was being formed (ILO (1923, pp. 47–8, 51–2, 93–4, 188–9, 296, 577); and Shotwell (1934, vol. II, pp. 406–9)). This, of course, remains an important problem.

15. Introduced in the McKinley Tariff on 1890, this prohibition then continued in the United States, and was soon adopted by New Zealand, Australia, Canada, and Newfoundland. For the discussion of prison labor at the formation of the ILO, see ILO (1923, pp. 218–19, 227–9). The restrictions on prison labor were a long time interest of Samuel Gompers and the American labor movement. Quite recently the US Congress has debated the Child Labor Deterrence Act (or Harkings Bill and the Sander's Amendment) aimed at restricting imports made by child labor, to prevent imports of goods produced by unfree or bonded child labor.

16. For state regulations in 1892, see US Commissioner of Labor (1892). Some of this legislation, much of doubtful constitutionality, included special markings or labels placed on these goods when sold, while in several states these goods could be sold only by persons with special licenses.

17. The nature of inspection, and its effectiveness, has always been a source of contention. While some early labor standards legislation did not require inspections, they ultimately did become a specific requirement. For a history of inspection in the United States up to 1897, see US Department of Labor (1897), which includes a detailed breakdown of the duties of factory inspectors. The English case is described in Keeling (1914), Thomas (1948), and Hutchins and Harrison (1966). For a discussion of health and safety standards in the United States, Germany, and Great Britain, see Teleky (1948), and for more details on the United States, see Brandeis in Commons (1935).

18. See the data and discussion presented in Engerman et al. (2000).

19. See Keeling (1914) on England and Goldin and Sokoloff (1982) on the United States.

20. Agriculture was spread out in rural areas, not concentrated in urban areas as was manufacturing, and much of the labor in agriculture was either by family members or transient workers. There had been earlier controls regarding servants in agriculture and poor relief, at times tied to wage rates, covering rural, agricultural areas. These, however, differed from the form of standards applied to industry. Several nations imposed codes on shop labor and on workshops in the late nineteenth century, but the size of most firms in these sectors made inspection and enforcement difficult.

21. This summary is based on several essays in Shotwell (1934, vol. I), and the documents in Shotwell (1934, vol. II).

22. See Keeling (1914) and Hutchins and Harrison (1966), who argue that the 1802 Act was more of an extension of the Elizabethan Poor Laws relating to apprentices than a new form of policy. There was clearly some carry-forward from the terms of regulating apprentices to those introduced with the factory acts.

23. See Keeling (1914).

24. See Brooke (1898); US Department of Labor (1900d); see also Zelnick (1968) and Tugan-Baronovsky (1970). The early legislation concerned state operated serf-factories and not privately owned establishments of the type that were covered by later forms of legislation. There seems some uncertainty in the literature on the exact dates, but there were several Russian initiatives regarding serf-factories in the eighteenth century.

25. See Brooke (1898); Bloss (1938), and US Department of Labor (1900c).

26. See Keeling (1914).

27. For details, see Brooke (1898) and Bulletins 25–28, and 30 of the US Department of Labor, authored by W. F. Willoughby (1899–1900).

28. See US Department of Labor (1899), and the discussions in Stone (1985, pp. 123–59), Weissbach (1989), and Lynch (1988) regarding child labor and other aspects of labor standards in France.

29. See also the essays by Mahaim and Delevingne, in Shotwell, (1934, vol. I); Follows (1951); Lowe (1935); and Ayusawa (1920). It might be noted that Owen's textile factories in Scotland had initially employed many children in its labor force, but had reduced their numbers over time. See Hutchins and Harrison (1966, pp. 21–6).

30. See the advocacy of Hindley in Follows (1951, pp. 10–21, 190–6). This was the same year, 1833, that Britain successfully passed legislation to bring about the ending of slavery in its colonies.

31. See Follows (1951); Lowe (1935); Périgord (1926); and Shotwell, (1934, vol. I, pp. 453–97).

32. See, in particular, Lowe (1935).

33. See, for example, Alcock (1971); Dillon (1942); Johnston (1970); Lowe (1935); National Industrial Conference Board (1928); Périgord (1926); Shotwell, (1934, vols I and II); Solano (1920); and Thomas (1948) for detailed histories by participants and subsequent authors.

34. See the essays in Bhagwati and Hudec (1996) and Sengenberger and Campbell (1994).

35. The US federal government introduced a ten-hour day for workers on government public works projects in 1840. See Richardson (1896, p. 602). In 1868 this requirement was reduced to an eight-hour day for all federal government workers (Kelly, 1950). In some cases states and nations did introduce labor standards covering government workers before they introduced legislation regarding private firms. For the legislation regarding seamen in the US, see Farnam (1938). Similar legislation regarding seamen also existed in Great Britain, including the deduction of the seamen's sixpence.

36. See US Department of Health, Education, and Welfare (1974). There have been subsequent publications on this information, but this will not effect the points made here. Analysis of other provisions such as social insurance provides a similar pattern.

37. In the 1973 volume, two of the Asian nations were listed as not having had work injury provisions. Subsequent publications list the dates of introduction for Fiji and Nepal at 1965 and 1959, respectively.

38. These are based on Ambrosius and Hubbard (1989); Bradlaugh, (1972, pp. 61–83); Brooke (1898); de Connick-Smith, et al. (1997); Cunningham and Viazzo (1996); Gordon (1988); Hayes (1963); Huberman and Lewchuk (1999); Martin

(1990), Rimlinger (1960a, b, 1989); Tugan-Baronovsky (1970); Turin (1935); US Department of Labor, Bulletins 25–28, 30 (1899–1900); van Leeuwen (2000), and Zelnik (1971). For more details on England, see Baernreither (1889, pp. 95–151); Bradlaugh, (1972, pp. 29–59, 85–123); Gray (1996); Nardinelli (1990), and Schmiechen (1984).

39. See Stewart (1926).

40. See Sinclair (1959) and Parsons (1904) on New Zealand and Clark, (1955, pp. 604–732), and Fitzpatrick (1941) on Australia. Australia had earlier nineteenth-century legislation concerning the terms and treatment of convict labor.

41. See the basic material by Adams and Sumner (1910); Baker (1925); Brandeis in Commons (1935); Commons and Andrews (1916, pp. 200–60, 295–353); Felt (1965); Nelson (1975, pp. 122–39); Ogburn (1912); Persons et al. (1911, pp. 1–129); Steinberg (1982); US Commissioner of Labor (1892), US Department of Labor (1967); and US Department of Labor, Women's Bureau (1929); For a broad examination of government policy at this time, see Fine (1956). In 1836, Massachusetts passed a statute linking employment for children under 14 to prior attendance in school. For a useful examination of the activities of a leading reformer see Sklar (1995, esp. pp. 85–102), and for the expected gains from legislation, see Kelley (1905). On the timing of the introduction of workmen's compensation see Fishback and Kantor (2000).

42. For India: Morris in Kumar (1983); Tripathy (1989); and Weiner (1991). For Japan: ILO (1933); Solano (1920, pp. 85–102). For China: Chesneaux (1968); and Henry (1927). For Egypt: Issawi (1947, pp. 97–8). For the developments in Latin America, see Fitzgibbon (1948), on twentieth-century constitutional provisions setting labor standards; and Poblete-Troncoso (1928a, b). For a discussion of labor legislation in the Dutch East Indies, see Angelino, (1931, pp. 492–591); and for a statement of French policy in colonial Africa, see Conklin, (1997, pp. 212–45). The ILO distinguished between colonies of European nations (with "native labor") to whom standards presumably did apply (except where local countries prohibited their application or necessitate modification) and self-governing areas, see ILO (1931, pp. 220–7); and ILO (1923, pp. 68–71.) The ILO has extended its interests in these matters while it had earlier used its concerns with forced and coerced labor to attempt to influence colonized areas.

43. See sources listed in fn. 41, above. For some contemporary discussions of "The Child Labur Problem," see *Annals of the American Academy of Political and Social Science*, xx (July, 1902, pp. 151–232), and on "Child Labor" see *Annals*, xxix (January, 1907, pp. 1–183).

44. See Seltzer (1995).

45. See n. 35.

46. See the comment of Lord Ashley in 1844 (*Hansard*, 1844, 1100). Ashley notes, further, that the "wives and daughters" bear a burden for which "at least during pregnancy, . . . they would be exempted even in slave-holding states."

47. See, for example, the points made in Keeling (1914). This linking can be found in all debates on child labor legislation. There are also arguments made to justify state intervention in the case of child labor, claiming its purpose was

to offset any exploitative behavior of parents regarding their children, thus forcing parents back into the labor force. See Bland et al. (1933, pp. 495–6) for an early comment.

48. See Bowley, (1937, pp. 269–70). A similar debate, within the feminist movement, regarding policy as well as historiography, has emerged concerning special standards for women in the United States. See Kessler-Harris (1990). For the argument that the opposition by Senior to the Factory Acts was more due to expediency, based on its effects on international competitiveness than to a consistently laissez-faire position, see Bowley, (1937, pp. 255–8). For discussions of the nature of opinions on Factory Acts by contemporary economists, see Blaug (1958); Marvel (1977); and Robbins (1953). On the beliefs of the economists in parliament, see Fetter (1980, pp. 57–77). For another interesting contemporary view, see McCulloch, (1849, pp. 184–5, 303–9, 426–30). Marvel argues that advocates of labor standards were aiming at the elimination of smaller manufacturing units using older technologies, a point that has been raised about many of the reforms of Progressive Era America.

49. Bowley (1937, p. 271) and Levy (1928, pp. 249–51, 305–11).

50. Bowley (1937, pp. 255–6).

51. The Georgia example is cited in Atack and Bateman (1991a). See Evans et al. (1993, p. 315) on Australia. They claim that this legislation had the purpose of raising the costs of having Chinese workmen in the industrial labor force and thus would limit their participation.

52. See n.15. But see also the discussion below on the British Sugar Duties of the 1840s.

53. Aldrich (1997, pp. 41–75). See also, on the extension of safety regulations into the manufacturing sector (pp. 76–121). For a discussion of municipal regulations regarding safety in the nineteenth-century United States, see Novak (1996, pp. 51–82).

54. See Hunter (1949, pp. 520–46, 618–19); Hunter (1985, pp. 353–85); and Maust (2000). See also Novak (1996).

55. See, e.g., Adams and Sumner (1910, pp. 113–41).

56. A forthcoming study by Ha-Joon Chang includes discussion of the comparative levels of per capita income at which various political and economic changes have been introduced in developed and developing nations. He concludes that, in general, in today's developing nations such reforms have been made at lower levels of income per capita than by those that developed in the past.

57. There were frequent early claims that not only would the long-run impact of reducing hours for children and women be positive because of better education and physical prowess, as well as, better maternal conditions and childcare, but also that lowering the hours worked would lead to a sufficient increase in output per hour that the total output would increase. Needless to say, all these remain continuous issues to the present day. For a still interesting discussion of the relation of hours to output, see Florence (1924).

58. See Marshall in Dankert et al. (1965); Owen (1969); and Whaples (1990). For the debate on the effects of female labor standards legislation, see Goldin (1988, 1990); Jones (1975); and Landes (1980). For a discussion of the impact of child labor legislation, see Cunningham and Viazzo (1996); Moehling (1999); and

Sanderson (1974). See also Atack and Bateman (1991a) on the United States in 1880. Most broadly on the issue of child labor, see Basu (1999).

59. This had been argued for the case of compulsory schooling in both the United States and England. See Landes and Solmon (1972); and West (1994, pp. 180–7).
60. See Green (1976, pp. 229–60); and Temperley (1972, pp. 153–67).
61. See Lowe (1935).
62. For a listing of bilateral agreements, see ILO (1952, pp. 1105–10); and Lowe (1935, pp. xiv, 137–68, 171–229).
63. See Lowe (1935, p. 406).
64. ILO (1923, pp. 189, 299–301) on Japan and India; Ayusawa (1920, pp. 207–34). Not as successful was Belgium, which requested special treatment because of war damage.
65. See ILO brochure *Promoting Social Justice* (ca. 1999).
66. For some background on the United States, see Destler in Collins (1998), and for a discussion of alternative measures to achieve labor standards, based on the Latin American case, see Frundt (1998, pp. 36–55, 64–5, 275).

REFERENCES

Abbott, Edith (1910) *Women in Industry: A Study in American Economic History*, New York: D. Appleton.

Adams, Thomas Sewall and Helen L. Sumner (1910) *Labour Problems: A Text Book*, New York: Macmillan.

Alcock, Antony (1971) *History of The International Labour Organization*, London: Macmillan.

Aldrich, Mark (1997) *Safety First: Technology, Labour, and Business in the Building of American Work Safety, 1870–1939*, Baltimore: Johns Hopkins University Press.

Ambrosius, Gerold and William H. Hubbard (1989) *A Social and Economic History of Twentieth Century Europe*, Cambridge, MA: Harvard University Press.

Angelino, A. D. A. de Kat (1931) *Colonial Policy, Volume II. The Dutch East Indies* (trans G. J. Renier), Chicago: University of Chicago Press.

Annals of the American Academy of Political and Social Sciences, vol. xx (1902), vol. xxix (1907).

Atack, Jeremy and Fred Bateman (1991a) "Whom Did Protective Legislation Protect? Evidence from 1880," (unpublished).

Atack, Jeremy and Fred Bateman (1991b) "Louis Brandeis, Work and Fatigue at the Start of the Twentieth Century: Prelude to Oregon's Hours Limitation Law," (unpublished).

Ayusawa, Iwao Frederick (1920) *International Labour Legislation*, New York: Longmans, Green.

Baernreither, J. M. (1889) *English Associations of Working Men*, London: Swan Sonnenschein.

Baker, Elizabeth Faulkner (1925) *Protective Labour Legislation: With Special Reference to Women in the State of New York*, New York: Longmans, Green.

Basu, Kaushik (1999) "Child Labor: Cause, Consequence, and Cure, with Remarks on International Labour Standards," *Journal of Economic Literature*, 37 (September), pp. 1083–119.

Bhagwati, Jagdish and Robert E. Hudec (eds) (1996) *Fair Trade and Harmonization: Prerequisites for Free Trade?: Volume I: Economic Analysis*, Cambridge, MA: MIT Press.

Bland, A. E., P. A. Brown, and R. H. Tawney (comps and eds) (1933 [1914]) *English Economic History: Selected Documents*, London: G. Bell and Sons.

Blaug, Mark (1958) "The Classical Economists and the Factory Acts: A Re-examination," *Quarterly Journal of Economics*, 72 (May), pp. 211–26.

Bloss, Esther (1938) *Labour Legislation in Czechoslovakia: With Special Reference to the Standards of the International Labour Organization*, New York: Columbia University Press.

Bowley, Marian (1937) *Nassau Senior and Classical Economics*, London: George Allen & Unwin.

Bradlaugh, Charles (1972 [1891]) *Labour and Law*, Clifton: Augustus M. Kelley.

Brooke, Emma (1898) *A Tabulation of the Factory Laws of European Countries*, London: Grant Richards.

Brownlie, Ian (ed.) (1992) *Basic Documents on Human Rights* (3rd edn), Oxford: Oxford University Press.

Chang, Ha-Joon (forthcoming) *Kicking Away the Ladder?*

Charnovitz, Steve (1987) "The Influence of International Labour Standards on the World Trading Regime: A Historical Overview," *International Labour Review*, 126 (September), pp. 565–84.

Chesneaux, Jean (1968) *The Chinese Labour Movement, 1919–1927*, Stanford: Stanford University Press, (first published in French, 1962).

Clark, C. M. H. (ed.) (1955) *Select Documents in Australian History, 1851–1900*, Sydney: Angus and Robertson.

Collins, Susan M. (ed.), (1998) *Imports, Exports, and the American Worker*, Washington, DC: Brookings Institution Press.

Commons, John R. (intro) (1935) *History of Labour in the United States, 1896–1932: Volume III: Working Conditions* (by Don D. Lescohier), *Labour Legislation* (by Elizabeth Brandeis), New York: Macmillan.

Commons, John R. and John B. Andrews (1916) *Principles of Labour Legislation*, New York: Harper and Brothers.

Coninck-Smith, Ning de, Bengt Sandin, and Ellen Schrumpf (eds) (1997) *Industrious Children: Work and Childhood in the Nordic Countries 1850–1990*, Odense: Odense University Press.

Conklin, Alice L. (1997) *A Mission to Civilize: The Republican Idea of Empire in France and West Africa, 1895–1930*, Stanford: Stanford University Press.

Cunningham, Hugh and Pier Paulo Viazzo (eds) (1996) *Child Labour in Historical Perspective, 1800–1985: Case Studies From Europe, Japan, and Colombia*, Florence: UNICEF.

Cunningham, W. (1922 [1882]) *The Growth of English Industry and Commerce During the Early and Middle Ages* (5th edn), Cambridge: Cambridge University Press.

Dankert, Clyde E., Floyd C. Mann, and Herbert R. Nothrup (eds) (1965) *Hours of Work*, New York: Harper and Row.

Dillon, Conley Hall (1942) *International Labor Conventions: Their Interpretation and Revision*, Chapel Hill: University of North Carolina Press.

Engerman, Stanley L. (1996) "Emancipations in Comparative Perspective: A Long and Wide View," in Gert Oostindie (ed.), *Fifty Years Later: Antislavery, Capitalism and Modernity in the Dutch Orbit*, Pittsburgh: University of Pittsburgh Press, pp. 223–41.

Engerman, Stanley L. (2000) "Comparative Approaches to the Ending of Slavery," in Howard Temperley (ed.), *After Slavery: Emancipation and its Discontents*, London: Frank Cass, pp. 281–300.

Engerman, Stanley L. (2002) "Changing Laws and Regulations and Their Impact on Migration," in David Eltis (ed.), *Coerced and Free Migration: Global Perspectives*, Stanford: Stanford University Press, pp. 75–93.

Engerman, Stanley L., Seymour Drescher, Robert Paquette (eds) (2001) *Slavery: A Reader*, Oxford: Oxford University Press.

Engerman, Stanley L., Elisar Mariscal, and Kenneth L. Sokoloff, (2000, unpublished) "Schooling, Suffrage, and the Persistence of Inequality in the Americas, 1800–1945."

Epstein, Steven A. (1991) *Wage Labour and Guilds in Medieval Europe*, Chapel Hill: University of North Carolina Press.

Evans, Raymond, Kay Saunders, and Kathryn Cronin (1993) *Race Relations in Colonial Queensland: A History of Exclusion, Exploitation and Extermination* (3rd edn), St. Lucia: University of Queensland Press.

Farnam, Henry W. (1938) *Chapters in the History of Social Legislation in the United States to 1860*, Washington, DC: Carnegie Institution of Washington.

Felt, Jeremy P. (1965) *Hostages of Fortune: Child Labor Reform in New York State*, Syracuse: Syracuse University Press.

Fetter, Frank Whitson (1980) *The Economist in Parliament, 1780–1860*, Durham: Duke University Press.

Fine, Sidney (1956) *Laissez Faire and the General Welfare State: A Study of Conflict in American Thought, 1865–1901*, Ann Arbor: University of Michigan Press.

Fishback, Price V. and Shawn Everett Kantor (2000) *A Prelude to the Welfare State: The Origins of Workers' Compensation*, Chicago: University of Chicago Press.

Fitzgibbon, Russell H. (ed.) (1948) *The Constitutions of the Americas* [as of January 1, 1948], Chicago: University of Chicago Press.

Fitzpatrick, Brian (1941) *The British Empire in Australia: An Economic History, 1834–1939*, Melbourne: Melbourne University Press.

Florence, P. Sargent (1924) *Economics of Fatigue and Unrest and the Efficiency of Labour in English and American Industry*, New York: Henry Holt.

Follows, John W. (1951) *Antecedents of the International Labour Organization*, Oxford: Clarendon Press.

Frundt, Henry J. (1998) *Trade Conditions and Labour Rights: U.S. Initiatives, Dominican and Central American Responses*, Gainesville: University Press of Florida.

Furniss, Edgar S. (1965 [1920]) *The Position of the Laborer in a System of Nationalism: A Study in the Labor Theories of the Later English Mercantilists*, New York: Augustus M. Kelley.

Goldin, Claudia (1988) "Maximum Hours Legislation and Female Employment: A Reassessment, *Journal of Political Economy*, 96 (February), pp. 189–205.

Goldin, Claudia D. (1990) *Understanding the Gender Gap: An Economic History of American Women*. New York: Oxford University Press.

Goldin, Claudia and Kenneth Sokoloff (1982) "Women, Children, and Industrialization in the Early Republic: Evidence from the Manufacturing Censuses," *Journal of Economic History*, 42 (December), pp. 741–74.

Goodrich, Carter (ed.) (1967) *The Government and the Economy: 1783–1861*, Indianapolis: Bobbs Merrill.

Gordon, Margaret S. (1988) *Social Security Policies in Industrial Countries: A Comparitive Analysis*, Cambridge: Cambridge University Press.

Gray, Robert (1996) *The Factory Question and Industrial England, 1830–1860*, Cambridge: Cambridge University Press.

Green, William (1976) *British Slave Emancipation: The Sugar Colonies and the Great Experiment*, Oxford: Clarendon Press.

Hansard's Parlimentary Debates: Third Series (1844) vol. LXXIII, The Twenty-Second Day of February, to the Second Day of April, 1844 (London: Thomas Curson Hansard).

Hartz, Louis (1948) *Economic Policy and Democratic Thought: Pennsylvania, 1776–1860*, Cambridge, MA: Harvard University Press.

Hayes, Carleton J. (1963 [1941]) *A Generation of Nationalism, 1871–1900*, New York: Harper and Row.

Heckscher, Eli F. (1935) *Mercantilism* (2 vols), London: G. Allen and Unwin (first published in Swedish, 1931).

Henry, P. (1927) "Some Aspects of the Labour Problem in China," *International Labour Review*, 15 (January), pp. 24–50.

Huberman, Michael and Wayne Lewchuk (1999) "Globalization and Worker Welfare in Late Nineteenth Century Europe," (unpublished).

Hunter, Louis (1949) *Steamboats on the Western Rivers: An Economic and Technological History*, Cambridge, MA: Harvard University Press.

Hunter, Louis (1985) *A History of Power in the United States, 1780–1930, Volume II: Steam Power*, Charlottesville: University Press of Virginia.

Hutchins, B. L. and A. Harrison (1966 [1903]) *A History of Factory Legislation* (3rd edn), New York: Augustus M. Kelley.

International Labour Office (1923) *Official Bulletin, Volume I, April 1919–August 1920*, Geneva.

International Labour Office (1931) *The International Labour Organization: The First Decade*, London: George Allen and Unwin.

International Labour Office (1933) *Industrial Labour in Japan*, London: P. S. King.

International Labour Office (1952) *The International Labour Code, 1951, Volume II, Appendices*, Geneva.

International Labour Office (ca. 1999) *Promoting Social Justice*.

Issawi, Charles (1947) *Egypt: An Economic and Social Analysis*, Oxford: Oxford University Press.

Johnston, G. A. (1970) *The International Labour Organization: Its Work for Social and Economic Progress*, London: Europa.

Jones, Ethel B. (1975) "State Legislation and Hours of Work in Manufacturing," *Southern Economic Journal*, 41 (April), pp. 602–12.

Keeling, Frederic (1914) *Child Labour in the United Kingdom: A Study of the Development and Administration of the Law Relating to the Employment of Children*, London: R. S. King and Son.

Kelley, Florence (1905) *Some Ethical Gains Through Legislation*, New York: Macmillan.

Kelly, Matthew A. (1950) "Early Federal Regulation of Hours of Labour in the United States," *Industrial and Labour Relations Review*, 3 (April), pp. 362–74.

Kessler-Harris, Alice (1990) *A Woman's Wage: Historical Meanings and Social Consequences*, Lexington: University Press of Kentucky.

Klein, Herbert S., Stanley L. Engerman, Robin Haines, and Ralph Shlomowitz (2001) "Transoceanic Mortality: The Slave Trade in Comparative Perspective," *William and Mary Quarterly*, 58 (January), pp. 73–117.

Kumar, Dharma (ed.) (1983) *The Cambridge Economic History of India, Volume II, c. 1750–c. 1970*, Cambridge: Cambridge University Press.

Landes, Elisabeth M. (1980) "The Effect of State Maximum Hours Laws on the Employment of Women in 1920," *Journal of Political Economy*, 88 (June), pp. 476–94.

Landes, William M. and Lewis C. Solmon (1972) "Compulsory Schooling Legislation: An Economic Analysis of Law and Social Change in the Nineteenth-Century," *Journal of Economic History*, 32 (March), pp. 54–91.

van Leeuwen, Marco H. D. (2000) *The Edge of Charity: Amsterdam, 1800–1850*, New York: St. Martin's Press.

Levy, S. Leon (ed.) (1928) *Industrial Efficiency and Social Economy by Nassau W. Senior, Volume II*, New York: Henry Holt.

Lowe, Boutelle Ellsworth (1935) *The International Protection of Labour: International Labour Organization, History and Law*, New York: Macmillan.

Lynch, Katherine A. (1988) *Family, Class, and Ideology in Early Industrial France: Social Policy and the Working Class Family, 1825–1848*, Madison: University of Wisconsin Press.

Martin, Benjamin (1990) *The Agony of Modernization: Labor and Industrialization in Spain*, Ithaca: ILR Press.

Marvel, Howard P. (1977) "Factory Regulation: A Reinterpretation of Early English Experience," *Journal of Law and Economics*, 20 (October), pp. 379–402.

Maust, Peter (2000) "'Congress Could Do Nothing Better': Promoting Steamboat Safety in Antebellum America," *Prologue*, 32 (Summer), pp. 101–13.

McCulloch, J. R. (1849 [1825]) *Principles of Political Economy* (4th edn), Edinburgh: Adam and Charles Black.

Minchinton, W. E. (ed. and intro) (1972) *Wage Regulation in Pre-Industrial England*, New York: Barnes and Noble.

Moehling, Carolyn M. (1999) "State Child Labour Laws and the Decline of Child Labour," *Explorations in Economic History*, 36 (January), pp. 72–106.

Mummery, A. F. and J. A. Hobson (1956 [1889]) *The Physiology of Industry: Being an Exposure of Certain Fallacies in Existing Theories of Economics*, New York: Kelley and Millman.

Nardinelli, Clark (1990) *Child Labor and the Industrial Revolution*, Bloomington: Indiana University Press.

National Industrial Conference Board (1928) *The Work of the International Labour Organization*, New York: National Industrial Conference Board.

Nelson, Daniel (1975) *Managers and Workers: Origins of the New Factory System in the United States, 1880–1920*, Madison: University of Wisconsin Press.

Novak, William J. (1996) *The People's Welfare: Law & Regulation in Nineteenth-Century America*, Chapel Hill: University of North Carolina Press.

Ogburn, William F. (1912) *Progress and Uniformity in Child Labour Legislation: A Study in Statistical Measurement*, New York: Longmans, Green.

Owen, John D. (1969) *The Price of Leisure: An Economic Analysis of the Demand for Leisure Time*, Montreal: McGill-Queen's University Press.

Owen, Robert (1818) *Two Memorials on Behalf of the Working Classes*, London: Longman, Hurst, Rees, Orme, and Brown.

Parsons, Frank (1904) *The Story of New Zealand*, Philadelphia: Equity Series.

Périgord, Paul (1926) *The International Labour Organization: A Study of Labour and Capital in Cooperation*, New York: D. Appleton.

Persons, Charles E., Mabel Parton, and Mabelle Moses (1911) *Labour Laws and Their Enforcement: With Special Reference to Massachusetts*, New York: Longmans, Green.

Poblete-Troncoso, Moises (1928a) "Labour Legislation in Latin America: I": *International Labour Review*, 17 (January), pp. 51–67.

Poblete-Troncoso, Moises (1928b) "Labour Legislation in Latin America: II," *International Labour Review*, 17 (February), pp. 204–30.

Richardson, James D. (ed.) (1896) *A Compilation of the Messages and Papers of the Presidents, 1789–1897, Volume III*, Washington, DC: Government Printing Office.

Rimlinger, Gaston V. (1960a) "Autocracy and the Factory Order in Early Russian Industrialization," *Journal of Economic History*, 20 (March), pp. 67–92.

Rimlinger, Gaston V. (1960b) "The Management of Labour Protest in Tsarist Russia, 1870–1905," *International Review of Social History*, 5 (August), pp. 226–48.

Rimlinger, Gaston V. (1989) "Labour and the State on the Continent, 1800–1939," in Peter Mathias and Sidney Pollard (eds), *The Cambridge Economic History of Europe, Volume VIII; The Industrial Economies: The Development of Economic and Social Policies*, Cambridge: Cambridge University Press, pp. 549–606.

Robbins, Lionel (1953) *The Theory of Economic Policy in English Classical Political Economy*, London: Macmillan.

Sanderson, Allen R. (1974) "Child Labour Legislation and the Labour Force Participation of Children," *Journal of Economic History*, 34 (March), pp. 297–9.

Schmiechen, James A. (1984) *Sweated Industries and Sweated Labour: The London Clothing Trades, 1860–1914*, Urbana: University of Illinois Press.

Seltzer, Andrew J. (1995) "The Political Economy of the Fair Labour Standards Act of 1938," *Journal of Political Economy*, 103 (December), pp. 1302–42.

Sengenberger, Werner and Duncan Campbell (eds) (1994) *International Labour Standards and Economic Interdependence*, Geneva: International Institute for Labour Standards.

Shotwell, James T. (ed.) (1934) *The Origins of the International Labour Organization* (2 vols), New York: Columbia University Press.

Sinclair, Keith (1959) *A History of New Zealand*, Harmondsworth: Penguin.

Sklar, Kathryn Kish (1995) *Florence Kelley and the Nation's Work: The Rise of Women's Political Culture, 1830–1900*, New Haven: Yale University Press.

Slack, Paul (1990) *The English Poor Law, 1531–1782*, Basingstoke: Macmillan.

Solano, E. John (ed.) (1920) *Labour as an International Problem: A Series of Essays Comprising a Short History of the International Labour Organization and a Review of General Industrial Problems*, London: Macmillan.

Steinberg, Ronnie (1982) *Wages and Hours: Labour and Reform in Twentieth Century America*, New Brunswick: Rutgers University Press.

Stewart, Bryce M. (1926) *Canadian Labour Law and The Treaty*, New York: Columbia University Press.

Stone, Judith F. (1985) *The Search for Social Peace: Reform Legislation in France, 1890–1914*, Albany: State University of New York Press.

Teleky, Ludwig (1948) *History of Factory and Mine Hygiene*, New York: Columbia University Press.

Temperley, Howard (1972) *British Antislavery, 1833–1870*, Columbia: University of South Carolina Press.

Thomas, Maurice Walton (1948) *The Early Factory Legislation: A Study in Legislative and Administrative Evaluation*, Leigh-on-Sea: Thames Bank Publishing Company.

Tripathy, S. K. (1989) *Child Labour in India*, New Delhi: Discovery Publishing House.

Turin, S. P. (1935) *From Peter the Great to Lenin: A History of the Russian Labour Movement with Special Reference to Trade Unionism*, London: P. S. King and Son.

Tugan-Baronowski, Mikhail I. (1970) *The Russian Factory in the 19th Century*, Homewood: Richard D. Irwin, [translated from 3rd Russian edn, first published 1907].

US Bureau of Labor Statistics (1913a) Bulletin no. 117 *The Prohibition of the Night Work of Young Persons*, Department of Labor, Washington, DC: Government Printing Office.

US Bureau of Labor Statistics (1913b) Bulletin no. 118 *Ten-Hour Maximum Working Day for Women and Young Persons*, Department of Labor, Washington, DC: Government Printing Office.

US Bureau of Labor Statistics (1920) Bulletin no. 268 *Historical Survey of International Action Affecting Labor*, Washington, DC: Government Printing Office.

US Commissioner of Labor (1892) Second Special Report, *Labour Laws of the Various States, Territories and the District of Columbia*, Washington, DC: Government Printing Office.

US Congress (1900) House of Representatives, 56th Congress, 1st Session (Document No. 476), *Report of the Industrial Commission on Labour Legislation, Volume V*, Washington, DC: Government Printing Office.

US Department of Health Education and Welfare, Social Security Administration (1974) *Social Security Programs Throughout the World, 1973* (Office of Research and Statistics, Research Report No. 44), Washington, DC: Government Printing Office.

US Department of Labor (1897) Bulletin no. 12, W. F. Willoughby, *The Inspection of Factories and Workshops in the United States*, Department of Labor, Washington, DC: Government Printing Office.

US Department of Labor (1899) Bulletin no. 25, *Foreign Labor Laws* in (Great Britain, France), Department of Labor, Washington, DC: Government Printing Office.

US Department of Labor (1900a) Bulletin no. 26, *Foreign Labor Laws* in (Belgium, Switzerland), Department of Labor, Washington, DC: Government Printing Office.

US Department of Labor (1900b) Bulletin no. 27, *Foreign Labor Laws* in (Germany), Department of Labor, Washington, DC: Government Printing Office.

US Department of Labor (1900c) Bulletin no. 28, *Foreign Labor Laws* in (Austria), Department of Labor, Washington, DC: Government Printing Office.

US Department of Labor (1900d) Bulletin no. 30, *Foreign Labor Laws* in (Russia, the Netherlands, Italy, Norway, Sweden, Denmark), Department of Labor, Washington, DC: Government Printing Office.

US Department of Labor (1967) *Growth of Labour Law in the United States*, Washington, DC: Government Printing Office.

US Department of Labor, Women's Bureau (1929) Bulletin no. 66, *History of Labour Legislation for Women in Three States; Chronological Development of Labor Legislation for Women in the United States*, Washington, DC: Government Printing Office.

West, E. G. (1994 [1965]) *Education and the State: A Study in Political Economy* (3rd edn), Indianapolis: Liberty Fund.

Weiner, Myron (1991) *The Child and the States in India: Child Labor and Education Policy in Comparative Perspective*, Princeton: Princeton University Press.

Weissbach, Lee Shai (1989) *Child Labor Reform in Nineteenth Century France: Assuring the Future Harvest*, Baton Rouge: Louisiana State University Press.

Whaples, Robert (1990) "Winning the Eight-Hour Day, 1909–1919," *Journal of Economic History*, 50 (June), pp. 393–406.

Zelnik, Reginald E. (1968) "The Peasant and the Factory," in Wayne S. Vucinich (ed.), *The Peasant in Nineteenth Century Russia*, Stanford: Stanford University Press.

Zelnik, Reginald E. (1971) *Labor and Society in Tsarist Russia: The Factory Workers of St. Petersburg, 1855–1870*, Stanford: Stanford University Press.

COMMENTARY 1.1

The Parallels Between the Past and the Present

Jane Humphries

Stanley Engerman is the kind of economic historian who looks at the past through the frame of the present and asks what we can learn from historical experience. His account of the origins and evolution of labor standards, including child labor legislation, is resonant with contemporary discussions. Let us follow him through his argument, pausing only to introduce additional historical evidence, which may have implications for how we think about labor standards today.

The Parallels Between the Past and the Present

Engerman shows that although the language may be quaint and different the arguments for and against labor standards in the eighteenth and nineteenth centuries were very similar to the arguments advanced today. Like today's, early arguments for labor standards fell into two main categories: ethical and economic. Early ethical arguments differed from their modern counterparts in two ways. They were more likely to be founded on religious belief than on the humanitarian moral stance, which underpins modern ethical arguments, and, as Engerman reminds us, they drew from contemporaneous soul-searching on the morality of slavery. The eighteenth- and nineteenth-century economic arguments sound unfamiliar. No late-eighteenth-century political economist demanded "Show me the market failure." Engerman thinks Dr Percival's late-eighteenth-century advocacy of child labor standards awkwardly expressed. But strip away the linguistic differences and the arguments are the same. The early advocates did not have the jargon of the modern economist, but their presentation of labor standards' contribution to the creation of a healthier, better-educated and more productive working class and citizenry is still recognizable as an argument about potential positive externalities. The external benefits proposed were both very general and very particular. Advocates drew attention to the dangers for all implicit in epidemics of infectious diseases, and they sketched now familiar links from working conditions to productivity.

Champions of labor standards also noted that chronically unequal bargaining power could lead to inefficient labor market outcomes. Their arguments appeared most pertinent to certain classes of labor, particularly to workers whose ability to make informed decisions and bargain for themselves was suspect. Victorian standards threw women and children together in this category. Both women and children were also "naturally" located within the externalities framework: women because their reproductive capabilities and related responsibility for children's early socialization gave them a determining influence over the quality of future generations; and children because they were the living link into the future. Following any of the early legislative interventions through the British political process also shows the practical importance of a range of arguments in recruiting champions from different interest groups and building a coalition of support.

The arguments against labor standards are also timeworn. As today, so historically the basic concern was the impact of higher costs on profits and competitivity. Opponents were anxious to underscore the knock-on effects of higher labor costs on employment levels, well-meaning intervention thus rebounding on those who were to be protected. More abstract arguments also came into play. Extending labor standards from (infantilized) women and children, to adult males challenged the prevalent belief in "free" contract and confronted the dominant political philosophy. Commentators of a more bureaucratic mind-set pointed to the difficulties and costs of such meddlesome regulation and the likelihood of evasion in the absence of effective policing. Thus in the past as in the present, opponents of labor standards often argued in one and the same breath that intervention would be both inefficient and ineffective. Early opponents of intervention also played the international trade card, noting that domestic standards not followed elsewhere could harm exports, a potent argument in the British case given the focus of legislative intervention on the export-intensive cotton industry.

The creation of coalitions of interests both for and against, as Engerman notes, suggests skepticism about motivation. Were groups' professed intentions in line with their real aims? The historical material offers plenty of scope for exploring cases of possible hijacking. These direct our attention away from alliances between "protectionists" and humanitarians in advanced industrial countries, the main basis of anxiety about hijacking today, to consider a broader set of potentially shared interests.

It has been widely argued that early trade unions supported limitations on the length of the working day for women and children in the hope that this would make long hours inefficient and promote shorter hours for all.

Adult males thus campaigned for a shorter working day "from behind the women's petticoats;" strategically using Victorian middle-class sex-role standards to achieve their own ends (Hutchins and Harrison, 1903; for a summary of the arguments see, Rose, 1992). Some feminist historians have gone so far as to argue that male-dominated trade unions' support for protective labor legislation was a thinly disguised strategy to exclude women from the better paid jobs (Honeyman and Goodman, 1991). Thus gendered labor standards and the accompanying campaign for a family wage promoted the male bread-winner family system in which women were trapped into domestic labor and made dependent on men and male wages (Creighton, 1996; Seccombe, 1986). Alternatively, the early trade unions' attempt to combine the campaign for labor standards for women and children with the demand for a family wage for adult men can be seen as a politicized version of Kaushik Basu's (1999) model of a labor market with multiple equilibrium. Protective labor legislation, which banned women and children's work outright in some jobs and prevented them from working in excess of certain hours in others, in effect moved the labor market from one equilibrium (with child and female labor and relatively low adult wages) to another equilibrium (with less child and female labor and higher adult wages). The intervention here is "benign." Because the equilibrium with intervention was an equilibrium of the original economy, once the economy has adjusted, the law banning women and children's labor is no longer needed. Both equilibria are Pareto optimal, so neither dominates. But worker households are better off at the equilibrium with intervention. So if equality is a positive argument in the social welfare function this equilibrium may be preferred. (Basu's argument depends on a number of assumptions, in particular the "luxury" axiom, but I would argue that these assumptions are reasonable and supported by empirical evidence in the historical context.)

One other coalition of interests that has been explored in this context is that which linked male employers with their male employees in defense of patriarchal subordination of women (Lown, 1990; Rose, 1992). Whatever the intentions of the many actors involved, patriarchal rhetoric was certainly a crucial factor in many of the campaigns for gendered standards and the increasing dominance of the male breadwinner family undoubtedly a consequence.

Modern arguments for labor standards reflect very different views on gender. Indeed internationally agreed standards rule out gender discrimination. However there are still tensions between culturally determined views about appropriate behavior for women and labor-force participation. Thus the earlier debate has a modern counterpart in the tricky reconciliation of local cultural imperatives with international anti-discrimination standards.

Other historical cases of hijacking have contemporary interest. There is strong evidence for example of specific producers seeking to gain a competitive march by embracing a labor standard that would disadvantage rivals who were using a more vulnerable technology. Thus early British legislation on the length of the working day was allegedly supported by those cotton magnates who had made the transition to steam because it was held likely to disadvantage their competitors who remained dependent on water power with its naturally discontinuous flow (Marvel, 1977). Similarly the 1842 Mines Regulation Act, which banned women and children under the age of nine from underground work was supported by coal owners whose seams were thick and who had mechanized underground transport (Humphries, 1981). Many such owners had dispensed with underground child transport workers. In contrast the Act put the owners of thin seam pits who needed to use small child workers to move the coal underground at a competitive disadvantage. Not even Sir Robert Peel has been above charges of self-interest. In evaluating his role in the genesis of the early protective labor legislation in Britain it is important to note that Peel's own interests were not entirely located in spinning. Peel also had major investments in warehouses and weaving as well as calico printing. When spinning and weaving interests clashed at the turn of the century over whether exports of cotton twist should be freely allowed (as the spinners wanted) or discouraged in order to keep down the price of weavers' raw material, Peel was on the weaving side of the debate. This puts his support for the Health and Morals of Apprentices Act (1802) in a less rosy light. Many contemporaries interpreted this act as representing a victory of weaving over spinning interests; an important objective was to restrict the output of cotton yarn (Innes, 1998). Perhaps Sir Robert's weaving interests predisposed him in favor of the Bill, certainly he would have been less threatened.

But if the historical literature throws up evidence of possible hijacking it also suggests that the inclusion of self-interested groups in coalitions for change was often needed to raise standards. In this case the record can be read as supporting Pahre's (1998) argument that hijacking may help achieve humanitarian goals or be "benign" as in the multiple equilibrium example argued above.

The search for optimal intervention requires some clear understanding of what causes, for example, children to be put to work. Only if we know why children work can we remove those causes and trace the implications both in terms of the costs and the benefits. Again this has long been recognized. Seminar papers provide us with the usual suspects in the contemporary context: poverty; adult unemployment; employers' demand; a technology that requires the small stature and nimble fingers of the child worker; family preferences; and a lack of alternatives for children other than idleness. There is agreement on this list though perhaps less consensus on ranking these causes in order of importance. The historical debate on child labor for instance anticipated the modern discussion of its likely causes, including but not limited to poverty. Like today's development economists, eighteenth-century commentators recognized that there were worse things than child labor (child starvation for example) and feared that labor standards by exacerbating family poverty could leave children worse off. They saw too that if standards were sector specific, the likely effect would be an exodus of children into unregulated employment where their experiences may be even worse.

Thus Engerman concludes: "The introduction and extension of standards depends more on shifts in political power, effective rhetoric, changing attitudes regarding the role of men, [and] new empirical data . . . than upon the introduction of new justifications or new claims for what the policies will achieve" (p. 00). But perhaps they may be some lessons for looking in more detail not just at the parallels between the past and the present but some of the disjunctures. I follow this path next.

The Macroeconomics of Child Labor

The first protective labor legislation and therefore the original labor standard occurred in Britain at the very beginning of the nineteenth century. The question whether universal standards are possible or appropriate in very diverse conditions, a question that haunts writers on child labor, occurs in a chronic form in contemplating historic cases. It is useful to put the British legislation in its social and economic context.

There is little doubt that the early industrial British economy utilized child labor intensively though modern historians have been less inclined than contemporaries or the authors of classic accounts to focus on child workers (Cunningham and Viazzo, 1996; Humphries, 2003, forthcoming). Translating this intensive usage into participation rates for comparative purposes is more difficult as census counts of working children and base populations were not made until 1851 and even then may under-record (particularly young) working children. Census figures for 1851 give the participation rates of boys and girls aged 5–9 as 2.0 percent and 1.4 percent, rising to 36.6 percent and 19.9 percent for boys and girls aged 10–14. The 1871, census counted 32.1 percent of boys and 20.5 percent of girls aged 10–14 as working. My own (1995) estimates (with Sara Horrell) for the pre-census period suggest that something like a quarter of all children in families worked from the late eighteenth century until the mid nineteenth century. For children aged 10–14, the participation rate was much higher, probably well over 50 percent (Horrell and Humphries, 1995). Other recent work from a second data source, working-class autobiographies, confirms this level of participation (Humphries, 2003, forthcoming). Using this data we can compare the British experience with contemporary levels of child labor using Alan

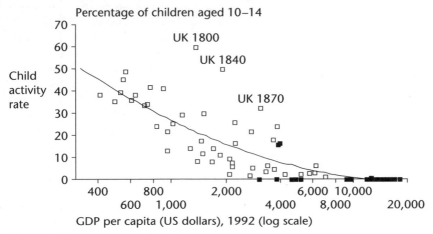

Figure 1.1 Child labor and GDP per capita

Note: 1870 – boys only.

Source: Krueger (1997); historical observations based on Crafts (1985); Horrell and Humphries (1995); Humphries (2003, forthcoming).

Krueger's (1997) figure (see figure 1.1). What can we make of the relatively high participation rates of children in the first industrial revolution?

At a basic level these data suggest the importance of child labor in a poor country, especially one experiencing rapid population growth and high dependency ratios. Child labor enabled the first industrial revolution. Its importance is underlined in new interpretations of British industrialization. These emphasize not technology nor high productivity, but the rapid growth of labor-intensive industries, a comparative advantage based on low labor costs, and an organizational leap into factory production, this latter being particularly important in the cotton industry. Child labor was pivotal in all three aspects.

The cotton industry and especially its early factories employed astonishingly high proportions of children. The water frame automated spinning so that the only tasks were mending broken threads and removing bobbins, tasks that required little physical strength and that could be done by children. In one Arkwright-type mill in 1779 "children" were said to constitute 90 percent of the workforce; in Robert Owen's New Lanark in 1799, 70 percent of the workforce were under 18, the majority under 13 (Innes, 1998; Tuttle, 1999). In mule-spinning supervision remained an adult employment, but children were still required as piecers and doffers. In 1816 in a number of mills around Preston, some 70 percent of the workforce were still under 18, though the corresponding figure for Manchester was 50 percent, and for Scotland 45 percent. The mechanization of preparatory processes reduced the proportions of child workers. By 1816 at Arkwright's Mill at Crompton only 7 percent of the employees were children under 13 and 37 percent children under 18 (Bolin-Hort, 1989). However, overall growth in the industry helped to ensure that demand for child labor remained buoyant, probably increasing in absolute terms until the 1830s at least. Peel said that his 1818 Act would help 20,000 children which provides us with an estimate of the children employed in the cotton (and perhaps woolen) mills at that date. By 1835 the cotton industry alone employed 56,000 children under 13 (Innes, 1998; Nardinelli, 1990).

But the factory production of cotton and even of textiles more generally was not the only source of child employment. Children were widely employed in another growth-pole of the industrializing economy: the coal industry. Many mines had as high a proportion of child employees as did mills (Tuttle, 1999). Children were also extensively employed in other more traditionally organized manufacturing. Indeed, Pinchbeck and Hewitt (1973) believed that it was domestic manufacture and not the factories that saw the high-water mark of child labor in British industrialization. Finally children were also widely employed in more traditional spheres, as plow boys, crow scarers, and shepherds in agriculture, as farm and domestic servants, and as apprentices in the multitude of trades that crisscrossed the traditional and modernizing sectors of the economy.

But can we really read this historical experience as confirming the inevitability of child labor at low-income levels and with high dependency ratios? Britain in 1800, 1840 and 1870 was poor but not that poor (Deane, 1979). Projecting the historical experience of Britain into the world of today's poor countries highlights the importance of factors other than a low standard of living in promoting children's work.

In Britain, industrialization was grafted onto an early-modern economy in which child labor was ubiquitous. Children's work was widely accepted and parents who sent their children to work encountered no social stigma. Economic growth and the development of manufacturing in particular increased the demand for child labor in a context when sending children to work was perfectly normal. Of course the nature of children's work changed dramatically as work shifted out of the home and into the factory, as farms became more commercialized, and domestic manufacture became sweated in competition with mass batch production. The social acceptability of child labor in the pre-industrial economy smoothed its metamorphosis into new forms of work in the early industrial setting and boosted child participation rates. Later on in the nineteenth century, sending children to school became part of the respectability so sought after by artisans while the ideal of the male breadwinner was extended to cover the needs of children who could therefore be kept out of the labor force until their mid teens. Whether social norms changed in advance of declines in child labor and so played a causal role in children's movement out of the labor force, or whether they changed in line with the decline in child employment is less certain. But the British case, along with other historical experience (see Saito, 1996) suggests an important role for ideas about childhood, about society, and about propriety.

The British case also illustrates another aspect of child labor that seems relatively neglected in the seminar papers: the importance of demand. Modern analyses of the growth process have underscored the extraordinary role of the cotton industry in the first industrial revolution and the more general importance of labor-intensive industries and processes. Without access to child labor the initial establishment of water-powered textile mills in isolated rural valleys would have been much more difficult and costly. Much of the early textile machinery was explicitly designed to be operated by children either for technical reasons (wooden machinery had to be low to the ground) or for reasons of relative cost. Christine Macleod notes in her (1988) survey of eighteenth-century patents, that many early innovations to textile machinery were explicitly motivated by the desire to substitute child for adult labor. Employers' pursuit of higher profits and their desire to introduce new methods of working that circumvented the structures of restraint and opposition, which workers had evolved, contributed to the demand for child labor.

Like many countries today, the British used child labor in a labor-intensive industry, a high proportion of whose products were exported. Modern interpretations of British comparative advantage in the late-eighteenth and early-nineteenth centuries are likely to emphasize low wage costs, to which child labor was a contributing factor. Interestingly, the other country that industrialized in the nineteenth century and emphasized the same spectrum of industries, including textiles and coal, Belgium, was probably the only European industrializer to approach Britain in its use of child labor (De Herdt, 1996). In contrast, France produced higher-quality manufactures, and, outside agriculture, at least appears to have had much lower child participation rates (Heywood, 2001).

But finally if the British case seems to suggest that child labor was an inevitable phase it also warns against too complacent an attitude. As is well known, British economic dominance did not last through the second half of the nineteenth century. Ironically those same factors that promoted industrialization have featured as causes of this relative decline. Thus the reliance on low-skilled and labor-intensive industries made it more difficult for the British economy to develop the industries at the core of the second industrial revolution. Similarly some of the later difficulties of the British economy in the nineteenth century have been linked to poor human capital formation. Stagnating, even declining, literacy and biological standard of living may well relate to the intensity and persistence of child labor. If the British case suggests that early use of child labor might be inevitable, indeed desirable, it also suggests that prolonging such reliance can adversely affect subsequent growth performance.

The Microeconomics of Child Labor

Many seminar papers focus less on the macro picture with which I have begun than the microeconomics of child labor. Economists have been heavily influenced by the individualism at the heart of their methodology and the elegance of models of household decision-making descended from Gary Becker. Models of family decision-making dominate the literature on child labor and the altruism or not of parents has been widely discussed. This inspiration has led to a strange oversight. It is one that Engerman's survey of labor standards could have exposed. But he too misses an important aspect of early industrial child labor clearly built into the first legislative concern, and an aspect that has important implications in the contemporary context. Many of the child workers of the industrial revolution did not live in families with parents altruistic or otherwise.

Life expectancies in pre-industrial England varied between the late twenties and early forties. Between one-half and two-thirds of young women would have lost their fathers by the time they married. Of 10-year-old children, 17 percent would be fatherless, as would 27 percent of children aged 15 (Laslett, 1977). Lists of apprentice registrations in Bristol on which the deaths of fathers were recorded show that up to one third of those apprenticed had lost their fathers before apprenticeship began (Ben-Amos, 1994). Nor did this situation improve in early industrialization. Large numbers of homes continued to be broken by the death of the father or the mother. And new sources of de facto orphanage increased. Urbanization and the opening of empire provided escape routes for men who might in earlier times have knuckled down to fatherhood (Humphries, 1998). Bastardy increased. Lower infant death rates meant more children survived to face a life alone. The bellicose climate of the late eighteenth and early nineteenth centuries, with large proportions of prime age males serving in the army and navy, deprived many households of their male heads. Thus the industrial revolution saw a bulge in the proportion of children left without a father or abandoned completely to the care of other family members or the state.

Why is this important? Increasing proportions of children without family support put intolerable pressure on normal levels of charitable provision and state-provided care. Vulnerable children fell through the various safety nets into earlier working and harsher working. Their public and visible employment inured the general population and shifted social norms towards greater tolerance of child labor, with knock-on effects for children in poor but intact families. I believe something like this happened in the British industrial revolution. My own work has shown that children who were fatherless, or worse still orphaned, were likely to be put to work at a younger age and to work in less tolerable surrounding (Humphries, 1998). The timing and nature of their work crowded out education and training and left fatherless children less productive as adults (Horrell et al., 2001). In particular, it was children in state care who became the first factory labor force. It appears that poor law officials overwhelmed by the dramatically rising costs of relief at the end of the eighteenth century, collaborated with manufacturers to institutionalize a supply of labor in the form of pauper apprentices to the early factories (Rose, 1989). The traditional solution to orphanage and abandonment, the parish apprenticeship, however harsh, had provided a lifeline back to economic independence and social inclusion. But in the face of a seeming rising tide of needy children and a new kind of demand for their labor, the parish apprenticeship mutated. It became a form of bonded labor, shedding all pretence at providing training and guidance (Dunlop and Denham, 1912). Significantly it was these children, who were the original focus of legislative intervention. The Health and Morals of Apprentices Bill (1802) applied only to parish apprentices in cotton and woolen factories.

Does this aspect of child labor in the past have any implications for child labor today? I suggest that it does, for orphanage and abandonment are increasing dramatically in many parts of the world today driven by civil war, ethnic conflict, large scale refugee migration, environmental disaster and epidemic disease, such as AIDS. In China alone 100,000 children a year are abandoned. The flood of vulnerable children left behind by these man-made and natural disasters could overwhelm initiatives to impose standards unless policy makers are prepared.

Labor Standards and Social Policy

There is one final lesson from historical experiences, one, which is anticipated in the contemporary debate. There is agreement, that both the causes and consequences of low labor standards are wide ranging. Thus there are many reasons for low standards but poverty alone, however important, is not to blame. The effects of intervention are held to impact widely even affecting future generations. What this suggests is that for optimal impact labor standards need to be packaged with other social and economic reform. For example, if a prime objective is to improve the health and education of children, it may not be adequate to ban child labor without ensuring the availability of health care and schooling. In fact it may be possible to combine health care and schooling with some acceptable labor for children, labor which is not physically oppressive and which has a training component. Similarly although it is not possible to eliminate poverty, the root cause of child labor, the identification of other aspects of vulnerability (fatherlessness, many siblings, gender) many facilitate the effective targeting of income support.

In the past, the issue of labor standards was recognized as multidimensional. The first British legislation concerning labor standards, for example, is often seen as part of poor law history rather than as part of the history of protective labor legislation. It can also be read as a contribution to the body of law regulating the institution of apprenticeship. It was not the only piece of apprenticeship legislation passed in that session (Innes, 1998). Moreover this legislation was the first to require the formal education of any English children. Maybe there are lessons that can yet be learned from the past about how labor standards were approached from different directions and embedded in different types of legislative intervention.

Finally, maybe the historical record can also help with another tricky issue: whether it is possible to draw lines around labor standards or whether compromise is appropriate. One important issue here is whether all child work is bad and should be outlawed or whether some work is worse than other work. It may be hard for us to accept, but our forebears, clearly distinguished between different kinds of work, and it may be necessary for policy makers in the Third World to do so as well. The ways in which parents, guardians, employers, and the state identified different kinds of child work as bad or not so bad – even positively good – may afford the basis for designing strategic interventions. Physically damaging work is abhorred. Work that can be combined with schooling either seasonally or daily is obviously preferred to work which crowds out education completely. Work with a training component was much more popular in the past than other kinds of work so much so that parents and children would make financial sacrifices in choosing this option. (Note too that schooling which involved a training component was often preferred by working parents to schooling of a more abstract kind.) The apprenticeship, a now under-valued institution, played a key role in the ability to combine education and work for generations of nineteenth century European children (Humphries, 2002). Perhaps it is time to look again at this and other institutional manifestations of the need to combine work and education.

Conclusion

In conclusion, I return to Engerman's claim: "The introduction and extension of standards depends more on shifts in political power, effective rhetoric, changing attitudes regarding the role of men, [and] new empirical data . . . than upon the introduction of new justifications or new claims for what the policies will achieve" (Chapter 1 of this volume, p. 29). It is possible to see conferences providing better rhetoric – though some of Shaftesbury's speeches are difficult to top – and new empirical data. But perhaps one new justification is possible in 2002. It derives from the shift in the idea of development away from increasing opulence and towards human development, as pioneered in the work of Amartya Sen and reflected in HDI indicators. Following Sen, Martha Nussbaum (1995) has proposed a list of human capabilities, firmly founded in humanist philosophy (see, Appendix). This list provides a rationale for the pursuit of labor standards. We advocate labor standards not as a humanitarian good to be purchased with the fruits of development nor for their externalities which contribute to development, but because they are constitutive of development itself. Consider in conclusion the "rhetoric" of a long dead child worker, Charles Shaw who makes the claim better than any development economist for child non-work as a human right. In a chapter of his autobiography entitled *First Knowledge of Disadvantage*, Shaw explained that as a child he had played like any other, but had accepted that at the age of about seven he would have to abandon his games and go to work. About a year later while enjoying a brief moment of leisure he came across another boy reading a book. "Now, I had acquired a strong passion for reading, and the sight of this youth reading at his own free will, forced upon my mind a sense of painful contrast between his position and mine. I felt a sudden sense of wretchedness. There was a blighting consciousness that my lot was harder than his and that of others. What birds and sunshine, in contrast with my work had failed to impress upon me, the sight of this reading youth accomplished with swift bitterness. I went to my mould-running and hot stove with my first anguish in my heart. I can remember, though never describe, the acuteness of this first sorrow" (Shaw, 1903).

Appendix: Nussbaum's List

1. Being able to live to the end of a human life of normal length thought of in universal comparative terms.
2. Being able to have good health; to be adequately nourished; to have adequate shelter; having opportunities for sexual satisfaction, and for choice in matters of reproduction; being able to move from place to place.
3. Being able to avoid unnecessary and non-beneficial pain, so far as possible and to have pleasurable experiences.
4. Being able to use the senses; being able to imagine, to think, and to reason – and do these things in a way informed and cultivated by an adequate education, but by no means limited to, literacy and basic mathematical and scientific training.

5. Being able to have attachments to things and persons outside our-
    selves; to love, to grieve, to experience longing and gratitude.
6. Being able to form a conception of the good and to engage in critical
    reflection about the planning of one's own life. This includes being able
    to seek employment outside the home and to participate in political
    life.
7. Being able to engage in social interaction; to have the capability for
    both justice and friendship.
8. Being able to live with concern for and in relation to animals, plants,
    and the world of nature.
9. Being able to laugh, to play, and to enjoy recreational activities.
10. Being able to live one's own life and nobody else's. This means having
    certain guarantees of non-interference with choices that are personal.

REFERENCES

Basu, Kaushik (1999) "Child Labor: Cause, Consequence, and Cure, with Remarks on
    Labor Standards," *Journal of Economic Literature*, 37, September, 1083–119.
Ben-Amos, Ilana Krausman (1994) *Adolescence and Youth in Early Modern England*,
    New Haven: Yale University Press.
Bolin-Hort, Per (1989) *Work, Family and the State: Child Labour and the Organization
    of Production in the British Cotton Industry, 1780–1920*, Lund: Lund University Press.
Crafts, N. F. R. (1985) *British Economic Growth during the Industrial Revolution*, Oxford:
    Clarendon Press.
Creighton, Colin (1996) "The Rise of the Male Breadwinner Family: A Reappraisal,"
    Comparative Studies in Society and History, 38, pp. 310–37.
Cunningham, Hugh (1996) "Combating Child Labour: The British Experience," in
    H. Cunningham and P. P. Viazzo (eds), *Child Labour in Historical Perspective 1800–
    1985*, Florence: UNICEF.
Cunningham, Hugh and Pier Paulo Viazzo (eds) (1996) *Child Labour in Historical
    Perspective 1800–1985*, Florence: UNICEF.
Deane, Phyllis (1979) *The First Industrial Revolution*, Cambridge: Cambridge University
    Press.
De Herdt, Rene (1996) "Child Labour in Belgium", in H. Cunningham and P. P.
    Viazzo (eds), *Child Labour in Historical Perspective 1800–1985*, Florence: UNICEF.
Dunlop, O. J. with a supplementary section on the modern problem of juvenile
    labour by O. J. Dunlop and Richard D. Denman (1912) *English Apprenticeship and
    Child Labour. A History*, London: T. Fisher Unwin.
Heywood, Colin (2001) *A History of Childhod*, Cambridge: Polity Press.
Honeyman, Katrina and Jordan Goodman (1991) "Women's Work, Gender Conflict,
    and Labour Markets in Europe 1500–1900," *Economic History Review*, XLIV,
    pp. 608–28.
Horrell, Sara and Jane Humphries (1995) "'The Exploitation of Little Children':
    Child Labor and the Family Economy in the Industrial Revolution," *Explorations
    in Economic History* 32, 4, October, pp. 485–516.

Horrell, Sara, Jane Humphries and Hans-Joachim Voth (2001) "Destined for Deprivation: Human Capital Formation and Intergenerational Poverty in Nineteenth-
Century England," *Explorations in Economic History*, 38, 3, July, pp. 339–65.

Humphries, Jane (1981) "Protective Legislation, the Capitalist State and Working-
Class Men: The Case of the 1842 Mines Regulation Act," *Feminist Review*, 7,
Spring, pp. 1–35.

Humphries, Jane (1998) "Female-headed Households in Early Industrial Britain: The
Vanguard of the Proletariat," *Labour History Review*, 63, 1, Spring, pp. 31–65.

Humphries, Jane (2002, forthcoming) "English Apprenticeship: A Neglected Factor in the
First Industrial Revolution," in Paul A. David and Mark Thomas (eds), *The Economic
Future in Historical Perspective*, Oxford: Oxford University Press/British Academy.

Humphries, Jane (2003, Spring, forthcoming) "At What Cost was Pre-eminence Pur-
chased? Child Labour and the First Industrial Revolution," in Peter Scholliers and
Leonard Schwarz (eds), *Experiencing Wages: Social and Cultural Aspects of Wage
Forms in Europe since 1500*, Oxford-New York: Berghahn Books.

Hutchins, B. L. and A. Harrison (1966 [1903]) *A History of Factory Legislation*, New
York: Augustus Kelley.

Innes, Joanna (1998) *The Origins of the Factory Acts: The Health and Morals of Apprentices Act, 1802*, mimeo, Oxford.

Krueger, Alan (1997) "International Labor Standards and Trade," in *Proceedings of
the Annual World Bank Conference on Development Economics, 1996*, Washington:
World Bank.

Laslett, Peter (1977) *Family Life and Illicit Love in Earlier Generations*, Cambridge:
Cambridge University Press.

Lown, Judy (1990) *Women and Industrialization: Gender at Work in Nineteenth-century
England*, Cambridge: Polity.

Macleod, Christine (1988) *Inventing the Industrial Revolution: The English Patent System*, Cambridge: Cambridge University Press.

Marvel, Howard P. (1977) "Factory Regulation: A Reinterpretation of Early English
Experience," *Journal of Law and Economics*, 20, October, pp. 379–402.

Nardinelli, Clark (1990) *Child Labor and the Industrial Revolution*, Bloomington: Indiana
University Press.

Nussbaum, Martha (1995) "Introduction," in Martha C. Nussbaum and Jonathan
Glover (eds), *Women, Culture and Development: A Study of Human Capabilities*, Oxford:
Clarendon Press.

Pahre, Robert (1998) "Comments on Conference Version of Paper: Labor Standards,
Trade Sanctions and the Hijacking Hypothesis," comments on chapter 12 in Alan
Deardorff and Robert Stern (eds), *Constituent Interests and US Trade Policies*, Ann
Arbor: University of Michigan Press.

Pinchbeck, Ivy and Hewitt, Margaret (1973) *Children in English Society*, vol. 2, London: Routledge and Kegan Paul.

Rose, Mary (1989) "Social Policy and Business: Parish Apprentices and the Early
Factory System 1750–1834," *Business History*, XXI, pp. 5–32.

Rose, Sonya O. (1992) *Limited Livelihoods: Gender and Class in Nineteenth-Century
England*, London: Routledge.

Saito, Osamu (1996) "Children's Work, Industrialization, and the Family Economy
in Japan, 1872–1926," in H. Cunningham and P. P. Viazzo (eds), *Child Labour in
Historical Perspective 1800–1985*, Florence: UNICEF.

Seccombe, Wally (1986) "Patriarchy Stabilized: The Construction of the Male Bread-winner Wage Norm in Nineteenth Century Britain," *Social History*, 11, pp. 53–76.

Shaw, Charles (1903) *An Old Potter*, London: Methuen.

Tuttle, Carolyn (1998) "A Revival of the Pessimist View: Child Labor and the Industrial Revolution," *Research in Economic History*, 18, pp. 53–82.

Tuttle, Carolyn (1999) *Hard at Work in Factories and Mines: The Economics of Child Labor during the British Industrial Revolution*, Boulder, CO: Westview.

COMMENTARY 1.2

Legislation Versus Bargaining Power: The Evolution of Scandinavian Labor Standards

Karl-Ove Moene and Michael Wallerstein

In his overview of the evolution of labor standards Stanley Engerman traces the basic historical trends of labor standards from the English Factory Act of 1802 to the adoption of international labor standards as an inherent part of present-day trade agreements. He recognizes the special role of the ILO and identifies the problems of control and the lack of adequate enforcement mechanisms. Engerman also explores the sources of agitation for higher labor standards, their moral and economic causes as well as their social and private benefits. He discusses the arguments used in the initial agitation of labor standards, such as better health and more education for children, and more controversially the need to protect women in the labor market. He identifies the possible self-serving bias in the arguments of unions, factory owners, and governments.

Engerman covers a wide range of events, industries, and countries. It is, therefore, understandable that he limits his attention to how required labor standards are specified in laws and rules that regulate the labor market. Yet, a standard is something that is commonly adhered to, irrespective of whether it is regulated by law or not. Thus it is not obvious that legislation is more important for labor standards than a continuous exercise of bargaining power, whether this bargaining power is protected by law or not.

There may also be important complementarities between legislation and bargaining power and between economic policies and bargaining power for the achievements of labor standards. The history of labor standards is in fact difficult to separate from the history of other social reforms and policy developments. Thus in order to understand more of the political economy of labor standards, maybe Engerman's picture should be supplemented by a more explicit treatment of labor unions. We shall try to do so by focusing on some aspects of the Scandinavian experience. Policy makers, who are concerned with the low labor standards in poor countries today, may learn from the struggles to reduce poverty and increase workers' security in Northern Europe in the past.

In Scandinavia the present level of labor standards emerged from a long process of piecemeal reforms with continual adjustments and modifications that were politically expedient. The essence of the political strategy of social democrats in Scandinavia centered on the cumulative nature of political mobilization and legislative reforms that started long before social democrats obtained governmental power. The more workers were organized in unions and mobilized as voters, the social democrats thought, the less employers and governments would be able to resist workers' demands. At the same time, each victory in parliament or at the bargaining table would increase workers' political and economic strength. No reform was revolutionary in itself, but the cumulative impact of incremental increases in workers' power would transform society in the long run (Moene and Wallerstein, 1993).

The battle over universal suffrage was prototypical. Political democracy allows the most numerous class to prevail. Yet insecurity, poverty, and ignorance stood as obstacles to the political mobilization of workers as a class. Thus reforms to ameliorate the living conditions of workers were not only desirable in order to create a more humane society. Such reforms were also important towards building a working-class movement capable of winning elections. In theory, each reform created the conditions that would enable the next reform to be gained. From political rights to social rights, and from social rights to economic rights, so the formula went.

Today Scandinavia must be ranked high on realized labor standards by any measure. Most other countries have elementary standards such as minimum wages set by law, however, the Scandinavian countries of Denmark, Sweden, and Norway do not. One way to view this is that minimum wages regulated by law are simply redundant in societies with strong and encompassing unions. Union officials may even try to prevent the adoption of such laws in order to raise the private value of union membership. To some extent, strong unions can therefore be a substitute for explicit laws on minimum standards. Among advanced industrial countries the effective level of minimum wages, the lowest pay in common use, is most likely to be highest in countries without minimum wage laws.

Labor standards in Scandinavia were also raised by policies designed for other purposes. The active labor market policy, for example, keeps open unemployment down by sending the unemployed back to school for vocational training. The other part of the social democratic employment strategy was the use of macroeconomic policies to maintain full employment. The emphasis on full employment reflected, perhaps, the trade union base of the social democratic movement. The way to maximize workers' power inside the factory, the thinking went, was to maintain conditions where workers could always quit and obtain another job across the street if they were dissatisfied with working conditions or safety procedures.

In a comparative context, the Swedish and Norwegian commitment to full employment was extraordinary. Full employment was maintained for at least 40 years after World War II. In particular, Norway and Sweden kept unemployment below 3 percent throughout the 1970s and most of the 1980s, when unemployment rates were rising above 10 percent in much of Europe. Even today unemployment in Scandinavia is lower than the European average.

The single most important union policy for higher labor standards in Scandinavia was solidaristic wage bargaining. In order to illustrate how solidaristic wage bargaining affected labor standards we can apply the metaphor of good and bad jobs. Good jobs are more productive, but more expensive to establish, than bad jobs. In a decentralized labor market good jobs have high standards both in pay and working conditions, while bad jobs have low pay and unsafe working conditions. Equilibrium is obtained when profits from both types of jobs are equalized.

To raise minimum labor standards in the conventional way implies that bad jobs become more expensive and less prevalent. Higher standards imply lower employment. This is not so with solidaristic bargaining. Wage compression via solidaristic bargaining requires that employers with bad jobs offer better terms. At the same time, however, solidaristic bargaining prevents workers in good jobs from obtaining higher wages. The result for employers with good jobs is higher profits and good jobs expand as bad jobs are closed down (Moene and Wallerstein, 1995, 1997).

This type of productivity enhancing creative destruction via an egalitarian wage policy also extends to industries. Solidaristic bargaining applied over the national economy, limits the ability of the most efficient industries to pay a wage premium, and prevents the least efficient industries staying in business by lowering their labor standards. In fact, the elimination of different labor standards between industries can be understood as a subsidy of industries with good jobs and a tax on industries with bad jobs. The consequence is a national economy composed of more modern industries with higher labor standards than would be the case with more decentralized bargaining or with a conventional law-imposed increase in minimum standards.

Many economists think that this dramatic union-sponsored wage equalization or centralized wage compression is irrelevant in today's globalized free trade regime. It is natural since economists think that strong unions and trade protection go hand in hand. Yet, the Scandinavian variety of solidarity via centralized wage setting was associated, not with protectionism and monopolistic pricing, but with free trade and the subsequent need to remain competitive in export markets.

The centralization of bargaining in Sweden and Norway were essentially actions by employers and workers in the metal working sector to control wages throughout the economy in line with prices in the traded goods sector. Construction workers were the target in Sweden and Norway because they were highly paid, militant and sheltered from foreign competition. When foreign demand collapsed in the 1930s, metal workers accepted large wage reductions in order to stem the decline of employment. Construction workers came under no such pressure, but since they were employed in the export sector as well as in home construction, higher construction wages raised labor costs in the export sector. The more construction workers were paid, the more metal workers had to reduce their wages in order to maintain employment (and the more metal workers had to pay for housing). In gaining control over the wage demands of workers in the non-traded goods sector, metal workers and their employers were able to force all workers to share the burden of lowering wage costs in the export sector. Centralized bargaining was created as a mechanism for allowing those workers who were directly subject to international competition to set the pace of wage increases for the entire economy.

The political economy of solidaristic wage bargaining is also worth emphasizing. The beneficiaries of egalitarian wage compression were low-paid wage earners and employers, particularly employers with modern plants. The principal losers were the relatively highly paid wage and salary-earners whose incomes were held back in the name of wage equality. Thus solidaristic wage leveling is a policy of the 'the ends against the middle,' based on an implicit coalition between employers and low paid workers.

In Sweden the political coalition that prevailed in the 1950s and established the pattern of centralized and solidaristic bargaining that was to last for 25 years was comprised of the low-wage unions inside the LO and Swedish employers organized in the Swedish Employers' Confederation, SAF. High-paid unions were prevented from leaving the centralized negotiations by the threat of lockouts as in 1955 and 1957 (Swenson, 1989, 1991). It is unlikely that the low-wage unions and the LO leadership would have been able to force the high-wage unions to accept an egalitarian wage policy without the backing of Swedish employers and the threat of lockouts against recalcitrant unions. Initially solidaristic bargaining was supported by important actors who were opposed to redistribution in general. When support for solidaristic bargaining was reduced to those who welcomed its redistributive impact, the policy declined.

The Scandinavian strategy of enhancing labor standards via solidaristic wage bargaining also had consequences for other important policies. Take social insurance, for example, a policy that constitutes a normal good in the sense the demand goes up with income. Thus richer countries spend more than poorer countries on social insurance arrangements. As the distribution of pay in Scandinavia became more compressed via solidaristic wage bargaining, the income of the majority of voters increased. This implied higher support for social insurance spending just as if the country became richer. Consequently, Denmark, Sweden, and Norway have better social insurance and lower rates of poverty than equally rich countries with higher inequality in pre-tax and transfer labor incomes (Moene and Wallerstein, 2001).

Yet, all is not well with centralized wage negotiation in Scandinavia. In Sweden the system has become somewhat more decentralized after the metal working industries made separate offers to the metalworking union in 1983. In Norway the system is maintained, but with less employer enthusiasm than before. Moreover, Norway has been accused of violating international labor rights by the ILO for the frequent use of compulsory arbitration to coordinate wage setting.

In any case union-sponsored wage compression played a positive role in raising labor standards for a long period in Scandinavia. It was not the only policy followed, but the one that made social democracy distinct. The lessons for poor countries are that encompassing unions that are not projectionist or hostile to market competition may, nevertheless, be effective in raising labor standards. In fact, it is difficult to solve the problems of control and enforcement that Engerman mentions, if poor countries do not have interest organizations with self-interest to monitor labor standards. Unfortunately the World Trade Organization has been unwilling to include rights of association and wage bargaining in its present regulations. It is not surprising that among the countries most opposed to including bargaining rights as part of the WTO regulations are poor countries where such rights are not present.

So the characterization Adam Smith gave of England more than 200 years ago, as "no acts of parliament against combining to lower the price of work, but many against combining to raise it," is still true for many developing countries today. But as Adam Smith also said: "No society can surely be flourishing and happy, of which the far greater part of the members are poor and miserable" (Smith, 1976, pp. 74, 88).

REFERENCES

Moene, Karl and Michael Wallerstein (1993) "What is Wrong with Social Democracy," in P. Bardhan and J. Roemer (eds), *Market Socialism. The Present Debate*, Cambridge: Cambridge University Press.

Moene, Karl and Michael Wallerstein (1995) "How Social Democracy Worked," *Politics and Society*, 23, (2, June), pp. 185–211.

Moene, Karl and Michael Wallerstein (1997) "Pay Inequality," *Journal of Labor Economics*, 15 (3), pp. 403–30.

Moene, Karl and Michael Wallerstein (2001) "Inequality, Social Insurance and Redistribution," *American Political Science Review*, 95 (4, December), pp. 859–74.

Smith, Adam (1976 [1776]) *An Inquiry into the Nature and Causes of the Wealth of Nations*, Chicago: Chicago University Press.

Swenson, Peter (1989) *Fair Shares: Unions, Pay and Politics in Sweden and West Germany*, Ithaca: Cornell University Press.

Swenson, Peter (1991) "Bringing Capital Back In, or Social Democracy Reconsidered," *World Politics*, 43 (4), pp. 513–44.

PART III
The Theory of International Labor Standards

CHAPTER 2

The Impact of International Labor Standards: A Survey of Economic Theory

Nirvikar Singh

Introduction

The main question guiding this chapter is whether international labor standards will benefit the poor, in particular, developing countries and the poor in those countries. We survey the theoretical literature on international labor standards, and give an overview of the analytical framework and main arguments provided in this literature. Among the situations in which a case for labor standards may arise are imperfections in labor markets, market power effects in international trade, and concerns that consumers or general individuals may have about the working conditions or rights that other individuals enjoy. We emphasize the importance of making clear the value judgments being used, and discuss the different institutional issues that may arise in considering the implementation of labor standards. In general, while there are contexts in which promoting labor standards through some form of collective action is beneficial, we argue that such policies ought to be incorporated into a broader perspective on well-being, and a package of policies that can promote the well-being of the poor.

While there is a large literature on international labor standards, much of its focus has been on evaluating the appropriateness of linking labor standards with trade. Excellent recent surveys include those of Brown et al. (1996), Golub (1997b), and Maskus (1997). This chapter goes back to basics, in some respects, and reviews some of the key economic arguments in favor of labor standards. We also emphasize the welfare judgments that are involved in debates about labor standards, and how to think about them rigorously. We do examine some of the links to international trade, and update previous surveys in this respect. We gather together some of the political economy and, more broadly, collective action issues that arise in considering international labor standards. Most importantly, perhaps, we follow some recent writings by development economists such as Pranab Bardhan and Kaushik Basu in tying the issue of international labor standards to broader perspectives on development and issues of helping the poor.

The structure of the chapter is as follows. Following this introductory section, we lay out some of the practical ways in which concerns about workers rights and working conditions have been delineated for policy discussion. Doing so highlights the importance of value judgments and normative concerns in this sphere. Because rights are an important component of how labor standards are framed in policy debates, we go on to a discussion of how rankings of processes or rights as well as outcomes can be combined, and the implications of such an approach. This more general approach helps in bringing out the potential conflicts or tradeoffs between outcomes and processes, and therefore in evaluating the impacts of labor standards.

We then examine several possible labor market problems, what their consequences might be in terms of worker welfare, how to evaluate them in terms of labor-market processes, and finally, what the impacts might be of different interventions that come under the broad heading of "labor standards." Among the issues we consider are imperfect competition due to market power, lack of information, and survival constraints. In conducting this review, we connect some innovative new analyses to the labor standards literature, such as conflicts between the right of voluntary contracting and welfare outcomes for workers. We clarify the nature of these tradeoffs. We also clarify some of the modeling assumptions that have been used by other authors with respect to labor-market competition, and suggest some generalizations to incorporate working conditions into conventional models such as that of monopsony in the labor market.

Following this, we consider a range of economic models that place international and domestic labor standards in the context of the world economy with international trade. We describe how the standard competitive model of international trade can be used to evaluate the impact of labor standards, and the comparison of international labor standards with other policies, including purely domestic interventions. We examine models in which countries have "pricing power" in international markets, so that international terms of trade can be affected by domestic choices. We examine possible distributional impacts of trade in developed and developing countries, either in terms of the effects on labor versus capital, or on unskilled versus skilled labor. When labor standards are chosen domestically, their choice may be distorted by the potential for influencing the terms-of-trade, and we review recent analyses that suggest a possible method for integrating international labor standards with international trade negotiations. We consider the general case of various international coordination problems, typically clustered under the heading of "races to the bottom." We review several different possibilities here, including new analysis of such potential problems among developing-country exporters. This model fails to support the use of trade sanctions by developed countries as a way of improving labor standards and welfare in developing countries.

We then examine the rather contentious questions of "who decides and how?" in the context of international labor standards. We begin with an analysis of issues raised by the possibility that consumers in one country may care about the methods used to produce the goods that they consume, when those goods are imported from abroad. We develop the argument that such consumers ought to be willing to pay more for products that are made according to "acceptable" labor standards, and we discuss the practical problems that might arise in implementing such a solution in the market, including issues of lack of information and effective monitoring. The case where concerns over another country's working conditions and worker rights are not tied to consumption of imports raises a public good problem, and we consider various collective action problems and possible institutional solutions that might arise. We discuss the possibility that groups with different interests might cooperate on international labor standards, and we examine the issue of where to draw the line in cases where there are spillovers in concerns of citizens of one country to those of another country.

Finally, we consider the impact of international labor standards on the poor. We examine the case that international labor standards can end up hurting those they are supposed to help, unless they are part of a broader policy package. We link this to an argument that the proper concern, even where processes matter as well as outcomes, is with a more basic set of capabilities and rights than is typically encompassed by proponents of international labor standards. Labor standards may certainly have a role to play, but they must be put in context, both conceptually and in terms of implementation. We also review work on the links between the markets for education, credit, and labor, and examine the role that labor standards might play. Such concerns are particularly important for child labor, but apply more broadly as well. We also examine some possible connections between international labor standards, technological progress, and economic growth, but we find no obvious theoretical case in which imposing labor standards on poorer countries will help their long-run growth. On the other hand, we argue that policies that promote basic nutrition and health, and broader access to education and credit are likely to help growth, as well as having intrinsic benefits. Labor standards may well be a component of such policies, but must be implemented in context. The final section reviews the chapter and summarizes our main conclusions.

Delineating Labor Standards

Labor standards can be seen as falling into two broad categories. The first category specifies standards as procedural rights, emphasizing that individuals or groups may do, or not do, certain things without penalty. The second category specifies standards in terms of outcomes, specifying that individuals or groups should be able to enjoy certain minimum levels of income or consumption in particular dimensions. These two categories overlap. They are also connected respectively to two somewhat different ethical views, which might be, albeit somewhat simplistically, characterized as the "rights" and "welfarist" perspectives. We shall discuss these theoretical issues after we have provided some practical examples of labor standards. We shall not go at all into the history and evolution of current formulations of international labor standards, since that task is performed in Engerman (2003), which forms part of the same project as this chapter.

Examples of current labor standards

Portes (1990) provides a classification of different kinds of labor standards, which is summarized in table 2.1 (taken from Maskus, 1997). The first category encompasses fundamental human rights, as recognized in various UN declarations. The second category, that of civic rights, deals with workers' positions with respect to their employers. In some respects, these rights are derived from basic rights (e.g., protection from physical coercion is the basis for free association and expression), and are related by involving some aspect of free choice. However, in practice the boundaries of these civic rights are often much less clear than those of basic rights. For example, it may be considered quite acceptable that employers are able to fire and replace striking workers, and this places practical limits on the right to collective representation. Hence, almost from the start, we begin to encounter practical problems with what, at first sight, seem to be very straightforward and obvious virtues. Therefore, we will discuss matters such as hierarchies of rights, and the relationship of rights to welfare later in this section and at other points in the paper.

Survival and security rights are the third and fourth categories of rights listed in table 2.1. They relate to conditions of work that affect workers' well being, but do not necessarily directly impact freedom of choice. One might argue that being fully informed about job hazards is as fundamental a right as those in the first two categories, and, indeed, a choice that is uninformed as a result of deliberate concealment of information is hardly a free choice. Again, we postpone a more detailed discussion of such issues. Note, also,

Table 2.1 Labor standards as rights

Type	Examples
Basic Rights	Right against involuntary servitude
	Right against physical coercion
	Right to compete without discrimination
	Right against exploitative use of child labor
Civic Rights	Right to free association
	Right to collective representation
	Right to free expression of grievances
Survival Rights	Right to a living wage
	Right to full information about hazards of job conditions
	Right to accident compensation
	Right to limited hours of work
Security Rights	Right against arbitrary dismissal
	Right to retirement compensation
	Right to survivors' compensation

Source: Maskus (1997), Portes (1990).

that the standards in the third and fourth categories include economic out-comes pertaining to working conditions, such as "a living wage," "limited hours of work," and various kinds of compensation, but they are couched in terms of the language of rights.

Perhaps the best-known expression of a fundamental subset of labor stand-ards is the Organization for Economic Cooperation and Development's (OECD, 1996) set of core labor standards (CLS), which also corresponds closely with the International Labor Organization's (ILO) core standards. These are summarized as follows:

1. Prohibition of slavery and compulsory labor, such as bonded labor;
2. Nondiscrimination in employment among genders, ethnic groups, etc.;
3. Prohibition of exploitative forms of child labor;
4. Freedom of association (the right to organize workers' groups); and
5. Freedom of collective bargaining over working conditions.

We can see that this list corresponds quite closely to the first two categories in table 2.1. The second pair of categories in table 2.1 is totally omitted, however, from this OECD CLS list.

In contrast, the United States' formulation of labor standards, as expressed in various legislation related to international trade, gives working conditions a more prominent role. The following list is taken from Golub (1997b), and represents a condensation of a more detailed list provided in the appendix of Brown et al. (1996):

1. Freedom of association;
2. The right to organize and bargain collectively;
3. Prohibition on forced or compulsory labor;
4. A minimum age for the employment of children; and
5. A guarantee of acceptable working conditions (possibly including maximum hours per week, a weekly rest period, limits to work by young persons, a minimum wage, minimum workplace safety and health standards, and elimination of employment discrimination).

Finally, Engerman (2003) provides a categorization of labor standards that very much takes an economist's perspective. He divides standards into three groups:

1. Labor market conditions, such as wages and hours, with different provisions according to age and gender;
2. Working conditions pertaining to safety and sanitation; and
3. The general range of arrangements between labor and management, including general rights as well as some contractual arrangements.

It can be seen that Engerman's third category includes most of the general rights that are spelled out in detail in the OECD and US lists.

Both the OECD and US lists, as given above, are appealing in terms of the ideals that they express. Both lists are dominated by considerations of rights and processes, though the working conditions category in the US list includes a mixture of process and outcome concerns. More recently, the US has endorsed the ILO/OECD list, leaving out working conditions, except for nondiscrimination. However, despite this convergence, and as we have noted, the details can be quite problematic. Conflicts can arise between different ideals. Defining the practical limits of various rights can be extremely difficult. Since actual policies will require working out such details, it is important to examine the differing justifications for various international labor standards, as well as their potential impacts. It is not clear, for example, that even the two lists combined cover all fundamental issues. For example, neither list explicitly mentions the right to full information about job hazards (pertaining to process rather than outcome), which Fields (1996, 2000) has argued is a fundamental right.

Framing labor standards

We have alluded to outcome- versus process-based standards, and to rights-based versus welfarist ethical perspectives. We next discuss these theoretical issues in greater detail. While some abstraction is involved, it is essential because it helps to clarify some of the bases for disagreement in practical debates on labor standards.

We begin with a discussion of rights and welfare.[1] Standard welfare economics focuses only on the consequences of institutions and policy for individuals who make up a society (however we choose to define it – community, nation, or globe, for example[2]). This consequentialist approach has two components. First, the welfare of individuals is typically taken to depend only on their consumption of material goods and services. Individuals are assumed to have rankings over all different possible bundles of such goods and services (e.g., 3 lb. of rice for 4 hours of work in a day is preferred to 2 lb. of rice for 3 hours of work). These rankings, if well-behaved enough, can be replaced by utility functions, which are simply numerical indices of preference ("higher utility" is equivalent to "better preferred"). Actually, consequentialism can be broader, allowing one individual's utility to depend on the outcomes of all members of society.

The second aspect of a consequentialist approach refers to the evaluation of the welfare of members of a society in the aggregate. Again, a consequentialist is only concerned with the preference rankings or utility functions of the individual members of society in evaluating aggregate welfare. The application of consequentialism to such concerns as evaluating individual welfare and the overall welfare of a group can be termed "welfarism."

To put the above ideas in context, consider the various rights listed earlier when we gave example lists of labor standards. For example, the right to free association is included as a fundamental or core standard. A consequentialist or welfarist position would be that such a right should not matter in itself, but only if it affects the outcomes for the individual. These may be explicitly material, e.g., if they enable the individual to bargain more effectively with an employer, or gather information about job safety from fellow workers. They may also be purely "psychological," such as the pleasure a worker may derive from exchanging banter with colleagues. Ultimately what matters is if the worker through free association is thereby able to make choices that increase her or his utility.

Lindbeck (1988) and Sen (1997) have articulated an alternative view. They suggest that the opportunities available to an individual matter, beyond consideration of the value of the best opportunities. In other words, the size of the choice set, or the freedom to choose from a bigger set, has intrinsic value. This concern with opportunities, however, seems to unnecessarily mix the general benefits of choice with the issue of the size of the choice set. Being freer to choose, even actions that are harmful to oneself, can instead be viewed as one kind of procedural consideration. It is procedural matters, therefore, that are central to the "rights" perspective. Aside from freedom, fairness may be the other broad category of procedural consideration that matters.

At this point, we may note that the connection between process-based labor standards and rights-based ethical approaches is close but not perfect. A procedural standard may be justified purely because we care about the right to certain kinds of freedom and fairness, or it may be justified on outcome-based grounds. For example, in the former case, the right to be fully informed about job risks is desirable irrespective of whether it has any positive or negative impact on the worker's behavior or utility (he may just feel more anxious, without anything else changing). In the latter perspective, full information is good only if it improves the worker's well being – he directly or indirectly enjoys greater utility.

Having sketched some of the essentials of the welfarist and rights approaches to evaluating policy, we explore some of the possible conflicts between these approaches, and the extent to which one can find pragmatic compromises that will allow one to go forward with practical decision-making. If there were no conflict between the two approaches, our task would be much simpler. However, it is very easy to construct examples where valuing procedures or rights conflicts with consequentialist or welfarist approaches. This point was first made in general by Sen (1970), and we illustrate it with an example from Pattanaik (1999).

In the example, there are two individuals, say Adam and Bob, who each can choose whether to wear a red or a white shirt. Their rankings of the overall choice by both of them are shown in table 2.2. The first element of each pair is Adam's shirt color choice, while the second is Bob's choice. The columns give each person's ranking in descending order, so that a combination that is higher in the column is preferable to one that is lower. Each person prefers to wear a white shirt, whatever the other person chooses to wear. For example, Bob prefers white to red if Adam chooses red (top two elements of Bob's column), and also if Adam chooses white (bottom two elements of Bob's column). Note that there is some degree of concern for others' consumption or choices in these preferences. Thus, whatever Adam wears (white or red), he prefers that Bob wear red. These preferences might be considered to be "meddlesome," but they seem to be so in a mild sort of way. In any case, they reflect each person's true rankings.

Table 2.2 Preferences that lead to a conflict between rights and outcomes

Adam's Ranking	Bob's Ranking
(White, Red)	(Red, White)
(Red, Red)	(Red, Red)
(White, White)	(White, White)
(Red, White)	(White, Red)

The problem that arises in this example is as follows. If one believes that rights such as freedom over personal choices matter, then clearly Adam and Bob should be allowed to make their personal choices, and each will choose to wear white, irrespective of the other's choice. However, Adam and Bob would *unanimously* agree that (Red, Red) is a better outcome than (White, White). A consequentialist would be obliged to say that the former outcome is therefore superior, even though it overrides the free choices of the two individuals. Thus we have a basic conflict between the rights and welfarist perspectives.

One way around the conflict illustrated by the above example is to allow individuals to have rankings over processes as well as over outcomes. To elucidate this in the context of the previous example, suppose there are two possible institutions, one in which Adam and Bob are both empowered to choose the colors of their own shirts, and another in which the shirt colors are specified collectively or cooperatively. Let us denote these two cases by the letters I (for individualistic) and C (collectively). Then if Adam and Bob both care strongly enough about their individual rights, each may prefer the outcome–process combination (White, White, I) to the combination (Red, Red, C), even though the outcome (Red, Red) is unanimously preferred.[3]

Allowing individuals to care about rights or processes in their rankings at least partially resolves the tension between the rights-based and welfarist perspectives. If these extended rankings are well-behaved enough, individuals still may have utility indexes that indicate their welfare, but utility now depends on processes as well as the outcomes. This expanded approach to evaluating social situations is important in general, but is particularly useful in clarifying the manner in which an important subset of labor standards is framed, since they emphasize basic rights.

While the right to wear the color of shirt one pleases, used in the example, may seem trivial, it is, of course, illustrative of "[t]he desire to be governed by myself . . . as deep a wish as that of a free area for action, and perhaps historically older."[4] Other examples of rights that may be considered important include rights to non-discrimination on the basis of race or gender, the right to practice one's religion, the right not to be imprisoned without due legal process, the right to an education, and so on. Some workplace rights might be deemed to fall easily within the broad class of basic rights: rights to a safe workplace and free association are possible examples. Other rights, such as those to a job or to a "living wage" may be considered to be less fundamental or absolute. On the other hand, the broader right to the basic means of existence might well be ranked as a fundamental right. While labor standards often focus on rights, we wish to suggest that, rather than de-emphasizing rights, a broader approach to rights is more appropriate: promoting the broader right to the basic means of existence may be more fruitful than focusing on the right to a job or a "living wage."

This point will be more fully developed in the penultimate section of the chapter.

We have already noted the potential conflict between the rights approach and pure consequentialism. This issue may be more serious than just the color of the shirt one wears. If there are substantial losses in efficiency that result from enforcing some rights, such as can arise when entitlements create moral hazard or other incentive problems, then we may be willing to sacrifice some rights in some circumstances. This is precisely what the extended ranking of outcome–process combinations allows – individuals may explicitly incorporate tradeoffs between outcomes and procedures in their judgments. Recognizing these tradeoffs explicitly may sometimes be unpleasant, but it can help to clarify debates over the appropriate nature and enforcement of labor standards.

A further issue that must also be called out in more detail is that different rights may conflict with each other: they are rarely completely absolute. For example, the right to free expression is limited by the rights of others not to be injured, including by such free expression. Such conflicts may ultimately boil down to tradeoffs between rights and outcomes, but they may also be pure tradeoffs between different rights. For example, the right to free expression may conflict with someone else's right to be fully informed, if the free expression involves withholding or distorting information, even if that distortion causes no material or psychological harm.[5]

Typically, rights conflicts will be interpersonal (one person's rights conflict with another's), though one can concoct examples where one person exercising a right may harm his ability to enjoy another right. While the ranking of outcome–process combinations solves the problem of single-person rights tradeoffs, the aggregation of individual rankings into a social ranking is required to resolve interpersonal rights' tradeoffs. This is a deep issue that also must be faced up to in considering international labor standards. When we have a list of labor rights, how are different rights in the list to be weighed against one another, or ordered in terms of the degree to which they are fundamental? Furthermore, how are these judgments to be made when other rights – not just labor-related rights – are included in the mix? One may respond by throwing up one's hands and saying that only consequences matter, but that does not resolve these issues, which, while abstract, underlie the theoretical and practical debates about labor standards.

Labor Markets and Labor Standards

Having provided a brief discussion of what labor standards mean in practice, and how they may be viewed within a general normative perspective, we turn to examining more specific justifications or rationales for various kinds of labor standards. Our starting point in this section is standard models of labor markets. We outline the standard model of competition, consider variants of this model, and explore how market failures may arise, creating a case for government intervention in the form of labor standards. This analysis is couched in familiar welfarist terms. Aside from market failures, a case for government intervention in the labor market may be made on grounds of concern for equity. This, too, fits into the welfarist approach. In both these cases, one may also question the ability of governments to effectively achieve objectives of increased efficiency or equity through their interventions – we discuss this briefly as well. Finally, in this section we examine issues that intersect with concerns for rights, in particular the right to voluntarily engage in labor contracts. As we have explained in the previous section, welfarist concerns are not thereby excluded, but tradeoffs between processes and outcomes are more explicitly recognized.

The basic competitive model

In the standard model of competitive labor markets, workers and firms are small relative to the market, and take market conditions, particularly the wage, as given. Workers can specify a quantity of labor they will supply at each possible market wage rate, while firms can likewise specify a quantity of labor they will demand at each possible wage rate. The market wage rate itself is determined by the condition that there be no excess supply or demand in the labor market. This is illustrated in figure 2.1, where w^c is the competitive equilibrium market wage rate, determined by the equality of quantities supplied and demanded (point A).

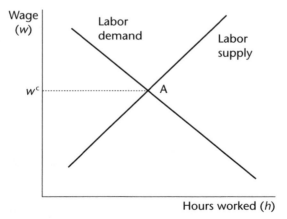

Figure 2.1   Competitive equilibrium in the labor market

The supply curve of labor in figure 2.1 is derived from the worker's simultaneous utility-maximizing choices of market-purchased consumption goods and leisure – the decision on the number of hours of work to supply is equivalently the decision on the number of hours of leisure to give up for work. The worker's utility may also be affected by a range of nonpecuniary job characteristics, which we shall lump together as "working conditions," and which will be a major focus of the discussion of labor standards in this section. The demand curve for labor in figure 2.1 comes from profit maximization by the firm, which decides how much labor, capital, and any other inputs to employ, taking all output and input prices as market-determined. The firm knows its technological possibilities perfectly. We assume for the moment that working conditions are fixed by technological factors, but they may affect the productivity of the firm's inputs, and labor in particular.[6]

It is useful to relate this simple model to Engerman's three-part classification of labor standards. First, wages and hours here are outcomes determined by the competitive market process, without any other restraint. Second are working conditions, such as safety and sanitation. Third are the conditions determining labor-management interactions: here these involve atomistic agents, with no bargaining power. In this outcome, there is no efficiency problem, in the sense that, taking all other economic conditions as given, no intervention in this market will improve the allocation of resources. We have said nothing so far about working conditions, taking them to be exogenously given, and therefore there is not yet any efficiency issue to be tackled with respect to working conditions.

However, it is possible that we may still find the competitive equilibrium of figure 2.1 to be unsatisfactory on equity grounds, because we think that the outcome, either in terms of the workers' wage, or her total income, or her overall utility is too low. The theoretical solution to that problem is lump-sum transfers of endowments, as T. N. Srinivasan points out in his comments. Often, however, informational and political constraints (touched on later in the chapter) make such policies infeasible in practice, and other, second-best, remedies are used. For example, a minimum wage above the competitive wage will benefit some of the workers in this situation, but hurt others, as firms reduce the hiring of labor, in numbers, hours or both. One might, alternatively, allow workers to bargain collectively with firms. That solution might also be preferred on rights-based grounds. The outcome in that case, however, will also be somewhat ambiguous effects on the welfare of the workers, as firms cut back on hiring. In both cases, the effect on the efficiency of resource allocation is negative (as Srinivasan implicitly emphasizes in his comments). One policy that may not have negative efficiency effects suggests itself if workers' productivity is inefficiently low. It may be best to raise workers' income and utility by making it possible to increase their productivity. This is a simple point, but one that will crop up repeatedly in our discussion as a counterpoint to the too ready imposition of labor standards.

Firms decide working conditions

We have presented the most basic competitive story, and we have not given job characteristics or working conditions any role so far, except to allow them to exogenously affect output as well as utility. The justification for allowing working conditions to affect output is that more pleasant or safer working conditions may affect the productivity of workers, presumably positively. Therefore, we next consider the case where the firm can make choices that affect working conditions. For simplicity, we can assume that while there may be many dimensions of job characteristics, these can be aggregated into a one dimensional index of working conditions that affects output − nothing essential is lost with this assumption.

Realistically, providing better working conditions will also cost the firm more, at least beyond some point − some minimum level of working conditions might be technologically determined, and incorporated in some fixed cost term. The firm will then choose the level of working conditions so that the marginal benefit in terms of higher output equals the marginal cost of improving working conditions, provided that such a possibility exists. Otherwise, if the marginal benefit is always too low, the firm will choose the minimum level of working conditions determined by technological constraints (see Appendix 2). In particular, if there is no impact of working conditions on productivity, then the firm will always choose the minimum feasible level of working conditions, even if workers benefit (derive higher utility) from better working conditions. Even in the case where the firm chooses working conditions above the minimum level, its calculations ignore the benefits to workers, and therefore the chosen level of working conditions is not socially efficient.

The problem of suboptimal working conditions that we have just outlined arises because there is no mechanism whereby the workers' desire for better working conditions is incorporated into the firm's choice. There are several plausible ways to introduce this possibility. For example, workers might be able to purchase improved working conditions in some way. If improved working conditions do not affect output, and if workers can choose their individual levels of working conditions through purchase on competitive markets (e.g., safety glasses, protective clothing), then this would be efficient (see Appendix 2). However, this is a very limited solution, precisely because neither requirement is likely to be met in practice.

It is more realistic to assume that firms explicitly or implicitly specify working conditions, along with the wages for different jobs. Workers can then evaluate the combinations of wages and working conditions that are available, thus allowing their own benefits from better working conditions to be introduced into their decision-making, and firms' responses. Firms will, of course, take account of their own benefits from better working conditions, in terms of higher productivity. The difference from the basic competitive model is that firms do not take wages as determined by competitive market forces. Instead they make offers of wage–working conditions pairs. Competition may still occur, in the form of free entry that drives firms' profits to zero. Alternatively, one can consider the case where firms do not compete, but workers instead receive their "reservation utility," the minimum utility from a job that the worker will accept, rather than choosing an alternative occupation. Both formulations are possible under this approach, which is well known as the theory of equalizing differences or compensating differentials.[7]

We can illustrate the workings of a labor market with equalizing differences. In order to do so, we assume that firms and workers have already determined what their best choices of other variables (labor and capital levels for firms, hours worked and consumption decisions for workers) will be, for any given wages and working conditions. Thus we can focus on market determination of wages and working conditions. Suppose that there are many firms and many potential workers. The profit of a typical firm, i, depends on the combination (w, s) of wages and working conditions that it offers. Similarly, the utility of a typical worker, j, also depends on the combination (w, s) that she accepts. A firm will make higher profits whenever w or s is lower, other things equal, while a worker will be better off with a higher w or s, other things equal. If firms are competitive due to free entry (which is most in keeping with the basic competitive model), then each firm must make zero profits in the competitive equilibrium. In figure 2.2, we show the combinations (w, s) that give two different firms zero profits. The thicker line shows the upper envelope curve for all firms' zero-profit combinations: these are the best combinations of wages and working conditions that the market can provide. Finally, there are two curves showing combinations (w, s) that give the workers their best choices among those the market can provide.

As we have constructed figure 2.2, worker 1 is best off working for firm 1. Worker 2, who prefers better working conditions, finds them with firm 2, but at a wage that is lower. Alternatively, we can say that worker 1 receives a compensating differential of a higher wage for tolerating worse working conditions. In fact, worker 2 would also have to be compensated with a higher wage for worse working conditions than her choice, but that would require combinations of (w, s) that no firm can provide and still break even. The main point here is that the outcome is efficient, in the sense that resources cannot be reallocated to make any worker better off, without hurting some

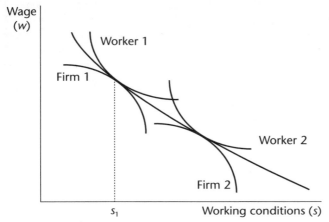

Figure 2.2 A labor market with compensating differentials

other worker.[8] From a strict consequentialist perspective, therefore, there is no room here for labor standards.

One could still take the position that worker 1 has a right to some minimum level of working conditions. In this case, imposing a minimum level of working conditions above s_1 will make worker 1 worse off in terms of her ranking over outcomes, because she will be forced to accept a less-preferred combination (w, s), given the constrained choice of combinations offered by the market. Hence there is the kind of conflict between rights and welfare that we have discussed earlier. If workers have extended rankings over combinations and procedures, they may agree that procedures that allow workers to accept jobs with poor working conditions are to be ruled out. In this case, how this aggregation of individual rankings over outcomes and processes is made becomes crucial. Therefore this is an issue we will return to in greater detail later.

There are two further points to consider in the model of compensating differentials. First, we have assumed that firms' profits are driven down to zero by competitive entry. This may be an unrealistic assumption. In many cases, especially in developing countries, workers may instead be competing for jobs in a manner that pushes them down to their reservation utilities – measures of how well off they would be in alternative occupations (working on the family farm, being a street vendor, or perhaps even begging).[9] In this case, the thick line in figure 2.2 can be interpreted as combinations that give workers reservation utilities. In the market equilibrium, firms now make positive profits. The market outcome is still allocationally efficient, but it may be considered undesirable on distributional grounds.

In theory, a redistributional policy may work here. For example, if worker 1 is in an industry that is inherently unsafe, imposing a higher standard of working conditions while requiring the wage to be maintained at the same level would make the worker better off at the expense of the firm: there is room to do so because the firm is making a positive profit. The combination (w, s) that results from this policy creates an allocational inefficiency, but it improves the equity of outcomes.[10] There are also practical issues of enforcement or implementation, but these exist with any policy intervention. If the wage condition is not included, however, the firm's response to a higher safety standard would be to lower the wage it pays, reducing the worker to her reservation utility again.

The second point to be added to the discussion of the compensating differential model concerns the hiring of multiple workers by a firm. If there are many workers and many firms in many industries, the outcome will be much like figure 2.2. Firm 1 will simply be the representative firm in its industry, and each such firm will be able to hire as many workers as it wants at the combination (w, s) that is shown as chosen by worker 1. Suppose, instead, that there are only two industries, with technological possibilities represented by the zero profit combinations available to firms 1 and 2 in figure 2.2. A worker with preferred tradeoffs over wages and working conditions that are intermediate between workers 1 and 2 will not be able to select a point on the thick line, but will instead have to select a combination (w, s) that is on one of the two firms' zero-profit curves. This assumes that a firm can offer different levels of working conditions to different workers. It may be that the firm has to choose the same level of working conditions for all its workers (the air quality in the factory, for example). Then the firm has to balance the preferences of its different workers in making its offers – compensating differentials cannot be perfect in this case. The case where working conditions are a good that is jointly consumed by workers (and by the firm if it enjoys higher productivity from better conditions) raises some significant new issues that are taken up in the next subsection.

Working conditions as a public good

To the extent that the same working conditions are shared by all workers in a firm, and those conditions affect their well-being directly, as well as their productivity, working conditions have the character of a public good. The essence of a public good is that it is shareable or non-rival: in other words, one worker's consumption does not reduce the amount available for other workers to consume. Clean air in a factory, safety information, and general safety procedures are examples that fit this category quite well. A pure public good is also non-excludable, so, for example, if clean air is provided in a building to some workers, other workers in the building cannot be excluded from also enjoying the clean air.

If there is some exclusion mechanism, even partial, a public good can be termed a club good, with the analogy being to a club where membership is required, but all members enjoy the same amenities. Public goods and club goods may also be subject to congestion effects, in which case they are partly like private goods: one person's consumption tends to reduce the amount available for others. All these ideas are surveyed in, for example, Cornes and Sandler (1986).

Public goods pose a general problem for market-based resource allocation, because they create incentives for individuals to not reveal their true benefit from consuming the public good, and therefore to not pay a share of the cost that reflects their true benefit.[11] This occurs because an individual can benefit from the public good if others are willing to pay for it. This problem is well known as the "free-rider" problem, and it results in underprovision of the public good relative to the efficient level, as measured by standard ways of assessing overall welfare. It does not arise in the case of private goods because there is no shareability or jointness in consumption. While several aspects of working conditions have the character of public goods, the implications of this have not been explored in analyses of regulation of working conditions such as those of Dickens (1984) and Brown et al. (1996). We therefore provide some discussion below.

Consider first the case where there is just one worker, who benefits from better working conditions. Thus better working conditions increase her utility (her index of material well-being). Furthermore, the same working conditions simultaneously affect the worker's productivity, and hence the profit of the firm (before costs of providing working conditions are factored in). The optimal provision of working conditions requires that the *sum* of the marginal benefits of the worker and the firm be equated to the marginal cost of improving working conditions at the best possible level of those conditions.[12] If the firm and worker can cooperate honestly, they can achieve this best level of working conditions. However, each has an incentive to let the other pay, and free ride, at least partially. This "noncooperative behavior" will lead to underprovision of working conditions, that is, they will be worse than the efficient level.[13]

Can this resource allocation problem be solved to ensure the optimal outcome? One theoretical answer is the Lindahl model, where the firm and the worker are assumed to pay personalized prices that reflect their individual marginal valuations. The supplier of s receives payments from both parties, and supplies the optimal amount. At first sight, this seems a rather unrealistic suggestion. However, it turns out to be equivalent to a noncooperative situation where each side contributing chooses its contribution taking the other side's cost share as given.[14] Again, this may seem an unlikely assumption for the case of a firm and a worker trying to agree on working conditions. However, it may have some relevance to the case of many workers trying to reach an agreement among themselves (see below), or of a union collectively representing workers in trying to reach agreement with a firm. The point of this discussion is to suggest that there could be mechanisms for overcoming free-rider problems that do not involve the direct imposition of labor standards by some external policy maker. Appropriate processes or institutions that allow for collective bargaining by workers may have some value in overcoming the public goods resource allocation problem, which is precisely a collective action problem.[15] Thus labor standards that support rights of collective action by workers may have a justification in terms of promoting more efficient outcomes, as well as a direct justification from a rights-based perspective. Of course the latter justification is broader, since it presumably applies even when collective action worsens outcomes.

To round out our earlier analysis of the public goods problem, we may note that in the case of many workers the problem is essentially the same. The optimal level of working conditions is determined by the condition that the sum of the marginal benefits of all the workers and of the firm be equated to the marginal cost of improving the level of working conditions.[16] There is a free-rider problem not only between the firm and workers, but also among all the workers. It is this latter problem that might be directly addressed by a union as an institution for collective action. The union may also provide a mechanism for workers to collectively negotiate a level of provision of working conditions with the firm, as we have discussed earlier. In fact, it seems that this has been one of the main roles of unions in practice, in addition to bargaining over wages and hours.

We close our discussion of working conditions as a public good by returning to the compensating differentials model of labor markets. If a firm competes simultaneously for many workers, and faces free entry that will push its profits down to zero, it will choose a wage for each worker and a common level of working conditions so that it maximizes the total utility of its workforce. It must do this to avoid being outbid for workers by a competing firm. In this case, competition also solves the public good problem with respect to working conditions, with the firm acting much as a club that maximizes the utility of its membership. This point is demonstrated more formally in Appendix 2. Even if firms are not constrained to zero profits by free entry, in this case of compensating differentials they will push workers down to their reservation utility levels in an efficient way, as they set wage–working conditions combinations to maximize their profits. This can raise concerns about equity, and workers' tradeoffs between wages and working conditions will be different at lower levels of utility, but there is no longer a straighforward problem of underprovision of working conditions as a public good. Allowing collective action by workers may still be supportable on distributional and rights grounds, but not on the basis of improving efficiency.

Monopsony

The model of compensating differentials allows for a kind of perfect wage discrimination by firms. This overcomes inefficiency problems that are sometimes associated with imperfect competition. Competition through free entry in the compensating differentials model redistributes from firms to workers, but does not affect efficiency. It is possible, however, that firms may have market power but not be able to discriminate among workers with different tradeoffs between consumption and work/leisure or to pay different wages for different hours worked. In such cases, we have the familiar inefficiency associated with market power, where the market wage does not properly reflect the value of the marginal product of workers.

In fact, market power leads to a wage that is below the value of the marginal product of labor. One can therefore also object to this outcome on grounds of inequity. Finally, the unequal position of the firm and the worker in the labor market might be considered to be unacceptable on the basis of procedural considerations. We will illustrate the market power outcome, and then discuss implications for labor standards policy. We have titled this subsection "monopsony," which is the case of a single buyer of labor, but the discussion also carries over to any firm with labor market power in the sense of a realization that the wage rate that it offers will affect the quantity of labor that is supplied to it.

In figure 2.3, the firm faces an upward sloping supply curve of labor. If it seeks to hire more labor (either more hours by a worker or more workers), it realizes that the wage offered must rise. The assumption here is that all hours worked receive the same wage. Hence, in this case, the firm's marginal expense of labor is above the wage rate it pays, and the firm maximizes its profit by choosing the amount of labor that equates its marginal labor expense to the value of the marginal product of labor. This is shown by the intersection of those two curves, and the market wage in this case is w^m, which is the wage at which this amount of labor will be supplied. The inefficiency and the possibly unacceptable distributional aspects of this outcome are both reflected in the fact that the equilibrium wage (the opportunity cost of the marginal hour worked) is less than the value of the marginal product of that hour.

This analysis is presented mathematically in Appendix 3. Mathematical analysis allows one to consider the simultaneous choice of working conditions

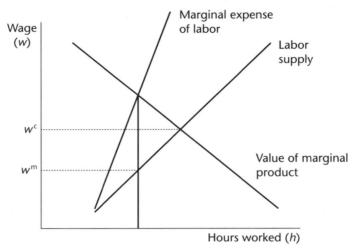

Figure 2.3   Monopsony in the labor market

by the firm. The monopsonistic firm will, in choosing the level of working conditions to offer, take account of its own costs and benefits, but also the impact of changes in working conditions on the supply of labor. It turns out that one cannot say anything in general. The monopsonist may choose working conditions that are too high or too low.

In any case, with or without the issue of working conditions, one policy response to the inefficiency illustrated in figure 2.3 is to impose a minimum wage. If appropriately chosen, the minimum wage can ensure the conditional optimality of the firm's choice of labor (so that the marginal value product equals the wage). In particular, this efficient minimum wage level is w^c as shown in figure 2.3. This is the level at which the value of the marginal product of labor and the opportunity cost of the last hour worked are equated. Of course this does not lead the firm to take account of the marginal benefit to workers in determining its choice of the level of working conditions. The inefficiency in that dimension is not caused by monopsony in the choice of labor input, so it requires a separate policy response. Furthermore, Dickens (1984) has shown that the effect on welfare of imposing a labor standard alone (without a minimum wage to correct the monopsony distortion) is also indeterminate. Our conclusion is the familiar one that multiple distortions require multiple policy instruments. Finally, another option is collective bargaining over working conditions and wages, the case of countervailing power highlighted by T. N. Srinivasan in his comments. Tore Ellingsen, in his comments, sketches a model of bilateral bargaining where some regulation of standards can help workers in the overall bargaining outcome.[17]

Survival

The typical competitive story does not consider survival constraints for workers. In the presence of a survival constraint, there might be a role for a minimum wage even in the case of competition, as suggested by Raynauld and Vidal (1998). The survival constraint leads to multiple equilibria, and the minimum wage can ensure that the "bad" equilibrium for poor workers is ruled out. Thus the policy justification is based on equity rather than efficiency grounds – in the case of monopsony, both equity and efficiency can be enhanced by an appropriately chosen minimum wage.

Suppose that workers maximize their utility over income (which in turn is used for consumption) and work/leisure hours, where they take the competitive wage as given. Furthermore, they are subject to an additional constraint, namely that a worker's income must be at least some minimum level that permits survival. If this survival constraint does not bind the worker, she will satisfy the usual marginal conditions, which imply a supply curve that will typically be upward sloping, that is, a lower wage *decreases* the number of working hours (neglecting the possibility of a backward-bending supply at high incomes). On the other hand, if the survival constraint binds, then the usual marginal conditions are overridden, and the worker simply chooses enough working hours to survive: in this case, a lower wage *increases* the number of working hours.[18]

The two components of the supply curve are shown in figure 2.4, along with a competitive demand curve, which slopes downward. The demand curve is based on the standard assumption that firms demand the amount of

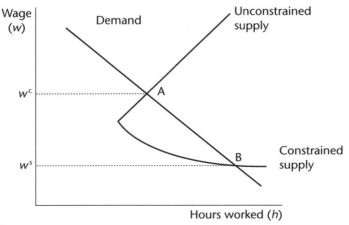

Figure 2.4 Multiple competitive equilibria with survival constraint

labor at which the value of the marginal product equals the wage, taking the wage as given by the market. The supply and demand curves intersect twice, so there are two equilibria. At point A, the worker earns above subsistence income with a wage of w^c, but at point B he is held to a lower, subsistence wage, w^s. If firms can make wage offers as in the compensating differential story outlined earlier, then the subsistence equilibrium cannot survive, since there are wage–hours contract offers that will generate a profit and make workers better off. However, since the standard competitive story has wage-taking firms, such a situation would allow the worse equilibrium to persist. Note that if there is competition in the product market, firms will earn zero long-run profits in either equilibrium, and consumers are the ones who benefit from the workers' "bad" outcome.

In the above framework, a minimum wage above the subsistence wage will rule out the subsistence-wage case, and lead to the higher-wage equilibrium, making the poor workers better off. This is the essence of the Raynauld–Vidal argument. This kind of argument seems to formalize the thinking of many who are concerned about "sweatshop" wages being forced on workers through their necessity. However, this model may not capture the real concern, for the following reason. The subsistence-wage equilibrium marked by point B in figure 2.4 is not stable. A small perturbation that pushes the wage above w^s creates excess demand rather than excess supply, and in this case the wage should rise all the way to w^c, the usual competitive wage, which would be the only equilibrium that persists. Note that the instability of the low-wage equilibrium is behind the fact that competitive wage contract offers by firms will rule out that equilibrium, as discussed in the previous paragraph.

The survival issue can be considered in a different light, however. In this alternative, the survival equilibrium is the only competitive equilibrium. In this case, a minimum wage is not the appropriate policy, because it would endanger workers' survival. This is illustrated in figure 2.5: point B is the only intersection of the supply and demand curves, and is the unique, stable competitive equilibrium.[19] In the absence of the subsistence constraint, the equilibrium would have been at C, with a higher wage and fewer hours worked. In the given situation, however, a minimum wage above w^s simply creates excess supply, and reduces workers' ability to survive. In this circumstance, the only way to improve the lot of workers may be to increase their productivity, shifting the labor demand curve up, and getting them above subsistence income levels. In figure 2.5, this is illustrated by the starred demand curve, with a new equilibrium at A. The contrast between figures 2.4 and 2.5, and their policy implications, illustrates one of the differences in perspectives that lead to debates about the appropriate nature and role of labor standards. In the case of figure 2.5, the correct policy intervention if one wishes to improve the lot of poor workers is one that raises their

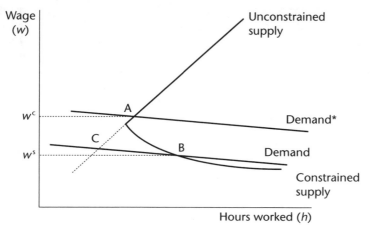

Figure 2.5 Unique competitive equilibrium at subsistence

productivity. We return to such approaches in the penultimate section of this paper.

In the consideration of survival constraints up to this point, we have not allowed any role for working conditions, beyond the wage and number of hours worked. However, working conditions may also be affected by the existence of survival constraints. This can happen in several ways, depending on what one assumes about the markets for labor and for working conditions (standards). Let us assume first that there is no productivity benefit from improving working conditions but that workers are better off with better conditions. In the absence of a market for working conditions, firms will choose the minimum feasible level of those conditions, whether there is a survival constraint or not. If there is a competitive market for working conditions as a private good (e.g., workers can buy safety glasses), then we get optimality in the absence of a survival constraint. Adding the survival constraint does not change the tradeoff at the margin between more leisure and better working conditions, but since the worker is working longer hours to survive, her marginal utility of leisure is higher, implying that adding the survival constraint raises the marginal utility of working conditions in equilibrium, so these must be at a lower level in this equilibrium. In the extreme case, the worker's demand for working conditions could be reduced to zero: intuitively, this just reflects the poverty of the worker. Imposing standards that mandate higher than equilibrium working conditions (with costs borne by the firm) in this case simply shifts the firm's demand downward, requiring the worker to work longer hours at lower pay to survive.

Finally, consider the case where firms can make offers combining wages and working conditions, as in models of compensating differentials. Recall that competing firms make zero profits with free entry, and workers' utility is maximized subject to this zero profit constraint. The zero profit constraint determines a locus of wage–working-conditions combinations that are feasible, irrespective of whether a survival constraint is present or not. A higher wage paid must be compensated for by worse working conditions in order to keep profit at zero. Adding a survival constraint changes workers' tradeoffs between wages and working conditions, in favor of the former, so that a given worker would prefer a combination with a higher wage and lower working conditions. Again, the survival constraint worsens working conditions, but there is no simple remedy: mandating higher standards will simply make workers worse off as firms adjust by reducing wages.[20]

Information

The smooth working of all markets can be derailed by asymmetries of information (see Stiglitz, 2000, for an overview and references). Under conditions of imperfect or incomplete information, market outcomes may be inefficient relative to a situation of perfect or complete information. Less obviously, market outcomes may sometimes not even be efficient given the constraints imposed by the available information. Depending on the situation, potential remedies may be policies to directly influence outcomes, or policies that are designed to do so indirectly, by improving the collection and exchange of information. Since information has public good characteristics, some of the issues discussed above will arise in the context of the production and consumption of information, but we will not repeat the earlier discussion. One can also take a rights-based approach, and argue that market participants are entitled to certain kinds of information, independently of the impact on market outcomes. Here, worker outcomes in the labor market are wages, hours, and working conditions in general. For employers, outcomes are the productivity or output of their employees. To the extent that employers are relatively privileged and that we care about equity, the focus is typically on the outcomes and rights of workers.

An area where workers and employers may commonly lack full information is that of safety and risks. These may include the possibility of accidents, negative health consequences from chemicals, and so on. One side effect of the industrial revolution has been the vastly greater complexity of the workplace, and the multiplication of potential risks. Even traditional occupations may have unknown long-term consequences, such as injuries from repetitive motions. Given this complexity, it is not surprising that both employers and workers may be uninformed, or poorly informed about safety, risks, and so on. Public good problems can hinder the efficient private collection of the relevant information. Even if information is available, participants may not have incentives to disseminate it optimally, or they may not be able to credibly exchange information. For example, workplace risks could conceivably be handled by insurance, but this can be made difficult to achieve efficiently, or at all, by problems of moral hazard and adverse selection.

In the compensating-differentials model discussed above, workers are fully informed about working conditions, including on-the-job risks. However, the empirical evidence appears to be that workers commonly underestimate job risks. This can potentially create inefficiencies in the labor market. Oi (1973) shows that the existence of workers who underestimate job risks is not by itself sufficient to cause a misallocation of workers to dangerous jobs – the risk assessments of marginal workers is what matter. Under plausible conditions, however, the market equilibrium does involve suboptimal levels of working conditions. There are numerous models with variations on this theme, surveyed in Dickens (1984), which support the basic theme that informational gaps may or may not cause problems in the efficiency of resource allocation, in particular, exposing workers to more risk than would be socially optimal in a world of full information, according to any standard welfarist objective.

The rationale for government intervention in cases of nonoptimality must be based on the assumption that the government is better informed or that it can become so at lower cost than individuals or firms. For many kinds of health and safety information, this is a very plausible and realistic assumption. The natural policy then might be simply to inform workers about the true risks of jobs. However, if this does not succeed in informing workers perfectly (because the government's information transmission is noisy, or because workers do not interpret it perfectly) Dickens (1984) shows that workers may be worse off with such partial improvements in information. In such cases, government mandated standards (if properly enforced, of course) might be superior.

Note that the presence of imperfect information on the part of workers, and possibly also firms, means that competition where firms offer compensating differentials is not enough to make the market equilibrium efficient. For example, suppose that worker preferences over wages and working conditions are heterogeneous, but that firms cannot distinguish workers according to these preferences. With complete information, firms would be able to vary wages across workers, even if, by assumption, they must offer the same working conditions to all workers. Lacking information on preferences, this is no longer possible, because a worker will always claim the highest wage offered, and therefore a firm must pay all its workers the same wage. Even if firms can screen workers by offering them nonlinear wage schedules to induce self-selection, the outcome is not necessarily efficient, and competition can even destroy the possibility of a market equilibrium. More realistically, firms are unlikely to be able to engage in such complex strategies.

Brown et al. (1996) consider a model, in which there is a distribution of workers and firms in two different industries, but firms cannot directly identify worker preferences. The job characteristic is treated as job safety, but it could be any aspect of working conditions that affects workers' welfare. In the model, there are more workers than firms, and levels of safety will differ across firms in the market equilibrium. A marginal worker in a firm will be indifferent between that firm and the alternative firm with the closest safety level. Brown et al. show that if the distribution of worker preferences is more concentrated in the middle (as would be realistic), firms that are safer than average will actually be less safe than would be optimal based on the preferences of the workers that they employ, while firms that are less safe than average are actually safer than would be optimal for the workers they employ. Thus firms' offered safety levels are also skewed toward the middle.[21]

While the result obtained by BDS is theoretically interesting, it does not seem to be very significant from the perspective of labor standards policy, because the least safe firms are "too safe." Empirically, we observe firms with different levels of working conditions, and it is unlikely that we would recommend that the safer firms tighten up their standards, while the less safe ones become more lax. Clearly, when we observe variation in working conditions, the situation is likely to be driven by other factors than differing worker preferences, and attempting to apply the Brown et al. model would be misleading.

Free contracting, rights, and welfare

In this subsection, we turn more explicitly to questions that revolve around rights. Earlier, we noted the importance of rights-based perspectives in practical formulations of labor standards, and we examined the manner in which such perspectives interact with welfarist approaches that focus on consequences or outcomes. Here we examine two models that illustrate these interactions in more specific situations. One right that is often supported is what Basu (1999) has termed the "principle of free contracting," which asserts that an individual should have the right to voluntarily enter into any contract, since voluntariness implies a welfare improvement.[22] This seems like an eminently reasonable right, supporting free choice, which does not appear to conflict with welfarist objectives. However, the models described below illustrate some possible limitations both with the principle of free contracting and with the argument that no voluntary contracts should be prohibited. In his comments, Tore Ellingsen provides two further possible cases for restricting contracting. In one, private information about productivity leads to an inefficient "rat race" because of informational externalities.[23]

Second, restrictions on giving up workplace and related civic rights may be efficient because they prevent free riding in the provision of a public good, a problem that was analyzed earlier.

Bonded labor

Once bonded, a worker is unfree, but the act of choosing to be bonded can be voluntary. Bonded labor can include peonage, debt slavery, attached labor, and even contract labor can be included in the term "bonded labor." The argument in Genicot (2000) is based on showing that the existence of bonded labor can hinder the development of welfare-enhancing credit opportunities for laborers. In her framework, the set of opportunities for the worker is so limited that these contracts may represent their best option. One can, of course, make a case for banning bonded labor on rights-based grounds alone, with the principle of free contracting subordinated to the right to remain "free to choose." Alternatively, one may argue that the workers have limited rationality or incomplete information, possibly combined with moral hazard on the part of employers. Furthermore, nonlinear discounting and endogenous preferences have been used to explain the suboptimality of bonded labor. Genicot provides a plausible alternative to some of these narrower, more technical justifications.

Genicot shows that a ban on bonded labor can enhance the welfare of the laborers affected by the ban. The crux of the argument is that the set of choices available to the individual facing the bonded labor option is endogenous. In other words, banning bonded labor improves the overall set of options that the worker faces. The way this works in her model is as follows. Formal credit institutions may refuse credit to the poor in the presence of bonded labor, because the presence of the bonded-labor option raises the risk that the borrower will default and switch to that alternative. As a result, the worker is not offered formal credit, and instead must choose the bonded labor contract. In this case, the landlord has greater enforcement power than the formal credit institution. To the extent that the existence of the formal credit option influences the landlord's choice, he is making a strategic decision that results in bondage, i.e., he is choosing a contract that destroys the option of a formal credit contract being offered. Side payments from the landlord to the worker may, in some cases, have the same effect as commitment in destroying the formal credit equilibrium.

The above argument in favor of banning bonded labor is ultimately based on grounds of equity and not of efficiency. Banning bonded labor makes the worker better off at the expense of the landlord. It is not a Pareto improvement, which would mean that one individual is made better off without reducing the welfare of any other individual. Philosophically, the issue may be deeper. Basu (1999) points out that the distinction between "coercion" and "free choice" entails a prior opinion on what constitutes basic human rights. The question in this case is whether the worker's right to borrow from a formal credit institution is such a basic right. However, if this right is conditional on the level of income of the worker, then it seems that it is not really basic. The basic right must be something else, such as that of making choices from a set that allows the chooser to preserve a level of autonomy and dignity, or to achieve a basic standard of living. This illustrates again the broader issue of what rights we should care about, taken up in the chapter's penultimate section.

Working conditions

Basu (1999) also considers problems with the principle of free contracting, in a manner somewhat different than Genicot. He asks, "Is there a case for banning violence and sexual harassment when these occur as a consequence of voluntary contracting?" Here, violence and harassment can be taken as two important examples of a particular category of working conditions. Basu postulates that an entrepreneur advertises for workers, openly saying he will pay a wage above the market wage rate, but this goes with reserving the right to harass his workers (other working condition may be substituted for harassment). In this case, workers who are averse to harassment will be worse off if harassment is allowed.

The supporting argument for the above assertion is as follows. Suppose there are two types of workers, those with no aversion to harassment and those with an infinite aversion. Each type has an upward sloping supply, as a function of the wage rate. Employers and workers are competitive wage takers. If the employer receives a constant additional benefit per worker that he can harass, this will be the difference in wages in two types of contracts that can be signed (harassment and no-harassment). However, at the margin, the wage is determined by the marginal product to the employer of those who are averse to harassment. Note that freedom from harassment is different from overall safety or sanitation, as discussed earlier, in that it is not a pure public good, but can be provided at a cost to a subset of workers. Banning harassment contracts reduces the wage of those who are willing to endure harassment (since their value to the employer is lower), and therefore their equilibrium supply. However, it increases the wage of those who are averse to harassment. Thus the latter are worse off if harassment contracts are allowed: this is a standard pecuniary externality.

As in the case of Genicot's analysis, banning harassment contracts does not lead to a Pareto improvement. Employers and workers who are not averse to harassment are worse off as a result. Basu notes that the argument hinges on going "beyond economics" to identify preferences that are "fundamental," in the sense that "no one should have to pay a penalty for having such a preference." Sexual harassment seems to fit this criterion (for most societies). Minimal levels of safety at work would also seem to be appropriate. However, there are two points to note. First, there is a very explicit value judgment that must be made here. Second, following the first point, there can be legitimate disagreement on such values, in particular, where one draws the line. Basu argues that the same issues arise in the case of child labor, where households that are averse to sending their children to work can be penalized in the market if child labor is allowed. We take up the issue of where and how one draws the line in such cases later.

Labor Standards in the Global Economy

In the previous section, we provided an overview of possible reasons for labor standards, either as regulations that directly set standards for outcomes (such as wages or working conditions) or as requirements on labor market processes (such as collective action or individual contracting rights). These issues with respect to the working of labor markets arise in a closed economy, and are not necessarily driven by concerns that transcend national boundaries. We now turn to some aspects of the links between international economic flows and labor standards. Some of the issues that arise with respect to the appropriateness and nature of these links are taken up in the next section.

In this section, the general theme is the impact of international trade on labor standards that are determined endogenously. We first examine whether international trade in goods has a causal link to inefficient labor standards. We briefly also discuss the link between trade negotiations and labor standards, as analyzed by Bagwell and Staiger (2001). However, we do not go in much detail into general issues of enforcement of labor standards, and whether trade sanctions are an appropriate tool for enforcing international labor standards. The second issue we address is whether trade hurts the poor (low-skilled) through its impact on labor standards. Thus the focus here is on distributional concerns rather than problems of inefficiency in resource allocation. Finally, we consider the choice of labor standards by competing countries, in which capital flows as well as international trade in goods are often given a role. There can be efficiency issues as well as distributional concerns in such "races to the bottom," where the term describes the lowering of labor standards by one country in strategic competition with other nations.

International trade and labor standards

Srinivasan (1994, 1996, 1998a, chapter 8; see also Bhagwati and Srinivasan, 1996) provides a lucid benchmark analysis of the possible links between international standards and international trade. He uses a model of a small open economy with perfectly competitive markets. He shows that labor standards will be chosen efficiently – none of the problems discussed earlier are present. This result, not surprisingly, does not depend on whether international trade occurs or not. In particular, he considers an economy with two regular traded goods and a third nontraded good, which is the economy-wide level of the labor standard. As is standard in international trade models, there are given endowments of the inputs, labor, and capital, and the feasible frontier is defined by a production possibility frontier that relates the outputs of the three goods, given the aggregate input endowments. Aggregate social welfare is captured in a Samuelson social utility function, which depends on the consumption of the two traded goods and the level of the labor standard.[24] Thus the labor standard enters social utility positively, while maintaining a higher standard entails a resource cost.

In this framework, the small open economy faces a given relative price of the two traded goods. With perfectly competitive markets, the economy's choices of consumption, production, and the labor standard are equivalent to those determined by maximizing social utility subject to the production constraint, nonnegativity constraints, and the trade balance requirement.[25] It is a straightforward and standard result that the outcome here is Pareto optimal, *including* the choice of the labor standard. In other words, no one can be made better off without making someone else worse off. This is a natural extension of the first welfare theorem of economics to incorporate labor standards. Srinivasan also points out that this Pareto optimal level will diverge across countries whenever preferences and resource endowments are heterogeneous.

Note that this conclusion tells us nothing about distributional issues, since the model is too aggregate to address such concerns. Here the implementation of standards is uniform within a country, and maximizes some unambiguous measure of aggregate social welfare. We will turn to distributional concerns in the next subsection, in examining the issue of winners and losers from trade. Public good problems in implementing standards – which we addressed earlier – are also put aside in this formulation. Nor is there any consideration of processes or rights independently of welfare outcomes. Finally, political economy issues are also treated separately by Srinivasan. Nevertheless, the results provide a useful benchmark for judging international labor standards, both in terms of rationale and precise implementation. Furthermore, one can argue that any such problems are ones of domestic implementation, and can or should be handled by domestic policies.

Srinivasan goes on to show that, even without balanced trade in each country, any world Pareto optimum of production, consumption, and standards (possibly different for each country) can be supported as a competitive equilibrium, i.e., as a free trade equilibrium. Unbalanced trade means that lump sum transfers may be required to support a particular world Pareto optimum. Srinivasan's contribution here is to show that the standard second welfare theorem of economics extends easily to include labor standards. Again, labor standards will in general be heterogeneous across countries.

Srinivasan also discusses the possibility that one can find a world Pareto optimum even when a minimum global labor standard is required. On the other hand, if the minimum standard is too high, a full Pareto optimum will be ruled out, and a restricted Pareto optimum, with a binding minimum standards constraint for some countries, will instead apply. In this case, there is a wedge between the marginal rate of substitution (MRS) between either consumption good and the standard on the one hand, and the marginal rate of transformation (MRT) in production between the same consumption good and the standard. Srinivasan points out *domestic* taxes and subsidies in countries where the minimum standard is binding will implement the Pareto optimum. There is no role for trade restrictions or other international policies.

Why should a minimum global labor standard be imposed at all, if it reduces welfare? Here one can introduce concerns about rights, taking the approach that the standard represents a consensus that countries agree to impose on themselves collectively, because it represents a concern about more fundamental rights that transcend immediate welfarist concerns. This is not too different from constitutional restraints within countries, which tie the hands of future governments even if they are acting in a "benevolent" manner. In the current example, there is an added international dimension. Srinivasan plausibly equates the minimum global standard in the abstract model with ILO conventions, and, together with his conclusions on the role of lump-sum international transfers and domestic taxes and subsidies, is led to state, "Indeed one could view the international assistance and domestic compliance measures associated with implementing ILO Conventions as precisely the right approach. *There is no need for any social clause.*" (emphasis added)

International consumption externalities are also considered in Srinivasan's framework.[26] With such externalities, the MRT in production between either consumption good and the standard in a country – call it A – is equated to a weighted sum of the MRS between that consumption good and country A's standard, where the sum is over all countries which care about A's standard. Again, the appropriate policy response to this externality is domestic taxes and subsidies that directly address the externality.

Srinivasan's use of Pigovian welfare economics to analyze issues of international labor standards is a useful benchmark. He extends it to a discussion of other market failures, such as capital market imperfections. Again, he argues that the best policy is to correct the externality at its source. Srinivasan notes that informational requirements may make such policy interventions difficult or impossible. We consider separately a further possible implication of this observation, that second-best policies may involve targeting in ways that include a focus on labor standards. The targeting issue also is relevant to income distribution considerations, where efficient direct income transfers may not be feasible because of informational constraints. This may apply to international as well as domestic transfers. We touch on these issues later.

Brown et al. (1996) examine many of the same issues as Srinivasan (1996). They also show that in a small open economy, correcting a labor market externality through a domestic standard improves domestic welfare, using a utilitarian criterion. In an importing sector, imports go up as a result of the standard. A common international standard has potentially different effects. While the loss to domestic producers is partly made up by the increase in the world price resulting from the global reduction in supply, domestic consumers are hurt, and the net gain may now be negative. Net exporters, on the other hand, definitely benefit from common standards. Common standards create terms-of-trade effects, and these may by themselves provide a motivation for imposing labor standards in a large country. This examination of terms-of-trade effects distinguishes the Brown et al. analysis from that of Srinivasan.

In the case where economies are specialized, the Brown et al. analysis implies that large countries acting noncooperatively will set standards too high, relative to the world optimum, since each tries to influence the terms of trade in its favor by raising its standard. Cooperation, or harmonization, will lead to lower standards. In a general equilibrium Heckscher–Ohlin model, the effect of a labor standard depends on how the factor requirements of the standard compare to the factor requirements of world production. For example, a labor standard that is more labor intensive than the world labor–capital ratio will raise the world relative price of the labor-intensive traded good, regardless of who exports the good. This means a terms-of-trade effect that benefits the labor-intensive country. Alternatively, Brown et al. also consider standards that are industry-specific. The results in that case are quite similar.

Therefore, in this framework, to the extent that most forms of labor standards are primarily or wholly labor using, they will increase the world relative prices of labor-intensive goods, improving the terms of trade of countries with labor-intensive exports. This analysis would suggest that, purely from the terms-of-trade perspective, less-developed countries (developing countries) would want higher labor standards, and developed countries would not. Therefore the analysis seems to be at odds with the current debates on international labor standards. Of course this conclusion neglects different interests within countries. For example, owners of capital may disproportionately influence policy.

Bagwell and Staiger (2001; see also Staiger, 2003) also consider the links between labor standards and international trade. As in the Brown et al. analysis, they allow for terms-of-trade effects. Unlike Brwon et al., they assume that countries can choose optimal tariffs as well as their national standards. Standards are assumed to matter directly only at the domestic level in each country. Thus cross-border externalities, such as when consumers in one country care about the production methods used in a different country, are ruled out: we discuss such possibilities in the following section. The domestic standards can be policies that are applied to production (specifying working conditions, for example) or to consumption (restricting consumption of products made using some kinds of processes).

The Bagwell and Staiger analysis works with reduced-form welfare functions for national governments. National welfare as perceived by a government depends on local prices, world prices, and domestic standards. Since the wedge between local and world prices is created by tariffs, welfare also depends on tariff levels. Each government is able to choose its domestic standards and tariffs. While this reduced-form approach is able to accommodate many different assumptions about domestic political economy, it may obscure some features of the model. In particular, Bagwell and Staiger focus throughout their analysis on the case where an increase in the national standard would worsen the terms of trade for every country. This is at odds, therefore, with the Brown et al. analysis, in which the direction of impact of a standard on the terms of trade depends on the relative factor intensity of the export good.

The Bagwell–Staiger model also allows efficient policy choices, as measured by any weighted sum of all countries' welfare functions, to include positive tariff levels. Optimal domestic standards are also specified in the efficient outcome. On the other hand, if each government chooses it tariffs and standards independently, the resulting noncooperative Nash equilibrium involves inefficient levels of tariffs and standards. In this equilibrium, trade volumes are inefficiently low. The source of this inefficiency, as one might expect, is the desire of each government to affect the terms of trade in its favor. However, since national standards can indirectly influence the terms of trade, international agreements that only negotiate improved cross-border market access through lower tariffs will distort national standards choices. This makes a theoretical case for tying international negotiations on domestic standards to international trade liberalization.

There are, of course practical difficulties with the connection of domestic issues to international trade, as Bagwell and Staiger acknowledge and discuss. These include questions of where to draw the line in terms of what is included in trade negotiations. They also point out the difference in their analysis from arguments for a WTO "social clause," which proposes linking access to one's markets to the choice of standards by a trading partner, or the meeting of some minimum international standards by all trading partners. Instead, Bagwell and Staiger's approach emphasizes the need to formulate negotiating procedures in a way that will allow governments to *raise* their *own* domestic standards from inefficiently low levels. We discuss practical issues and policies in the subsection, after the next, on "races to the bottom", as well as in the following main section.[27]

Trade, labor standards, and skills

Brown et al. provide some consideration of the distributional impacts of international trade, and the consequences for labor standards within countries. Casella (1996) provides a general equilibrium analysis of labor standards and trade that specializes some of the assumptions as compared to Brown et al. and Srinivasan. This allows a closer consideration of income distribution effects. In Casella's model the two factors are high-skill and low-skill labor, and the two consumption goods each requires labor of only one type: the outputs can be interpreted as high-tech and low-tech goods. As is standard, trade reduces the relative wage of the factor that is relatively scarce in autarky. Trade leads to a rise in the real income for low-skill labor in the country that has a relative abundance of low-skill labor, what we can treat as the developing country. Similarly, it leads to a rise in the real income of high-skill labor in the other, developed country.

Labor standards are modeled as an economy-wide public good, financed through labor taxes. If the technology for producing the public good is such that the relative demand for the two private consumption goods is unaffected, then relative prices are unchanged, and the level of the standards in one country has no effect on the other country. All workers prefer to be taxed proportionally to their income, with the constant of proportionality being the same. This means that higher income workers desire higher standards. If there are fewer high-skill than low-skill workers in each country, then high-skill workers in each country will prefer higher standards than will low-skill workers. This result is quite intuitive, since it is driven by income effects alone. Furthermore, since trade can make everyone better off if there are suitable domestic transfers, those transfers will also lead to higher standards with free trade than with autarky. On the other hand, if there are no such transfers, changes in the demand for standards by any group will depend precisely on how their real income is affected by opening up to trade.

Note that in this model, since standards are an economy-wide public good, there is no possibility of a differential imposition of standards. If, on the other hand, standards can be imposed at differing levels across industries, then different groups' ranking of them will differ even more. For example, a standard implemented only in the low-skill sector will not be supported by workers in the high-skill sector (in terms of their willingness to be taxed), even though the latter would prefer a higher level of an economy-wide standard. However, if there were a positive externality, so that workers in the high-skill sector cared about the working conditions or other labor standards for those in the low-skill sector, then this conclusion would change. We examine such externalities in the following main section.

Races to the bottom

The idea of a race to the bottom is quite pervasive in discussions of international labor standards. The broad idea in all of these discussions is that international competition will drive down labor standards in all countries, to levels that are too low, in terms of the allocational efficiency of outcomes, their distributional impacts, on the basis of criteria that emphasize rights and procedures, or some subset of these concerns. It turns out that there are many different possible formalizations of the "race-to-the-bottom" idea, and in this subsection we trace out some of these differences, and their implications for rationales for labor standards.

Much of the literature on the race to the bottom is situated in the area of local public economics. Since capital has always been relatively quite mobile within national boundaries, the concern has been that local or other subnational governments would compete for mobile capital by lowering local labor or environmental standards to attract firms to the benefit of local economies. The extension of this argument to the case of countries competing for internationally mobile capital is immediate.

Local public economics also provides a counter-argument to the idea of a race to the bottom. Tiebout (1956) formulated a model, in which individuals could move freely between jurisdictions, effectively "voting with their feet." In such a case, local government competition for residents can lead to efficient outcomes, as long as the local governments maximize land values, and have sufficient tax instruments at their disposal. While labor is certainly not freely mobile across countries, the Tiebout insight can be applied to mobile capital. The implication is that inefficiency and a race to the bottom are the result of some restriction on the tax instruments available to competing governments.

Relevant models of local government competition include those of Bucovetsky and Wilson (1991), Oates and Schwab (1988), Revesz (1992), and Zodrow and Mieszkowski (1986). Wilson (1996) re-examines and extends this set of models to clarify when races to the bottom could conceivably occur. As noted, the starting point of many of these models is a Tiebout-type framework in which jurisdictions compete for mobile capital. A race to the bottom occurs in such models when standards for some aspect of firm operations (pertaining to working conditions, environmental effects, and so on) are set inefficiently low. In general, with perfect competition and a complete set of tax-subsidy instruments, this inefficiency cannot occur. Therefore Wilson examines a range of possible limitations on the policies of jurisdictional governments.

One possibility is that mobile capital is taxed, because more efficient tax instruments are not available, and this, in turn, leads to standards that are more lax than is optimal, as a way of attracting capital. This result can occur even in the absence of capital taxation. If a jurisdiction's provision of a public good (even when financed through wage taxes) increases the supply of capital to other jurisdictions, then this externality implies that the public good (which may be related to working conditions, human rights, etc.) is underprovided relative to the optimum.

Alternatively, Wilson considers some different possibilities with respect to imperfect competition, which might be expected to lead to nonoptimal outcomes. If jurisdictions are large enough demanders of capital that they influence the equilibrium after-tax rate of return on capital, net importers of capital have an incentive to tax it to improve their terms of trade. However, the optimal tax on capital does not cause a deviation from choosing optimal labor standards. One has to appeal to inefficiencies in the collection of capital taxes to generate a possible race to the bottom.

Several other models of imperfect competition also do not support races to the bottom. The complications arise because imperfect competition among firms itself creates inefficiencies, and taxation has impacts on these inefficiencies, as well as on the possible levels of working conditions or labor rights. A further complication occurs when competing jurisdictions are assumed to be exporting to a different jurisdiction, or seek to attract firms owned outside any of their jurisdictions. Whether the welfare of the "non-residents" is counted can affect the welfare evaluation of the outcome. The conclusion from the local public economics literature appears to be that the possibility of an international race to the bottom, taken to mean inefficiently low domestic labor standards, is highly dependent on the particular set of assumptions made about competition and policy instruments.

The above conclusion carries over to newer analyses of possible races to the bottom, specifically in the context of international trade and independent choices of domestic labor standards. These international trade models do not have factor mobility, but similar problems can arise as goods are traded across jurisdictions. For example, the Bagwell–Staiger analysis summarized earlier has a race-to-the-bottom interpretation, as they point out. Their model is one of imperfect competition among governments, since terms-of-trade effects are crucial to their analysis. As Bagwell and Staiger put it, "trade pressures associated with a country's WTO market access commitments could cause it to delay the introduction or enforcement of stricter labor or environmental standards." They go on to discuss how this result depends on the particular policy restrictions that are incorporated in their model. Another illustration of the sensitivity of such results lies in a comparison of Bagwell and Staiger with Brown et al.'s analysis, where standards may actually end up being inefficiently *high* – the opposite of a race to the bottom.

General theoretical analyses of possible races to the bottom do not typically distinguish between different levels of development of jurisdictions. This is also true of the Bagwell–Staiger reduced-form approach. On the other hand, analyses that relate terms-of-trade incentives to factor endowments can admit the interpretation of differences in development levels. For example, a country that is relatively more labor-abundant, or low-skilled labor abundant (as in Brown et al. or Casella, respectively) can be interpreted as a developing country. Such models may also be used to analyze fears that low labor standards in developing countries (the South) may create a race to the bottom with developed countries (the North).

Chau and Kanbur (2000), take a different perspective, focusing instead on possible races to the bottom among developing country exporters to the North's markets. Their model has two large countries in the South, plus a competitive fringe, all exporting a good to the North. Labor standards have two effects in all exporting countries. They raise production costs, and they provide some utility benefit to the residents of the country (the reasons for this may have to do with altruism, conscience, etc., and are taken up in the following section). In the model, there are two levels of labor standards, high and low. Chau and Kanbur assume that the net gain from high labor standards is negative. Thus the competitive fringe always chooses low standards. However, for the two large exporters, there is a positive terms-of-trade effect from high standards. This implies that a high standard may lead to a higher level of welfare for a *large* country.[28]

A key aspect of the model is the nature of the strategic competition between the two large exporters, which depends on the nature of the demand curve in the importing North. Standards will either be strategic substitutes or strategic complements.[29] Chau and Kanbur characterize the Nash equilibrium of the standard-setting game between the two large countries, for different sizes of the competitive fringe of exporters, and different relative sizes of the two large countries themselves, as well as separately for the cases of strategic substitutes and complements. Depending on the situation, the Nash equilibrium may involve low standards being set by both large countries, high standards by both, or an asymmetric outcome where the larger country chooses a high standard while the relatively smaller country chooses a low standard. The symmetric equilibria are, in fact, dominant strategy equilibria.

Can the Nash equilibrium be improved upon, and can coordination on a welfare-enhancing outcome be sustained? Smaller countries are always better off with higher standards. The analysis is not extended to the welfare of the importing North, but the concern here is welfare in the South. Starting from a symmetric, low-standards equilibrium, if standards are strategic complements, the high standards outcome is better for both large countries if the labor endowment in small countries is below a critical level. In the case of substitutes, the result holds if that endowment is above a critical level. Thus the symmetric equilibrium in each of these cases represents a standard prisoners' dilemma problem. Starting from an asymmetric equilibrium, moving the low standard country to a high standard must involve a side payment to make it better off. Under some conditions, this will be possible, so that both countries are better off.[30]

Chau and Kanbur discuss protectionism in the North, and show that if such protectionism is precommitted, high-standards equilibria become more likely. On the other hand, in the more likely case that protectionism in the North is an optimal response to Southern standards, high-standards equilibria in the South will never exist. The latter conclusion acts as a warning on the use of Northern trade policy to promote standards in the South, if it is likely to end up maximizing Northern welfare. In that case, the outcome will instead be damaging to the South's standards – note that this contrasts with the Bagwell–Staiger results, reflecting their different assumptions. On the other hand, the analysis suggests that Northern policies to promote cooperative implementation of high standards by large South exporters may be appropriate as a way of achieving that goal.

Basu (1999) also considers a model that can be interpreted as a race-to-the-bottom situation. In his model, there are multiple equilibria, and an international ban on child labor will lead to coordination on the good equilibrium (which involves a Pareto improvement), whereas the imposition of a ban by a single country will not, due to the mobility of capital. This therefore seems to be a variant of a race to the bottom. In the extreme version of this race to the bottom, there may be only one equilibrium (as in a prisoners' dilemma game), and one needs to change the parameters of the game to create a better noncooperative equilibrium. Alternatively, one can think of binding agreements as enforcing cooperation. This kind of possibility again raises institutional as well as conceptual issues, which we discuss in the next section.

Who Decides and How?

Earlier, we introduced and discussed different possible factors that might enter into individual value judgments about social situations. In particular, we distinguished between concerns about outcomes and about procedures. This discussion was motivated by practical lists of labor standards, which include both kinds of concerns. One general approach that encompasses both outcomes and processes involves considering individual rankings over both classes of concerns. In taking this approach, we also permit outcomes to include more than just individuals' own consumption of goods and services, and processes to encompass more than their own enjoyment of particular rights.

The question that remains is how different individuals' differing rankings of such complex alternatives are to be aggregated to arrive at an overall social ranking. For example, one person may believe that the right to collective representation and action by workers comes before any consideration of their wages, though given the said right, higher wages (or incomes) are considered better (and may be promoted by the exercise of the right). Another person may view material outcomes as paramount, with the right to collective action nice to have, but not essential. It may be that the set of feasible social situations does not force a sharp tradeoff between these different rankings, but on the other hand, it might. If a choice does have to be made between more rights and better outcomes, whose values should carry weight? It almost certainly should matter if one of the individuals is the worker who is affected, and the other is not. Alternatively, does it matter where the two individuals live?

In earlier sections we have presented various reasons why outcomes might not be efficient, and some specific issues of outcomes and processes having to be balanced against each other (e.g., banning some kinds of voluntary labor contracts). In the third section, we focused almost exclusively on problems related to the functioning of labor markets themselves. The implicit assumption underlying our discussion was that if a problem could be identified, it could potentially be fixed. For example, if banning certain kinds of voluntary contracts would benefit a majority of people, it should be possible to legislate and enforce such a ban. Here we see how a particular institution for aggregating individual rankings would be used in practice – in this case, majority rule.

In the fourth section we examined the interaction of different economies, where strategic behavior on the part of policymakers was assumed, and could sometimes lead to inefficient or undesirable outcomes. The issue here is also an aggregation problem. While national governments in such analyses are assumed to maximize some aggregate measure of the welfare of the residents of their jurisdictions, there is not necessarily any institutional mechanism for balancing the concerns of residents of different countries. In a world of perfect competition without nonpecuniary externalities, this does not matter – decentralized decision-making leads to outcomes that are optimal, in the sense that no one can be made better off without making someone else worse off.

Problems arise, however, when there are imperfections in competition, externalities (including public good problems under this general heading), or both. In particular, caring about rights may almost *require* allowing for externalities, since rights are, by conception, often public or shared in nature. Finally, distributional concerns are not removed by the working of competitive markets. The upshot is that some form of international coordination in making decisions, which represents aggregation of rankings across countries, *may* be better than purely decentralized behavior. In this section, we explore some of the issues surrounding such international decision-making in greater depth than in previous sections, while seeking to tie possible approaches to the underlying reasons for cross-border aggregation of preferences.

Consumption externalities and product labeling

In this subsection, we focus particularly on how individuals in general in a society view working conditions and worker rights, rather than on the direct impacts on workers themselves. In an extreme case, these approaches can be completely orthogonal. For example, an important example of a well-defined group of individuals is the consumers of a particular product. These consumers may care about how the product is made. Even if the choice of production process has no effect on the welfare or rights of workers, or on the cost of firms, if buyers care about it, and are willing to pay for it, these preferences can potentially be accounted for in the marketplace. In this case, working conditions or other aspects of how a product is made are just like a product characteristic, such as whether a shirt is red or white. On the other hand, individuals may have preferences over working conditions or worker rights that are not linked to their own consumption of the products made. This is an externality that is more difficult to accommodate through the market. We discuss both these kinds of preferences, and possible policy responses.

Freeman (1994a, b) has emphasized the possibility that labor standards can be an economic commodity. If consumers are willing to pay more for products made using higher labor standards, such products are essentially equivalent to "high quality" products (though fashion or other taste variables are also no different in their effects). If this quality can be directly and costlessly observed by consumers, then labor standards will be provided at the efficient level from the perspective of meeting consumer wants.

To illustrate the argument, suppose there are two levels of labor standards, denoted by s_L and s_H. Suppose initially that all consumers are identical, and each buys one unit of the good. An individual consumer's willingness to pay for the good is u_L or u_H, depending on the level of labor standards used in production. If $u_H > u_L$, then the consumer is willing to pay something for the product that is made with higher labor standards.

Suppose that there are many competitive firms, each of which can choose the level of labor standards in production. The unit (average and marginal) cost is c_L or c_H. It is reasonable to assume that $c_H \geq c_L$. This could conceivably hold with equality, in which case there is no problem at all. The more interesting case is where higher standards are costly to the firm. Then, with competition, firms earn zero profits, and these are the prices that prevail in the market. Consumer surplus is, therefore, either $u_L - c_L$ or $u_H - c_H$. High labor standards will prevail in the market if and only if $u_H - c_H > u_L - c_L$, that is, the extra gain to consumers outweighs the extra cost.

The market outcome is optimal if the costs of the firm properly reflect the social costs of production. On the other hand, if the firm does not take proper account of all costs, then the consumer's decision is not based on the socially optimal calculation. For example, if workers are exposed to risks that they are uninformed about, and which are not reflected in c_L, consumers' marketplace decisions will not necessarily capture this. Consumers are guided by market prices, which do not reflect true social costs. Note that this problem is much more general than just with respect to working conditions or other labor market issues. Any externality in production, such as pollution, or other unpriced environmental impacts, will lead to the same conclusion.

To make the point more explicitly in the context of labor standards, suppose that the benefit to workers from the higher standard is $v_H - v_L$. For the kinds of reasons discussed earlier, the labor market may not adequately be able to account for this worker benefit in determining the rewards and working conditions of employees, even when the gain outweighs the marginal cost, $c_H - c_L$. It may also be true that $v_H - v_L < c_H - c_L$, so that worker benefits alone are not enough to justify higher labor standards. The higher standard is optimal in this case if the combined benefits to consumers and workers outweigh the costs, that is, $(u_H - u_L) + (v_H - v_L) > c_H - c_L$.[31] If the second term in brackets on the left hand side is zero, then we have the pure case of consumer preferences with which we began.

Returning, therefore, to the pure focus on consumer preferences, now consider the case where consumer preferences are heterogeneous. In this case, some consumers may be willing to pay more for higher labor standards, while others are not. Therefore goods may be produced both with high and with low labor standards, and consumers will buy those goods that suit their preferences. As long as information about quality is complete, there is no inefficiency in the product market.

We next consider a possible complication to the analysis. So far, we have assumed that the cost of higher standards is a variable cost. In fact, we assumed away all fixed costs, so that scale did not matter for producers. If higher labor standards are achieved through higher fixed costs, as would be the case where they involve safer or cleaner factories, for example, then the efficient scale of firms may increase. Therefore, it is possible that if there is only a small segment of consumers who are willing to pay more for higher standards, the extra cost of serving them will be quite high, reflecting the inefficient scale of the producers that serve these consumers. This is not inefficient from an allocational perspective, but simply highlights possible benefits of increasing the size of the market for goods produced according to high labor standards.

As Freeman (1994a, b) points out, it is difficult for consumers to assess the conditions under which a product is made. This distinguishes the consumer's problem from that of the worker, in a parallel between compensating price differentials and compensating wage differentials (see note 31). Therefore, now consider the case where consumers cannot identify at all the labor standards used in production. Suppose that their estimate of the probability that a product was produced with low labor standards is α. In equilibrium, this estimate should reflect the true proportion of such products. Based on this probability estimate, a consumer's expected utility is $\alpha u_L + (1 - \alpha)u_H - p$, where p is the price paid. Since high-standard producers cannot identify themselves, they receive the same price as low-standard producers. Low-standard producers earn economic profit, and will enter, driving out high-standard producers once the price falls below c_H. In equilibrium, $\alpha = 1$. This is a well-known argument, and can be characterized as adverse selection or moral hazard, depending on the precise assumptions made.[32]

One approach to solving the information problem identified above is to use product labeling. Products can be labeled as meeting certain minimum labor standards. However, firms have an incentive to cheat, and so product labeling cannot be self-enforcing. In some markets, reputation solves the cheating problem, as consumers discover the true quality of the good after purchase. This possibility is not relevant, however, in the case of labor standards.

An alternative mechanism is third-party certification. Thus, if firms use a third party that can monitor labor standards and enforce accurate product labeling, the information problem can be overcome. In fact, if product labeling can be enforced costlessly and perfectly, it restores the full information equilibrium. More realistically, monitoring and enforcement are costly. Firms with high labor standards can pay fees to be certified to cover these costs. Such costs must then be passed on to consumers in the price of the product that is certified to have been produced with high standards.

The remaining problem here is that the certification authority now has an incentive to cheat, if such cheating cannot be detected by consumers. In this case, reputation effects will again fail to come into play. The incentive to cheat is particularly strong if the organization's objectives are profit maximization. Alternatively, if those who are responsible for monitoring and enforcement share the preferences of those consumers who want their products made according to high labor standards, the cheating incentive is mitigated. NGOs or public agencies may fit this bill. In the latter case, the enforcement of labeling becomes a public policy matter, requiring legislation.

Finally, note that it would be prohibitively costly for an individual to monitor labor standards directly. Monitoring involves high fixed costs, and has the nonrival characteristic of a public good. However, private provision is at least possible as one method of monitoring, because free rider problems are overcome in including monitoring costs in the product price. Alternatively, we can think of NGOs and government policy as collective action mechanisms that partly overcome free rider problems: consumers then pay for the monitoring service through voluntary contributions or through taxes.[33] One could also think of the firm paying the tax, and collecting it from purchasers of the "high standard" product through the higher price they pay.

At various points in the above discussion, we have introduced considerations of worker welfare, which may complement or be orthogonal to consumer concerns. We wish to emphasize that the discussion encompasses both outcomes and processes. Workers' welfare may depend not just on working conditions, but also on the rights that they enjoy. In the framework we outlined earlier, workers can have an extended ranking of different combinations of their own working conditions and rights. Consumers can also have an extended ranking of social situations that include the working conditions and the rights enjoyed by the workers who make the product they buy. This may be quite different from workers' rankings. For example, workers may only care about their working conditions, whereas consumers may only care about workers having the rights to collective action. The logic of the market is that whoever is willing *and* able to pay can influence the choices made.

The issue of differential willingness and ability to pay also has a bearing on the approach to implementing labor standards. In particular, if the consumers are in developed countries and the workers in developing countries, the potential for consumers to pay for their desire for better working conditions or worker rights has more scope for making a difference than do the preferences of relatively poor workers over the same dimensions. To the extent that a product labeling strategy makes it possible for consumers to pay, it is preferable to policies that put the burden on workers. For example, if labeling cannot be made to work, and the policy response is to ban the good that is produced under low standards, if the outcome is that the industry in the developing country shuts down, workers may be still worse off. This kind of issue is, of course, at the heart of debates about the impact of international labor standards, and we will examine it later. However, the point we wish to emphasize here is that policies of quantitative regulation may have very different impacts than price-based mechanisms.[34]

We now return to possible public good problems, which are more central when individuals care about working conditions or worker rights, irrespective of whether they purchase and consume the product or not. Thus the externality is not linked to the consumption of a product, but simply to the existence of a situation. In this case, all consumers with these preferences still should be willing to pay for improvement in labor market outcomes or processes. However, paying through the market, even with truthful labeling, is no longer sufficient for efficiency.

Consumers who do not purchase the product do not contribute payments toward improved labor standards, but receive the benefits. This is a free-rider problem, which might be solved partially or completely in various ways that are used for tackling public good provision. Individuals who care might make voluntary contributions that are then used to raise standards. Alternatively, they might agree to be taxed, with the proceeds earmarked for the same purpose. If the workers who are the subject of concern are in a different country, the difficulties and costs of implementation may be great, but the economic logic points in this direction. The difficulties may be viewed as insurmountable, if the other country's political or social structure does not permit implementation. This issue of conflicting jurisdictions is taken up later in this section.

One might take the view that consumers *ought* to care about worker rights and working conditions, irrespective of whether they purchase the products made or not.[35] In other words, labor standards ought to be a public good. At one level, this argument is easy to understand. If we care about human dignity or welfare, then the importance of human rights in the workplace must not be merely dependent on consumer preferences as expressed in the marketplace. At another level, this is a difficult approach to analyze. It involves having a ranking of social situations that encompasses other individuals' rankings in the definition of social situation. In practice, individual rankings of social situations are rarely fully formed and articulated, and the political process is at least partly about resolving such issues. We take this up in the next subsection, and also in the following section, where we, in fact, make our own argument concerning what individuals *ought* to care about.

Political economy and collective action

The discussion in the previous subsection, on the preferences of consumers, and of individuals in general, with respect to worker rights and working conditions, led into a consideration of how these preferences might be satisfied through collective action, in cases where the market mechanism is insufficient to achieve that objective. This is, in fact, a general problem of political economy, since one aspect of the political process and political institutions is precisely the use of collective action to determine how public goods are to be produced and paid for, how external effects are to be resolved, and what kinds of redistribution (implicit or explicit) are to be made. In fact, the usual emphasis is on how political processes are used to promote pure self-interest, rather than the interests of an altogether different set of individuals.

An important example of the self-interest perspective is the possible danger that enforcing international labor standards through trade policy or related sanctions will result in concerns over human rights being 'hijacked' by interest groups that directly benefit from the enforcement of higher standards in other countries. Alternatively these interest groups may gain from the imposition of trade-related sanctions against those other countries that do not conform to the higher standards. Srinivasan (1996, 1998b) has been most forceful in articulating the danger of hijacking, though many other economists would agree with this perspective. It is worth noting that an interest group could conceivably benefit from higher labor standards in another country, without using sanctions or trade policy in general. For example, if soccer balls produced abroad under poor working conditions are being imported to the US, competing with domestic producers, the importers could be paid to not produce, or the workers could be directly "bought off." One might view this as a form of targeted foreign aid, which happens to help a group of domestic workers and firms. Even if this seems far-fetched, such thought experiments can help to put policy alternatives in perspective.

Pahre (1998), in commenting on Srinivasan, raises the possibility that hijacking may actually help achieve a humanitarian goal. The essence of Pahre's argument is as follows. Imposing a trade sanction against a human rights violator will create domestic winners and losers, and the credibility of a threat to sanction requires that winners outnumber losers. Interest groups representing those who benefit directly (whom we may term "protection-ists"), as well as human rights groups (with the kinds of preferences we have discussed earlier), are winners if the sanction is imposed against a foreign country that does not raise its standards. This combination of groups with different motivations may create a large enough winning coalition so that the threat to sanction is credible, whereas without this coalition the policy would fail. A credible threat in this case leads to the foreign country raising its standard. If either interest group is large enough on its own, it will choose a different policy (e.g., antidumping for "protectionists," or direct international transfers – such as were discussed above – for rights groups). International labor standards become an issue that allows the two groups to find common ground when they cannot succeed otherwise.

Srinivasan's rejoinder to the above argument is that the central point made by Pahre is the value of credibility, not the role of protectionist inter-est groups. The implication is that credibility may be achieved by other, better means. However, if credibility requires a large enough coalition of supporters, a policy that benefits enough constituents is required. For example, one reason direct transfers are not used is that they do not garner enough political support. Protectionism may therefore serve a role that is difficult to finesse. Two other issues remain, however. First, is the outcome of higher standards truly better for the objects of concern, even without the imposition of sanctions? Second, is a unilateral threat of this nature, or even one that is jointly agreed to by importing nations, consistent with international norms or conventions of sovereignty? We tackle these issues below.

Pahre also suggests that second-best policies may serve a signaling role when the strength of a human rights group is unknown to the target country. For example, suppose that a sanctioning country may be of two types, one where the human rights group is large enough to tip the scales in favor of some first-best policy being supported by a majority of constituents, and the other where the rights group is not large enough to make a difference even for sanctions. In the absence of the second type, the first best policy would be used by type one, but this is subject to mimicking by the second type, which affects the credibility of the threat. The first type therefore uses the second-best policy of tying human rights to trade to make a credible threat. This seems appealing at first sight, but the nature of the first-best policy is unclear – direct transfers, for example, are not a threat.

We next return to the case of individuals who explicitly care about workers in other countries, independently of the impacts that those workers' rights and working conditions may have on the income and consumption of the concerned individuals. This category may include consumers of products made by the workers who are the object of concern, as well as human rights groups and other concerned individuals. The Pahre argument can be bypassed if the coalition of such individuals can be made large and influential enough to implement a preferred policy directly, without having to team up with "protectionist" interests. Earlier, we highlighted the argument that such individuals should be willing to pay for higher labor standards, including the costs of monitoring that would be required, since firms do not have an incentive to report truthfully. Alternatives to payment would be quantitative regulation. Fung et al. (2001) have presented a proposal that is a hybrid of monitoring through collective action, quantitative regulation, and sanctions. We next discuss some aspects of their proposal.

Fung et al. propose monitoring by third parties, governed by a council that would represent a coalition of interests – not just concerned individuals in developed countries, but also multilateral agencies, intergovernmental organizations, NGOs, and representatives of worker interests in the organized and informal sectors of developing countries. Thus Fung et al. are suggesting a new collective action mechanism for implementing the preferences of various groups of individuals for better working conditions and/or worker rights, rather than the "unholy" alliance of protectionists and rights advocates. In a standard political economy framework, we can characterize this as a proposal for political entrepreneurship.[36]

Monitoring would be delegated to specialists, and would, if successful, lead to greater transparency and opportunities for comparison across competing producers than is available currently. However, departing from the economic logic pursued earlier, Fung et al. suggest that sanctions be imposed on firms that either do not meet certain labor standards or evade monitoring altogether. Unfortunately, the nature of these sanctions is unclear. Fung et al. suggest that sanctions should be more than civic action, but have absolutely no specifics to offer on actual institutional details of the nature and implementation of sanctions. Ultimately, therefore, the Fung et al. proposal seems to founder on some fundamental issues.[37]

It is also worth noting that the Fung et al. proposal does not necessarily have any significant role for developing-country governments or labor unions. They discuss the possibility that such bodies would view their council and associated monitors as substitutes for their traditional activities, and they make the counterargument that they would be complements. In practice, however, the perception of overstepping jurisdictions is likely to be a serious issue.[38] The exclusion of firms from the proposed coalition of interests also poses a problem since, even though the multinational firms that are the main target in the FOS proposal care about reputation, unless it is clear that their reputations are at stake in a monetarily significant way, through the loss of sales in particular, any serious impact is unlikely. As we have noted, the implementation of sanctions on firms seems institutionally improbable.[39] In fact, Bardhan (2001a) points out that the problem of competitive undercutting at the firm level − in cases where the greater willingness to pay of consumers for higher labor standards is not enough − needs to be overcome by cooperation among firms. He cites as a reasonably successful example the agreement among the main sporting goods firms, the ILO, UNICEF, NGOs, and the Pakistan government to work toward eliminating child labor in the production of soccer balls. As the analyses of Basu (1999, 2001a) and Chau and Kanbur (2000) demonstrate, a further coordination issue arises at the level of nations, precisely because the firms have multinational production facilities − Bardhan also highlights this issue.

Drawing the line

Cross-border externalities, whether based on consumption or on general moral concerns (where rankings may include combinations of outcomes and processes in other countries as well as one's own), raise complex issues of appropriate jurisdiction. If the residents of one political jurisdiction care about the rights or welfare of residents of another jurisdiction, what policies are appropriate to pursue? One possible pragmatic answer to the general issue of where to draw the line with respect to policy is to say that the outcomes of the democratic process properly determine how these concerns are aggregated into social policy.[40] However, this does not solve the problem of what to do where the democratic decision of the citizens of the United States, for example differs from the democratic decision of the citizens of India, both with respect to the appropriate level of labor standards for *Indian* workers. To illustrate this issue, and possible solutions, we describe the approach taken by Dani Rodrik, and the debate it opened up.

Rodrik (1996) argues that international labor standards are justified, based on cross-border externalities such as those associated with moral considerations. His argument is as follows. He notes that citizens of developed countries have agreed, as expressed in their countries' legislation, that certain production technologies are unacceptable domestically, because workers' rights or employment conditions associated with those technologies are unacceptable. This proscription typically extends to all technologies within a country's jurisdiction, even if they involve noncitizens. Rodrik argues that importing goods from countries with unacceptably low labor standards is equivalent to importing foreign workers and allowing them to work under unacceptable conditions.

Srinivasan (1998b) has countered Rodrik's argument by pointing out that there is a wide range of government regulations that affect the cost of production and the welfare of citizens in the producing country. Environmental regulations, building codes, zoning laws also differ across countries. Are goods produced in an Indian factory that does not meet US building codes to be deemed unacceptable for import? One can extend Srinivasan's critique by noting that regulations may differ across states or regions within a country. If California has a higher minimum wage than the rest of the US, would it be morally justified in prohibiting trade with the rest of the country? Of course California cannot do so, because of the US interstate commerce clause, but the question helps to highlight the potential fuzziness of what initially seems to be a clear-cut argument.

Can one reconcile the differing positions of Rodrik and Srinivasan? Clearly, proscribing "unacceptable" technologies indirectly by restricting the import of goods that use them cannot be a fully general argument, independent of the particular case of unacceptability. This is the point that Srinivasan makes with his counter arguments. We can bring out more explicitly two separate considerations that limit the scope of Rodrik's argument. These involve sovereignty and democracy on the one hand, and the universality or fundamental nature of human rights on the other.

First, the extension of moral concerns about rights violations involves an indirect exercise of sovereignty beyond the jurisdiction's borders. In the example of California, the state has explicitly ceded some dimensions of sovereignty to the federal government. In international trade, this issue is less clear, but the country with the lower standard has, presumably, made a sovereign decision to have that lower standard. If the democratic process in the low standard country is flawed or absent, enforcement of international labor standards may be a possible second-best response, but should be recognized as such.[41] If lower standards are the result of a reasonable aggregation of the preferences of the citizens of the other country, then we may make the case that the social rankings of the citizens of India with respect to Indian labor standards should take precedence over the ranking of the citizens of the US, just as the citizens of the US should not determine what religion Indians should profess, even if they care deeply about it.[42] If we accept this, then attempting to enforce international labor standards must appeal only to the second reason, which we now present.

The second justification for, as well as limitation on, Rodrik's argument is that the violation of human rights must be serious enough to warrant overriding all other considerations. The use of slave labor, prison labor, or other forced labor is typically considered abhorrent enough that issues of sovereignty and democracy are overridden.[43] Thus, Rodrik's argument is really one about balancing sets of possibly competing rights, and possibly also about enforcing wider sets of rights. It is not based merely on a neutral extension of an accepted principle. Srinivasan's critique implicitly follows these lines.[44] For example, the reason that Indian building codes and zoning laws are not the subject of discussion with respect to international standards is precisely because US citizens do not care about them, and probably should not care about them, in whatever rankings they have over combinations of outcomes and processes in other countries as well as their own.

Given that we are dealing with a complex problem of aggregation (usually implicit) of complex individual rankings, we should not be surprised there is no easy agreement on where to draw the line. For example, Freeman (1994), taking a self-described pragmatic view, suggests that many "standards that specify processes for determining labor outcomes (freedom of association, use of slave or convict labor) . . . can be met without high levels of income and thus might be viewed as fundamental social rights," which have a universal character. On the other hand, Sachs (1997) has given the example of South Korea joining the OECD, where he argues that the OECD had "no business pushing Western-European style labor relations" on the new entrant. Freeman also notes problems with being totally flexible on issues of outcome-based standards, in allowing them to vary with income. Even if we can theoretically reconcile the positions of Rodrik and Srinivasan, the practical difficulties remain, whether one is a pragmatist or not.

While we have focused our discussion of where to draw the line on the case of direct or nonpecuniary externalities, Bagwell and Staiger (2001) have shown lucidly that even pecuniary externalities can matter when there is not perfect competition. Of course, this is precisely what we should expect from the theory of competitive markets. As we discussed earlier in the chapter, Bagwell and Staiger suggest a particular way of tying labor standards to trade negotiations, and raise the issue of drawing the line, "Why stop at labor and environmental standards? Virtually all domestic policy choices of large economies . . . could be the subject of an analysis similar to what we have undertaken here." Bagwell and Staiger sidestep this issue, however, by saying that the WTO "social clause" and minimum standards approach is subject to the same problem of where to draw the line, while being more invasive of sovereignty. While this certainly rationalizes the Bagwell–Staiger approach as preferable, it does not address at all the issue of what aspects of domestic standards ought to be tied in some way to international trade negotiations. Our point is that this is not a *neutral* decision, but involves balancing different and complex sets of rights of different groups of individuals.[45]

What Happens to the Poor?

If the unifying concern of those who pursue international labor standards is an improvement in the lot of those who are less well off, however this improvement is measured by different individuals, and however it is to be implemented institutionally, then the title of this section poses the central question for all those concerned. There are, of course, further distinctions one can make in tackling this question. To what extent are we concerned about the poor in developed countries, versus in developing countries? Furthermore, what is the time horizon that we have in terms of the desired improvements?

In earlier sections we have provided some answers to the question of the impacts of labor standards, in the context of static resource efficiency and the distribution of income. In this section, we expand on this discussion in the context of some of the institutional mechanisms discussed in the previous section. Next, we discuss some issues concerning the dynamics of investment in human capital, and problems created by subsistence or general resource constraints. We go naturally from these issues to examining longer-run welfare issues in the context of models of endogenous innovation and growth. Finally, we return to some of the issues raised initially in the second section, which were touched upon at several subsequent points in the chapter, and discuss the role of labor standards in protecting the fundamental rights of the poor. Here we suggest what we *ought* to care about, and put international labor standards in a broader development perspective.

Unintended consequences?

One major concern that crops up repeatedly in discussions of international labor standards is whether they will have the impact that is intended. For example, in 1994, the manager of the ILO's Program on the Elimination of Child Labor stated, "Abolishing child labor in one sector alone, such as the export sector, cannot eliminate child labor in a country – it may simply push it into other activities, including some more hazardous to children." (ILO, 1994, quoted in Freeman, 1994a). Such consequences may not be those that are intended by a policy of imposing international labor standards. On the other hand, there are cases where one may not care. If consumers in developed countries care only about how products that they consume are made, then such consequences are irrelevant. Alternatively, if the concern is with the welfare of workers in an import-competing industry in a developed country, then again, the impact on workers in developing countries is irrelevant to those concerns.

The second of the above positions is more likely to be held with some conviction. There are certainly plausible theoretical arguments that support the contention that trade between North and South can hurt the incomes of unskilled or low-skilled workers in the North. It is theoretically less clear that trade will lead to lower labor standards in the North, though this is also possible. We have reviewed some of these arguments earlier. However, it is also true that the best response to negative impacts on incomes, according to theory, is to use some form of worker adjustment assistance to deal with the impact of trade (see Fung and Staiger, 1996, and the references therein). Even in the presence of political constraints, the use of international labor standards for developing countries as a form of worker protection is likely to be relatively costly, as compared to methods based on adjustment assistance.[46] In any case, the use of international labor standards explicitly to protect domestic groups violates international trade agreements as currently structured. A further, though distinct, practical counterargument is that it is unlikely that much of the harm to the poor in developed countries has come from the impacts of trade, with technological change and a rising skill premium in all likelihood playing a much greater role.[47]

Bardhan (2001a, b) clearly argues the case that international labor standards such as banning child labor in exporting industries will only shift the problem out of the export sector. Since the proportion of overall child labor that is in export-related industries is quite low (only 5 percent in India), just tackling that small proportion has, at best, no significant impact. At worst, it can significantly harm the lives of the displaced children. Similar issues arise with other kinds of labor standards that are implemented for all workers in export sectors of developing countries. Note that, in the case of child labor,

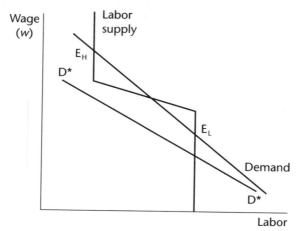

Figure 2.6 Multiple equilibria with and without child labor

the kind of analysis performed by Basu and Van (1998) and Basu (1999), in which a ban on child labor improves welfare, assumes that the ban is economy-wide. Thus the children who are displaced are taken care of, because their parents' income goes up as a result of the ban on child labor.

We illustrate this point more explicitly. The Basu–Van model assumes that adults and children can do the same work, with the latter's productivity being some fraction of that of adults. Furthermore, it assumes that a household would not send its children out to work if its income from non-child labor sources is high enough. In this model, there are multiple stable equilibria. In one (see figure 2.6, point E_H) there is a high wage, and adults do not have to send their children to work. In the other (point E_L), there is a low wage and child labor.

The debates about consequences extend to other examples of labor standards, including working conditions and worker rights. These debates ultimately rest on differing assumptions about competition and its effects, and on varying implicit distributional judgments. At one extreme (e.g., Rothstein, 1994) with respect to assumptions about competition is that monopsony drives a substantial wedge between marginal products and wages, as outlined in the section on monopsony. In that case, there is room to extract some of the firm's excess profits, through higher wages, better working conditions, or both. On the other hand, if firms are competitive, and operate in competitive labor markets, any policy designed to improve the lot of workers will make at least some workers worse off. This is the point made by Srinivasan, Bardhan, and numerous other economists.

The mobility of capital (and the lack of international mobility of labor) poses a problem even for cases where implementing worker rights would otherwise improve workers' bargaining power, and hence their incomes (Bardhan, 2001a). When firms can relocate, the implementation of international standards requires some form of coordination among developing countries. However, coordination is probably much more difficult to achieve in the case of worker rights, as opposed to working conditions. To illustrate the point about competition and adverse consequences in another way, we can see that as the demand curve in figure 2.6 becomes more elastic (curve D*D*), reflecting greater competition from workers elsewhere, the high wage equilibrium disappears (Dixit, 2000).[48]

Distributional concerns raise different issues from the negative impacts that might follow from international labor standards in the presence of competition. Even if standards improve the lot of workers in the export sector, these workers may be a privileged subset of the privileged subset of workers in the formal sector. This itself is not bad, but the distributional implication that those who are most in need of assistance – according to standard welfare criteria that include a concern for equity – are not being helped, is disturbing. Other, more benign, distributional issues can also arise. In the Basu and Van model, since working households are all encompassed in the model and parents are altruistic, the fact that income is redistributed from children to adults in moving to the high wage equilibrium does not matter. In the kind of situation discussed by Bardhan, however, while there may be redistribution to poor adults (who would otherwise be unemployed) as a result of banning child labor, this must be weighed against the negative consequences on the displaced children. Baland and Robinson (2000) also point out that the high wage equilibrium in the Basu–Van model involves a redistribution away from firms – again, this is an implication that those who are concerned with equity will be comfortable with.[49]

Investment in human capital

With the exception of the model of Genicot (2000), discussed earlier, which involves multiple periods in an essential way, we have focused on static analyses of labor standards. This is in keeping with much of the literature. In this subsection and the next, however, we examine some dynamic issues.

A dynamic structure is critical, for example, in looking at child labor, to the extent that investment in human capital by children is a central issue. Basu (1999), adapting Basu and Van (1998), models this as follows. He assumes that children and adults are perfect substitutes after adjusting for the fact that a child is a fraction of an adult in terms of productivity. He assumes that there is a unique equilibrium in a single period case, so that the Basu–Van result does not hold. The model is one of overlapping generations, where each person lives for two periods. Children can either work or go to school, and this is decided by the adult(s) in the household. Productivity, and therefore the wage as an adult, is a function of human capital acquisition as a child. If the adult wage is high enough, the adult will send the child to school, in which case the child becomes educated and earns a high wage as an adult, and so on. There can be multiple stable steady-state equilibria in this model, one where every parent sends his or her child to school and the adult wage is high, supporting this behavior, and another where every parent makes his or her child work, so that the adult wage is low. Policy intervention can move the economy toward the higher equilibrium, through a large effort to educate one generation, getting the economy out of the "child labor trap."

Baland and Robinson (2000) also examine a model in which there is a tradeoff between child labor and the accumulation of human capital. In their model, parents are altruistic, but may run out of resources needed to educate their children. The option of borrowing against their children's future income is not available to them because such intergenerational contracts cannot be enforced. Besides the practicality of such contracts, they are subject to problems of moral hazard by parents borrowing against children's future income and then using the money for their own consumption. This points out some of the difficulties in relying on obvious interventions such as improving capital markets to improve education of children and reduce child labor.

The Baland–Robinson model leads to an equilibrium that is Pareto inefficient, even without the existence of positive externalities to human capital accumulation – an idea that has been pursued by Grootaert and Kanbur (1995). The idea that subsistence and capital market constraints on households force children into work seems empirically plausible, and more compelling than an argument based on social returns exceeding private returns. Baland and Robinson also examine endogenous fertility decisions by parents. They show that the general impact of a reduction of child labor on fertility is ambiguous, though under special circumstances, the effect is to reduce fertility. This latter result was also obtained by Eswaran (1996), who showed that when parents need children for old-age security, allowing child labor could induce parents to have larger, but less-educated families. The advantage of the Baland–Robinson analysis is a clear-cut welfare ranking of possible outcomes.

If, as in the Baland and Robinson analysis, child labor is Pareto inefficient, why is it difficult to abolish in practice? The answer that they provide to this question is that heterogeneity may create some losers from a ban, necessitating compensatory transfers that are themselves infeasible or costly to implement. For example, rich people and those firms that have adopted technologies that do not require skilled workers may be affected by a ban, the former by having their wages depressed, the latter by being put at a competitive disadvantage. In the absence of such factors, however, government subsidies of education, financed by a tax on adult earnings, could be Pareto-improving. Baland and Robinson also suggest that foreign bans on imports of goods produced with child labor can be Pareto-improving, but this assumes away some of the problems noted by Bardhan (2001a) and others, as discussed in the previous subsection.[50]

Long-run effects

Investment in human capital is relevant for all workers, not just for children, though it is particularly important in their case. Thinking about retraining and education naturally leads one to a more general discussion of long-run issues in weighing labor standards. Long-run development can depend on technological change as well as on investment. Piore (1990, 1994) argues that there can be multiple equilibria in an economy, and that labor standards can move firms and workers out of a "sweatshop" equilibrium. This much is similar to our earlier discussion of multiple equilibria with a subsistence constraint. Piore goes on to suggest that forcing up labor costs induces technological change and growth.

The induced technological change hypothesis is an old one, but it is hard to justify formally. If profitable opportunities for technological improvement exist, then the firm should be able to take advantage of them irrespective of its current strategy. Tying technological change to current or past factor intensities requires either some kind of localized learning about possible innovations, switching costs that lock the firm into its current technology, or some other reason for path dependence.[51] Alternatively, there must be some positive externality associated with the high-wage equilibrium that fuels growth. For example, if workers are better off than the subsistence level of income, they may be able to invest in their own or their children's education.[52] Consumers, who are worse off in the high-wage equilibrium, may simply curtail consumption of goods that do not affect growth. This simply brings one back to the kinds of models analyzed by Basu and Baland and Robinson.

Explicit models of growth appear not to have been considered in the literature on international labor standards. However, Amsden (1994) provides a discussion based implicitly on a structuralist model of developing-country economies and their growth. Amsden distinguishes between "wage-led" growth, in which real wages rise with productivity, and this fuels aggregate demand, investment, and, ultimately, higher incomes, and "profit-led growth", in which profits are the source of investment and growth. The former economies are identified with large countries that have substantial domestic markets, while the latter are equated to smaller, open economies. Amsden argues that international labor standards would be consistent with, and might even support, wage-led growth, but that they would very probably hurt growth in small, open developing-country economies. While Amsden does not provide a full model, she appears to be assuming that there are some structural rigidities or imperfect competition effects, which can create a wedge between real wages and marginal products. Growth is assumed to be determined by investment, and there is no role for endogenous technological progress.

One possibility for formally examining the relationship between labor standards and growth that would allow for endogenous technological progress (as highlighted by Piore) is to use the framework of Grossman and Helpman (1991, chapter 10). For example, they consider a two-country model where each country has three sectors: traditional manufacturing, high-tech manufacturing, and R&D, in order of increasing human capital intensity. R&D ultimately determines innovation and growth, and it is not surprising that a subsidy to R&D in one country increases its rate of innovation and growth.

Production subsidies are more surprising in their effects. A production subsidy to the high-tech sector reduces innovation and growth, because it draws human capital (skilled labor) from the R&D sector. A production subsidy to the low-tech sector in one country spurs growth in that country, but at the expense of the other country. If we interpret a labor standard as analogous to a tax on the low-tech sector, which uses low-skill labor more intensively, then the Grossman–Helpman analysis suggests that a labor standard would actually be harmful to growth in the country where it is applied, and therefore to the long-run welfare of low-skill workers in that country. This perspective would suggest some caution in accepting Piore's assertions on labor standards and growth, though alternative models might bear out his analysis. Note that the imposition of an international labor standard on the low-tech sector of the country with relatively less human capital would seem to cause long-term harm to that country's growth, if the analogy with a tax is reasonable.

In another way, the results of the thought experiment of introducing labor standards into the endogenous growth model are not surprising. Growth in that model is driven by technological progress, and there is nothing tying technological progress to working conditions, or to worker rights. Piore tries to make this connection through a discussion of firms' business strategies, but the argument is ultimately unclear. The detailed modeling of firm decision-making along the lines discussed in Milgrom et al. (1991) might provide some insights. Tore Ellingsen, in his comments, also provides a hint of a fruitful approach in this area. He points out that, in an incomplete contracting framework, such as that analyzed by Grossman and Hart (1986) and Hart and Moore (1999), workers with no rights may be reluctant to invest in firm-specific human capital (and, to extend the argument, firm-specific innovation). Thus assigning some control rights to workers might have positive impacts on efficiency and growth.

Rights and the poor

One of the distinguishing features of the debate on international labor standards is its emphasis on human rights in general, and on the rights of the poor in poor countries, in particular. The emphasis on rights poses some difficulties for standard welfare economics but, as we have indicated previously in the chapter, these difficulties are not insurmountable for a rigorous and consistent analysis, incorporating concerns about rights or processes as well as outcomes or consequences.

If we accept that fundamental rights, including labor rights, are of overriding importance in themselves, then improving the extent to which all workers enjoy such rights provides immediate and lasting benefits. This argument in favor of fundamental rights is almost tautological. The practical difficulty, as we have seen, comes about in deciding where to draw the line around fundamental rights. Debate is particularly useful here, because it can clarify which rights are to be considered fundamental, and it can help to achieve something that approaches a consensus. The ILO/OECD core labor standards are not necessarily the final word on this topic, as Fields (1996, 2000) lucidly argues. In any case, it is typically the poor in every country whose rights deserve the most protection, so a general strengthening of concern for fundamental rights would presumably help them the most.

However, there is a further difficulty that might work against the last statement: a concern for rights may conflict with outcome-based measures of welfare. This is a fundamental problem in the abstract, with regard to situations where preferences are other-regarding, as illustrated by the conflict between the Pareto principle and libertarian rights (Sen, 1970), or variants of it (the "shirt colors" example cited earlier). More concretely, for example, enforcing strict rights of collective bargaining can conceivably deter hiring, and make workers worse off through job loss. We might still argue that such a right is important enough that it must transcend narrow welfarist considerations: this case is easy to accept for prohibitions against slavery or bondage, even if "voluntary".

A further response could be that in such cases it is not sufficient to enforce the labor right in isolation – human beings are entitled to a set of minimum rights that must be provided or ensured as a bundle. If this bundle of rights includes access or entitlement to sufficient education and credit opportunities, the poor person's bargaining power is increased in a manner that mitigates the possible adverse effect of labor rights.[53] In many poor countries, an even more basic right that is still not universally available is the right to some minimum level of physical or biological well-being. Lack of adequate nourishment and unwarranted exposure to various hazards are examples of a failure to meet such minimum standards.

In highlighting such an approach, we are not being particularly novel. Sen (1985a, b) has developed and emphasized the importance of human capabilities in thinking about the objectives of development. Dasgupta (1993), and Ray (1993, 1998, see also Ray and Streufert, 1993) have examined the importance and consequences of nutritional deprivation. Numerous authors and developmental institutions have emphasized the crucial need to "invest in people," based on a tripartite framework that includes nutrition, skills, and financial assets.[54] In such cases, again, we are emphasizing capabilities, which may include endowments as well as rights, along with outcomes.

How does this impact the debate on labor standards? We suggest that those who care about worker rights and working conditions of the poor in poor countries ought to do so in a broader context. If the fundamental rights at stake are the ability to achieve minimum standards of physical and mental well-being,[55] narrowly focusing on labor standards may not be the right approach to thinking about rights. One needs a broader perspective. To illustrate this concretely, consider once again the case of child labor. Bardhan (2001a, b) reviews several different policies that can be and have been tried to tackle this issue, including making schools more attractive or less costly to attend, having firms employing child labor finance some of these efforts, improving the productivity of adult workers in the same industry, and so on. The point is that the focus is on the broader rights and welfare of the children, rather than on child labor per se. Of course unsafe and unhealthy working conditions are still to be controlled, but this is again properly part of a broader concern with physical well-being. It is the fundamental rights to capabilities that enable achievement of minimum well-being that individuals, whether in developed or developing countries, *ought* to care about.[56]

All this is not to say that labor standards are unimportant, merely that they must be placed in perspective. In general, the interaction of the credit and education markets with the labor market provides examples of how labor standards may be beneficial, or alternatively, where the policy focus may need to be different. In Genicot's (2000) analysis of bonded labor, restricting one set of voluntary contracts that may be signed can actually help poor workers because it allows another, more attractive set of credit contracts to become available. An alternative approach might be to improve the working of rural credit markets through micro-credit schemes or similar approaches. In the Baland–Robinson (2000) analysis, the credit market imperfection cannot be directly removed to make it possible for parents to finance their children's education and avoid child labor. Banning child labor may solve the problem in the theoretical model, but in practice, targeted subsidies for education for the poor may be a good alternative policy.

The same policies that improve basic capabilities, through access to minimum levels of physical well-being, education, and credit opportunities, are likely to be quite consistent with concerns about outcomes alone. To the extent that outcomes include educational outcomes, the correlation is obvious. Even if we care only about low incomes, and measure poverty accordingly, improving access to nutrition, education, and credit may be the proper primary areas of policy focus, rather than labor standards. For example, job provision or protection schemes typically work less well than policies aimed at more fundamental capabilities, even if efficient targeting in the presence of incomplete information requires in-kind rather than cash transfers.[57] These observations are just as true for developed countries as they are for developing countries, and it is safe to say that they reflect the thinking of most economists, whatever weight they put on non-consequentialist concerns in their own views.

Conclusion

In this conclusion, we summarize our main arguments. This survey has gone beyond the issue of linking labor standards with trade, to review key economic arguments in favor of labor standards. As the comments by Srinivasan and Ellingsen suggest, even this attempt has not been comprehensive. However, we have accomplished several things in this chapter.

Methodologically, we showed how value judgments and normative concerns about rights can be rigorously incorporated into discussions of international labor standards. In fact, rigor helps in bringing out the potential conflicts or tradeoffs between outcomes and processes. After setting the methodological stage, we reviewed at least a significant subset of possible labor market problems, what their consequences might be in terms of worker welfare, how to evaluate them in terms of labor market processes, and finally, what the impacts might be of different interventions that come under the broad heading of "labor standards." The general conclusion of this survey of models of the labor market is a familiar one for economists: there are many potential sources of market failure, and devising policies to correct them can be complex and circumstance specific. Nevertheless, careful economic analysis can aid in appropriate policy choices, whatever the objectives may be (including concerns about processes).

We next considered a range of economic models that place (international or domestic) labor standards in the context of the global economy. Again, impacts are often model-specific, and this suggests that international labor standards policies must be applied with caution, even if policy coordination issues are at the heart of the problem. Even when cooperation on international labor standards may be desirable, the case for linking standards to trade negotiations remains problematic. We then turned to the contentious questions of "who decides and how?" in the context of international labor standards. Our discussion highlighted the importance of explicitly recognizing the value judgments being made, issues of collective action, and those of sovereignty.

Our final topic was the impact of international labor standards on the poor, and here we reviewed some of the possibilities raised earlier in the chapter, as well as some new issues. We examined the case that international labor standards can end up hurting those they are supposed to help, unless they are part of a broader policy package. We linked this to an argument that the proper concern, even where processes matter as well as outcomes, is with a more basic set of capabilities and rights than is typically encompassed by proponents of international labor standards. Policies that promote basic nutrition and health, and broader access to education and credit are likely to help growth, as well as having intrinsic benefits. Our final conclusion, therefore, is that this is what individuals and policy-makers ought to care about, rather than labor standards in isolation. Labor standards may well be a component of such policies, but must be implemented in context.

Appendix 1: Basic Competitive Model

We model a worker's utility as being a function of a vector of market-purchased consumption goods (x), leisure (l), and a vector of nonpecuniary job characteristics (s), so that the function is $u(x,l,s)$. We assume that job characteristics are defined and measured so that "more is better" always. Thus the function is increasing in all its arguments. The worker has an endowment, T, of time, and receives a wage, w, which she takes as given. She chooses how much to work at this wage, and how much of the various consumption goods to buy with her earnings from work, but job characteristics are taken as given. Then her maximization problem is described as:

$$\max_{xl} u(x,l,s)$$
$$\text{subject to } p{\cdot}x = w(T - l),$$

where p is the vector of goods prices.

In this formulation, the individual's labor supply decision in terms of time receives attention, as well as how income is spent, but the characteristics of the job are not in the individual's choice set. The above maximization will give demand functions for goods and a supply function for labor, which can be substituted in the objective function to yield the indirect utility function, denoted by $v(p,w,T,s)$. This is the maximum utility that the worker can obtain given the existing market conditions. If market prices of consumption goods are taken as given, we can suppress them in the arguments of the indirect utility function. Furthermore, we can suppress the individual's time endowment, since this is determined by nature. Hence the indirect utility function can be written as $v(w,s)$.

Now consider the decision-making of the competitive firm producing the single consumption good. If it chooses total labor and capital to maximize profits, given wages and prices, it solves the following maximization problem

$$\max_{L,K} Q - wL - rK$$
$$\text{subject to } Q = F(L,K,s),$$

where r is the rental rate (price of capital) and $F(L,K,s)$ is the production function.[58] This problem will yield demand functions for labor and capital. We focus on labor only, suppressing the role of the rental rate and the market for capital. In that case, the wage rate can be viewed as determined by the equality of supply and demand for labor.[59] If there are n firms and N workers, then this condition is simply

$$Nh^{S}(w,s) = nL^{D}(w,s),$$

where $h^{S}(w,s) = T - l^{S}(w,s)$ is the labor supply function of an individual worker. For the above equation to determine the wage rate, both N and n must be determined. We can simply assume that each of them is exogenous. Alternatively, the number of firms may be determined by a zero profit condition, implied by free exit and entry in competition. In that case the labor market clearing and zero profit conditions simultaneously determine the wage rate and the number of firms. Of course, with constant returns to scale, the number of firms is indeterminate, since profits are always zero.

Appendix 2

Firms decide working conditions

Suppose that the cost of a level, s, of the index of working conditions is $c(s)$, a differentiable, convex, strictly increasing function. Furthermore, suppose that there is some minimum level of s that is technologically feasible, say s_0. The firm's maximization problem is now:

$$\max_{L,K,s} Q - wL - rK - c(s)$$
$$\text{subject to } Q = F(L,K,s),$$
$$\text{and } s \geq s_0.$$

If the inequality constraint is not binding, we get the straightforward condition that marginal benefit equals marginal cost, or $Fs = c'$, as determining the job characteristic (where the subscript denote the partial derivative). Clearly the left-hand side of this marginal condition depends on L and K, so these are determined simultaneously with s, by the marginal conditions for input choice. In fact, from the firm's perspective, labor, capital, and working conditions are all inputs into its production. The difference in the case of working conditions is that these will typically directly affect the worker's welfare, and the firm does not take this into account in its calculations.

The above formulation assumes that the cost of providing a given level of working conditions is independent of the firm's other choices. This assumption can be relaxed. For example, the cost function for working conditions may be $c(s,L,K)$. For example, having more equipment or more workers can raise the cost of providing a safe factory. In this case, the simultaneity of determination of L, K and s is also driven by this cost function, as well as the production function with the first-order condition becoming $F_s = c_s$, the right hand side now being a partial derivative.

Competitive demand and supply of working conditions

Suppose that each worker can individual choose her working conditions, and their level, s, does not affect productivity. Let us also suppose that there is a competitive market in s. For example, there may be competing specialists that provides such features to all firms. Let the price of the good be m. Now each worker can purchase s in the marketplace, so her maximization problem is:

$$\max_{x,l,s} u(x,l,s)$$
$$\text{subject to } x + ms = w(T - l).$$

Suppliers of s maximize $ms - c(s)$, so that in equilibrium we get $us = c'$, which, together with the price-taking choices of x and l, is optimal, through the standard market mechanism of price mediation. Hence, if job characteristics do not affect productivity, and they are competitively supplied, we get the optimal outcome.

Compensating differentials

Suppose that firms' maximized profits (with respect to labor and capital inputs) given w and s are denoted by $\pi(w,s)$, where the dependence on the rental rate is suppressed. Suppose that competition by firms for workers is such that firms offer wage and job characteristic combinations that maximize workers' welfare, subject to a nonnegativity constraint on profit. Free entry will make this constraint bind, i.e., profits will be zero in equilibrium. That is, the firm maximizes workers' indirect utility $v(w,s)$ subject to $\pi(w,s) = 0$. In this case, we are assuming that the firm hires one worker, or that all workers it hires are identical. As noted in the main text, this formulation is not competition in the sense of price-taking behavior. Let the multiplier associated with the constraint be λ. Then the first order conditions for the equilibrium are:

$$v_w + \lambda \pi_w = 0, \text{ and}$$
$$v_s + \lambda \pi_s = 0.$$

Thus we see that in this case, s is chosen to maximize a weighted sum of the worker's utility and the firm's profit. This will be equivalent to maximizing the sum of profit and utility if $\lambda = 1$. In any case, the wage and job characteristic combinations that result are optimal, in the sense that the worker's utility cannot be increased without causing firms to make losses and become nonviable. We may also work out the marginal expressions in terms of the underlying utility function and production function. From the envelope theorem applied to v and π, we have that:

$$v_w = u_x(T - l(w,s)) \qquad \pi_w = -h^D(w,s)$$
$$v_s = u_s \qquad\qquad\quad \pi_s = F_s - c'(s).$$

The above formulation results in firms offering different wage and job-type combinations to workers who have different tradeoffs between money income and job characteristics. Since firms are competing for workers, even if they hire multiple workers, the above result will still hold, with the firm maximizing the sum of the utilities of its workers, subject to the zero profit constraint. Even if workers are heterogeneous in their preferences, the firm's decisions yield Pareto optimality. Explicitly, the firm maximizes $\Sigma_i v_i(w_i,s)$ subject to $\pi(w,s) = 0$.

This is a standard problem in allocating a public good. In this formulation, the firm is constrained to offer the same level of s (the public good) to all its workers, but it can adjust its wage offers based on workers' preferences. With many competing firms, as discussed in the main text, one can get sorting of workers so that workers with similar preferences (w–s tradeoffs) work for the same firm. This is, in fact, very similar to Tiebout-type models of competing jurisdictions, where local governments set tax-expenditure policies to attract residents. The original reference is Tiebout (1956).

Appendix 3: Monopsony

For simplicity, we can consider the case of one worker, and we can suppress the analysis of the firm's choice of capital. We use the notation given in Appendix 1 for the worker's supply of labor, which also depends on the level of working conditions. Hence the firm chooses w to maximize

$F(h^S(w,s),s) - wh^S(w,s)$, which yields the first order condition
$F_L h_w^S = h^S + wh_w^S$.

This condition implies that the value of the worker's marginal product exceeds her wage rate. Now if the firm also chooses the level of working conditions in a similar fashion, the first order condition is

$$F_L h_s^S + F_s = wh_s^S + c'.$$

Note that were the firm to be setting the wage equal to the marginal value product, the first term on each side of this equation would be equal and cancel out, and we would get the optimality condition for the choice of the job characteristic level. Since the wage is below the value of the marginal product, it follows that $F_s < c'$. If job characteristics did not enter the utility function of the worker, this would imply that the level of the job characteristic is also nonoptimal – but too high – given the wage rate. In actuality, since the optimality condition is $u_s + F_s = c'$, and using the first order condition for w, the appropriate comparison is of us with $h^S h_s^S / h_w^S$. This comparison is indeterminate.

ACKNOWLEDGMENTS

This study is part of a larger project on international labor standards, initiated and funded by the Swedish Ministry of Foreign Affairs and the Expert Group on Development Issues, Sweden. I am grateful to Lisa Román of the Department of International Cooperation, Swedish Ministry of Foreign Affairs, as well as Henrik Horn and Kaushik Basu, for extremely helpful comments and guidance. T. N. Srinivasan and Tore Ellingsen, the discussants of this paper at the Seminar on International Labor Standards in Stockholm, August 2001, made excellent comments and suggestions that I have acknowledged in the present version, but have not been able to fully incorporate into the present study. I am also grateful to Kimberly Elliott, Robert Fairlie, Michael Hutchison and John Isbister for comments received when I presented a preliminary version of these ideas at a workshop of the Santa Cruz Center for International Economics. I am solely responsible for all errors and omissions, and the views expressed here are not those of any of the individuals or organizations mentioned.

NOTES

1. Our treatment of this deep area with an enormous literature will have to be brief. Some of the important writers on this topic include Kenneth Arrow, James Buchanan, Robert Nozick, Prasanta Pattanaik, Amartya Sen, Robert Sugden and Kotaro Suzumura. Selected works that provide more references to the literature include Pattanaik (1999), Sen (1985a, b) and Suzumura (1999).
2. T. N. Srinivasan, in his comments, infers that this generality of the abstract theory, in terms of its applicability to different societies, means that I think "it does not matter . . . how a society came to be established and whether it is the community, nation or the globe." As a reading of the third subsection in the fifth section of this chapter will show, this is not at all the case. His comments on restricted domains of preferences are, nevertheless, quite useful.
3. More formally, procedural institutions can be modeled as game forms, which specify the set of individual actors, their admissible strategy sets, a set of feasible outcomes, and an outcome function that maps strategy profiles to outcomes. The "rules of the game," such as the admissible strategy sets or outcome function, may result in certain strategies being excluded (denying me a job because of my race) or punished (legal damages against someone who discriminates in hiring on the basis of race), as ways of capturing rights. This approach originates with Nozick (1974). See Pattanaik (1999) and Suzumura (1999) for further details.
4. Berlin (1969), pp. 15–16, quoted in Suzumura (1999).
5. One can argue that if there is no harm, then the conflict of rights does not matter, but then this is a consequentialist judgment.
6. Appendix 1 provides a simple formalization of the model, which will be used to provide a parallel formal treatment of some of the issues to be tackled later in the main body of the chapter.
7. The theory is comprehensively surveyed in Rosen (1986), who describes its origins in the writings of Adam Smith. A significant theoretical analysis in the context of job safety is by Thaler and Rosen (1975). Dickens (1984) also discusses various aspects of working conditions in the context of this approach.
8. A formal mathematical analysis of the situation illustrated in figure 2.2 is sketched in Appendix 2.
9. In fact, as T. N. Srinivasan has emphasized in his comment, a large fraction, even a majority, of the workforce in developing countries is self-employed. In such cases, we can think of the worker as owning the firm, as well as being the sole employee, and the efficiency argument following figure 2.2 applies.
10. Presumably the firm is owned by better-off individuals, so a reduction in the firm's profits is truly a redistribution from richer to poorer. The allocational inefficiency may or may not be of concern – while lump-sum taxes are the

nondistortionary ideal, they are practically impossible, and many kinds of dis-
tortionary policies are used in practice to achieve redistribution. The practical
policy question is typically how to minimize overall inefficiencies.

11. This problem of revelation of true benefits applies even if the public good
     provider (the firm in this case) can tax the beneficiaries – only quite complex
     schemes can implement efficient levels of provision: see Cornes and Sandler
     (1986) for more detail. I am grateful to Kaushik Basu for helping me clarify this
     point.

12. Mathematically, if s denotes the level of working conditions, u the worker's
     utility, F the firm's production function, p the price of output, and $c(s)$ the cost
     of providing the working conditions at level s, the marginal benefits to the worker
     and firm are, respectively, u_s, $F_s > 0$. The condition for optimality (maximizing
     the sum of benefits) is then $u_s + pF_s = c'$. See Appendix 2 for a further discussion
     of the cost function, which may be generalized to depend on the size of the firm.

13. In a voluntary contribution game, the firm and worker noncooperatively decide
     on contributions. Let the contributions be s_w and s_f, measured in terms of the
     job characteristic itself, and the reduced form benefit functions be $v(s_w + s_f)$ and
     $\pi(s_w + s_f)$, where the other arguments are suppressed. Then the worker chooses
     sw to maximize $v(s_w + s_f) - c(s_w + s_f)$, taking the firm's contribution as given.
     The firm makes a similar choice. The Nash equilibrium of this game does not
     yield the optimal amount.

14. This equivalence is shown in Cornes and Sandler (1986).

15. Olson (1965) is the classic reference on this perspective, though he highlights
     also many of the practical difficulties and inefficiencies of collective action.

16. The mathematical condition, modifying that in note 12, is now $\Sigma_j u_s^j + pF_s = c'$,
     where j indexes different workers.

17. Ellingsen also suggested Datta and Chowdhury (1998) and Fairris (1995) as
     additional references.

18. Formally, the worker maximizes $u(x,l)$ subject to $x = wh$, $h = T - l$, and $x \geq x_0$,
     where x is both consumption and income, l is leisure, h is hours worked, w is
     the wage rate, T is the endowment of time, and x_0 is the minimum consumption
     level for survival. The standard equilibrium is given by the interior first order
     condition, $u_x/u_l = 1/w$, which can be solved for the supply function $h^S(w)$.
     However, this may involve violating the survival constraint. If that constraint
     binds, the supply curve is given by $h^S = x_0/w$.

19. Note that the demand curve may or may not intersect the constrained part of
     the supply curve again, depending on its continuation. Whether it does or not
     is inessential to the analysis. In this case, competitive wage offers by firms also
     do not affect the outcome.

20. These negative conclusions on the efficacy of policy can be tempered if firms
     make positive profits. Adding a survival constraint may allow firms to offer
     lower working conditions as well as lower wages. Imposing standards relating
     to working conditions may then benefit workers even in the absence of a
     minimum wage.

21. A technical point is in order here. Brown et al. (1996) suggest that Pareto
     optimality implies that the average marginal rate of substitution between wages
     and safety in each firm is equal to the price of safety, which is defined as the

cost of providing a unit of safety. However, if the latter is the actual marginal cost, the condition for Pareto optimality is that this be equal to the sum of the workers' marginal rates of substitution. Implicitly, therefore, the price of safety in Brown et al. must be the marginal cost divided by the number of workers.

22. More precisely, as stated by Basu (1999), "Economists usually take the line that a voluntary contract between two agents that does not involve negative externalities on uninvolved outsiders ought not to be banned." Here Basu means direct and not pecuniary externalities. As will be seen in the subsequent discussion of Genicot's analysis, there may be pecuniary externalities when the availability of one type of contract drives out another type. Srinivasan suggests in his comments that this endogeneity of contracts being offered calls into question the applicability of the free contracting principle – however, this critique is less relevant for Basu's model.

23. Thus this model is related to those discussed in the previous subsection. The general analysis of Aghion and Hermalin (1990) has its antecedents in Akerlof's (1976) seminal article.

24. The formal notation is as follows. Q_i and C_i ($i = 1, 2$) are the production and consumption, respectively, of the two goods. S is the level of the labor standard. $U(C_1, C_2, S)$ is the Samuelson social utility function, and $Q_1 = F(Q_2, S; L^o, K^o)$ is the production possibility frontier, given the endowments L^o, K^o of labor and capital.

25. Let the world relative price for good 2 in terms of good 1 be p. Using the notation of the previous note, the equation for the trade balance requirement is $C_1 + pC_2 = Q_1 + pQ_2$.

26. We will consider these in more detail in the following section, along with a discussion of product labeling.

27. Further references to the issue of international labor standards and trade may be found in Brown (2000a, b). See, also Basu (2001b), Brown et al. (1997), de Waart (1996), Deardorff and Stern (1998), Stern (2000) and Enders (1996).

28. Henrik Horn has pointed out that an export tax would serve the same purpose more effectively. This illustrates the earlier general point that races to the bottom typically rely on restrictions on policy instruments.

29. These terms were introduced by Bulow et al. (1985). In the Chau and Kanbur model, if the inverse import demand function is logconvex, then the net gain to a country from adopting a high standard increases with the number of workers in other countries who are already under the high standard: standards are strategic complements. If instead the inverse demand function is logconcave, then standards are strategic substitutes, so that the net benefit to a country from the high standard decreases with the number of workers in other countries that have the high standard. Since the competitive fringe also enters into country welfare calculations, the size of the fringe will have similar effects to strategic choices by the other large country. While the shape of the demand curve affects the precise analysis, in either case there can be a race to the bottom, so T. N. Srinivasan's concern, in his comments, about policy relevance of such analysis, is met to some degree.

30. Sustainability through repeated interaction is also considered. When the Nash equilibrium is symmetric with low standards, then in a repeated game, a high

enough discount factor will sustain the high standards outcome that is better for both large countries. However, the required minimum discount factor increases as the large countries become more asymmetric in size. If the one-shot Nash equilibrium is asymmetric, there is no discount factor that will support an alternative to the static equilibrium.

31. One might object that, to the extent that consumers' benefits do reflect workers' welfare, there is some double counting going on, but this is unavoidable. In fact, if satisfaction is shared, it presumably should count more. A related point is Freeman's observation that consumer willingness to pay for better working conditions for the worker parallels workers' willingness to pay for better conditions, which can be captured through compensating differentials. In the case of compensating differentials, some or all of the extra cost of the better working conditions may be factored into the worker's compensation.

32. If firms are taken to be exogenously low- or high-standard producers, then the situation is one of adverse selection, for which the classic reference is Akerlof (1970). If firms are assumed to endogenously decide their standards of production, then we have a moral hazard problem: one early analysis in the context of consumer preferences for quality is by Shapiro (1982).

33. This kind of approach is related to the proposal of Fung et al. (2001), which we discuss in the next subsection.

34. In particular, Freeman's (1994) referencing of Weitzman (1974) may not be the best analogy, since Weitzman's analysis is specific to a situation of market uncertainty, in which either price or quantity regulation may on average be better, depending on where in the market the uncertainty is greatest. In the current context, the issue is more whether consumers pay for their wants or not.

35. One can further argue that labor rights are salient in the minds of developed country consumers precisely *because* such consumers now routinely buy products made in places where labor rights are lower than in developed countries. This is probably correct, but again, it does not justify this particular focus, rather than a broader concern with the general rights and welfare of those in poorer countries. Instead, one can argue that consumers need to be educated on what polices will best meet their concerns.

36. The fact that Fung et al. propose a new kind of "club" to produce a public good is reminiscent of Casella's (1996) discussion of standards provision through voluntary coalition formation. However, in Fung et al.'s proposal, the ultimate producers of the good (firms) are explicitly not in the club, and their compliance is to be obtained by coercion.

37. Fung et al. also emphasize continuous improvement, which gives their proposal its name – Ratcheting Labor Standards. This aspect of the idea is subject to its own problems, on which see the various comments in the same issue of the *Boston Review.*

38. See the comments on Fung et al. by Broad (2001), Levinson (2001) and Moberg (2001).

39. It is not impossible that a government could pass appropriate legislation. For example, US firms are prohibited by US law from using bribery in doing business abroad. On the other hand, European firms have no such restriction.

40. A separate issue is the wide degree of variation possible in the details of democratic institutions (or even their absence), and in their consequent outcomes. A further consideration is that the democratic process also includes persuasion, for good or bad. All participants may choose to present their preferences in ways that attempt to win over other citizens. Thus arguments about what is moral or right in terms of social policy are presented, and must be evaluated, even if the final policy outcome is determined by democracy rather than logical superiority.

41. It is also important to point out that the incursion on sovereignty is asymmetric: the country imposing the standard does not simultaneously provide assistance to those who are adversely affected. As Panagariya (2001a, b) points out, and as was also noted by Alan Winters in the discussion in Stockholm of the paper on which this chapter is based, this is quite different from a domestic standard, where domestic safety nets are part of the overall policy package.

42. While this involves comparing two groups, it is similar in spirit to the idea that individuals should have the right to decide matters pertaining to themselves, irrespective of what others' preferences are. Recall our earlier discussion of the "shirt colors" example.

43. For example, as Henrik Horn has pointed out to me, forced labor is already included in the GATT (Article XX).

44. Srinivasan here also expresses concern about interest group capture as a result of rights concerns: this is a separate issue that we have addressed in the previous subsection.

45. This point might also be applied to the Chau–Kanbur model, in which the possibility of Northern support of Southern cooperation to raise standards is raised. Implicitly, in that case, the Southern exporters are unanimous not only in their goals, but also in what they wish to include in the cooperative agenda.

46. Bardhan (2001a) notes the importance of *domestic* labor standards in the dimension of worker rights, where centralized collective bargaining offers more income protection to workers than decentralized unions.

47. See, for example, Krugman (1994). However, there is a large empirical literature that continues to try to test both sides of the argument.

48. On the other hand, as T. N. Srinivasan points out in his comments, growth can move the demand curve upward, eliminating the low wage equilibrium. This is related to the discussion of growth and consequences for the poor.

49. The issue of redistribution arises in another way in Basu and Van's model. Swinnerton and Rogers (1999) show that if workers own shares of firms sufficiently broadly, and receive dividends, the low wage equilibrium will disappear. Basu and Van (1999) show that this would require a massive redistribution of ownership from any likely initial conditions. This issue is related to the discussion in the "Rights and the poor" subsection.

50. Additional analysis of child labor issues may be found in Brown (2000c) and Brown et al. (2001).

51. See the discussion of these issues in the context of development in Singh (1994) and Marjit and Singh (1995).

52. Piore seems to make the human capital argument as well. See also the discussion of Ellingsen's comments at the end of this subsection.

53. One might even argue that sufficient access to education and credit make the satisfaction of rights automatic. For example, Silicon Valley engineers are well treated because of their skills, and not because of any labor rights that they are endowed with by law. This cannot be a general counter argument, however, since it involves a somewhat extreme case of skills, and even such workers need to be informed about potential job hazards, or protected from certain kinds of restrictive labor contracts.

54. For a comprehensive "textbook" treatment, see Ray (1998). For an overview with recent examples, placed in the context of globalization, see Bardhan (2001a).

55. Note that in accepting this position, rights advocates are not too far from T. N. Srinivasan's philosopher friends (see his comments) who agree that it is "virtually impossible to rank processes without considering their potential consequences." In the example at hand, consequences are built in to the rights that are classified as fundamental. On the other hand, freedom to choose remains a process-based right. Srinivasan's comments about the importance of social and temporal context are relevant here. See the "Drawing the line" subsection as well.

56. Of course, this does not have to diminish concern about rights such as freedom of speech and association: any supposed tradeoff between these is likely to be a false one. I am grateful to Ulf Edström for bringing out this point in the discussion at the seminar.

57. See Singh and Thomas (2000) for such an analysis.

58. There is, of course, no difficulty in adding more inputs or incorporating fixed costs into this formulation.

59. More generally, the wage and rental rate can be taken as simultaneously determined by the supply and demand of labor and of capital. Even more generally, there are multiple markets for labor, capital and goods that all clear simultaneously. We are taking a simple partial equilibrium view here.

REFERENCES

Aghion, Philippe and Benjamin Hermalin (1990) "Legal Restrictions on Private Contracts Can Enhance Efficiency," *Journal of Law Economics and Organization*, 6 (2), pp. 381–409.

Akerlof, George (1970) "The Market for Lemons: Quality Uncertainty and the Market Mechanism," *Quarterly Journal of Economics*, 84, pp. 488–500.

Akerlof, George (1976) "The Economics of Caste and of the Rat Race and Other Woeful Tales," *Quarterly Journal of Economics*, 90, pp. 599–617.

Amsden, Alice (1994) "Hype or Help?," *Boston Review*, 20 (1, December–January), online at: http://bostonreview.mit.edu/BR20.6/Amsden.html

Bagwell, Kyle and Robert Staiger (2000) "The Simple Economics of Labor Standards and the GATT," in Deardorff and Stern (eds).

Bagwell, Kyle and Robert W. Staiger (2001) "Domestic Policies, National Sovereignty and International Economic Institutions," *Quarterly Journal of Economics*, 116 (2, May), pp. 519–62.

Baland, Jean-Marie and Robinson, James (2000) "Is Child Labor Inefficient?," *Journal of Political Economy*, 108 (4, August), pp. 663–79.

Bardhan, Pranab (2001a) "Social Justice in the Global Economy," *Economic and Political Weekly*, February, pp. 3–10.

Bardhan, Pranab (2001b) "Some Up, Some Down," *Boston Review*, 26 (1, February–March), online at: http://bostonreview.mit.edu/BR26.1/bardhan.html

Basu, Kaushik (1999) "Child Labor: Cause, Consequence, and Cure, with Remarks on International Labor Standards," *Journal of Economic Literature*, 37 (September), pp. 1083–119.

Basu, Kaushik (2001a) "On the Goals of Development," in Gerald Meier and Joseph Stiglitz (eds), *Frontiers of Development Economics: The Future in Perspective*, Washington, DC: World Bank and Oxford University Press.

Basu, Kaushik (2001b) "The View from the Tropics," *Boston Review*, 26 (1, February–March) http://bostonreview.mit.edu/BR26.1/basu.html

Basu, Kaushik and Van, Pham Hoang (1998) "The Economics of Child Labor," *American Economic Review*, 88, pp. 412–27.

Basu, Kaushik and Van, Pham Hoang (1999) "The Economics of Child Labor: Reply," *American Economic Review*, 89 (5), pp. 1386–8.

Berlin, Isiah (1969) *Four Essays on Liberty*, Oxford: Oxford University Press.

Bhagwati, Jagdish (1995) "Trade Liberalization and 'Fair Trade' Demands: Addressing Environmental and Labor Standards Issues," *World Economy*, 18, pp. 745–59.

Bhagwati, Jagdish and Robert Hudec (eds) (1996a) *Fair Trade and Harmonization, Vol. 1: Economic Analysis*, Cambridge MA: MIT Press.

Bhagwati, Jagdish and Robert Hudec (eds) (1996b) *Fair Trade and Harmonization, Vol. 2: Legal Analysis*, Cambridge MA: MIT Press.

Bhagwati, Jagdish and T. N. Srinivasan (1996) "Trade and the Environment: Does Environmental Diversity Detract from the Case for Free Trade?," in Bhagwati and Hudec (eds), 1996a.

Broad, Robin (2001) "A Better Mousetrap?," *Boston Review*, 26 (1, February–March), online at: http://bostonreview.mit.edu/BR26.1/broad.html.

Brown, Drusilla (2000a) "International Labor Standards in the World Trade Organization and the International Labor Organization," Discussion Paper 2000–03, Department of Economics, Tufts University.

Brown, Drusilla (2000b) "International Trade and Core Labor Standards: A Survey of the Recent Literature," Discussion Paper 2000–05, Department of Economics, Tufts University.

Brown, Drusilla (2000c) "A Transactions Cost Politics Analysis of International Child Labor Standards," in Deardorff and Stern (eds).

Brown, Drusilla, Alan Deardorff, and Robert Stern (1996) "International Labor Standards and Trade: A Theoretical Analysis," in Bhagwati and Hudec (eds) 1996a.

Brown, Drusilla, Alan Deardorff, and Robert Stern (1997) "Issues of Environmental and Labor Standards in the Global Trading System," Working Paper 97–10, Department of Economics, University of Michigan.

Brown, Drusilla, Alan Deardorff, and Robert Stern (2001) "Child Labor: Theory, Evidence and Policy", (this volume).

Bucovetsky, S. and John D. Wilson (1991) "Tax Competition with Two Tax Instruments," *Regional Science and Urban Economics*, 21, pp. 333–50.

Bulow, Jeremy, John Geanakoplos, and Paul Klemperer (1985) "Multimarket Oligopolies," *Journal of Political Economy*, 93 (3), pp. 488–511.

Casella, Alessandra (1996) "Free Trade and Evolving Standards," in Bhagwati and Hudec (eds), 1996a.

Chau, Nancy and Ravi Kanbur (2000) "The Race to the Bottom, From the Bottom," Working Paper, Cornell University, November.

Cornes, Richard and Sandler, Todd (1986) *The Theory of Externalities, Public Goods, and Club Goods*, Cambridge: Cambridge University Press.

Dasgupta, Partha (1993) *An Inquiry into Well-Being and Destitution*, Oxford: Clarendon Press.

Datta, S. and P. R. Chowdhury (1998) "Management Union Bargaining under Minimum Wage Regulation in Less Developed Countries," *Indian Economic Review*, 33 (2), pp. 169–84.

de Waart, Paul (1996) "Minimum Labor Standards in International Trade from a Legal Perspective," in van Dijk and Faber (eds).

Deardorff, Alan and Robert Stern (eds) (1998) *Constituent Interests and U.S. Trade Policies*, Ann Arbor: University of Michigan Press.

Deardorff, Alan and Robert Stern (eds) (2000) *Social Dimensions of U.S. Trade Policies*, Ann Arbor: University of Michigan Press.

Dickens, William (1984) "Occupational Safety and Health Regulation and Economic Theory," in William Darity, Jr. (ed.), *Labor Economics: Modern Views*, Boston: Kluwer-Nijhoff.

Dixit, Avinash (2000) "Comment on A Transactions Cost Politics Analysis of International Child Labor Standards," in Deardorff and Stern (eds).

Enders, Alice (1996) "The Role of the WTO in Minimum Standards," in van Dijk and Faber (eds).

Engerman, Stanley (2003) "The History and Political Economy of International Labor Standards", (this volume).

Eswaran, Mukesh (1996) "Fertility, Literacy and the Institution of Child Labor," manuscript, Vancouver: University of British Columbia, Department of Economics.

Fairris, D. (1995) "Do Unionized Employers Reappropriate Rent through Worsened Workplace Safety," *Eastern Economic Journal*, 21 (2), pp. 171–85.

Fields, Gary (1996) "Trade and Labor Standards: Final Report on the Meeting," Working Paper No. 7, Paris: Organization for Economic Cooperation and Development.

Fields, Gary (2000) "The Role of Labor Standards in US Trade Policies," in Deardorff and Stern (eds).

Freeman, Richard (1994a) "A Hard-Headed Look at Labor Standards," in US Department of Labor.

Freeman, Richard (1994b) "A Hard-Headed Look at Labor Standards," in Sengenberger and Campbell.

Fung, Archon, Dara O'Rourke, and Charles Sabel (2001) "Realizing Labor Standards," *Boston Review*, 26 (1, February–March), online at: http://bostonreview.mit.edu/BR26.1/fung.html.

Fung, Kwok-Chiu and Robert Staiger (1996) "Trade Liberalization and Trade Adjustment Assistance," in M. Canzoneri, W. Ethier, and V. Grilli (eds), *The New Transatlantic Economy*, Cambridge: Cambridge University Press.

Genicot, Garance (2000) "Bonded Labor and Serfdom: A Paradox of Voluntary Choice," Working paper, University of California, Irvine.

Golub, Stephen (1997a) "Are International Labor Standards Needed to Prevent Social Dumping?," *Finance and Development*, December, pp. 20–3.

Golub, Stephen (1997b) "International Labor Standards and Trade," Working paper WP/97/37, Research Department, International Monetary Fund.

Grootaert, Christiaan and Kanbur, Ravi (1995) "Child Labor: An Economic Perspective," *International Labor Review*, 134 (2), pp. 187–203.

Grossman, S. and O. Hart (1986) "The Costs and Benefits of Ownership: A Theory of Vertical and Lateral Integration," *Journal of Political Economy*, 94, pp. 691–719.

Grossman, Gene and Elhanen Helpman (1991) *Innovation and Growth in the Global Economy*, Cambridge, MA: MIT Press.

Hart, Oliver and John Moore (1999) "Foundations of Incomplete Contracts," *Review of Economic Studies*, 66 (1), pp. 115–38.

ICFTU (1999) "Development, Environment and Trade: Statement to the High-level Symposia of the WTO on 'Trade and Environment', Geneva, 15–16 March 1999," mimeo: ICFTU, Geneva and Washington.

ILO, Washington Branch (1994) *Washington Focus*, Spring, p. 9.

Krugman, Paul (1994) "Does Third-World Growth Hurt First World Prosperity?," *Harvard Business Review*, 72 (4), pp. 113–21.

Levinson, Mark (2001) "Wishful Thinking," *Boston Review*, 26 (1 February–March), online at: http://bostonreview.mit.edu/BR26.1/levinson.html.

Lindbeck, Assar (1988) "Individual Freedom and Welfare State Policy," *European Economic Review*, 32, pp. 295–318.

Marjit, Sugata and Singh, Nirvikar (1995) "Technology and Indian Industry," in Dilip Mookherjee (ed.), *Indian Industry*, New Delhi: Oxford University Press.

Maskus, Keith (1997) "Should Core Labor Standards be Imposed through International Trade Policy," paper prepared for World Bank International Trade Division.

Milgrom, Paul, Yingyi Qian, and John Roberts (1991) "Complementarities, Momentum, and the Evolution of Modern Manufacturing," *American Economic Review*, 81 (2, May), pp. 84–8.

Moberg, David (2001) "Unions and the State," *Boston Review*, 26 (1, February–March), online at: http://bostonreview.mit.edu/BR26.1/moberg.html.

Nozick, Robert (1974) *Anarchy, State and Utopia*, Oxford: Basil Blackwell.

Oates, Wallace and Robert Schwab (1988) "Economic Competition among Jurisdictions: Efficiency Enhancing or Distortion Inducing," *Journal of Public Economics*, 35, pp. 333–54.

OECD (1996) *Trade Employment and Labor Standards*, Paris: Organization for Economic Cooperation and Development.

Oi, Walter (1973) "Workmen's Compensations and Industrial Safety," *Supplemental Studies for the National Commission on State Workmen's Compensation Laws*, Volume I, Washington, DC: US Government Printing Office, pp. 41–106.

Olson, Mancur, Jr. (1965) *The Logic of Collective Action: Public Goods and the Theory of Groups*, Cambridge MA: Harvard University Press.

Pahre, Robert (1998) "Comments on Conference Version of Paper: Labor Standards, Trade Sanctions and the Hijacking Hypothesis," in Deardorff and Stern (eds).

Panagariya, Arvind (2001a) "Trade Labor Link: A Post-Seattle Analysis," in Zdenek Drabek (ed.), *Globalization under Threat: The Stability of Trade Policy and Multilateral Agreements*, Cheltenam, UK: Edward Elgar, pp. 101–23.

Panagariya, Arvind (2001b) "Labor Standards and Trade Sanctions: Right End Wrong Means," paper presented at the conference "Towards An Agenda for Research on International Economic Integration and Labor Markets," January 15–16, 2001, East-West Center, Hawaii.

Pattanaik, Prasanta (1999) "Individual Rights and Social Choice," public lecture delivered at Deakin University, Victoria, Australia, November.

Piore, Michael (1990) "Labor Standards and Business Strategies," in Stephen Herzenberg and Jorge Perez-Lopez (eds), *Labor Standards and Development in the Global Economy*, Washington, DC: US Department of Labor, Bureau of International Affairs.

Piore, Michael (1994) "International Labor Standards and Business Strategies," in US Department of Labor.

Portes, A. (1990) "When More can be Less: Labor Standards, Development, and the Informal Economy," in *Labor Standards and Development in the Global Economy*, US Department of Labor, Washington, DC: Government Printing Office.

Ray, Debraj (1993) "Nutrition, Adaptation and Labor Markets," in P. Bardhan, M. Datta-Chaudhuri, and T. N. Krishnan (eds), *Essays in Honour of K. N. Raj*, Delhi: Oxford University Press.

Ray, Debraj (1998) *Development Economics*, Princeton: Princeton University Press.

Ray, Debraj and Peter Streufert (1993) "Dynamic Equilibria with Unemployment Due to Undernourishment," *Economic Theory*, 3, p. 61–85.

Raynauld, André and Jean-Pierre Vidal (1998) *Labor Standards and International Competitiveness: A Comparative Analysis of Developing and Industrialized Countries*, Northampton, MA: Edward Elgar.

Revesz, Richard (1992) "Rehabilitating Interstate Competition: Rethinking the 'Race-to-the Bottom' Rationale for Federal Environmental Regulation," *New York University Law Review*, 67, pp. 1220–54.

Rodrik, Dani (1996) "Labor Standards in International Trade: Do They Matter and What Do We Do About Them?," in Robert Lawrence, Dani Rodrik, and John Whalley (eds), *Emerging Agenda for Global Trade: High Stakes for Developing Countries*, Washington, DC: Overseas Development Council.

Rosen, Sherwin (1986) "The Theory of Equalizing Differences," in Orley Ashenfelter and Richard Layard (eds), *Handbook of Labor Economics*, vol. I, Amsterdam: North Holland.

Rothstein, Richard (1994) "The Case for Labor Standards," *Boston Review*, 20 (1, December–January), online at: http://bostonreview.mit.edu/BR20.6/rothstein.html.

Sachs, Jeffrey (1997) "Re-thinking International Labor Standards," Lecture, January 22.

Sen, Amartya (1970) "The Impossibility of a Paretian Liberal," *Journal of Political Economy*, 78, pp. 152–7.

Sen, Amartya (1985a) *Commodities and Capabilities*, Amsterdam: North Holland.

Sen, Amartya (1985b) "Well-being, Agency and Freedom: The Dewey Lectures 1984," *Journal of Philosophy*, 82, pp. 169–221.

Sen, Amartya (1997) *On Economic Inequality,* (expanded edn), Oxford: Clarendon Press.

Sengenberger, Werner and Duncan Campbell (eds), (1994) *International Labor Standards and Economic Interdependence,* Geneva: International Institute for Labor Studies.

Shapiro, Carl (1982) "Consumer Information, Product Quality, and Seller Reputation," *Bell Journal of Economics,* 13 (1, Spring), pp. 20–35.

Singh, Nirvikar (1994) "Some Aspects of Technological Change and Innovation in Agriculture," in Kaushik Basu (ed.), *Agrarian Questions,* New Delhi: Oxford University Press.

Singh, Nirvikar and Ravi Thomas (2000) "Welfare Policy: Cash Versus Kind, Self-selection and Notches," *Southern Economic Journal,* 66 (4, April), pp. 976–90.

Srinivasan, T. N. (1994) "International Labor Standards Once Again!," in US Department of Labor.

Srinivasan, T. N. (1996) "International Trade and Labor Standards from an Economic Perspective," in van Dijk and Faber (eds).

Srinivasan, T. N. (1998) *Developing Countries and the Multilateral Trading System: From the GATT to the Uruguay Round and the Future,* Boulder CO: Westview Press.

Srinivasan, T. N. (1998) "Trade and Human Rights," in Deardorff and Stern (eds).

Staiger, Robert W. (2003) "A Role for the WTO", (this volume).

Stern, Robert (2000) "Labor Standards and Trade," Discussion Paper no. 457, Research Seminar in International Economics, School of Public Policy, University of Michigan.

Stiglitz, Joseph (2000) "The Contributions of the Economics of Information to Twentieth Century Economics," *Quarterly Journal of Economics,* 115 (4, November), pp. 1441–78.

Suzumura, Kotaro (1999) "Consequences, Opportunities and Procedures," *Social Choice and Welfare,* 16, pp. 17–40.

Swinnerton, Kenneth and Carol Rogers (1999) "The Economics of Child Labor: Comment," *American Economic Review,* 89 (5), pp. 1382–5.

Thaler, Russell and Sherwin Rosen (1975) "The Value of Saving a Life: Evidence from the Labor Market," in Nestor Terleckyj (ed.), *Household Production and Consumption, Studies in Income and Wealth,* vol. 40, NBER, New York: Columbia University Press.

Tiebout, Charles (1956) "A Pure Theory of Local Public Expenditures," *Journal of Political Economy,* 64, pp. 416–24.

US Department of Labor (1994) *International Labor Standards and Global Economic Integration: Proceedings of a Symposium,* Washington DC: US Department of Labor.

van Dijk, Pitou and Gerrit Faber (eds) (1996) *Challenges to the New World Trade Organization,* The Hague: Kluwer Law International.

Weitzman, Martin (1974) "Prices vs. Quantities," *Review of Economic Studies,* 41 (4, October), pp. 477–91.

Wilson, John D. (1996) "Capital Mobility and Environmental Standards: Is There a Theoretical Basis for a Race to the Bottom?," in Bhagwati and Hudec (eds), 1996a.

Zodrow, G. R., and Peter Mieszkowski (1986) "Pigou, Tiebout, Property Taxation, and the Underprovision of Local Public Goods," *Journal of Urban Economics,* 19, pp. 356–70.

COMMENTARY 2.1
Old Wine in New Bottles?

T. N. Srinivasan

I very much enjoyed reading Nirvikar Singh's study. It is clear and well exposited. After reading it I wondered whether the major issues in the debates and controversies over labour standards are of economic theory. First, most of the theory surveyed so admirably in the paper, to use a cliché, amounts to pouring the not so new wine of labour standards in very old bottles of externalities, market failures, public goods, multiple equilibria, second best and so on. If there were new analytical insights that emerged from the theory that were specific to labour standards, and helpful for thinking through policy issues more clearly than would have been possible otherwise, I missed them! In saying this I mean no offence to the excellent theorists who have contributed to this literature. In fact it may just be my incapacity to understand the depth and subtlety of their analysis.

Second I could not see how the models exposited could be empirically estimated and tested. Without empirical support their policy relevance will remain limited. Diverse aspects of labour standards are simply ignored for analytical convenience. It is difficult even to think of what sorts of data one would collect for estimating, for example, the Chau–Kanbur model and testing whether the inverse demand function for imports was logconvex on logconcave! Their results depend on this.

Third, the theory did not seem to be based on labour market realities of poor countries. In India, the most recent national sample survey of employment and unemployment for the year 1999–2000 shows that less than one-fifth of the labour force is employed in regular wage employment and more than 50 percent is self-employed. Theoretical models however assume that the entire labour force is employed for wages. Fourth, is the absence of any discussion of growth. Many types of poor labour standards such as caste discrimination in employment and wages tend to disappear in a tight labour market and with urbanization, both of which are associated with rapidly growing economies. Moreover, a dominant cause for children working, rather than being in schools, is the poverty of their parents. Since rapid growth is again associated with reduction in poverty, models with no dynamics of growth are deficient for analysing labour standards. For example, in Basu's model of multiple equilibria, the one with child labour will disappear over time if growth shifts the demand for labour sufficiently to the right.

Singh starts the chapter with the question whether international labour standards would benefit the poor, presumably poor everywhere, the developing countries and finally, the poor in developing countries. The meaningfulness or otherwise of this question can be judged only by answering some prior questions. First, it is not evident that all the advocates of international labour standards view them as instruments to improve the welfare of the poor anywhere, least of all in developing countries. I would not put, for example, the labour union AFL-CIO in the US as having the poor in its mind in its strong advocacy of international labour standards. Second, how are international labour standards to be determined? Third what is the mechanism by which international standards get translated into national and international action? Fourth, what are the mechanisms linking labour standards to the poor, if by poor one meant, as one should, individuals and households who are deemed poor by some national or international norms? Singh's survey partially answers some of these. But given his focus, his answers are more from theoretical, and less from empirical and practical policy, perspectives.

In his second section, Singh delves into issues such as process versus outcomes, rights versus welfarism, interdependent preferences, preference aggregation and so on. Some friends of mine, who are more knowledgeable about philosophy than I am, tell me that the view that it is virtually impossible to rank processes without considering their potential consequences, and as such, the process approach collapses to the consequentialist approach, is dominant among contemporary philosophers. In any case, to my simplistic mind, talking about rights in abstract philosophical terms, without grounding them in a social and temporal context is not particularly useful. It is vacuous to simply list something as a right, without inquiring how an individual or group came to be endowed with it; whether it has the characteristics of Rawlsian primary goods or it has only an instrumental value in obtaining primary goods; to whom those endowed with a right can assert their claim to that right; and if denied, what recourse do they have, and so on.

Of course, one can appeal to a presumed creator as having endowed each individual with certain rights. The founding fathers of the United States did so when they said in the declaration of independence that "We hold these truths to be self-evident, that all men are created equal, that they are endowed by their Creator with certain unalienable Rights, that among these are Life, Liberty and the pursuit of Happiness." But for many, Creationist approaches make little sense, whether it is about biology or about rights. Equally unappealing is to say that all human beings, just because they are human beings, have certain rights.

I would not have chosen to raise those quibbles except for the sweeping claim of universality and eternity made by President Clinton's Council of Economic Advisors for a particular set of "core" labour standards, with the assertion they represent "fundamental human and democratic rights in the work place, rights that should prevail in *all societies whatever their level of development* [my emphasis]" (CEA, 1995). If accepted, any diversity in the content and scope of core labour standards would be deemed a violation of fundamental human and democratic rights and would be illegitimate. Apparently the rest of the world has gone even further than the Council: barring a few, most states have signed and ratified a set of conventions that recognize a number of civil, economic, political, and social rights that include, and go beyond, the core labour standards enunciated by the Council. This being the case, whether labour standards are rights-based or welfarist is a moot question. They have already been enshrined as rights and the only question is how they are to be enforced.

Singh is casual about how one defines a society, in effect implying that it does not matter to his arguments how a society came to be established and whether it is the community, nation, or the globe. It does matter. For example, Arrow's general possibility theorem about preference aggregation (Arrow, 1951) postulates the domain of preferences to be unrestricted. Individual members of Arrow's society are allowed to rank them in any possible order. However, as is well known, if we drop this postulate and consider suitably restricted domains, aggregation becomes possible. It is natural to think of restricted, rather than unrestricted domains, if only individuals with sufficient similarity of preference from societies. Thus prudes and lewds with diametrically opposite preferences are unlikely to form a society!

It also matters whether one is considering an existing society of individuals, say, a nation state, from which they cannot opt out and form a new state if they wished (secession is impossible) or a group of individuals contemplating the formation of a state, its constitution and the decision-making processes of the state behind the Rawlsian veil of ignorance. Obviously in the first situation initial conditions matter and in the second not.

Singh uses an example of Pattanaik to illustrate the conflict between rights and welfarist approaches. If I understand it correctly, the preferences of the two individuals, in particular, that each one's choice of shirt to wear, enters the welfare ranking of the other, is common knowledge. In such a case, to deem one's choice of a shirt to wear as exclusively in one's personal domain, and as such, personal freedom implies one is free to choose whatever coloured shirt to wear is not convincing. Further, given no additional information, such as whether the other party will cheat, it is plausible that both will choose, in the example, to wear a red shirt in a one-shot simultaneous choice play of the game.

Let me turn to a few of the models. Consider the competitive model. The first welfare theorem says that a laissez-faire competitive equilibrium is a Pareto optimum. But if it is deemed unsatisfactory on equity grounds, the second welfare theorem, assures us that under appropriate conditions, a more equitable Pareto optimum can be sustained as a competitive equilibrium, provided either initial endowments or incomes of individuals can be suitably redistributed in a lump sum. As such, it is not clear why Singh thinks that "the solution to the problem [of competitive equilibrium being unsatisfactory on equity grounds] is not obvious." It is true that lump transfers are impractical from informational and policy perspectives. But Singh is surveying theory and not practical policy! Leaving this issue aside, it is clear that if labour standards can be bought and sold, as in one of Singh's competitive models, one can easily imagine an employer supplying it to his employee at a price (just as employers charge them for health insurance) over which she has no control (she takes its market price as given). Then in a world where workers and employers are atomistic competitors who take the price of labour standard and the wage rate as given, a competitive equilibrium, if it exists, will be efficient and a Pareto optimum. Also Singh's comment that equilibria in competitive models do not take into account rights such as collective bargaining seems odd. If both employers and employees are atomistic competitors, collective bargaining, unless the collection is large enough to have market power, has no instrumental value. Traditionally collective bargaining is viewed as creating market power for workers that countervails the employer's market power. In atomistic competition, neither a worker nor his employer has market power.

In the monopsony model, there are two distortions, namely, that from monopsony and the other, due to the fact that labour standard is an externality that affects the labour supply decision of workers but does not enter the profit calculus of the monopsonist. With two distortions, conventional theory has shown that one would in general need two instruments to achieve efficiency, and setting a minimum wage by itself would not ensure it. Also it is well known from second best theory that setting one instrument (say the minimum wage) at a level that would have been optimal in the absence of the externality created by labour standards, could end up with an equilibrium which is worse, from the point of view of the worker's welfare than in one with no intervention at all. All of this is well known and illustrates my earlier point that by applying this standard theory in the context of labour standards does not yield additional insights.

Finally, Singh interprets the Genicot model of bonded labour as illustrating the limitations on the principle of free contracting. I am not entirely persuaded. My understanding of the principle is that, given an *exogenous* set of contracts available to two parties, the contract voluntarily chosen by them, is as good, from the perspective of both, as any other that they could have chosen, but did not. In the Genicot model, one party, namely the formal credit institution (FCI) does not offer *any* contract, if bonded labour contracts offered by the landlord are available to the worker. If the latter contracts are banned, then by definition only the contracts offered by the FCI are available. I would interpret this saying that one party's choice of her partner, and the contract voluntary chosen by both, are affected by a third party's (namely the government's) action whether or not to ban bonded labour. As such the principle of voluntary contracting does not apply to this case.

Singh is very generous in discussing my contribution to the analysis of labor standards in an international economy. Let me conclude by saying that the crux of the debate is not whether having children at school rather than at work, freedom of association and other dimensions of core labour standards are desirable objectives. Nor is it about large number of countries, developing and developed, having endorsed by signing and ratifying international conventions relating to them. Indeed by signing and ratifying the Universal Declaration of Human Rights of 1948, the community of nations endorsed rights that cover and go beyond child labour and core labour standards. The debate is about the desirability of using trade sanctions for enforcing them. On this the answer is very clear to most economists. It is emphatically that it is not.

REFERENCES

Arrow, Kenneth J. (1951) *Social Choice and Individual Values*, New York: John Wiley.
Council of Economic Advisers (CEA) (1995) "Economic Report of the President," Washington, DC: Council of Economic Advisers.

COMMENTARY 2.2
Governing Labor Relations

Tore Ellingsen[1]

My views on international labour standards are those of an outsider. Hence, I cannot credibly judge whether Singh's survey in this volume gives a balanced picture of the relevant research. On the other hand, I do have the advantage of being quite representative of the intended readership of the chapter, which I take to be interested non-experts who want to get a first grasp of this very hot topic.

As expected, I learnt a lot from Singh's carefully written study. Some of the analysis was pleasantly surprising. In particular, I appreciate that Singh does not take welfarism for granted. There is considerable evidence that people care about processes as well as outcomes. For example, in bargaining people often reject proposals that yield an unequal split of the surplus, but only if it was in fact possible for the proposer to suggest a more even split (for evidence, see Falk et al. (2002)). I am also convinced that a bad outcome is much easier to accept if one initially had a fair chance, than if the scales were tipped to begin with. Economists have been all too willing to ignore arguments that are not based on concern for final outcomes, and for this reason our analysis of rights has tended to be much too narrow. The existence of non-welfarist values could well be a respectable reason for opposition to conventional economic analysis.

This being said, I still think that the standard welfarist approach admits worthwhile insights – even about rights. And while Singh's survey demonstrates that much good work has been done, it seems to me that economists do not understand either the causes or the consequences of labour standards as well as we might. Below, I shall discuss briefly two of the questions that strike me as needing more attention.

Incomplete Contracts and Workers' Rights

Until quite recently, economists tended to study hypothetical worlds in which people could easily write complete contracts. This was not because this assumption appeared realistic, but because we lacked the tools to handle alternative assumptions. From the point of view of discussing labour standards, that framework is however particularly unsatisfactory. To the extent that rights are present at all, they are implicit and deep in the background.

With the help of game theory, we are now finally in a position to study incomplete contracts in a rigorous way, and thus allow *control rights* to take a place at center stage. In fact, this is one of the most active areas of research in corporate finance, which is a sign as sure as any that the approach is useful.

A central insight from the theory of incomplete contracts is that the allocation of rights not only affects distribution but can also have an effect on efficiency.[2] In other words, giving rights to workers may well be in the general interest. Basically, the idea is that workers with no rights will be afraid of exploitation by employers in the future and hence be unwilling to invest in any form of firm-specific human capital. A recent investigation touching on this issue is Booth and Chatterji (1998). An implication of the argument is that workers' rights could be an important component in the development of new industries that require high levels of human capital. Note here that there is a built-in conflict between old and new industry. Old firms with low human capital requirements would not welcome workers' rights, whereas new firms that depend on firm-specific human capital investment may not even be able to enter before such rights are established (because of their inability to credibly promise to pay fairly for human capital).

It is hard to say on theoretical grounds whether improved bargaining power plays a major role in a worker's decision to acquire human capital. For a variety of reasons, the effect is likely to vary across time and place. First, the degree of specificity depends on whether there is competition among employers for workers with the relevant skills. With a monopoly employer, any skill that is useless in home-production is firm-specific. Second, large employer power does not necessarily imply exploitation. An employer may find it profitable to establish a reputation for treating workers well in order to encourage human capital investments. However, this mechanism is only likely to function well if firms are quite large, are expected to be long-lived, and if information flows are good. Third, if workers are heterogeneous, a system of collective representation is not necessarily conducive to human capital investment. If the majority of workers perform tasks that require very little training, they may be tempted to vote in favor of "egalitarian" wage policies that effectively exploit trained workers.

As far as I know, there has not been much serious work on the relationship between workers' rights, human capital investments and industrial development. If anything, existing literature has emphasized the negative effects of trade unionism on technological development. The starkest example is perhaps Parente and Prescott (1999), who argue that workers' resistance to the introduction of new technologies could be a major reason why production technologies differ so much between countries.[3] Of course, only empirical studies can say whether workers' rights are conducive to human capital investment or not, and if so whether the effect outweighs any negative effects on capital investment.[4]

Working Conditions

Let me now comment on the politically hottest topic of all, namely the need for regulated working conditions. In my view, the primary arguments for such regulation must be either that it is hard to enforce private agreements or that there will be some kind of race to the bottom. Given that Singh discusses the latter in some detail, I shall focus exclusively on the former.

Let us neglect any externalities between workers in different firms. Suppose that workers can bargain over working conditions as well as wages, and that the resulting bargain will be somewhere on the "contract curve," i.e., at a point where it is impossible to find another combination of wages and working conditions that make both the firms and the workers better off. Regulation of working conditions through a minimum standard changes the contract curve by ruling out any outcome with poor working conditions. However, it does not rule out low wages. Thus, the question is to what extent the improvement in working conditions will be offset by lower wages. A standard bargaining model can be shown to yield the following quite intuitive insight: If the regulated level of working conditions is not too much higher than the level which would have been negotiated between the firm and the trade union, then the workers will benefit from the regulation. However, if the regulated level is much higher than the unregulated level would have been, the workers will suffer from the regulation too, because the negotiated wage becomes very low. This argument thus calls for regulatory caution. It could be very harmful to follow Rodrik's (1996) suggestion that we impose the same working conditions on firms in developing countries as those enjoyed by workers in developed countries.

Of course, the above argument presupposes that unions can negotiate working conditions in the first place. If working conditions are hard to regulate through firm-level contracting (due for example to high contract enforcement costs), the argument for intervention is much stronger. The reason is that, without regulation, workers in this case are typically always pinned down to their reservation utility. Even if they can bargain over wages, and such contracts are easier to enforce, there is no point in doing it, because the higher the wage, the worse will the working conditions become; see Fairris (1995) for a discussion. If regulated working conditions are easier to enforce, the downward adjustment in working condition is limited, and so it makes sense to bargain over wages again. Note however that even in this case one should not be overly ambitious with respect to the labour standard, as the solution will then once more be inefficient and wage reductions may be hurting workers.

Indeed, a general insight from this model is that overly ambitious labour standards will tend to harm the workers either through lower wages or through unemployment. This is a strong reason for not demanding similar working conditions all over the globe. Instead it makes sense to strive for working conditions that improve in tandem with economic growth, possibly with the aid of some regulation – as they have in the industrialized countries.

Conclusion

In conclusion, I found Singh's study highly informative and clearly written. It provides a valuable starting point for policy debate, and I completely agree with the main conclusion, which is that labour standards should be seen as part of a broader package of development strategies. Still, the study leaves me unsatisfied. Given the current state of the economics discipline and the importance of the problems at hand, we should have been able to say quite a bit more. Much important work remains to be done.

NOTES

1. This is an edited version of my comments given at the EGDI Labor Standards seminar in Stockholm, August 2001.
2. The modern theory of incomplete contracts was initiated by Grossman and Hart (1986); see Hart (1995) and Malcomson (1997) for surveys.
3. Acemoglu and Zilibotti (2001) argue that technology differences are indeed important for explaining cross-country productivity differences, but also point out that technology–skill mismatch can play a major role. The technologies that work well in highly developed countries are less productive when adopted in countries with a different skill composition (e.g., much fewer educated workers). Hence, even if new technologies were always adopted immediately, they are only fully productive if workers undertake sizeable human capital investments.
4. While there exist empirical studies of the relationship between unionization and training, it seems to me that these are not well suited answering the fundamental question asked here.

REFERENCES

Acemoglu, Daron and Fabrizio Zilibotti (2001) "Productivity Differences," *Quarterly Journal of Economics*, 116 (2), pp. 563–606.

Booth, Alison L. and Monojit Chatterji (1998) "Unions and Efficient Training," *Economic Journal*, 108 (447), pp. 328–43.

Fairris, David (1995) "Do Unionized Employers Reappropriate Rent through Worsened Workplace Safety?," *Eastern Economic Journal*, 21 (2), pp. 171–85.

Falk, Armin, Ernst Fehr and Urs Fischbacher (2002, forthcoming) "On the Nature of Fair Behavior," *Economic Inquiry*.

Grossman, Sanford and Oliver Hart (1986) "The Costs and Benefits of Ownership: A Theory of Vertical and Lateral Integration," *Journal of Political Economy*, 94 (4), pp. 691–719 .

Hart, Oliver (1995) *Firms, Contracts, and Financial Structure*, Oxford: Clarendon Press.

Malcomson, James M. (1997) "Contracts, Hold-Up and Labour Markets," *Journal of Economic Literature*, 35 (4), pp. 1916–57.

Parente, Stephen L. and Edward C. Prescott (1999) "Monopoly Rights: A Barrier to Riches," *American Economic Review*, 89 (5), pp. 1216–33.

Rodrik, Dani (1996) "Labour Standards in International Trade: Do They Matter and What Do We Do About Them?," in Robert Lawrence, Dani Rodrik, and John Whalley (eds) *Emerging Agenda for Global Trade: High Stakes for Developing Countries*, Washington, DC: Overseas Development Council.

Part IV
The Issue of Child Labor

CHAPTER 3

Child Labor: Theory, Evidence, and Policy

Drusilla K. Brown, Alan V. Deardorff, and Robert M. Stern[1]

Introduction

Over the past decade, child-labor practices in developing countries and their implications for international trade have become a focus for attention in the international arena. Pursuant to these concerns, some developing countries have adopted innovative programs designed to discourage the worst child-labor practices and to provide families and communities with incentives to reduce child labor and increase educational attainment. Additionally, some industrialized countries have considered a range of policy options, both punitive and non-punitive, intended to reduce imports of goods produced by children and to provide incentives and financial support to reduce child labor in traded and non-traded sectors. Given the increased attention to child labor and the threat of trade sanctions by industrialized countries for weak child labor protections, it is instructive to evaluate the policies that have been adopted with the *intent* of reducing overall child labor in terms of the impact they are *likely* have on the welfare of children.

There is a growing theoretical and empirical literature concerning the causes and consequences of child labor. The overriding objective of this chapter is to evaluate the policy initiatives targeted on child labor in light of the newly emerging theoretical argumentation and empirical evidence. We will focus in particular on programs to address child-labor practices, and we will attempt to evaluate these programs, given the empirical evidence concerning the primary determinants of when and why children work.

Particular attention will be given to the causes of child labor above and beyond poverty. It is widely accepted that child labor declines as per capita income rises. However, the process of economic development is a slow, and many developing countries have lost ground over the last decade both in terms of their standard of living and progress made in reducing child labor. Therefore, we would like to focus particularly on the other causes of child labor distinct from poverty and the policy remedies that theory and evidence suggest.

We begin with some of the theoretical arguments concerning family decision-making and the determinants of child labor. We then turn to the empirical evidence concerning the determinants of child labor and their implications for the types of policies that are likely to influence household decision-making in a manner that reduces the incidence of child labor and increases educational attainment. We then review the traditional methods for reducing child labor. This is followed by an overview and discussion of the likely effectiveness of recent initiatives targeting child labor by developing-country governments and initiatives underway by international agencies such as the World Bank and International Labor Organization. Next, we examine some of the motivations for including child labor on the international trade agenda and the likely implications of doing so. Conclusions follow.

Theories of Child Labor: Models of Household Decisions

The purpose of this section is to touch briefly on theories of household decision-making with regard to the employment of children. Greater emphasis will be placed on the more recent literature that addresses the role of market failure, particularly in the capital market, and its relationship to poverty. The ultimate objective of the review is to identify the household characteristics that ought to emerge in empirical analysis as statistically significant determinants of child labor.

Neoclassical models of household decision-making are commonly employed in the analysis of child labor and are typically derivative of Becker (1964). Models of household bargaining fall into two broad categories: those in which children have no bargaining power and those in which children have some intrinsic value in the family.

Children as household assets

In models in which children have no bargaining power in the household, parents make decisions that serve their own interests, without regard for the impact on the child. This class of models lends analytical support for public policies that constrain the choices that parents are allowed to make for their children, e.g., compulsory schooling, minimum age of work, a ban on bonded child labor, etc.

In this context, children are viewed strictly in terms of their value as assets. Parents first must choose the number of children they will have. They then weigh whether to invest in the quality of the child or to extract a current stream of services. Becker and Lewis (1973) argue that in the quality–quantity tradeoff, parents who choose a large number of children are less likely to invest in quality schooling. That is, the number of children and investment in the human capital of children are substitutes. Or, parents may choose to have a large number of children in order to diversify risk, formally educating some and putting the others to work.

Initial empirical analysis was quite supportive of both the quality–quantity tradeoff and the diversification hypothesis. Rosenzweig and Wolpin (1980) find that an exogenous increase in fertility lowers child quality, and Hanushek (1992) finds a tradeoff between family size and educational attainment in the United States. Indeed, there is considerable evidence that, on average, children in larger families in both developed and developing countries receive less schooling, perform more poorly on intelligence tests, and are less well nourished (Patrinos and Psacharopoulos, 1997). Closely spaced children receive the least investment (Powell and Steelman, 1993).

However, Montgomery et al. (1995) find contradictory evidence for Ghana and Cote d'Ivoire. Further, Patrinos and Psacharopoulos (1995) do not find that the number of siblings of Paraguayan children affect the level of enrolment. Nor is there a strong sibling effect in Brazil (Levison, 1991; Psacharopoulos and Arriagada, 1989). Chernichovsky (1985), studying schooling choice in rural Botswana, actually finds that family size raises educational attainment. Levison (1991) suggests that the positive correlation between family size and schooling may occur because there are decreasing returns in household production. With a large number of children available to engage in household work, the opportunity cost of education for any one child may be quite low.

Not only are child assets viewed in relation to one another, the labor of children may also be seen as a complementary input to other household capital. For example, the investment in physical capital to launch a family enterprise may be optimizing only if it can be combined with the labor of the household's children.

In fact, exploiting a household's assets may frequently require the inputs of child labor. One of the most well documented cases of complementarity concerns the work and school habits of girls whose mothers have marketable skills. Tapping the mother's human capital in the formal labor market may require her daughters to replace her contribution to home work. Thus, human capital embodied in a mother is complementary with *more* home work and *less* education for her daughters.

The poverty hypothesis

Although parental selfishness may play a role, it is a very commonly held view that child labor is fundamentally a by-product of poverty, strongly suggesting that policy should focus on economic development and increasing income (Nardinelli, 1990). Krueger (1997) notes a steep cross-country negative correlation between GDP per capita and the employment rate of 10–14 year olds in 1995. An important implication of the poverty hypothesis is that policies that focus on compelling parents to deviate from their optimizing choices may, in fact, make children worse off.

Although the poverty/child-labor link may seem obvious, Baland and Robinson (2000) formalize this idea, thus helping to isolate the precise nature of the mechanism. They take as a point of departure that all families make child-labor decisions to maximize the present discounted value of the household's income. In making child-employment decisions, parents weigh the present discounted value of the future income of an educated child against the foregone income while the child is in school. Child labor is only chosen if the return to education is not high enough to compensate families for the lost income of their children.

The obvious question then becomes "what is it about being poor that lowers the present discounted value of an education relative to current work?" In a world with perfectly functioning capital markets there are two possibilities: (1) poor people are impatient; that is, they discount the future more heavily than other families; and (2) the return to education for a poor child is lower than for children generally. A low return to education for poor children will occur if schools are far away, inadequately staffed, lack educational supplies and materials, etc. The return to education may also simply be unappreciated if the parents themselves are not educated.

A third possibility emerges when the parent's initial endowment is low relative to their child's future income (whether or not they are educated). In this case, parents would like to engage in consumption smoothing. That is, they would like to borrow against the household's future wealth to increase current consumption while lowering future consumption, thereby evening out the consumption profile of the family over time. Parents are particularly highly motivated to engage in consumption smoothing when the household's survival is threatened by a period of unemployment, drought, etc.

In such a case, parents could offer the child a deal whereby the parent borrows on behalf of the current household, expecting the child to provide the funds to repay the loan out of the income they will earn as an educated adult. The problem is that a child cannot pre-commit to compensate the parents from future income. Thus, the only option parents have for increasing current household consumption at the expense of the future is to put the child to work.

Baland and Robinson note that this type of bargaining failure occurs when the optimal bequest is negative. That is, over time, it is optimal (from some point of view) to transfer resources back in time from the future of the household to the present, rather than from the present to the future. Implicit in the Baland–Robinson analysis is the fact that child labor is a device for transferring income from the future into the present. A child who works today at the expense of acquiring an education will contribute to family income today at the expense of future productivity.

Evidence of intra-household bargaining problems of the sort identified by Baland and Robinson (2000) are found by Parsons and Goldin (1989) and Andvig (1997). Both studies find that children leave the household after receiving an education, making it difficult for parents to internalize the benefits of investing in their children. Further, and perhaps more to the point, Parsons and Goldin (1989) find from their analysis of the US 1900 Census, that working children received little of their earnings in the form of bequests. Child wages only raised current household consumption. One way to interpret this result is that working children were transferring income back to their parents. That is, the optimal bequest was negative, which is precisely the situation in which Baland and Robinson expect to observe working children.

It is important to note that while Baland and Robinson find an analytical role for poverty as a source of child labor, their analysis does not suggest that we should rely exclusively on economic development as a strategy for eradicating child labor. Rather, as we will see below, government policy can play a significant role in solving the intra-household bargaining problem.

Market failure and multiple equilibria

A second wave of models assumes that parents are altruistic and focuses on the interaction between market characteristics and child labor that point to certain market manipulations as a remedy. For example, Basu (1999) examines the case in which rigidities in the market for adult labor drive child labor. He considers a market in which the adult wage is downward rigid, giving rise to adult unemployment. Families with an unemployed adult may depend on the work of their children for survival. A policy aimed at restoring wage flexibility and improving labor-market function might lower child labor, as would a subsidy to the household during a period of unemployment.

Grootaert and Kanbur (1995) focus attention on the external benefit of an educated child on the general population. In this case, an education subsidy will help internalize the externality and may have the added benefit of reducing child labor.

Basu and Van (1998) analyze the case in which benevolent parents withdraw their children from the labor market once the adult wage reaches a critical level. Such a labor market may have two equilibria: one in which both children and adults work, giving rise to a large labor supply and low wages, and one in which only parents work, giving rise to a low labor supply and a high adult wage. A ban on child labor may have the effect of helping the high-wage, no-child-labor equilibrium emerge, thus redistributing income towards the supplying families and away from owners of other factors.

Hirshman[2] also suggests the possibility of multiple equilibria emerging when parents who put their children to work suffer a social stigma for doing so. The stigma is greater, the smaller the number of other children in the community who are working. Thus, as with Basu and Van, there may be two equilibria: one with many children working and a low social stigma attached to work and one with few children working and a high social stigma. Hirshman's analysis also suggests that a policy banning child labor might bring about the low child-labor/high social-stigma equilibrium. Similarly, it has been argued that compulsory education laws can play a role in affecting public attitudes toward child labor.

The most recent developments focus on capital-market failure. Baland and Robinson (2000) extend their approach discussed above, introducing the possibility that households might be liquidity constrained. Thus, they emphasize the importance of capital-market failure as a contributing factor to inefficient child labor.

Capital-market failure can emerge in several different guises. Consider first the case in which the present discounted value of an education is greater than the current value of a child's labor. In this case, it is clearly optimal for a family to borrow against the child's future income to finance the child's education. Or, to be more specific, it is in the interest of the child to make any requisite contribution to household income by borrowing against future income, thus freeing the child to attend school rather than work. Baland and Robinson note that the inability of the child to access the capital markets, or the inability of the child to pre-commit to repay education loans obtained by the parents on the child's behalf, may give rise to inefficiently low educational attainment.

To the extent that such intra-family bargaining failure is contributing to inefficient educational attainment, it is possible for government policy to correct the failure with properly configured educational loans to poor families. A government loan that is tied to the child's educational performance and becomes the liability of the child, rather than the parent, allows the child to access the capital markets to meet required contributions to the family. Such a loan is Pareto improving provided there is some reason to believe that the child would have voluntarily undertaken the loan if he/she had the cognitive ability to analyze the choices like an adult.

However, if parents treat their child's future as a contributing factor to their own sense of well-being, they may be willing to borrow against their own assets or future income in order to finance their child's education. In this case, a lack of collateral will prevent parents from accessing the capital markets, thus again giving rise to an inefficiently low level of education.

The dynamic implications of capital market failure have been studied by Ranjan (2001), with similar conclusions reached by Basu (1999). Ranjan considers, in particular, very poor families who would choose to educate their children if they had access to a capital market, but fail to do so due to capital-market failure. Such families produce poor, uneducated children who repeat the cycle for the next generation. In this model, a concerted effort to educate one generation of such children will pull the family away from the income level at which they depend on the labor of their children for survival. Thus, subsequent generations of the family will be able to educate their children, permanently enjoying a higher standard of living and educational attainment.

The central policy lesson of the Ranjan and Basu models is that government intervention is required for only one generation of children. For, once an educated child's future income is raised above a threshold level, the newly created parent will be able to choose education rather than child labor for the next generation.

Empirical Evidence on the Determinants of Child Labor

The purpose of this section is to review the empirical evidence on the determinants of child labor. The theoretical models considered above suggest several potential motivations for putting children to work. As noted in each case, knowing the cause of child labor is fundamental to making effective policy.

Evidence to support a view of selfish parents is provided by Burra (1995) and Parsons and Goldin (1989). Moehling (1995) also finds that the bargaining position of the children in the household varies with the child's contribution to income. Gupta's (1997) analysis of working children in West Bengal, India, suggests that children have very little bargaining power in the household. Thus, there is some evidence of at least a little *play* in the resources that a family can devote to the welfare of their children. At the margin, a properly configured policy may push some families to increase the investment they make in their children.

Household decision-making and child labor

In order to disentangle the conflicting determinants of child labor and to assess the relative importance of each of the factors influencing child-labor decisions, it is necessary to empirically estimate household decision-making in the context of a formal analytical model. In the most careful of such studies, households are assumed to use a sequential process for making child-labor decisions. In the first stage, parents decide whether a child should work. In the second stage parents decide whether the child will work part-time or fulltime. In the third stage, the type of work is chosen. Sequential probit analysis is undertaken on household survey data to identify the family characteristics that are determining the probability that a child works, the probability of schooling, and the type of work. Typically, such analysis will begin with the specific characteristics of the child such as age and gender. Parental characteristics such as educational attainment, age, and employment status are also included.

Household characteristics include, first and foremost, some measure of household income. Due to problems with endogeneity of income, most analysts include measures of household capital, welfare, poverty status, total expenditures or expenditure on food, in lieu of household income.

Household assets are also important in the absence of access to formal capital markets. Households that want to borrow against the future may be able to tap internal assets. The presence of the father in the household, the presence of an older sibling in the household (particularly a brother), the capacity of the mother to engage in market work, or property associated with a family enterprise can all be thought of as assets that can be drawn upon even if the family has no access to formal capital markets. For this reason, the presence of such household assets might be expected to lower child labor. Consequently, gender, birth order, the presence of older siblings, the mother's work opportunities, and the presence of a family enterprise are also important determinants of whether a child works, the type of work undertaken, the number of hours worked, and whether part-time schooling is an option.

The availability of schools in terms of quality, proximity, and cost will also affect child labor and schooling choices. Household expenditures on schooling are typically available from survey evidence. However, measuring school quality is extremely difficult. At best, some studies have evidence on the integrity of the school structure, whether or not the school is open most days of the week, and other services available to the general community such as running water or electricity.

Nearly every study includes some other characteristics such as region of the country, urban vs. rural, and other cultural characteristics including religion.

Table 3.1 Sequential probit analysis for selected countries in Latin America: Probability that a child works
Stage 1:

	Colombia		Bolivia	Peru
	Rural	*Urban*		
Year	1993	1993	1993	1991
Statistical technique		Sequential Probit		Logit
Population sampled	7–17 years	12–17 years	7–17 years	7–18 years
Child characteristics				
Age	7.72	7.16	1.76	
Male	9.03	10.86		3.62
Parent characteristics				
Age head of HH	1.98			
Father's education	−1.98	−1.02		−0.40
Mother's education	−1.95	−1.79	−0.37	
Mother working?	7.30	3.84		
HH characteristics				
Log expenditures	−10.81	−18.68	−4.63	
Rural				15.08
Indigenous				7.76
Family Enterprise	7.77			
Siblings				
Aged 0–6				2.70
Sisters 10–15	−13.53	−14.58	−4.76	
16+	−4.88	−8.91	−0.29	
Brothers 6–9	−6.69			
10–15	−16.72	−17.26	−3.96	
16+	−5.15	−8.77		
Cost of schooling	−8.41	−7.59	6.16	
Observations	1,829	9,821	4,730	1,727

Entries are probability derivatives at the mean of the explanatory variables. Variables significant at the 10% level.
Sources: Adapted from Cartwright, 1999, pp. 91–100, Cartwright and Patrinos, 1999, p. 126 and Patrinos and Psacharopoulos, 1997, p. 401.

Determinants of work and school

Consider first the decision as to whether children should work at all. Empirical results for Colombia, Bolivia, and Peru are reported in table 3.1. Each study uses a slightly different set of explanatory variables. Those significant at the 10 percent level are listed in the corresponding columns. Regression results reported in table 3.2 are probability derivatives evaluated at the mean of the explanatory variables.

Table 3.2 Sequential probit and logit analysis for selected countries in Latin America: Probability of fulltime work
Stage 2:

	Colombia		Bolivia	Peru
	Rural	Urban		
Year	1993	1993	1993	1991
Statistical technique		Sequential probit		Logit
Dependent variable	Probability of fulltime work	Probability of fulltime work	Probability of fulltime work	Age–grade distortion
Population Sampled	7–17 years	12–17 years	7–17 years	7–18 years
Child characteristics				
Age	6.78	4.59	3.64	22.20
Male	−31.35	−13.75		2.67
Parent characteristics				
Father's education		−1.10		−1.53
Mother's education		−1.21	−3.10	
Mother working?	−12.95	−8.25	−33.48	
Father union member			−30.47	
HH characteristics				
Log expenditures	−8.56		−34.88	
Family enterprise	−14.11			
No. of rooms				−2.84
Rural				11.11
Indigenous language			−27.42	−9.05
Siblings				
Sisters 0–5 years	−10.71			6.15*
10–15			−12.87	2.55*
16+		−5.70	−9.54	2.84*
Brothers 0–5 years	12.89	−7.06		
10–15		−3.90		
16+		−1.02	−21.49	
Cost of schooling	8.51	8.92		
Private school				−6.93
Observations	624	1,915	590	1,727

*Brothers and sisters.
Entries are probability derivatives at the mean of the explanatory variables.
Variables significant at the 10% level.
Sources: Adapted from Cartwright, 1999, pp. 91, 94 , Cartwright and Patrinos, 1999, p. 126 and Patrinos and Psacharopoulos, 1997, p. 399.

Cartwright (1999) analyzes 1993 survey data for rural and urban children in Colombia. As we will see below, gender usually plays a significant role in work and school decisions, but the role of gender varies across continents. In the case of Colombia, rural boys are 9 percent more likely to work than are girls. The age of the child is also significant in virtually every country studied. In Colombia, the probability of work increases by 8 percentage points for each year a child ages. As the child ages and becomes more productive, the opportunity cost of education rises, making work more attractive.

Poverty also plays a substantial role in driving children to work. For a one percent increase in household expenditure in Colombia, the probability of work declines by 0.11 percentage points for a rural child and 0.19 percentage points for an urban child.

Also, as expected, household assets are an important determinant of whether children work, although the direction depends on the nature of the asset. The presence of a household enterprise for rural families makes it easier to draw children into work. Children in rural Colombia whose families operate a household enterprise are nearly 8 percent more likely to work than are other rural children. The fact that the mother is working may also make child labor in the household necessary. Rural children are 7 percent more likely to work and urban children are 4 percent more likely to work if their mothers also work. These are household assets that are most effectively tapped when children are employed in the household work. Thus, for these two household assets, the asset and child labor are complementary.

The role of siblings is particularly interesting. There is little evidence that siblings increase child labor supply. The presence of younger siblings does not affect the probability of working, so older children do not appear to be engaged in childcare. However, the presence of other siblings in the same age range plays a significant role in *lowering* the probability of work, and the presence of older children in the household also lowers the probability of any one child working.

These results certainly provide very little evidence for a diversification in the investment in children. Siblings within an age-range, 10−15 years old, increase the probability that each other are in school. This is far more consistent with the notion of decreasing returns to household production than diversification.

One possible way to preserve the diversification hypothesis is to assume that parents with a single child diversify by having the child work part-time and in school part-time. Once additional children are born, diversification can be accomplished by putting some children to work exclusively and some in school exclusively. If this is the case, the presence of additional siblings should have the twin effects of increasing the probability of full-time schooling and increasing the probability of full-time work. That is, the larger the family, the less likely we are to observe a work–school combination.

However, as we will see below, the presence of other siblings in the household also typically *lowers* the probability of full-time work. The negative impact of other siblings in the household on full-time work is particularly notable for urban Colombia. The only exception is that very small brothers in rural Colombian households *increase* the probability that their older siblings will work full-time. Cartwright was somewhat skeptical of this result because the presence of very young sisters *lowers* the probability of full-time work for older rural Colombian siblings. She was unable to account for the distinction.

Nor does there appear to be evidence of a quantity-quality tradeoff. The only possible way to interpret the results in favor of the tradeoff hypothesis is that parents are putting their first-born to work and then investing in formal education for the younger children. However, this configuration defies conventional wisdom. Hanushek (1992) and others argue that appearing high in the birth order has significant advantages. Parents typically invest in the first child since first-borns have a higher probability of being in a small family than subsequent children.

It seems far more compelling to interpret the presence of older siblings in the household as evidence of household capital on which the parents can draw in lieu of tapping formal capital markets, making it possible to keep younger children in school full-time. This is an important conclusion because it lends support for the notion that improved access to capital markets for families with limited household assets might reduce the incidence of child labor.

Furthermore, the evidence also suggests that increasing the size of each cohort of children in the family, thereby increasing sibling density, lowers the probability of child work. We would expect the opposite if parents with a large number of closely spaced children were planning to put them to work rather than in school. Thus, we have far more evidence of decreasing returns to household production rather than a quality–quantity tradeoff. Children with a large number of similarly aged siblings share household chores and then also attend school.

We will also find that parental education plays a persistent, powerful and negative role in the family's decision to put a child to work. The more years of school both mothers and fathers have, the more likely they are to devote their children's time exclusively to school, even controlling for household income. This effect is more ubiquitous than any other in determining child labor. In the case of Colombia, as noted in table 3.1, the parental education effect is particularly pronounced. Each year of *each* parents' education lowers the probability that their child will work full time by 2 percentage points in rural Colombia. Note that the parental education effect exists above and beyond the contribution that the educated parent's human capital makes to family income. Thus, when parents become educated, this appears to impart some informational externality that affects the decisions that parents make for their children.

Finally, the cost of schooling in Colombia has a negative effect on child labor. That is, the more expensive school is, the less likely it is that the child will work. Cartwright suggests that the cost of schooling in this case is a proxy for school quality.

Results for the second stage of the estimation are reported table 3.2. The second stage includes only those children who are working and attempts to determine which of these children work fulltime. For children who work, the decision to work fulltime depends on many of the same variables as the decision whether to work at all, although there are some important exceptions and nuances. For example, even though boys are more likely to work, girls are more likely to work full-time, both in market work and household production. Further, there is some evidence that when children are taken out of school to work full-time, they are caring for very young male siblings.

It is also important to note the subtle role that a family enterprise and mother's work have on children in Colombia. Both of these household assets are complementary with some child labor. However, they also appear to make it possible to combine work and school. So, children in families with a household enterprise and/or a mother who works are more likely to be working than other children, but they are not put to work full-time. A household enterprise gives the family some flexibility in when and how hard their children work and also allows parents to supervise their children themselves. In such cases, child labor may not seem so egregious and may more readily be combined with formal schooling.

Cartwright and Patrinos (1999) find somewhat similar results for Bolivia as also shown in tables 3.1 and 3.2. Poverty plays a central role in driving child labor. The effect of poverty is mitigated only by a mother's educational attainment and the presence of other older siblings in the household. However the cost of schooling is also key. The more expensive that schooling is, the more likely children are to work, as one would expect.

But, for Peru, as analyzed by Patrinos and Psacharopoulos (1997), we have a dramatically different story. As can be seen from the last column of table 3.1, boys are more likely to work than girls, and the father's education has a small negative impact on the decision to work. There is also some evidence that older children are caring for younger children, but this effect does not appear to be driven by the mother's employment. What is noteworthy in Peru is that *none of the potential measures of household assets or income appear to play a significant role.* This is quite a surprising result in light of the strongly held popular notion that child labor is most importantly a consequence of poverty. (Similar results for Peru are found by Ray (2000).)

In order to tease out the more subtle aspects of Peruvian child labor, Patrinos and Psacharopoulos also try to determine why a child fails to advance in school. They use as a dependent variable a measure of the age–grade distortion, which indicates the extent to which a child is failing to advance through school with his/her cohort. Results are reported in the last column of table 3.2.

Neither family income *nor whether the child is employed* played a role in success in school. Neither of these variables is statistically significant in explaining the age–grade distortion. The only income or asset variable that does appear to be important is the number of rooms in the home. Children who fall behind in school have a large number of siblings who are also in school. Thus, child labor and educational attainment do not appear to be connected in Peru, with only one exception. Older Peruvian children are, in some cases, taken out of school to care for younger children. Otherwise, the type of work engaged in by Peruvian children does not appear to be a competitor with schooling for a child's time or intellectual energy. Consequently, it is not surprising that income and household asset variables play little role in the decision to work.

Patrinos and Psacharopoulos hypothesize the reason that Peruvian children can combine work and school without ill effect is that work makes it possible to afford to attend school. However, it is equally possible that these results point to the poor quality of school. Perhaps the value of schooling is so low that parents do not see school attendance in financial terms. The role of poor school quality should not be understated. Peru provides a particularly striking example. The deficiencies in the facilities, supplies, teacher salaries, and training seriously undermine the value of the time that children spend in school. A third of all schools have only one teacher, a problem most common in rural areas. In rural Amazon, it is typically the case that there is only one teacher to handle 50 to 60 students in four to six different grades. The poorest schools may not have even the most fundamental educational supplies such as books. In rural areas, 83 percent of schools have no running water, electricity or indoor plumbing. Even in metropolitan Lima, only 60 percent of schools have electricity (Ministerio de Educacion, 1993).

Given the deficiencies in the public education system, some children work for the explicit purpose of earning the tuition for *private* education. For example, in Ecuador, one in ten working children studies in a private school.

It is also important to note that the weak impact of child labor on academic performance in Peru is not evident elsewhere. For example, Psacharopoulos (1997) finds that a working child in Bolivia is 10 percent more likely to fail a grade than an unemployed child. Similar results are obtained for Venezuela.

Turning to evidence from Africa, we find several differences, one of which is that the cultural attitudes toward gender, work and school vary across continents. Canagarajah and Coulombe (1998), analyzing the work and school choices in Ghana, find that girls are more likely to work than boys and less likely to attend school, as can be seen from the first column of table 3.3. The differential rate is directly attributable to homework performed by girls. However, as with Peru, household income does not play a strongly positive role in whether children work. In fact, the correlation between income and child labor follows an inverted-U shape. Thus, child labor falls with income only in the upper range of the income distribution. This relationship is confirmed by Bhalotra and Heady (1998) and Levison (1991).

Table 3.3   Probability of child work and schooling for selected countries in Africa

Year	Ghana 1991–92		Cote d'Ivoire 1993			Zambia 1993
	Probability of		Probability of			
Dependant variable	Some work	Some school	School only	School and work	Work only	Probability of school
Sample population	7–14 year olds		Urban 7–17 year olds			7–14 year olds
Statistical method	Bivariate probit		Sequential probit and bivariate logit			
	Beta-coefficient		Probability derivatives at the variable mean			Beta-coefficient
Child characteristics						
Age	0.85	0.66		21.05	9.33	−0.20
Female	0.23	−0.37	−29.80	−16.40	−15.58	−0.22
Grade						0.30
Married						−2.94
Parent characteristics						
HH head age			2.91	2.73		
Father's education	−0.29	1.26	1.48	1.84		0.06
Mother's education		0.75		3.54		
Mother working?			10.63			
Girl with working mother					18.25	
Father in formal sector						0.15
Proportion of non-head of HH working						−1.59
Father in household		0.32				
Head not working						−0.29
Household characteristics						
Log expenditures/capita			0.28			1.55
Assets						0.16
Savings						0.06
Land						−0.36
Family enterprise	−0.22		−10.04	−12.62	9.22	
Protestant	0.26	0.61				
Catholic		0.46				
Other Christian		0.40				
Muslim		0.17				
Agriculture/animals		−0.34			29.22	0.55
Rural		−0.26				0.30
Rain forest	0.45	0.62				
Poor			−8.63	−12.51		
Other household members						
Boys 6–9				4.6		
10–15			3.65			
16–17				13.93		
Girls 6–9					6.33	
10–15		0.12	4.39	9.02		
15+	−0.21					
Aged 60+		−0.11				
Cost of schooling	0.16	0.11				
Distance to school						−0.03
Households	3,811		1,177			6,372

Variables significant at the 10% level.
Sources: Canagarajah and Coulombe, 1998, p. 36, Grootaert, 1999, pp. 44–5 and Jensen and Nielsen, 1997, p. 420.

We do see evidence that family assets influence school and work decisions. The presence of a *non-farm* family enterprise and older women in the household lower the probability of work for younger children. However, children are more likely to work if the parents are self-employed farmers. Years of parental education and the presence of older siblings also lower the probability of work and raise the probability of some schooling. Interestingly, school fees increase both the probability of work and the probability of school attendance. This strongly suggests both that children need to work to pay school fees, but that more expensive schools are higher quality.

Given the indication that household assets, as distinct from income, are playing a role in child labor decisions, it would be useful to have some more direct evidence from financial assets rather than simply trying to draw inferences from the presence of human capital. Jensen and Nielsen (1997) include several asset measures in their study of schooling decisions in Zambia. Results are presented in the last column of table 3.3. As in Ghana, girls are less likely to be in school than boys. This is particularly the case for girls who are married.

We also see some other familiar results. For example, educated fathers are more likely to school their children. Families with a wage earner are also more likely to school their children. However, children in households with more than one family member working other than the child are considerably less likely to be in school.

Income, again, has a strong positive effect on schooling, as do financial assets and household capital. However, if the family holds its assets in the form of land, children are less likely to be in school. Land and child labor appear to be complementary inputs in Zambia. Note, though, that children in the rural sector and whose family members work in the agricultural sector are more likely to be in school. It may be that such families have more flexibility in combining agricultural work and schooling. However, Jensen and Nielsen also suggest that rural schools may be of higher quality than urban schools, thus making schooling a more attractive choice for agricultural families.

Much of the same character of child labor in Zambia is evident for Cote d'Ivoire, as well. Grootaert (1999) uses sequential probit and bivariate techniques to analyze the sequence of child labor decisions for children aged 7 to 17. Results for urban children are reported in the middle columns of table 3.3. Grootaert first isolates the household characteristics for families that send their children to school only. Next, of those children who do some work, children are sorted between those who combine work and school and those who work only. Finally, of those who only work, children are divided between market/family-enterprise workers and home-workers. Several of the standard results are in evidence in Grootaert's estimates. Girls are 30 percent less likely to be in school fulltime and are also less likely to combine work and school and less likely to work in the market than boys.

Educated parents are more likely to send their children to school fulltime or to combine work and school than to put children to work only. Each year of a father's education lowers the probability of dropping out of school by 1.8 percentage points, and each year of a mother's education lowers the probability of dropping out by 3.5 percentage points. In fact, parental education is more important than any other variable in deterring fulltime employment by children. For rural children the impact is even more pronounced. (See Grootaert (1999) for rural results.) Each year of a father's education lowers the probability of dropping out by 7 percentage points and each year of a mother's education lowers the probability of dropping out by 3 percentage points. However, in both cases, the effect is weaker for girls than for boys.

Poor families are less likely to send their children to school or combine school with work. Urban families in the lowest income quintile are nearly 9 percent less likely to send their children to school fulltime and over 12 percent less likely to have children combine school with work rather than drop out completely.

Grootaert argues that his results suggest a strong role for income in determining child labor. However, he does not enter income directly into the equation due to problems with endogeneity, preferring instead to rely on measures of household capital. Coulombe (1998), evaluating a similar data set, finds that income, corrected for endogeneity, plays only a small role. Each one percent increase in household income lowers the probability of child labor by 0.3 percent.

The impact of household assets on child work, once again, depends on the nature of those assets. In Cote d'Ivoire, the presence of a family enterprise lowers the probability of school only and the probability of a work–school combination. One possible explanation is that a family that decides to invest in a family enterprise is doing so with the expectation that the children will work in the family enterprise and thus will not need an education.

Grootaert suspects that the household enterprise is a proxy for poverty, as most household enterprises in Cote d'Ivoire are run by very poor families. However, some corroborating evidence of the complementarity between child labor and household assets is offered by Coulombe (1998). In rural Cote d'Ivoire, the probability of working increases and the probability of school attendance decreases with the number of acres of land owned by the household.

The family enterprise also interacts in an unusual way with the work of mothers and daughters. In Cote d'Ivoire, it appears to be the case that mothers who work in a family enterprise draw their daughters in, working side-by-side both in the enterprise and in household production. Otherwise, unlike in some other studies, a working mother *increases* the probability of fulltime schooling.

In Cote d'Ivoire we see another by now familiar result. The presence of other work-age children in the household increases the chances of schooling and lowers the probability of work at all stages of decision-making. The distance to school also plays a role for rural children. The absence of a school in the local community increases the probability of dropping out for rural children by 18 percentage points.

Several studies above have pointed to the importance of school quality as a determinant of child labor. However, few studies incorporate any measure of school quality. Dreze and Kingdon (2000), in their study of child labor in India, do not have measures of school quality, but they do have some indication of desirable school characteristics that might be correlated with school quality, such as whether the building's roof is waterproof. They also include evidence as to whether the community has made a commitment to building infrastructure, such as whether homes have electricity, piped water, and phone service. The impacts of these variables on the probability of enrolment for boys and girls are reported in the first two columns of table 3.4. (Ray (2000) found similar results for Pakistan.)

Although factors such as school quality and village characteristics do not impact schooling decisions for boys, they are quite important for girls. In addition, the availability of a school-lunch program, which increases the short-term return to school attendance, and a positive attitude toward school attendance both increase the probability of school enrolment for girls.

Glewwe and Jacoby (1994), in their analysis of Zambia, also find an important role for school quality. For example, they find that repairing classrooms in schools that are unusable when it rains is more valuable than providing additional instructional material. Hanushek and Lavy (1994) find that Egyptian students attending higher quality schools tend to stay longer in school and complete more grades. Finally, San Martin (1996) finds that labor-force participation (LFP) rates for children aged 10 to 14 rise with the primary-school, student–teacher ratio across countries.

The demand for child labor

Up to this point we have focused on the supply side of child labor. On the demand side, it is sometimes argued that the demand for children derives from their special characteristics that make them indispensable for production; the so-called "nimble fingers" argument. Some employers claim that only children with small fingers have the ability to make fine hand-knotted carpets, pick delicate jasmine flowers, or scramble through narrow tunnels. However, like the argument that children work because parents are selfish, analysts have lost interest in the "nimble fingers" hypothesis. It is almost certainly the case that if employers had to pay the true social cost of employing

Table 3.4 Sequential probit analysis for selected countries in Asia

	India		Philippines
	Boys	Girls	
Year			
Statistical technique	Binary logit		Sequential probit
Age of sample population	5–12 years old		10–17 years old
Dependent variable	Probability of enrollment		Probability of work
Child characteristics			
Age			0.024
5 years old	−0.233	−0.317	
8 years old		−0.101	
10 years old		−0.117	
11 years old		−0.131	
12 years old		−0.175	
Parent characteristics			
Age head of household			
Father's education	0.009	0.020	
Mother's education		0.025	
Mother working?			0.011
Mother of girl working?			0.019
HH head of girl working?			−0.020
Female HH head working?			0.029
Household characteristics			
Poor			0.038
Rural			0.024
Member of caste or tribe	−0.044	−0.119	
Other backward caste	−0.042	−0.116	
Believe girls should be educated	0.097	0.303	
Male head of household			0.031
Married head of household			−0.027
Assets		0.006	
Family enterprise			0.278
Cow/goat		−0.011	
Siblings			
#children/#adults in HH		−0.050	
School characteristics			
School lunch program		0.149	
Building waterproof		0.146	
School open previous week		0.111	
Village characteristics			
Elect., P.O., Water, Phone		0.036	
Women's association		0.102	
Observations	1,405	1,067	23,062

Variables significant at the 10% level.

Entries are beta-coefficients of the explanatory variables.

Sources: Adapted from Dreze and Kingdon, 2000, table 4, and Sakalariou and Lall, 1999, p. 146.

children, they would find technological innovations to replace child workers. In fact, Levison et al. (1996) and Anker and Barge (1998) find that children are not necessary for the Indian carpet industry. Both sets of authors argue that it is more likely that children are attractive employees in spite of their low productivity because they are less aware of their rights and more willing to take orders, do monotonous work, and are less likely to steal. We can draw other bits evidence on the demand side as well. For example, Parsons and Goldin (1989) note that the LFP rates for children did not vary across sectors, as would be expected if children had some special characteristics that made them particularly valuable to industry. First, a cross-state analysis of the US 1900 Census of Population reveals that the LFP rates for males aged 10 to 15 was not significantly higher in manufacturing and mining than in agriculture, although, it should be noted that the LFP rate for girls aged 10 to 15 was higher in industry. However, those industries in which one would expect the special features of children to place them in high demand, such as textiles, boots and shoes, paper, and clothing, did not employ substantially more children than iron, steel, and mining. Rather, the industry in which a child was employed was overwhelmingly determined by the industry in which the parent was employed.

Concluding remarks on the determinants of child labor

Parental education

Parental education plays a persistent and significant role in lowering the incidence of child labor, above and beyond the impact on family income. The results presented on this are quite robust, as reviewed by Strauss and Thomas (1995). In some cases, such as Cote d'Ivoire, the parent's level of education overwhelms all other family characteristics.

Several theoretical contributions on the determinants of child labor emphasize the importance of educating a single generation of parents and its long-term implications for decision-making for future generations. The theoretical mechanism draws attention to the impact that an education has on the parent's human capital and income. That is, educated parents earn enough income to afford to educate their own children.

However, the empirical evidence very strongly suggests that a parent's education affects future generations above and beyond the impact on household wealth. There are several possible explanations. For example, educated parents have a greater appreciation of the value of an education or uneducated parents may simply want to believe that the human-capital decisions made by their own parents were correct. In any event, cost–benefit analysis of programs that concentrate on educational attainment must look beyond the impact that an education has on a future parent's income stream and incorporate the implications for human-capital formation by subsequent generations.

School quality

Several studies point to the importance of school quality as an important determinant of schooling and work. However, school quality is virtually never measured directly in any of the studies discussed. It is quite possibly the case that when a family poised to move children out of the workforce and into school fails to do so, the culprit is poor schools. Poor school quality is found to be weakly important in rural Ghana (Lavy, 1996) and very important for Africa generally (Bonnet, 1993). It should be noted though that even if poor school quality lowers the value of formal education, there is an abundance of empirical evidence across Latin America, Africa, and Asia that the return to education is still quite high and more than offsets the foregone income of children in school.

Household income

The role of household income in determining child-labor decisions needs further study. Clearly, there is a very strong cross-country negative correlation between child labor and per capita GDP. However, the role of family income is not so predominant in explaining variations within a community. We did observe, for some but not all countries, that household expenditures play a central role in child-labor decisions. This evidence suggests that there are some external effects across families that make it difficult to put children in school even as income rises or, equally, difficult to put children to work when income is critically low. In particular, none of the studies does a very good job of measuring school quality. The role of cost of schooling, when this is measured, suggests that it may be acting as a proxy for quality. In this case, parents who have the financial ability to forgo the income from the children may still not choose schooling if the quality of schools is very poor. It is also the case that regional dummies and cultural characteristics such as religion or caste have some significance, suggesting a nontrivial role for cultural factors.

Finally, it is important to reconsider when economic theory tells us to expect poor parents to put their children to work. Recall that, as argued by Baland and Robinson, child labor is a device for transferring resources from the future into the present. Children who work do not invest in human capital that will make them more productive in the future. A family will choose to make this inter-temporal shift in household resources when current income is low *relative* to future income. Thus, it is not the absolute level of family income that matters for the child-labor decision but, rather, the current level *relative* to future income. There may be families that are quite poor and do not have any reason to expect any change in the future. Such families have no reason to attempt to consumption-smooth by putting their children to work.

Household assets

Household assets play an important role in the child-labor decision. One might expect that the more assets a family has, the lower the probability of child labor. However, there are a number of assets that require a complementary input of labor, and families may expect to get that labor from their children. Tapping the human capital of mothers in the family also requires an increase in child-labor inputs in home production. Thus, a strategy of increasing access to capital markets may not always lower child labor, at least in the short run.

Nevertheless, the significant role of household assets lends some evidence to the possibility that incomplete credit markets give rise to inefficiently high levels of child labor. For example, the presence of older children in the home considerably reduces the probability of child labor. Note that there is a measurable impact *above and beyond* the contribution that older siblings make to family income. This is particularly the case for older brothers, who embody the greatest human capital. In addition, a parent's education reduces child labor for reasons other than the impact of education on the parent's productivity. It is possible that a parent's education is viewed as a marketable asset, or it may be a reflection of the informational externalities associated with the value of formal education.

What is not clear is why family assets matter. On the one hand, households with assets can more readily weather adverse events. That is, these assets provide the household with the ability to manage uncertainty and, as a consequence, child labor is not required for this purpose. However, families with assets may also have more access to capital markets or can, themselves, fund a child's education without a formal loan. That is, household assets help families transfer household income intertemporally.

In either case, expanding access to formal capital markets to families who otherwise lack collateral may lead to a reduction in LFP rates for children. However, it is also the case that placing constraints on household decision-making, such as mandatory schooling, may at least inhibit the family from turning to internal assets that can be accessed only if children work more. Providing working mothers with firm-level childcare may also help reduce the reliance on older daughters to care for their younger siblings.

Age of child

It is clear that older children are more likely to work than younger children. As children grow older and acquire skills, the opportunity cost of schooling rises. This is particularly the case for adolescent boys, who are increasingly able to perform physically demanding tasks as they approach maturity. Thus, it appears to be the case that it will be more challenging and costly from a policy point of view to induce older male children to remain in school.

The role of siblings

The role of siblings in the household does not appear to be a major deterrent to schooling *once we control for other household characteristics.* The only exception is that there is some evidence that in some cases, mid-aged children are caring for younger siblings.

When evidence that older children are caring for younger children is combined with the fact that the presence of an older sibling in the house generally raises the probability of schooling, it is possible to make a case that parents are diversifying their human-capital investments in their child assets. The oldest children acquire human capital in the form of on-the-job training and the youngest children receive formal education. However, this interpretation of the evidence does not accord well with the other significant result: the presence of siblings in the same age range tends to *raise* the probability of school and lower the probability of work.

Rather it seems more natural to, first, view children in the middle age range, 10 to 14, as complements, sharing housework and schooling opportunities. Second, when we observe older children making schooling possible for their younger siblings, this is likely evidence that older siblings help relax the liquidity constraint in the presence of capital-market failure. Third, when we observe mid-aged children caring for younger siblings, it is to help the family make optimal use of the mother's human capital in the form of marketable skills. Thus, policies that focus on lowering fertility may not be particularly effective in reducing child labor.

To the extent that parents diversify their child assets, this appears to occur along gender lines. In Latin America, parents are more likely to engage in the formal schooling of their daughters whereas in Africa parents are more likely to school their sons.

Needs of industry

Finally, we see little evidence that child labor is driven by the needs of industry. Children are far more likely to be working in a rural setting rather than an urban setting where factories are located. In addition, LFP rates rise with a child's age, strongly suggesting that the productivity of a child increases, the larger and stronger the child is. If child workers were valued for their small stature and tiny fingers, we should have observed the opposite. To the extent that child labor is a demand-side phenomenon, it appears to occur primarily within the household. Families with a household enterprise or a large tract of land tend to want to put their children to work. That is, the household's physical assets are most efficiently employed when the child's time is used as a complementary input.

Traditional Policies Targeting Child Labor and Education

We now turn to an examination of some traditional strategies for reducing child labor and increasing school attendance. As discussed in Engerman (2001), the initial strategies for circumscribing child labor in industrial England included limits on hazardous work, hours of work, minimum age of work, a prohibition against night work and minimum educational attainment for working children, and strategies to promote general economic growth.

Promotion of economic growth

Given the strong correlation between economic growth and the decline in child labor, some have argued that policies targeted explicitly on child labor are ill-conceived. There is certainly an abundance of evidence both that household income is an important determinant of whether and how much children work in developing countries, as well as a strong negative correlation between per capita GDP and income growth both across countries and across time. However, while economic growth undoubtedly offers the greatest promise for helping children in the long run, the well-being of today's children and perhaps even economic growth itself may depend on getting children out of the labor force and into schools *today*.

Minimum age and compulsory education

In the international arena, child-labor practices are also regulated by ILO Convention 29 that calls for the abolition of forced labor and Convention 138 that provides for a minimum age of employment. According to the language of Convention 138, children should not enter the labor market before having completed compulsory education or having reached the age of 15. Additional provisions allow for light work beginning at age 13 and hazardous work beginning at age 18. Furthermore, developing countries may permit light work at the age of 12 and non-hazardous work at age 14. Indeed, regulating minimum age and compulsory education has become the most common strategy globally for limiting child labor. Typically, children are required to attend school until the age of between 14 and 16 and are permitted to begin working at the age of 14.

There are several theoretical justifications for compulsory schooling and minimum age of work laws. Certainly if there is evidence that parents are overly selfish when making decisions concerning investing in the human capital of their children or if there is an external effect of education of the sort argued by Grootaert and Kanbur (1995), then requiring parents to provide for more education than they would freely choose can be justified on both equity and efficiency grounds. We might also be able to justify constraining family choice if parents are making school/work decisions to diversify the human-capital investment in their children. It may be legitimate to prevent parents from schooling some of their children and putting others to work on equity grounds if on-the-job training is less valuable than formal schooling once the child grows to adulthood.

In addition, Basu and Van's (1998) multiple-equilibrium argument in support of a ban on child labor can be implemented by establishing laws regulating minimum age of work with monitoring by examining school-attendance records. Finally, to the extent that labor standards established in the international arena require countries to control child labor, presumably all countries attempting to be in compliance with international standards would pass and attempt to enforce compulsory schooling and minimum age-of-work laws.

Minimum age of employment and years of compulsory education are reported for a selection of countries in table 3.5. We also report labor force participation rates for children covered by the legislation. Needless to say, many families in developing countries do not comply with the law. In Latin America, the LFP rate for children aged 5 to 14 is 17 percent even though in nearly all countries children are not legally permitted to work until the age of 14. A similar situation exists throughout Asia, in which the LFP rate for children aged 5 to 15 is 21 percent. In Africa, over 40 percent of 5 to 14-year olds are working even though the minimum age of employment is typically 14 years or even higher. Although these age ranges overlap somewhat with the ages of legal work, these numbers nonetheless indicate a good deal of illegal child employment.

Similarly, Krueger (1997) presents evidence from the 1990–91 waves of the World Values Survey[3] in which respondents were asked for the age at which they completed (or will complete) full-time education. His results are reported in table 3.6 for individuals born between 1959 and 1974 for a select group of countries. These results clearly indicate that while compliance is

Table 3.5 Child labor and education. Labor force participation rates, minimum age of work, and compulsory education

| Region | Child labor force participation | | Minimum age for work | | Compulsory education ages |
	Age range	Rate	Basic	Hazardous	
Africa	5–14	41.0			
Egypt	6–14	12.0	14	15–17	6–13
Kenya	10–14	41.3	16	16–18	
South Africa	10–14	4.3	15	18	7–15
Tanzania	10–14	39.5	12–18	18	7–13
Asia	5–14	21.0			
Bangladesh	5–14	19.1	12–15	18	6–10
India	5–14	5.4	14	14–18	
Nepal	5–14	41.7	14	16	
Pakistan	5–14	8.0	14	14–21	
Philippines	5–14	10.6	15	18	6–11
Thailand	10–14	16.2	15	18	6–11
Latin America	5–14	17.0			
Brazil	5–14	12.8	14	18–21	7–14
Guatemala	7–14	4.1	14	16	6–15
Mexico	12–14	17.3	14	16–18	6–14
Nicaragua	10–14	9.9	14	18	7–12
Peru	6–14	4.1	12–16	18	6–16
Europe	5–14				
Turkey	6–14	12.6	15	18	6–13

Source: Adapted from USDOL, 1998, pp. 14, 39, 57.

Table 3.6 Percentage of children leaving school, by age, for selected countries, 1959–74 birth cohort

School leaving age	Mexico	Argentina	Brazil	Nigeria	Chile	India	Portugal	UK	USA
12 or younger	25.2	6.6	80.2	4.2	2.4	40.5	17.4	0.0	0.6
13	1.3	5.9	5.8	2.0	2.0	4.2	7.4	0.4	0.2
14	1.8	5.9	3.7	7.5	2.7	5.1	10.7	0.0	0.0
15	5.1	3.5	3.5	8.6	3.7	3.2	4.6	5.3	1.8
16	4.0	4.5	2.1	6.4	5.2	3.6	5.4	50.1	2.6
17	3.8	10.8	2.1	6.6	12.3	4.3	4.6	10.3	15.0
18	7.8	16.0	1.0	14.3	6.5	6.5	7.8	11.2	29.7
19	5.3	8.0	0.7	7.8	10.4	4.9	0.0	0.0	4.4
20	6.5	4.2	0.4	8.5	8.1	4.5	10.6	7.4	4.9
21 or older	39.1	34.5	0.4	34.1	31.3	23.3	31.6	15.2	40.8

Source: Adapted from Krueger, 1997, table 3.

the norm in high-income countries, compulsory-education laws have little discernible effect in low-income countries.

In the United Kingdom, the law was changed in 1947, raising the age from 14 to 15, and then again in 1973, raising the age from 15 to 16. For each cohort, the modal age at which children left school coincided with the legal requirement and no more than 5 percent of children left school before the legal age.

However, when the law is somehow inconsistent with the equilibrium level of education, there is little effect. For example, Brazil increased the compulsory school age from 11 to 14 in 1971. Yet 85 percent of children still left school to join the work force before reaching the age of 14 whether or not they were covered by the revised regulation.

Furthermore, the evidence of compliance is corroborated with evidence from earnings, at least in the United States in the period 1960 to 1980. Angrist and Krueger (1991) and Harmon and Walker (1995) find that the earnings payoff to years of compulsory school is higher than for years of optional schooling.

Clearly, the casual empirical evidence does not suggest that laws regulating compulsory education and minimum age of work are very effective in controlling child labor in those settings in which child labor is problematic. In order to gain a sense of how laws regulating minimum age of work and compulsory education might operate in a developing country, it is instructive to analyze the effects of such laws during the period in which child labor was declining rapidly in industrialized countries.

Several studies look at the historical events surrounding the decline in child labor in Western Europe and North America throughout the nineteenth and into the twentieth centuries. Scholliers (1995) studied child labor in Ghent, Belgium and concluded that the incidence of working children under the age of 12 declined substantially by the middle of the nineteenth century *without* legal intervention. Brown et al. (1992) draw similar conclusions for the US fruit and vegetable canning industry between 1880 and 1920. While legislation played some role, economic forces dominated the decision to remove children from this sector. By contrast, Bolin-Hort (1989) argues that legal restrictions played a substantial role in the removal of child workers from the cotton mills in Manchester, England.

Thus, it is useful to consider some of the more careful statistical analysis of the impact of laws regulating entrance to the labor market and compulsory schooling. Angrist and Krueger (1991) develop a "natural experiment" type statistical technique for evaluating the impact of compulsory schooling laws on school attendance. The 1960–1980 US censuses collected information on the "quarter of birth" and "school attendance as of April 1." Angrist and Krueger argue that if compulsory school laws are effective, teenagers who are 16 years old as of April 1 and live in a state that requires students to remain in school only until they are 16 are less likely to be attending school at the time of the census than 16-year old teenagers who live in states with a mandatory school age of 17 or 18. They find a statistically significant effect of compulsory schooling laws for 1960 and 1970, thus supporting the hypothesis that laws affect schooling behavior.

Acemoglu and Angrist (1999) perform similar analysis on the same data looking for the impact of child labor laws on school attendance. They find, for example, that boys born in states that required 9 years of school before entering the work force spent 0.26 more years in school than boys born in states requiring 6 or fewer years of schooling.

The Angrist–Krueger technique was then applied to earlier periods in US history. Margo and Finegan (1996) analyze the schooling choices of 14-year olds reported in the 1900 federal census. In this study, 14-year olds are broken into two groups: (1) those teenagers who are already 14 at the beginning of the 1900 school year; and (2) those who are not yet 14 at the beginning of the school year. Margo and Finegan hypothesize that if mandatory school laws are effective, the younger 14-year olds living in a state with a compulsory schooling law should be more likely to be in school than older 14-year olds. However, no such difference should exist for 14-year olds in states without compulsory schooling laws. Margo and Finegan find that compulsory school laws have a positive and statistically significant impact on the decision to obtain *some* schooling for younger 14-year olds. However, the laws have no discernible effect on the probability of fulltime school attendance.

They then consider the impact of compulsory school laws combined with laws that regulate the minimum age of work. The addition of child-labor restrictions is likely to have an additional effect on school attendance because child labor laws were more aggressively enforced than mandatory education laws at that time. In this case, the combination of laws has a statistically significant impact on school choice. Young 14-year olds were 18 to 21 percent more likely to obtain *some* schooling if their access to the labor market was legally restricted. However, the laws did not significantly increase the probability of being in school *fulltime.*

The statistical evidence presented above has been criticized, most notably by Moehling (1999). She argues that the laws mandating school attendance are, themselves, endogenous and tend to follow the decline in child labor rather than precipitate it. That is, cross-state differences in technology, immigration, and real wages are driving both the change in educational attainment and the laws regulating school attendance. Thus, despite the fact that compulsory education laws, child labor laws and school attendance are correlated, it is not a causal relationship.

Moehling draws on the fact that most laws around the turn of the twentieth century applied to 13-year old, but not 14-year old children. Therefore, when work–school patterns for 13- and 14-year olds are similar, it is unlikely that legal restrictions are affecting household behavior. However, we can detect a role for legal restrictions if 13- and 14-year olds make different work choices particularly in those states with compulsory education laws.

Moehling looks at occupation rates – the proportions of youth that identify some form of employment as their main use of time, as opposed to school. Then, in order to control for differences in the economic conditions across states that might be driving both the legislative process and schooling choice, she first looks at the difference in occupation rates for 13- and 14-year olds in each state *prior* to the introduction of compulsory schooling laws. This gives a baseline against which to compare the difference in occupation rates for 13- and 14-year olds after some states passed compulsory education laws. Moehling also included a number of other economic and demographic variables that have been shown to play a significant role in child labor decisions, as discussed above.

Moehling finds that the probability a 14-year old boy would be working fell substantially between 1890 and 1900 in states with newly enacted compulsory education laws. However, she observes a statistically similar decline in labor force participation in states without such laws, thus suggesting that the laws themselves were *not* the causal factor for boys.

Similarly, the labor force participation rates for 13- and 14-year old girls in states that *did* pass compulsory education laws also fell between 1880 and 1990. By contrast, 13- and 14-year old girls in states that *did not* pass compulsory education laws had *increased* labor force participation during the decade. *Thus, for girls, there is a negative correlation across states between the passage of laws and the LFP rates for girls.*

The above evidence, thus, suggests that compulsory education laws might be affecting work–school choices made by (or for) girls. However, Moehling argues that such an inference is not correct. Her reasoning follows from the fact that there is no differential effect on girls covered and not covered by the law within a single state. That is, the employment choices by 13-year old girls covered by compulsory education laws is mirrored by 14-year old girls in the same state but not covered by the law. *From this, Moehling infers that the failure of some states to pass laws requiring 13-year old girls to attend school, and the increase in the employment of 13-year old girls in these same states, are being simultaneously driven by other economic factors. For, such factors are similarly driving behavior by 14-year old girls not regulated by legislation.*

Moehling then goes on to consider Margo and Finegan's hypothesis that schooling is affected by the combination of child labor and compulsory education laws. Once again, the laws do not seem to be driving behavior. The only case in which 13-year olds behave differently from 14-year olds occurs for boys in states with *no* legislative change. In states with no laws regulating either compulsory education or minimum age of employment, the LFP rate for 14-year old boys rose between 1890 and 1900, whereas the LFP rate for 13-year old boys declined during the same period. Thus, the results are running precisely counter to the expectation that laws affect behavior!

In response to the rising LFP rates for girls in the last decade of the nineteenth century, there was a burst of legislative activity shortly after 1900. In 1900, 24 states had laws regulating minimum age of employment. By 1910, 43 states had such laws. Perhaps more importantly, by 1909, 34 states had enacted legislation providing for inspectors assigned to enforce child labor laws.

Moehling then applied her statistical technique to the 1900 and 1910 censuses. In this case, the estimated effect of legal restrictions on school attendance, at least, appears to be positive but statistically insignificant for some groups. However, the impact is small relative to the time-series change.

What can we conclude from this evidence? First, the more carefully executed the statistical analysis, the weaker is the evident effect of legal restrictions on child schooling and labor decisions. Second, it does appear that for carefully crafted laws, such as those enacted in the last quarter of the twentieth century in England, there is some impact of legislation on behavior at the margin. However, when the age limits specified by the laws are substantially at odds with optimizing decisions by households, they have little effect. For example, the laws written in the United States around 1900 tended to specify 14 years as the cut-off between schooling and work. However, Moehling's evidence clearly suggests that 14 years of age was not viewed as a significant work–school boundary for many US households at that time. Similarly, recently enacted laws regulating work in Brazil have had no effect on household decisions. Thus mandatory school laws and minimum age of employment are at best, a complement to other policies designed to alter the family's perception of the appropriate age at which children should begin working.

Finally, the results of Margo and Finegan on the one hand, and Moehling, on the other, are not as inconsistent as they may at first seem. Margo and Finegan focus on the 1900 census because it not only asks whether a child views school as the main occupation but also whether the child is in school at all. Moehling, by contrast, looks at several decades of data and, so, is only able consider whether the laws are affecting a child's perception as to whether school is the main occupation. Neither study finds an impact of compulsory schooling laws or child-labor laws on the child's perception of his/her main occupation. That is, neither study finds that the legal restrictions increase the probability of fulltime schooling.

Recent Policy Initiatives Addressing Child Labor

Although the empirical results discussed earlier are by no means conclusive, they are certainly suggestive of the types of policies that might be effective in reducing the incidence of child labor. We turn now to consider some of the policy initiatives that have recently been undertaken in some developing countries.

Recently, several governments have implemented a range of positive strategies designed to improve compliance. For a more thorough description see USDOL (1998) and World Bank (2001), from which much of this section draws. See also Anker and Melkas (1996) for an overview of programs relying on economic incentives, worldwide. The programs include improvements in educational infrastructure, programs targeted at children who have fallen or are likely to fall behind in school, financial incentives and sector-specific programs. We discuss some of these below.

Educational infrastructure

Increased spending on books, supplies, buildings, and teacher training have been pursued by several governments. Brazil has been one of the most aggressive in this regard. Beginning in 1997, the Livro Didactico project has provided $142.5 million for textbooks. The television program TV Escola is targeted at raising the skill levels of teachers in rural areas. The program also includes the distribution of kits that contain instructional materials. Funds have also been made available to raise the wages of extremely low paid teachers and to build and improve public-school facilities.

Similarly, the Mexican government uses telecommunications to improve education quality for rural communities. By virtue of the Telesecundaria program, rural seventh, eighth and ninth graders can view educational programs broadcast by the Mexican Ministry of Education. The central government provides a teacher, television set, satellite dish, decoder, instructional material, and books for qualified schools.

Some poorer countries have had to rely on the one-room schoolhouse model in order to extend educational opportunities to all children. For example, The Ministry of Education in Egypt built 8,500 new one-classroom schools in rural communities during the mid-1990s and increased investment in teacher training. Similarly, the government of the Philippines established 1880 "incomplete" elementary schools, along with 900 elementary schools, thereby halving the proportion of *barangays* (political divisions of municipalities or cities) without a primary school.

The Turkish Ministry of Education has built 670 new primary schools and appointed 1,930 new teachers in order to implement a new compulsory school law requiring eight years of schooling. Nevertheless, many communities in Turkey still lack most of the items essential to a school, such as chalk, blackboards, teachers, books, etc.

Remedial teaching and flexible schedules

Working children, given the competing work and school demands on their time, are particularly likely to fail to complete each grade with their cohort. Some empirical evidence discussed above suggests that greater flexibility in school schedules would help working children remain in school. Nicaragua's remedial education program, *Extra Edad*, targets older children who have failed to complete the primary grades by the age of 14. Classes are offered after work in order to allow the child to continue to earn an income while pursuing an elementary education. Guatemala has also introduced a strategy of flexible schedules to keep working children in school. Classes begin after market work is completed and students make up missed schoolwork with independent study. Children of migrant workers are also offered a more flexible school calendar, allowing students to resume school attendance as soon as they are able. Mexico provides flexibility by allowing the children of migrants to attend school in whichever district they happen to be currently residing. Peru offers classes in three shifts throughout the day. This school schedule allows each student to combine work and school in a manner consistent with the requirements of the employer. Lapu-Lapu City in the Philippines offers a work-study program in which children attend school in the morning and then report for work in the afternoon. Child workers are directed toward less dangerous work and monitoring of working conditions is intensified in hazardous occupations such as firecracker assembly.

The state of Andhra Pradesh in India launched a program in 1997 targeting children who have left school or were never enrolled with two-month school camps. Typically eligible children are bonded child laborers, domestic servants and those from lower castes. Each camp comprises 100 children and 5 teachers. The pilot program was particularly successful as a stepping-stone to formal education. Of those children enrolled in the first year of the program, 74 percent subsequently enrolled in formal school. The Andhra Pradesh program is particularly attractive in light of the fact that 60 percent of children aged 5 to 14 never attend school.

Financial incentives

Governments rely on a wide array of financial incentives either to make school more attractive or even to make school attendance financially feasible for families. School meals are the most pervasive of such programs and are distinctive because they tie the aid to school attendance. Brazil launched *Marenda Escolar* in 1997, spending $453.4 million on breakfast and lunch. Urban Brazilian families who are likely to put their children to work also receive food baskets from the Foundation of Childhood and Adolescence. Like food distributed at school, the food baskets are contingent on school attendance. Mexico provides approximately 4 million breakfasts a day to poor children attending school. All Egyptian children are also given one meal/day in school. Similarly, the government of South Africa provides meals for five million children who attend school.

While food aid may make school more attractive, it may not provide a sufficiently strong incentive to induce families to give up the income earned by their children. As a consequence, some governments have instituted cash stipends or in-kind gifts for children attending schools. For example, the poor families in Bangladesh receive 15 to 20 kg of wheat per month if their children are attending school. In 1996, the program reached 1.14 million families. ILO-IPEC (1998a) finds that the program has a significant impact on enrolment, attendance and drop-out rates.

In Brazil, *Bolsa Escola* pays a monthly stipend to each family with an unemployed adult in the Federal District that keeps all of its children aged 7 to 14 attending school. In addition, the program deposits the equivalent of one month's salary into a savings account after each year of completed school through the eleventh grade. Funds are forfeited if the child fails to advance to the next grade.

Mexico introduced a similar, though not identical, program in 1997. The Program for Education, Health and Nutrition (PROGRESA) targets over 2.5 million families whose children are not attending school. The program pays a bimonthly stipend to the families of children who maintain an 85 percent attendance record. The stipend ranges from $7 to $63, depending on the age and gender of the child. The program also provides families with funds to purchase school materials and supplies, a basic package of primary health-care services, and food supplements for children and mothers. The health-care provisions of the program are tied to routine visits to medical facilities.

Although the Mexican and Brazilian programs appear similar, some key aspects are likely to make the Mexican program more effective at lowering child labor. The Brazilian subsidy to families with an unemployed adult has features that repair some of the effects of capital-market failure. In the absence of the program, families without access to capital markets are forced to turn to the labor of their children in order to survive periods of economic adversity, such as an unemployed adult. Thus, this program must be seen primarily as a program to deter child labor that occurs as a form of family insurance against income uncertainty. Children who work as a consequence of poverty proper may not be affected.

The educational savings account is even more deceptive. The family can access the account only after the child has successfully completed eleven years of education. Therefore, the savings account cannot serve as collateral for education loans, nor can the family access the account to pay ongoing expenses. In addition, the child cannot pre-commit to surrender the proceeds to repay their parents even if the parent could access the capital markets on behalf of the child. As a consequence, none of the problems with capital market failure are remedied with the Brazilian savings-account program.

The only impact the loan has is to raise the present discounted value of an education relative to current income. The increased return to education may affect the calculus in a family that is able to borrow in order attend school, but it cannot help families without access to capital markets.

By contrast, the Mexican program buys out the labor contract of the child from the parent. Participating children receive a stipend that partially replaces the income the child could earn by working in exchange for school attendance. Thus, all of the problems with capital-market failure and their implications for inefficient child work are sidestepped. Issues of collateral and intra-family bargaining are no longer relevant. Nor do policy-makers need to be concerned that providing access to capital markets will lead families to purchase assets that they intend to combine with the labor of their children.

Subsidy programs that replace the child's income boast some of the highest success rates. Between 1995 and 1996, the official dropout rate in the Brazilian Federal District fell from 11 percent to 0.4 percent, although the extent to which this should be attributed to any particular program is unknown. Similarly remarkable success is reported for the Brazilian Child Labor Eradication Program (PETI). Begun in 1996, PETI targets nearly 900,000 Brazilian children aged 7 to 14 working in the most harmful conditions in rural areas. Under the program, mothers in families earning half the minimum wage per capita receive a monthly stipend equal to US$13.50 per month for each child attending school and after-school programs fulltime. Children in school also receive three meals per day. An equal amount of money per child in the program is paid to the local municipality to finance salaries, materials and meals. In return, the municipality must pay 10 percent of the cost of the schools' infrastructure. Monitoring of school attendance is undertaken by teachers. The total cost of the program through 2006 is estimated to be on the order of $2 billion.

Anecdotal evidence suggests that PETI is profoundly successful. The town of Conceicao do Coite, a Brazilian sisal-producing community located in Bahia, provides a striking example. Children working in sisal harvesting are commonly permanently injured by both the sharp sisal stalks and the tools used for cutting. Evaluation of PETI undertaken by UNICEF suggests that child labor in Conceicao do Coite has been virtually eliminated.

One of the distinctive features of the PETI program is that it combines stipends to families that replace the child's earnings with financial support to develop and fund educational opportunities, all of which are embedded in a vigorously active local community committed to eradicating child labor. In addition, PETI, like Bolsa Escola, is a means-tested program targeting the very poor. Finally, the educational subsidy is quite large in comparison to the family's income. Although the size of the benefit and the income cut-off have varied over the life of the program, the educational subsidy has at some points been equal to the income earned by the parents.

However, it is difficult to judge the quality of the reported evidence. The teacher's report on school attendance is required to receive the subsidy and also serves as the basis for school-attendance statistics. Teachers may have an incentive to misreport, either in return for a bribe or out of concern for the welfare of the child.

Both Brazil and Mexico have designed additional income-support programs targeted at specific sectors. The Mexican government targets children working in the fruit and vegetable sector in the northeastern state of Sinaloa. Aid is paid in the form of food packages worth about 30 percent of an adult's monthly salary. As with the income supplement, families are required to demonstrate a substantial school-attendance record of their children. Local growers are required to contribute 30 percent of the cost of the food. Growers may also construct and furnish local schools. In such cases, the government provides teachers and supplies.

The ILO's International Program on the Elimination of Child Labor (IPEC) furnished seed funding to start a program sponsored by the Union of Rural Workers in Retirolandia in Brazil to provide families with assets that they could use to support their children in school rather than send them to work. The *Goats-to-School* program provides each eligible family with a goat and information on tending and rearing goats. Beneficiary families are required to use the milk to feed their children and to repay the program in goats without interest. This unique program provides families with the assets they need to find safer alternative employment for their children which does not interfere with schooling.

The *Goats-to-School* program is not very significant in terms of the number of children covered. Between 1996, when the program was begun, and 1998, 60 goats were distributed to 30 families affecting 100 children. However, the incentives and constraints built into the program are quite sensitive and responsive to the evidence currently available as to why children work and in what occupations. Clearly the program provides families with an asset that produces an income stream that the family can rely on rather than on the labor services of their children. That is, poor families are able to acquire capital that allows them to fund current education for their children, thus eliminating inefficient child labor associated with incomplete capital markets. In addition, the loan can be repaid through the efforts of the children tending the goats since the loan is repaid simply by returning one baby goat to the program for each adult goat received. Thus, the intra-family bargaining problem that arises because children cannot pre-commit to repay loans taken out on their behalf is eliminated because the children, through their efforts tending the animals, are able to repay the loan on their own.

Furthermore, the children tend the goats, thereby continuing to make some current contribution to the family. However, the times at which the goats need tending do not conflict with schooling, thus providing each child with sufficient flexibility in their work schedule to combine school and work. Nor is the work so onerous that the children are too exhausted to complete their schoolwork. Finally, receiving the benefit is contingent upon school attendance. As a consequence, the program provides a strong incentive to substitute education for work even if the family is far from the income level that would place them near the work–school margin. Thus, it is not necessary to wait until income reaches some critical level at which parents start withdrawing children from school and the implicit subsidy does not have to be so large as to raise income to the poverty line to be effective.

To the extent that *Goats-to-School* has a design weakness, it is the absence of time consistency. Families receive the asset based on a commitment to place their children in school. However, there is no mechanism for enforcing ongoing compliance other than the social pressure that might be brought to bear by the union implementing the program. The income subsidies described above that make a payment only after the teacher certifies attendance may prove to be more effective in lowering the level of child labor for a given level of expenditure. Another interesting feature of the *Goats-to-School* program is that it is self-sustaining. Animals repaid become assets for new families entering the program. Although IPEC provided the original funding, the program is now self-financing.

The programs discussed above provide financial support specifically targeted at replacing the contribution that working children make to household income. Others are targeted at helping families defray the cost of education. For example, the Egyptian government pays a grant equal in value to about US$4.17 to cover uniforms, books and supplies for families earning less than about US$29.41 per month.

Micro-credit programs

The education subsidy programs described in the previous section address the role that capital market failure plays in inefficient child labor by buying the child's time from the family in exchange for school attendance. As a consequence, most of the inadequacies of the capital market are simply side-stepped. However, there are several programs currently in place that attempt to operate directly on the market for credit.

One of the best-known of the micro-lending programs is administered by the Grameen (Village) Bank in Bangladesh. Small loans are provided to families that promise to place their children in school. IPEC has established a similar program in the Dominican Republic with the objective of drawing children out of hazardous agricultural work in Constanza. Parents are required to enroll their children in school and attend project meetings in order to be eligible for loans of $200 to $500. IPEC also targets children working in Guatemala's stone quarries and the Bridge Foundation provides micro-loans to families in India.

As with the education subsidy programs in Brazil, there is anecdotal evidence that micro-lending has a powerful impact on the poverty that gives rise to child labor. However, there is no supporting careful empirical analysis.

Programs to reduce child labor in targeted sectors

Conditions for working children in some sectors are sufficiently hazardous that programs have been tailored to the specifics of the relevant sector. In addition, cultural factors may be sufficiently complex that simply relying on financial incentives may be ineffective. Examples include the Vale dos Sinos Project initiated in 1996 to reduce the employment of children in the Brazilian footwear industry and the HABITAT project initiated in 1998 to reduce child labor in the stone quarries of Guatemala. Both projects have a public-education component designed to sensitize parents, employers, and the community to the risks to children employed in these sectors. Program objectives also include improved working conditions, medical services and flexible school options. The government of Peru has also targeted children who work turning bricks in the Huachipa brickfields outside of Lima. In addition to mentoring and tutoring young children, the program provides health care and small business loans to start a family enterprise.

Providing alternative employment opportunities has also been used as a strategy to draw children out of the quarries of Carabayllo, Peru. Mothers who agree to keep their children out of work receive financial and other help in establishing a micro-enterprise making plastic bags. Families are provided with equipment, raw materials and technical advice on beginning the business.

A similar program has been developed in Turkey. It is a common practice in the mountain villages of the Duragan district of Sinop to auction off male children aged nine to 15 to help during the harvest season on the farms of affluent families. The Development Foundation of Turkey has launched a program to train families in small-scale agricultural projects, such as bee-keeping and turkey-breeding, that allows the child to work productively while remaining at home. Children can, in some cases, earn more in these newly created family enterprises than as rented labor.

Several programs are targeted at raising awareness of the negative effects of work on children. For example, the African Network for the Prevention and Protection against Child Abuse and Neglect on the tobacco and tea plantations in Tanzania uses drama and theater to mobilize communities and to educate. Teachers report increased attendance and some employers have begun to provide financial help to schools for the purchase of supplies and school meals.

Children who have been formerly bonded frequently perform poorly in a formal education setting. In Nepal, rehabilitation is undertaken by the Informal Sector Service Center, which provides nine months of remedial training in language and arithmetic. Children are then channeled into elementary schools.

Several communities have reached formal agreements with employers to not employ children and to return currently employed children to school. For example, the Bangladesh Garment Manufacturers Association (BGMEA) signed a Memorandum of Understanding in 1995, which provides for dismissing children currently working if they can be placed in school. In addition, no under-age children should be newly employed. Children presenting themselves for employment shall be directed to NGO-run schools where they can receive a monthly stipend equal in value to about US$6.88 for attending school. The program appears to have been fairly successful. In 1995, 10,546 children were working in BGMEA factories. About 43 percent of member factories employed children. This figure fell to 32 percent in 1997 and 13 percent in 1998 (ILO-IPEC, 1998a, b).

Several US importers of soccer balls have signed the Partners' Agreement to Eliminate Child Labor in the Soccer Ball Industry in Sialkot, Pakistan. The program aims to provide children removed from employment and their younger siblings with informal education, alternative income-generating opportunities, formal schooling and awareness training for parents. The weakness of this program occurs in the monitoring component. It is commonly the case in Sialkot for women and their children to stitch soccer balls in between other household chores. In order to prevent families from putting their children to work stitching soccer balls, work has been moved from homes to stitching centers. However, as has been noted in a previous section, mothers who work outside of the home place their daughters at risk for fulltime home-work. However, when mothers work in a household enterprise, such as soccer ball stitching, daughters can more readily combine home-work with schooling. As a consequence, this program has the potential to undermine the efforts that Pakistani families are making to educate their daughters.

A rescue and rehabilitation program was initiated in 1995 by the National Society for Protection of Environment and Children in the Nepalese carpet industry. The program attempts to provide informal education for children removed from work but also conducts classes for children in the carpet factories. Children removed from work are either returned to their family or placed in youth hostels where they receive alternative skills training.

Empirical evidence on program effectiveness

Although programs that provide incentives to replace work with schooling seem like they ought to be effective, there is very little careful empirical analysis of these programs. Anker and Melkas (1996) surveyed administrators of 68 income-replacement and substitution activities in Africa, Asia, and Latin America. Respondents generally thought that their programs were effective. However, the authors doubted the value of such self-reporting and noted that none of the programs had evaluated the impact on the incidence of child labor either short-term or long-term.

Nevertheless, the survey provided some useful insights:

1. A package of school-based incentives, remedial education, income-generating activities for families, and awareness training for parents is more effective than any one of these components individually.
2. School-lunch programs themselves do not provide a sufficient incentive to draw children out of work and into school. As a consequence of the low financial value of the meal combined with the poor quality of schools, school-lunch programs do not generally alter the parents' calculation of the value of school relative to work. Children covered by the survey typically contributed 20–25 percent of the family's income, an amount that is far in excess of the value of a single mid-day meal.
3. Many respondents were concerned that cash grants could be misused and so preferred aid in-kind. However, it is also the case that cash provides families with flexibility that is sometimes essential to the effectiveness of the program. Most respondents preferred programs that had elements of both.

4. Programs that provided apprenticeships, school-work combinations, or "safe work" alternatives and other informal education were particularly effective in helping children leave dangerous or onerous occupations. This is partly a reflection of the very poor quality of schools that families frequently regard as irrelevant to their situation.
5. Several respondents raised concern with dependency and the role that incentives might play in luring children into work in order to qualify for benefits.

Although the survey evidence cited above is of some value, some programs have been carefully evaluated using statistical techniques. Ravallion and Wodon (1999) evaluate the Food-for-Education (FFE) program in rural Bangladesh. Participating households receive a food ration of rice as long as their children attend school. In 1995–6, 2.2 million Bangladeshi children benefited from the FFE program. The national government targets economically underdeveloped areas for benefits. Local community groups then select participants based on idiosyncratic local information. Children are required to maintain an 85 percent school attendance rate. Monitoring and food distribution are handled by each school's headmaster.

Based on the 1995–6 Household Expenditure Survey undertaken by the Bangladesh Bureau of Statistics, the typical participating household received 114 kg of rice per year. Using information on the local cost of rice, average family size, and local wages, Ravallion and Wodon calculate that the FFE stipend is the equivalent of 13 percent of the average monthly earnings of boys and 20 percent of that for girls.

Ravallion and Wodon estimate the determinants of the probability of work and school. A working child is one who regarded work as his/her "normal activity" in the previous week. The level of education is measured by the reported educational status for children aged 5 to 16 who have not completed primary school. Explanatory variables include distance to school, the type of school, school-quality variables, parental education, community religion, household demographics, land ownership, the child's age, and the size of the FFE stipend.

Ravallion and Wodon find that the stipend has a strong and statistically significant impact on both the probability of work and the probability of schooling. In particular, they find that an FFE stipend of 100 kilos of rice increases the probability that a boy will be in school by 17 percent and that a girl will be in school by 16 percent. Thus, there is some evidence from household survey data that corroborates the enrolment data provided by school administrators on the impact of education subsidies on school attendance.

However, the impact on child labor is much smaller. An extra 100 kg of rice lowers the probability of working as the main activity by 4 percent for boys and only 2 percent for girls. Therefore, of the children newly in school following the inception of the program, only a quarter of the boys and one-eighth of the girls are switching from work as the primary activity to school as the primary activity.

Of course, it may be the case that some children newly in school were formerly working only part-time, in which case the subsidy has had a positive impact on school attendance. Nevertheless, the subsidy appears primarily to increase school attendance at the expense of the child's leisure rather than work. These results strongly suggest that school quality or a failure to appreciate the value of school, rather than each family's need for their child's income, are deterring formal schooling. By contrast, for those children who are making a financial contribution to the family, a stipend that replaces less than 20 percent of the child's earnings is not sufficient to alter the family's calculation of the value of school relative to work.

Children nevertheless benefit from the program. On average, the total impact of the subsidy raises family income. The average loss in child wages as a consequence of the subsidy is only 19 percent of the average value of the subsidy. Furthermore, Wodon (1999) finds that completing primary school in rural Bangladesh increases per capita consumption by nine percent. Nevertheless, these results point more to school quality, an under-appreciation of the value of education, or direct school costs as the most important deterrents to schooling, rather than poverty and child labor.

Similar evidence has emerged for Thailand. Tzannatos (1996) finds that Thai children under the age of 12 do not initially leave school in order to work. Rather the direct cost of schooling, such as uniforms and supplies, relative to its value deters parents from keeping children in school. Uneducated Thai children do not begin to enter the labor force until they are 12 to 15 years old.

The importance of the physical presence of school buildings in a community in raising each family's perception of the value of education is further supported by Duflo (2000). Between 1973 and 1978, the Indonesian Government built over 61,000 primary schools at a cost of US$5 billion. She finds that children aged 2 to 6 in 1974 received 0.12 to 0.19 more years of schooling for each school constructed per 1,000 children. Duflo also finds a measurable impact on wages. Each school built per 1,000 children also raised wages by 1.5 to 2.7 percent.

PROGRESA, a school subsidy program operated in Mexico, was specifically implemented with the purpose of providing data that can be used to rigorously analyze the program's effectiveness. Design and implementation of the analysis was executed by the International Food Policy Research Institute (IFPRI, 2000). At the inception of the program in 1997, households in seven states[*] were randomly assigned to control and treatment groups. Of the 506 communities initially targeted, 320 were designated for treatment and 186 as control communities.

Before the program was implemented, PROGRESA surveyed rural households in the targeted states in order to determine their socioeconomic status. Employing the program's selection criteria, 78 percent of households were deemed eligible for benefits. Households were then surveyed in March 1998 before benefits were received and then again in October 1998, June 1999 and November 1999. Families were queried on their family background, assets brought to marriage, schooling, health status, parental attitudes, aspirations for their children, food and nonfood consumption, and time allocation for all household members and self-employment activities. Schools provided supplemental survey evidence on student achievement test scores.

In Mexico, completion of primary school is fairly comprehensive. The enrolment rate for primary school is about 93 percent. However, rural children typically leave school after completing the sixth grade, at which point the national enrolment rate drops to 55 percent. A second decline in enrolment occurs at the tenth grade at which point only 58 percent of those qualified to continue do so.

Benefits under the program are paid to the mother every two months. The size of the stipend varies with the age of the child and the child's gender, with higher stipends for girls. In addition, financial aid for school supplies is paid twice each year.

Enrolment rates for treatment and control groups were then compared, controlling for family and community factors. The impact of the program was found to be positive and statistically significant. At the primary level, at which enrolment rates are already 90 to 94 percent, PROGRESA stipends increase attendance for boys by between 0.74 to 1.07 percent and for girls by 0.96 to 1.45 percentage points.

The impact on secondary enrolment, however, is much more distinctive. Prior to the beginning of the program, the enrolment rate in secondary school was 67 percent for girls and 73 percent for boys. Considering children in grades one through nine, the PROGRESA subsidy increased the enrolment rate for girls by between 7.2 to 9.3 percentage points and by 3.5 to 5.8 percentage points for boys, as found by Schultz (2001). These preliminary results suggest that PROGRESA will increase overall educational attainment for poor rural children in Mexico by about 10 percent, thereby raising adult income by 8 percent. The impact of PROGRESA is largest for children making the transition to junior secondary school. Enrolment rates for girls of this age receiving the education subsidy are 20 percent higher for girls and 10 percent higher for boys as compared to the control group.

As a byproduct of the empirical analysis, which examined other determinants of child labor, the study also produced estimates of the effect of increasing the density of schools. In the sample, 12 percent of children travel more than four kilometers to a junior secondary school. If enough schools were built so that all children traveled less than four kilometers to their junior secondary school, secondary-school enrolment for boys would rise by less than one-half of one percent and enrolment for girls would rise by about one-third of one percent.

While PROGRESA has a substantial impact on most indicators of child welfare including food consumption, physical stature, illness, school attendance, and future income, the impact on child labor is disappointing. There is only a modest decline in labor force participation rates for children in the program, falling primarily on unpaid activities (Parker and Skoufias, 2000). Neither do enrolled children in the program spend more time on schoolwork at home nor exhibit higher achievement test scores than similar children who do not receive the stipend.

The efforts being made on behalf of children in the programs reviewed here are impressive and encouraging, even if the results are sometimes mixed. For the most, however, little has been done to compare the benefits from these programs to their costs. An exception is Schultz (2001), who calculates the rate of return on the resources put into the PROGRESA program. He finds a rate of return of 8 percent that is above and beyond both the role of the program in reducing current poverty and any consumption benefits from education.

Child Labor Standards Initiatives in the International Arena

In the international arena, it is commonly argued that countries with poor labor practices with regard to children should be sanctioned in some manner. Advocates are generally motivated either by concern for the impact of low cost child labor on wages in industrialized countries or by humanitarian concern for exploited children. We turn first to empirical evidence as to whether child labor practices affect export performance or comparative advantage. We then turn to the impact that trade policies are likely to have on the welfare of children.

Do national labor standards alter exports, competitiveness or comparative advantage?

It is arguably the case that child labor may lower the wages of unskilled workers in industrialized countries. A large volume of cheaply produced, unskilled-labor intensive exports made possible by the labor of children may have the effect of depressing the demand for such goods produced in industrialized countries and, thereby, lower the wages of unskilled workers. To the extent that child labor practices in developing countries have implications for industrialized country workers, industrialized countries may seek reform or redress.

In order to determine whether child labor practices affect trade performance, several researchers have examined a simple correlation between the existence and/or observance of core labor standards and various measures of trade performance. For example, Mah (1997) analyzes the trade performance of 45 developing countries and finds that each country's export share of GDP is strongly negatively correlated with rights to nondiscrimination, negatively correlated with freedom-of-association rights and weakly negatively correlated with the right to organize and collective bargaining.

However, such a correlation can have many reasons, and to gauge the marginal contribution of core labor standards, one must compare each country's trade performance against a baseline expectation as to what such a country should be trading given its factor endowments and other determinants of trade. Rodrik (1996) provides an excellent example of how such analysis can be undertaken.

He first considers the impact of core labor standards on labor costs per worker in manufacturing. He does this by calculating a regression using labor cost as the dependent variable and per capita income and various measures of labor standards as the independent variables. In this framework, per capita income is being used as a proxy for productivity in the economy. Labor standards are measured in a variety of ways: total number of ILO conventions ratified; number of ILO conventions ratified pertaining to labor standards; Freedom House indicators of civil liberties and political rights; statutory hours worked; days of paid annual leave; the unionization rate; and an indicator of child labor.

Rodrik finds that for the period 1985 to 1988, labor costs are overwhelmingly determined by labor productivity. However, the number of ILO conventions ratified, Freedom House indicators of democracy and the index of child labor are large and statistically significant, with laws regulating child labor playing a particularly important role in statistically explaining labor costs.

Rodrik then turns to the determinants of comparative advantage in labor-intensive goods. He uses the fraction of textiles and clothing exports in total exports as a proxy for measuring comparative advantage in labor-intensive goods. As a theoretical matter, comparative advantage is primarily determined by factor endowments. Therefore, the comparative advantage variable is regressed on the independent variables of population-to-land ratio (a measure of the labor endowment), average years of schooling in the population over 25 (a measure of the stock of human capital) and the labor standards variables. The population and human capital variables have the expected signs and are statistically significant. However, generally the labor standards variables, while having the expected sign, are not statistically significant.

The lone exception is statutory hours worked. The longer the workweek, the stronger is the comparative advantage in textiles and clothing.

Overall, the link from low labor standards in low-income countries to the wage of unskilled workers in industrialized countries is not especially strong. Child labor practices in developing countries are, at best, a secondary factor in determining comparative advantage and trade performance.

Labor protections and humanitarian concerns

While there may be some legitimate concern with the impact of labor practices on industrial country workers, we may be equally motivated by humanitarian concerns for children. However, while it is undoubtedly the case that voters in high-income countries are genuinely concerned with the welfare of foreign children, it is not at all clear that these concerns can be constructively addressed by applying trade disciplines. To understand the role that trade policy might play in mediating humanitarian concerns with the process of production, it is important to distinguish between two different forms in which these moral concerns might manifest themselves.

First, moral distaste may be a private good. For example, a consumer might prefer not to consume goods produced by children or under poor working conditions. In this case, consumers ought to have an opportunity to avoid goods produced in this manner, provided that they are willing to pay the additional cost of production. In some cases, this might be accomplished by attaching a product label detailing the conditions under which the good was produced (Freeman, 1994). But if moral distaste is also a public good, consumers preferring that their fellow citizens also refrain from such consumption, then one can make a case that countries that wish to do so should be allowed to state a broad definition of immoral working conditions and, acting as a country, refuse to import such goods.

However, this particular moral stance focuses only on alleviating the bad feeling that consumers may have knowing they have consumed a good produced under unpleasant circumstances. The welfare of the foreign workers themselves is not necessarily at issue. But if consumers in high-income countries can exhaust their moral commitments simply by avoiding consumption of goods produced in ways that they dislike contemplating, without regard for the welfare of the children involved, then the humanitarian argument begins to lose some of its moral gravity.[5] If, by contrast, humanitarian and moral concerns focus on the welfare of the children themselves, rather than on the discomfort of the consumer, then the ability of trade sanctions to address these concerns is highly limited.

In fact, trade sanctions in the face of weak child protections are as likely or even more likely to harm children as they are to improve conditions.

Maskus (1997) provides a detailed discussion of this point. Consider the problem of child labor in the case of a small open economy in which the export sector is adult-labor-intensive, the import sector is capital-intensive, and a nontraded intermediate input to the export sector is produced using child labor. The child's labor supply is increasing in the child's wage and decreasing in the adult wage. The marginal child worker is the youngest, since the opportunity cost in terms of foregone education falls as the child ages. In this setting, a foreign tax imposed on goods produced by children can lead to the social optimum in the sense of internalizing the external effect of child work on the well-being of western consumers. Those children no longer working who receive an education may also be better off, although the fact that they or their parents chose for them to work before makes this questionable. However, if, as a consequence of the tax, the newly unemployed children live in a household with lower income, less nutrition, and otherwise diminished life alternatives, the trade sanction has probably been counterproductive. Children who continue to work after the imposition of the tax are definitely worse off, since the firms who employ children have to pay a tax. In a small open economy, a tax must lower the after-tax wage of the working child.

One might wonder whether trade sanctions could be effective in the multiple-equilibria context of Basu and Van (1998), moving a country from a low-wage equilibrium to a high-wage equilibrium that could then be sustained without the sanctions. Leaving aside the daunting empirical question of how one could ever be sure that such multiple equilibria were present, Basu (1999) is explicit in rejecting this as a basis for trade sanctions, arguing only that coordinated enforcement of labor standards across countries might be appropriate. In fact, trade sanctions tend to reduce the demand for labor in poor countries, not increase it, and if anything this would move a country to a lower equilibrium, not a higher one.

The threat of sanctions will be particularly ineffective if the targeted country simply lacks the resources to respond to the threat. For example, Rogers and Swinnerton (1999) estimate that if GDP per worker falls below $5,020, families are so poor that they cannot survive without contributions to family income from children. Thus, no matter how intense the demand for a reduction in child labor, child labor practices will continue.

Furthermore, trade sanctions do little to address the underlying market failure that gives rise to offending child labor practices. For example, as discussed above, capital market failure arguably lies at the heart of the most egregious forms of child labor exploitation. If parents had access to capital markets, they would school their children while transferring wealth from the future to the present by borrowing against their own future income or the future income of their children. However, lacking collateral and facing other capital market pathologies, the only device that parents have available to them is to put their children to work. The end result, of course, is inadequate human capital formation.

Conclusions

Concern for the welfare of working children has taken on a new importance in the international arena over the past decade. While some participants in the global discussion focus on the implications that working children might have on the rights and wages of workers in industrialized countries, there is little evidence to support this concern. Although there are around 250 million children working worldwide, the value of their output is so small that it is unlikely to have much of an effect on the international wage structure. Furthermore, most children work in the informal sector or in home-work and, therefore, are not in direct competition with unskilled workers in industrialized countries. Neither of these reasons means that child labor has no effect at all on wages of other workers elsewhere, but those effects are surely small compared to the effects on the children themselves. For this reason, much of the discussion with regard to children focuses on the children, rather than on the implications for others.

When establishing policies with regard to children, it is essential therefore to have reasonable confidence that policies put in place will actually improve the lives of the intended beneficiaries. However, this is difficult to do given the wide array of factors that are affecting parents and the work–school decisions they make for their children. For this reason, recent policy initiatives have focused on providing incentives, for families to choose education, rather than punishments. Attempts to use legal restrictions to affect household decisions take away options that families are exercising and may leave children with worsened alternatives. By contrast, incentive schemes open up new and improved alternatives to families without taking away existing choices. Thus, if, in the presence of the incentive schemes, families choose less child labor than in their absence, there is reason to believe that the policy has been effective in improving the lot of children.

Although at this point the evidence is not clear that such incentive schemes will succeed in significantly reducing the incidence of child labor, they still currently represent the best hope for helping working children, while minimizing unintended negative effects. They deserve an opportunity to succeed. Recent policy innovations are receiving earnest support from the World Bank, the International Labor Organization, UNICEF and UNESCO, but they are in need of further financial assistance, technical support, and rigorous empirical evaluation.

The question then is which of the myriad policy configurations appears to have the greatest potential to improve the lot of working children? First and foremost, both theory and empirical evidence point very strongly to the role of capital-market failure in giving rise to inefficient child labor. From a theoretical perspective, families without access to capital markets may not be able to invest in their children even if it is optimizing for the family to do so.

As an empirical matter, it is generally the case that families with some household assets such as older children, a mother with marketable skills, and assets associated with a household enterprise are more likely to choose some education for their children than families without assets. However, providing access to capital markets is a double-edged sword. While access to capital markets may lead some families to borrow to finance an education for their children, there are at least some cases in which households borrow to finance assets that are then combined with more child labor. For this reason, those policies that offer assets in return for school attendance provide the liquidity that make schooling possible while cutting off the option of taking children out of school to work with household capital.

One of the striking results of the studies we have reviewed is that education subsidies that might normally be expected to draw children out of the work force and into school do, in fact, keep children in school. But we have very little statistically significant evidence that such subsidies alter the parent's decision as to whether the child should work. It is useful to consider why this might be the case. The evidence suggests several possible explanations.

First, the education subsidy may not be large enough to replace the child's contribution to family income. In this case, even if parents would like to put their children in school, they are too poor to do so even given the subsidy. In the case of the Bangladeshi program, the subsidy was not even replacing 20 percent or a working child's earnings. This alone is enough to explain why very few families returned full-time-working children to school. By contrast, the Brazilian programs, PETI and Bolsa Escola, are means tested and provide subsidies that are typically quite large, enough to pull a beneficiary family up to the poverty line.

Second, the families who do respond to the subsidy appear to be those with idle children, neither working nor in school. The question, of course, is why are parents allowing their children to remain idle? One possibility is that school quality (or the perception of it) is so poor that parents see little point in going to the effort or expense of schooling their children. If school quality is in fact poor, attending school may earn the subsidy but will have little impact on the formation of the child's human capital. Certainly, both empirical and anecdotal evidence point to school quality as an important factor in a family's work-school decision.

The issue of school quality may also help us understand the somewhat disappointing impact that the PROGRESA program had on child labor in rural Mexico compared to the stunning impact that PETI appears to have had on some working children in rural Brazil. Both programs combine education subsidies with other forms of support for children. PROGRESA emphasizes nutrition and health care. PETI emphasizes school structures and instructional materials. It may be the case that improving school quality is more important than is health care and nutrition for altering the family's work–school calculation. However, it may also be the case that the miraculous impact of PETI emerges in communities in which child labor is particularly pervasive or the work that children are undertaking is extremely dangerous. Without the type of careful empirical analysis applied to PROGRESA, it is difficult to draw conclusions.

Although the initial analysis of education subsidies appears to be disappointing, their performance is not worse and, in some cases, far better than laws that mandate minimum years of compulsory schooling and age of work. In fact, there appears to be very little evidence that such regulations have more than a marginal impact on the age at which children leave school and begin working. Therefore, a policy stance that requires the establishment and enforcement of child labor standards across all countries is unlikely to be effective or improve the lot of children.

Neither is it reasonable to believe that trade sanctions leveled against countries with a high rate of child labor are likely to make children better off. In fact, the threat of sanctions against non-compliant countries is all too credible because of political forces within industrialized countries that will promote them for a variety of reasons. But such threats are either disingenuous or misguided, because sanctions are very likely to harm children rather than help them.

NOTES

1. The authors would like to express their appreciation to Lisa Román and the Expert Group on Development Issues for sponsoring this project on international labor standards. We particularly appreciate the comments of Sarah Bachman, Kaushik Basu, Alan Krueger, Luis-Felipe Lopéz-Calva, Deborah Levison, T. N. Srinivasan, Ulf Edstrom, Dale Andrew, Jane Humphries, Eliot Berg, G. Rajasekeran, Bjorn Jonzon and other participating authors.
2. See Basu (1999).
3. The World Values Survey is undertaken by the European Values Systems Study Group.
4. Guerrero, Hidlago, Michocacan, Puebla, Queretero, San Luis Potosi, and Veracruz.
5. Product labeling does sometimes include provisions for improving the well-being of children who are displaced from jobs as a result. For more on this see Brown et al. 2001.

REFERENCES

Acemoglu, D. and J. Angrist (1999) "How Large are the Social Returns to Education? Evidence from Compulsory Schooling Laws," NBER Working Paper 7444, Cambridge, MA: NBER.

Andvig, J. (1997) "Child Labor in Sub-Saharan Africa – An Exploration," NUPI Working Paper no. 585.

Angrist, J. and A. Krueger (1991) "Does Compulsory Schooling Affect Schooling and Earnings?," *Quarterly Journal of Economics*, 106 (4), pp. 979–1014.

Anker, R. and S. Barge (1998) *Economics of Child Labor in Indian Industries*, Geneva: ILO.

Anker, R. and H. Melkas (1996) "Economic Incentives for Children and Families to Eliminate or Reduce Child Labor," Geneva: ILO.

Baland, J. and J. Robinson (2000) "Is Child Labor Inefficient?," *Journal of Political Economy*, 108 (4), pp. 662–79.

Basu, K. (1999) "Child Labor: Cause, Consequence, and Cure, with Remarks on International Labor Standards," *Journal of Economic Literature*, 37 (3), pp. 1083–119.

Basu, K. and P. Van (1998) "The Economics of Child Labor," *American Economic Review*, 88 (3), pp. 412–27.

Becker, G. (1964) *Human Capital*, New York: Columbia University Press.

Becker, G. and H. Lewis (1973) "On the Interaction Between the Quantity and Quality of Children," *Journal of Political Economy*, 81 (2, part 2), pp. S279–S288.

Bhalotra, S. and C. Heady (1998) Child Labor in Rural Pakistan and Ghana: Myths and Data, Bristol: University of Bristol, Department of Economics.

Bolin-Hort, P. (1989) *Work, Family, and the State: Child Labor and the Organization of Production in the British Cotton Industry, 1780–1920*, Lund: Lund University Press.

Bonnet, M. (1993) "Child Labor in Africa," *International Labor Review*, 132 (3), pp. 371–89.

Brown, D., A. Deardorff, and R. Stern (2001) "U.S. Trade and Other Policy Options and Programs to Deter Foreign Exploitation of Child Labor," in M. Blomstrom and L. Goldberg (eds), *Topics in Empirical International Economics*, Chicago and London: University of Chicago Press.

Brown, M., J. Christiansen, and P. Philips (1992) "The Decline of Child Labor in the US Fruit and Vegetable Canning Industry: Law or Economics," *Business History Review*, 66 (4), pp. 723–770.

Burra, N. (1995) *Born to Work: Child Labor in India*, Dehli: Oxford University Press.

Canagarajah, S. and H. Coulombe (1998) "Child Labor and Schooling in Ghana," Policy Research Working Paper no. 1844, Washington, DC: The World Bank.

Cartwright, K. (1999) "Child Labor in Colombia," in C. Grootaert and H. Patrinos (eds), *The Policy Analysis of Child Labor, A Comparative Study*, Washington, DC: The World Bank.

Cartwright, K. and H. Patrinos (1999) "Child Labor in Urban Bolivia," in C. Grootaert and H. Patrinos (eds), *The Policy Analysis of Child Labor, A Comparative Study*, Washington, DC: The World Bank.

Chernichovsky, D. (1985) "Socioeconomic and Demographic Aspects of School Enrolment and Attendance in Rural Botswana," *Economic Development and Cultural Change*, 32 (1), pp. 319–32.

Coulombe, H. (1998) "Child Labor and Education in Cote d'Ivoire," Washington DC: The World Bank.

Dreze, J. and G. Kingdon (2000) "School Participation in Rural India," Oxford: Oxford University Press.

Duflo, E. (2000) "Schooling and Labor Market Consequences of School Construction in Indonesia: Evidence from an Unusual Policy Experiment," NBER Working Paper 7860, Cambridge, MA: National Bureau of Economic Research.

Engerman, S. (2001) "The History and Political Economy of International Labor Standards," Rochester: University of Rochester.

Freeman, R. (1994) "A Hard-Headed Look at Labor Standards," in R. Sengenberger and D. Campbell (eds), *International Labor Standards and Economic Interdependence*, Geneva: International Labor Office.

Glewwe, P. and H. Jacoby (1994) "Student Achievement and Schooling Choice in Low-Income Countries: Evidence from Ghana," *Journal of Human Resources*, 29 (3), pp. 843–64.

Grootaert, C. (1999) "Child Labor in Cote d'Ivoire," in C. Grootaert and H. Patrinos (eds), *The Policy Analysis of Child Labor, A Comparative Study*, Washington, DC: The World Bank.

Grootaert, C. and R. Kanbur (1995) "Child Labor: An Economic Perspective," *International Labor Review*, 134 (2), pp. 187–203.

Gupta, M. (1997) *Unemployment of Adult Labor and the Supply of Child Labor: A Theoretical Analysis*, Calcutta: Jadavpur University.

Hanushek, E. (1992) "The Trade-off between Child Quantity and Quality," *Journal of Political Economy*, 100 (1), pp. 647–60.

Hanushek, E. and V. Lavy (1994) "School Quality, Achievement Bias, and Dropout Behavior in Egypt," LSMS Working Paper no. 107, Washington, DC: The World Bank.

Harmon, C. and I. Walker (1995) "Estimates of the Economic Return to Schooling in the UK," *American Economic Review*, 85 (5), pp. 1278–86.

IFPRI (2000) "Is PROGRESA Working? Summary of the Results of an Evaluation by IFPRI," Washington, DC: International Food Policy Research Institute.

ILO-IPEC (1998a) *Child Labor in Bangladesh: Its Context and Response to It*, Dhaka: ILO/IPEC.

ILO-IPEC (1998b) *Update Factory Monitoring per 01/05/90*, ILO/IPEC, Memorandum to Members of the Informal Steering Committee, Dhaka, May 13.

Jensen, P. and H. Nielsen (1997) "Child Labor or School Attendance? Evidence from Zambia," *Journal of Population Economics*, 10 (4), pp. 407–24.

Krueger, A. (1997) "International Labor Standards and Trade," in M. Bruno and B. Pleskovic (eds), *Annual World Bank Conference on Development Economics*, Washington, DC: The World Bank.

Lavy, V. (1996) "School Supply Constraints and Children's Educational Outcomes in Rural Ghana." *Journal of Development Economics*, 51 (2), pp. 291–314.

Levison, D. (1991) *Children's Labor Force Activity and Schooling in Brazil*, PhD Dissertation, Ann Arbor: University of Michigan.

Levison, D., R. Anker, S. Ashraf, and S. Barge (1996) *Is Child Labor Really Necessary in India's Carpet Industry?* Labor Market Paper no. 15, Geneva: International Labor Organization.

Levy, V. (1985) "Cropping Patterns, Mechanization, and Child Labor and Fertility Behavior in a Farming Economy: Rural Egypt," *Economic Development and Cultural Change*, 33 (4), pp. 777–91.

Mah, J. (1997) "Core Labor Standards and Export Performance in Developing Countries," *World Economy*, 20 (6), pp. 773–85.

Margo, R. and T. Finegan (1996) "Compulsory Schooling Legislation and School Attendance in Turn-of-the-Century America: A 'Natural Experiment' Approach," *Economic Letters*, 53 (1), pp. 103–10.

Maskus, K. (1997) "Should Core Labor Standards be Imposed Through International Trade Policy?", World Bank Policy Research Working Paper no. 1817, Washington, DC: The World Bank.

Ministerio de Educacion (1993) *Censo Escolar*," Lima: Ministerio de Educacion.

Moehling, C. (1995) "The Intra-household Allocation of Resources and the Participation of Children in Household Decision-Making: Evidence from Early Twentieth Century America," Chicago: Northwestern University.

Moehling, C. (1999) "State Child Labor Laws and the Decline of Child Labor," *Explorations in Economic History*, 36 (1), pp. 72–106.

Montgomery, M., A. Kouame, and R. Oliver (1995) "The Tradeoff between Number of Children and Child Schooling: Evidence from Cote d'Ivoire and Ghana," LSMS Working Paper no. 112, Washington, DC: The World Bank.

Nardinelli, C. (1990) *Child Labor and the Industrial Revolution*, Bloomington: Indiana University Press.

Parker, S. and E. Skoufias (2000) "The Impact of PROGRESA on Work and Time Allocation," Washington, DC: International Food Policy Research Institute.

Parsons, D. and C. Goldin (1989) "Parental Altruism and Self-Interest: Child Labor Among Late Nineteenth-Century American Families," *Economic Inquiry*, 27 (4), pp. 637–59.

Patrinos, H. and G. Psacharopoulos (1995) "Educational Performance and Child Labor in Paraguay," *International Journal of Educational Development*, 15 (1), pp. 47–60.

Patrinos, H. and G. Psacharopoulos (1997) "Family Size, Schooling and Child Labor in Peru: An Empirical Analysis," *Journal of Population Economics*, 10 (4), pp. 387–405.

Powell, B. and L. Steelman (1993) "The Educational Benefits of Being Spaced Out: Sibship Density and Educational Progress," *American Sociological Review*, 58 (3), pp. 367–81.

Psacharopoulos, G. (1997) "Child Labor Versus Educational Attainment, Some Evidence from Latin America," *Journal of Population Economics*, 10 (4), pp. 377–86.

Psacharopoulos G. and A. Arriagada (1989) "The Determinants of Early Age Human Capital Formation: Evidence from Brazil," *Economic Development and Cultural Change*, 37 (4), pp. 683–708.

Ranjan, P. (2001) "Credit Constraints and the Phenomenon of Child Labor," *Journal of Development Economics*, 64 (1), pp. 81–102.

Ravallion, M. and Q. Wodon (1999) "Does Child Labor Displace Schooling? Evidence on Behavioral Responses to an Enrollment Subsidy," Washington, DC: The World Bank.

Ray, R. (2000) "Analysis of Child Labor in Peru and Pakistan: A Comparative Study," *Journal of Population Economics*, 13 (1), pp. 3–19.

Rodrik, D. (1996) "Labor Standards in International Trade: Do They Matter and What Do We Do About Them," in R. Lawrence, D. Rodrik, and J. Whalley (eds), *Emerging Agenda For Global Trade: High States for Developing Countries*, Overseas Development Council Essay no. 20, Washington, DC: Overseas Development Corporation and Johns Hopkins University Press.

Rogers, C. and K. Swinnerton (1999) "Inequality, Productivity, and Child Labor: Theory and Evidence," Washington, DC: Georgetown University.

Rosenzweig, M. and K. Wolpin (1980) "Testing the Quantity–Quality Fertility Model: The Use of Twins as a Natural Experiment," *Econometrica*, 48 (1), pp. 228–40.

Sakalariou, C. and A. Lall (1999) "Child Labor in the Philippines," in C. Grootaert and H. Patrinos (eds), *The Policy Analysis of Child Labor, A Comparative Study*, Washington, DC: The World Bank.

San Martin, O. (1996) "Child Labor and Socio-Economic Development," in B. Grimsrud and A. Melchior (eds), *Child Labor and International Trade Policy*, Paris: Organization for Economic Cooperation and Development.

Scholliers, P. (1995) "Grown-ups, Boys and Girls in the Ghent Cotton Industry: The Voortman Mills, 1835–1914," *Social History*, 20 (2), pp. 201–18.

Schultz, P. (2001) "School Subsidies for the Poor: Evaluating a Mexican Strategy for Reducing Poverty," FCND Discussion Paper no. 102, Washington, DC: International Food Policy Research Institute.

Strauss, J. and D. Thomas (1995) "Human Resources: Empirical Modeling of Household and Family Decisions," in J. Behrman and T. N. Strinvasan (eds), *Handbook of Development Economics*, vol. 3, Amsterdam: North-Holland.

Tzannatos, Z. (1996) "Child Labor and School Enrollment in Thailand in the 1990s," The World Bank Social Protection, Human Development Network, Washington, DC: The World Bank.

US Department of Labor (1998) *By the Sweat and Toil of Children, Efforts to Eliminate Child Labor*, vol. 5, Washington DC: US Department of Labor.

Wodon, Q. (1999) "Cost–Benefit Analysis of Food for Education in Bangladesh," Policy Research Working Paper, Washington, DC: The World Bank.

World Bank (2001) *Spectrum*, Winter, Washington, DC: The World Bank.

COMMENTARY 3.1

The Political Economy of Child Labor

Alan B. Krueger[1]

To make conversation at a dinner party at the World Economic Forum in Davos, I once asked the then-finance minister of Pakistan whether child labor was a problem in his country. Perhaps thinking I was a potential investor, he replied, "No, child labor is not a problem. You can hire all the children you want." This story reminds me that there are many different perspectives that one can take on child labor.

There are many things I like about the perspective taken by Brown et al. in their study. Most importantly, they have the perspective of children's welfare in mind, and they provide a dispassionate and extensive analysis of policies intended to help improve child well-being based on the best available evidence. Alas, there are also a few points where I disagreed with their conclusions, or hoped further analysis would have been provided. Most importantly, I think the chapter should devote more attention to the political economy of child labor in both developed and less-developed countries. I'll begin with five aspects of the paper I liked and think are worth highlighting, and then will turn to some constructive criticisms.

First, Brown et al. rightly point out that laws concerning school enrolment and work restrictions are often not followed. Just because a compulsory schooling level is enacted, for example, does not mean that all – or even any – families will comply with the standard. This is the case in both rich and poor countries, but it is particularly true in poor countries that often lack the means to enforce the laws. Nevertheless, compulsory schooling laws do matter sometimes. My impression is that a skillfully set compulsory school-ing law can *nudge* behavior around the existing equilibrium schooling level, and may even cause educational attainment to increase faster than it other-wise would have increased, but such laws probably cannot not move an economy to a new equilibrium. In other words, if the minimum schooling age is set only slightly above the typical school-leaving age, it is more likely to have an effect than if it is set well above the typical school-leaving age. Indeed, if the compulsory schooling level or minimum work age is set at a level judged to be inappropriate or infeasible at the current income level and prevailing norms, it will be routinely ignored. Because compulsory schooling is a cheap policy, it may pass a cost–benefit standard even if there is little behavioral response. However, any investigation of legislated schooling or work requirements must first seek to determine whether the laws influence behavior before the benefits are considered.

Second, the authors rightly emphasize the overriding effect of poverty on children's activities. The impact of income (or its correlates) on child employment and education shows up in cross-country studies and in micro-econometric studies conducted at the family level. Brown et al. carefully review the micro evidence, which uniformly shows positive associations between income and school enrolment and negative associations between income and child labor. Indeed, I think they probably understate the importance of income because it is endogenous – all else equal, if a family has a child working it will have higher income, which works against finding a negative association between family income and the likelihood of children working.

One implication of this strong empirical regularity is that countries that do not exhibit falling child labor as their economy grows bear close scrutiny by the world community. Is it because they are exploiting children? Is it because aggregate income growth is concentrated among the wealthy, and the income of the masses is not rising?

Third, Brown et al. emphasize capital market failures and liquidity constraints as an explanation for many of their results. This seems to me to have a great deal of merit. For example, this seems a natural explanation for why first-born children obtain less education (although unlike the authors I would shy away from calling older children "assets").

Fourth, I particularly liked the careful attention the authors devoted to market-oriented programs to increase school enrolment. Indeed, this chapter provides a useful catalog of many programs in a diverse set of countries that subsidize families to send their children to school. I haven't seen the literature pulled together so comprehensively elsewhere. The most compelling evidence on the impact of these programs is from research on the PROGRESA program in Mexico. This program is unique in that it utilized random assignment to select the initial areas that participated in the program, while others served as a control group. As a consequence, evaluations of the program can be confident that observed changes in school enrolment and other behaviors are a response to the program, as opposed to other differences across regions.[2] The results indicate that educational subsidies are reasonably effective at increasing enrolment. Although less is known about the effect of educational subsidies on child labor, Parker and Skoufias (2001) find that eligibility for PROGRESA benefits led employment to decline by about 15 percent for boys and girls; this is a more optimistic result than Brown et al. would lead one to expect. It would be worth studying the impact of such programs on the wages and employment of adults.

Fifth, I also agree with the authors that it is very unlikely that unskilled workers in developed countries are in direct competition with many child laborers. Although there are an estimated quarter of billion child laborers throughout the world, most work in agriculture or in industries that are no longer existent in the developed world. I doubt very much that the job prospects or pay of a single worker in Newton, Massachusetts is affected by child labor in Pakistan. To put this in technical terms, the industries that employ child labor are outside the cone of diversification insofar as the developed nations are concerned. For this reason, I find it very unlikely that support for policies to restrict child labor among those in economically developed nations stems from disguised protectionism. The policies they seek may be irrelevant or counterproductive, but it is not accurate to simply dismiss them as a result of narrow, self-interested protectionism. More on this below.

While the chapter has many admirable features, I think it also has some limitations that are worth noting.

First, the chapter would be easier to read and more focused if a clear and consistent definition of child labor were employed. Indeed, one could imagine a useful distinction between potentially harmful and potentially helpful child labor. For example, child labor that occurs when school is out of session is probably less of a concern. Also, child labor in some industries or occupations is probably much more of a concern than it is in other industries and occupations. Likewise, the duration and physical demands of child labor is another dimension by which one could distinguish child labor. Many other dimensions are also worth considering. It does not seem right, however, to lump all forms of child labor together for the purposes of the present chapter, or present volume for that matter.

Second, the evaluation of the empirical literature could have been more discriminating. For example, some of the enrolment probit specifications controlled for both expenditures and parental education. The interpretation of expenditures in such a specification is different than in a specification that only controls for expenditures. In addition, the authors only present coefficients for variables that are statistically significant at the 10 percent level, as if there is no information in the other coefficients, or no information in knowing what other variables were held constant in the equation. And it would have been informative had Brown et al. compared the magnitudes of the effect of income on child labor from the studies conducted at the national and family level, and tried to reconcile any discrepancies that exist.

Third, the findings from the literature on school enrolment and income could have been integrated with the findings from education subsidies. In particular, education subsidies have both an income effect (families are richer so they desire more education for their children) and a substitution effect (school pays more than work so families should prefer to substitute children's time in school for time in other activities). In principle, the first empirical literature reviewed in the chapter estimates the pure income effect. This could be used to infer the substitution effect from the research on education subsidies. If the effect is primarily an income effect, then an elaborate subsidy program like PROGRESA is not necessary; income transfers would accomplish the same effect.

Fourth, the political economy of child labor *in developing countries* is given short shrift. The stylized view of child labor implicit in the chapter seems to be that all children voluntarily decide whether to work on the family farm or attend their local school. No external pressure is applied to their decision. No distortions exist. But in some countries children may be sold into slavery, or apprenticeship systems may exploit children. Employers may collude to block school construction and suppress wages below competitive market levels. Although such market imperfections may be rare, they are at least worthy of some consideration.

These were, after all, concerns of Adam Smith, who wrote, "When the regulation is in favor of the workers, it is always just and equitable; but it is sometimes otherwise when in favor of the masters." Smith even supported universal schooling at public expense because he feared that children's work was mind-numbingly dull and mentally debilitating. "When a person's whole attention is bestowed on the seventeenth part of a pin," he lectured, it is hardly surprising that he or she becomes "exceedingly stupid" (see Rothschild, 2001, p. 97).

Finally, it is common for trade economists to argue that support for international labor rights, such as restrictions on the importation of goods made with child labor, is motivated by disguised protectionism in economically developed nations, often at the instigation of labor unions. Because protectionism is bad, the argument goes, so are international labor standards, or even consideration of mutually agreed upon labor standards in trade negotiations. In my view, this argument is a red herring. Labor unions could support international labor standards for humanitarian as well as (or instead of) self-interested reasons. Moreover, even if international labor standards were motivated by self-interest, they nonetheless may raise welfare in less-developed nations (consider sanctions against apartheid in South Africa). And the converse is also true: even if international labor standards were motivated by humanitarian concerns they may hurt those they are intended to help in developing countries. There is no substitute for careful, direct empirical evaluation of the effect of policies designed to help certain groups.

In Krueger (1997) I examined the variables that were related to Congressional support for legislation that would ban importation of goods made by child labor.[3] For comparison, I also examined the correlates of support for the General Agreement on Tariffs and Treaties (GATT) in 1994 and the North American Free Trade Agreement (NAFTA). If the variables that were associated with support for the former differed from those that were associated with support for the GATT and NAFTA, then I would argue that political support for international child labor protectionism was not a form of disguised protectionism. The evidence as best as I can judge does not support the view that support for international labor standards is motivated solely from concerns for disguised protectionism. While self-interested protectionism may play a role, it is not the only factor behind political support for international labor standards.

I have been able to extend this analysis by considering two other recent votes in the United States House of Representatives. A bill concerning labor protection was voted on as an amendment to an appropriations bill for the Agriculture Department in August 2001. The amendment (H.R. 2330), which passed 290 to 115 but was not voted on in the Senate (as of this writing), directs the Food and Drug Administration to develop a label stating that enslaved child labor was not used to harvest cocoa beans used in chocolate products, and provides $250,000 for such labels. This is a fairly mild labor protection in the scheme of things. I doubt anyone in America supports the practice of enslaving children to produce cocoa beans for candy bars. Yet the bill does not prohibit consumption of candy bars made with ingredients produced with forced labor; it simply would notify consumers that their candy bar was not produced by enslaved children. Eliot Engel of New York was the main proponent of this legislation in the House, and Henry Bonilla of Texas was the main opponent. Mr. Engle justified his support for the amendment by arguing that there is "a moral responsibility for us not to allow slavery, child slavery, in the twenty-first century."[4] Since no cocoa is produced in New York, it is hard to see how he could be motivated by disguised protectionism. Mr. Bonilla objected to the amendment because he was concerned that "Additional money for food labeling will come from other vital areas."[5]

The second bill that I examine is the fast-track Trade Promotion Authority legislation passed in the House of Representatives by a razor-thin margin of 215–214 in November 2001. This legislation gives the President authority to negotiate bilateral or multilateral trade agreements, and then requires the Senate to vote up or down on the legislation without the opportunity to add amendments. Fast-track authority is generally considered to promote free trade, and consequently opposition to fast-track authority is a good indication of protectionist sentiment.

Table 3.7 reports estimates of probit models fit to the votes on these two bills. The unit of observation is an individual Congressman or Congresswoman. The dependent variable equals one if the representative voted for

Table 3.7 Probit estimates of determinants of Congressional support for labeling of cocoa products made with enslaved child labor and for fast-track trade promotion authority: US House of Representatives, 2001

Explanatory variable	Mean SD (1)	Voted for cocoa labeling (2)	Voted for trade promotion authority (3)
		Outcome variable	
Proportion less than	0.25	0.03	−1.03*
high school degree	(0.09)	(0.24)	(0.41)
Proportion union members	0.15	1.12**	−2.28**
	(0.06)	(0.34)	(0.60)
Democrat (1 = yes)	0.49	0.53**	−0.77**
	(0.50)	(0.04)	(0.03)
Pseudo-R^2	–	0.41	0.54
Sample size	429	405	429

Coefficients are expressed as the change in the probability the dependent variable equals one for a unit change in the explanatory variable.
For continuous explanatory variables the derivative is calculated for an infinitesimally small change in the explanatory variable; for the dummy variable a discrete change is used.
The probit equations also include an intercept.
Standard errors are shown in parentheses.
The one independent member of Congress is classified as a Democrat.
Mean of the dependent variable is 0.72 in column (2) and 0.50 in column (3).
* Statistically significant at 0.05 level.
** Statistically significant at 0.01 level.

the bill and zero if he or she voted against it. A relatively small number of explanatory variables are used to predict the votes: the proportion of individuals who live in the representative's district who left school without graduating from high school; the proportion of workers in the representative's state who are union members; and a dummy variable indicating whether the representative is a member of the Democratic or Republican party. The coefficients have been re-expressed so they may be interpreted as the change in the probability that the legislation was supported with respect to a one-unit change in the explanatory variable.

The main explanatory variable of interest is the proportion of the population with less than a high school degree. This is a measure of the skill-level of the constituents in the district. Because the United States is endowed with relatively skilled workers compared to the rest of the world, less-educated workers in the United States would benefit more than highly educated workers from trade restrictions. The results in table 3.7 – similar to

those found in Krueger (1997) – suggest that Congressmen who represent
districts with relatively many less-skilled workers are more likely to oppose
overt trade expansion (i.e., they oppose granting the President fast-track
for trade promotion authority). But support for labeling chocolate made
with enslaved child labor is virtually uncorrelated with the education level
of the representatives' constituents. Thus, insofar as the skill composition of
a district is concerned, support for international labor standards does not
look like disguised protectionism.

The other variables in table 3.7 are also worth noting. Congressmen who
represent states with a high proportion of union members are more likely to
oppose trade promotion and more likely to support international labeling.
Democrats are much more likely to support labeling and oppose fast-track
authority than Republicans – only 1 percent of the Democrats voted against
cocoa labeling, and only 10 percent supported fast-track trade promotion.
One interpretation of these results is that Democratic members of Congress
and those who represent many union members are more protectionist, and
this affects their vote on both overt protection and less direct protection. It
is also possible, however, that members who support legislation that would
protect child labor in developing countries do so out of humanitarian concerns, and that union members and leaders share those concerns. In any
event, it is not possible to infer the effects of international labor legislation
from the motives of the supporters, even if their motives could be unambigu-
ously inferred.

Conclusion

Countries that seek to raise the educational level of children and reduce
child labor would be well served to study Brown et al.'s chapter. Their
conclusion that capital market imperfections lead some families to send their
children to work instead of school seems to me to be an important problem
in need of policy redress. The solution to this problem, however, does not
have to involve improving access to capital. As Lawrence Summers has said
in a different context, it is not necessary to inflate a flat tire through the
puncture. Besides, other distortions may contribute to an inefficient level of
education and child labor, such as suboptimal provision of school resources.
Nevertheless, the mounting evidence on education subsidies suggests they
are very effective, probably because they help overcome capital constraints
and lower the cost of school attendance. A complete solution will probably
involve a portfolio of policies, such as school construction, improved school
quality, enforcement of compulsory schooling laws, educational subsidies
and loans, and enforcement of child labor laws. But educational subsidies are
probably a good margin to start.

Notes

1. Kenneth Fortson provided excellent assistance on the research reported in table 3.7.
2. Several studies on PROGRESA are available from www.ifpri.cgiar.org.
3. The legislation did not pass. In fact, it did not come to a vote. But the proposal did garner a number of co-sponsors. I modeled the determinants of co-sponsoring the bill.
4. Transcript of House debate on HR2330.
5. Transcript of House debate on HR2330.

References

Krueger, A. (1997) "International Labor Standards and Trade," in Michael Bruno and Boris Pleskovic (eds), *Annual World Bank Conference on Development Economics, 1996*, pp. 281–302, Washington, DC: The World Bank.

Parker, S. and E. Skoufias (2001) "The Impact of Progresa on Work, Leisure, and Time Allocation," mimeo, Washington, DC: International Food Policy Research Institute.

Rothschild, E. (2001) *Economic Sentiments: Adam Smith, Condorcet, and the Enlightenment*, Cambridge, MA: Harvard University Press.

COMMENTARY 3.2

Social Norms, Coordination, and Policy Issues in the Fight Against Child Labor

Luis-Felipe López-Calva[1]

The issue of child labor has been extensively analyzed in recent years. The study presented by Brown et al. (in this volume) is a thorough and very complete survey of the analysis of determinants, consequences, and possible solutions to the problem. The study presents evidence on policy experiments dealing with this phenomenon, discussion that is especially useful and illuminating. There are, however, some points that will be presented in this chapter to emphasize additional lines of research, as well as policy implications that should be considered to complete the picture.

The Role of Social Norms

An issue that has been ignored, to a certain extent, in the literature is the role of cultural aspects influencing child labor decisions. Specifically, the role of different types of informal social norms that might have an important effect on child labor incidence. I will discuss here two examples, namely, norms of filial obligations and norms of "social stigma" or social disapproval of parents who send their children to work. The latter idea has been proposed by Hirschman, as mentioned in Brown et al., and also briefly discussed in Basu (1999).

Filial interactions

There are two issues not discussed in Brown et al. that have shown to be important according to recent research. First, the so-called "intergenerational child labor trap," first discussed in Basu (1999) and later extended in Emerson and Portela (2000). The latter shows robust empirical evidence using Brazilian data. Controlling for relevant socioeconomic characteristics, children whose parents started working at a young age tend to start working earlier in their lives. Though not the main explanation provided by the authors, it has been argued that a cultural norm could be playing a role here, namely, the fact that parents who started working early consider that a value and something that is good for the education of their children – given that those children could also be in school. There are also communities, especially in rural areas, where the children's contribution to family work is a well-established cultural value.[2]

Another type of filial interaction is related to social security for old age among the poor. López-Calva and Miyamoto (2002) show that a filial obligations contract can be sustained as an intergenerational equilibrium, but the type of care parents receive during old age will depend on human capital investment in their own children. If the production of care for the old has a Cobb–Douglas form in which the inputs are time and monetary transfers, it can be shown that, depending on technological and productivity parameters in the economy, you may end up in either an equilibrium with low-child labor and money-intensive transfers or one with high-child labor incidence and time-intensive care. Just as an illustration, figure 3.1 shows the incidence of co-residence – time-intensive care – and child labor in low-income versus more developed countries, which tends to support this idea.

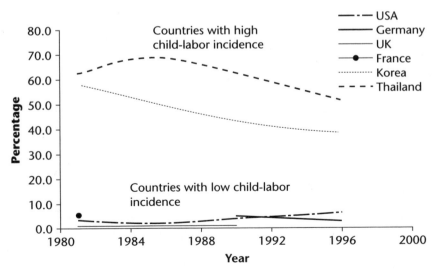

Figure 3.1 Member of household aged 60 and over living with grandchild

The discussion on norms should not be understood as an alternative to a typically rational, children-as-assets type of analysis. Rather, we suggest this is an additional route to understand fully the phenomenon. One has to also consider that, at the end, social norms might also be endogenous to the set of economic conditions in the longer run.

Social stigma

This section shows a simple example to show the multiplicity of equilibria arising through the social convention that imposes a social cost on those that send their children to work. An extended model is in López-Calva (2002). Also, empirical evidence from Mexico, using the National Urban Employment Survey from 1994 to 1998, shows that such a hypothesis cannot be rejected.

Stigma models have been previously used in the literature to analyze different issues like the welfare system (Besley and Coate, 1992; Lindbeck et al., 1998) and crime incidence and its persistence (Rasmusen, 1996). The internalization of such kinds of norm into the preferences becomes a self-enforcement mechanism. People may incorporate certain rules into their preferences and norms prevail through feelings of embarrassment, anxiety, guilt, and shame when they violate them (Akerlof and Kranton, 2000; Elster, 1989). Disapproval by members of the group a person belongs to may reduce that person's welfare by affecting the sense of belongingness, her identity. Akerlof and Kranton (2000) introduce a utility function that depends on:

1. consumption of goods and services;
2. the individual's own actions and *the actions of others*; and
3. a given "prescription" (something that *should* or *should not* be done, i.e., a norm).

This is the type of effect that can be modeled as a "stigma." There are other forms of enforcement mechanisms, as in the case where the convention requires a punishment or "social sanction" by the community in order for the norm to be sustainable, within a folk theorem type of argument (Coate and Ravallion, 1993). Yet one alternative role norms may play in economic interactions is that of focal points in interactions with multiple equilibria. Those are called "equilibrium-selection" norms (Basu, 2000).

As mentioned above, let us assume there is a social norm that says that should you send a child to work, you shall be considered a bad parent. Sending a child to work produces embarrassment – a *social stigma* cost – that is reflected in lower utility. That embarrassment, however, will be lower the higher the proportion of people that are violating the norm. The higher the level of child labor in the economy, the lower the social stigma cost, for a given level of child labor supply of a specific household.

In the model, the aggregate level of child labor, E, shall be taken as given by individual households. The effect of one individual's decision on the aggregate variable is seen as negligible by the concerned decision-maker. The expectation of what the aggregate level would be, though, will influence the optimal level of child labor for the decision-maker in the household.

Let us suppose that we have N households in the economy, each one composed of one adult and one child. The general specification of preferences is given by a utility function whose arguments are total household consumption (c), the child's effort level, $e \in [0,1]$, denotes the fraction of the child's non-leisure time spent at work, number of hours at work, and the aggregate level of child labor in the economy, E, $W = W(c,e,E)$. The last two arguments are related to what will be termed "stigma cost." It will be assumed that the utility function is separable in consumption and "stigma cost," the latter being a function of e and E. The social stigma reduces the parent's utility. There will be one decision maker in the household, the parent, following the tradition of the unitary model (Becker, 1965). The problem of the parents is then:

$$\text{Max}_{c,e} \; W(c,e,E) = U(c) - S(e,E) \tag{1}$$

such that

$$c \le w + w_c e, \tag{2}$$

where the wages of the adults and the children are w and w_c, respectively. Both w and w_c are later determined endogenously, though each household treats these (as well as E) to be given. The assumption on the functions $U(c)$ and $S(e,E)$ are $U_c > 0$, $U_{cc} \le 0$, $S_e > 0$, $S_{ee} \ge 0$, $S(0,E) = 0$, $eS_E \le 0$, and finally $S_{eE} < 0$, i.e., the marginal disutility from a child's effort is decreasing in the total amount of child labor in the economy. The first four assumptions are standard; $S(0,E) = 0$ captures the fact that stigma cost is zero if the child is not working. The latter implies that if $e = 0$, then $S_E = 0$. The condition $eS_E \le 0$ implies that if $e > 0$, $S_E \le 0$. In other words, an increase in aggregate child labor weakly diminishes the stigma cost, provided that the child is working in the first place. Note that thsese assumptions imply that $S(e,E) > 0$ whenever $e > 0$. Therefore, it is being assumed that even if E is very large, as long as one child works the stigma cost does not vanish. Thus, child labor is not a value neutral activity with reward for keeping up with the Jones. It is something that society considers to be inherently "bad."

Clearly, the constraint will always be binding, since $U_c(\ ) > 0$. Hence, we may insert (2) into the utility function of the agent, (1), and obtain the first order condition

$$U'(w + w_c e)w_c = S_e(e,E),\tag{3}$$

which simply states that the marginal benefit of an extra unit of child labor supplied in the market, measured in terms of utility from extra consumption, has to equal the marginal cost, as given by the stigma to be borne by the parent, as a function of individual and aggregate child labor supply. From (3), it is possible to obtain the optimal amount of child labor hours supplied by the individual household, given by $e^*(w,w_c,E)$. Hence, the agent considers the wage rates and the *expected* level of child labor in the economy, E, in order to optimally choose the number of hours that her child should work.

The aggregate level of child labor in the economy in equilibrium, E^*, must satisfy a natural aggregate consistency requirement (Basu, 1987; Becker, 1991; and Lindbeck et al., 1998). The consistency requirement shall be termed "rational expectations property." The set of E that satisfy such a property is defined as:

$$\psi(w,w_c) = \{E \mid E = Ne^*(w,w_c,E)\}.$$

Let us now turn to the description of firms. Firms maximize profit using a production function whose only input is "effective" units of labor, i.e., adult and child labor corrected by the adult equivalence parameter, γ, which tells us how productive a child is compared to an adult. In other words, it is being assumed, for analytical simplicity, that adult labor and child labor are substitutes, subject to an equivalency correction.

Thus, for a firm that employs A adults and C children, its effective labor input is $L \equiv A + \gamma C$. Given the assumptions, it is obvious that if $\gamma w < w_c$, no firm will employ children and if $\gamma w > w_c$ no firm will employ adults. Hence, whenever adults and children work, $\gamma w = w_c$. From now on, it will be assumed, without loss of generality, that this is the case. Then, whenever it is said that the adult wage is w, it should be presumed that child wage is γw.

With this in mind, notice that if the wage is w, then the representative firm maximizes $\pi = f(L) - wL$, and the first order condition is simply $f'(L) = w$. Assume there are constant returns to scale, so that profits are equal to zero. The optimal amount of effective units of labor demanded is

$$L^* = f'^{-1}(w).\tag{4}$$

Without loss of generality, let us assume that this economy has only one firm. We are now in a position to define an equilibrium. Intuitively, an equilibrium is a situation where the demand for child labor is equal to its supply, the demand for adult labor equals the demand of adult labor, and the amount of child labor satisfies the rational expectations property.

The *equilibrium* for this economy can now be defined formally as a triple (w^*, w_c^*, E^*) such that:

(i) $\gamma w^* = w_c^*$
(ii) $E^* \in \psi(w^*, \gamma w^*)$, and
(iii) $N + \gamma E^* = f'^{-1}(w^*)$.

Condition (ii) above establishes that the aggregate level of child labor must satisfy the rational expectations property at the equilibrium, i.e., parent's choice of e, given wages and expected level of E, must result in E^*. The third condition, (iii), is the market clearing in the labor market, in terms of effective units of labor. The wage w^* must be such that the firm's demand equals the summation of N (adult labor supply) and total child labor supply in effective units, γE^*.

In order to show in a simple way the multiplicity of equilibria introduced by the social interactions in this model, let us assume that $U(c) = \ln(c)$. Using this specification of $U(c)$ has the advantage that the optimal supply of labor will be independent of the level of wages, which will allow us to illustrate the main result in a simple manner. In the next section, this specification is changed so as to incorporate the interaction with wages. The first order condition is as follows:

$$\frac{\gamma}{(1 + \gamma e)} = S_e(e, E). \tag{5}$$

It is easy to show that the model yields strategic complementarity in terms of child labor supply, for any positive level of e. In this case, strategic complementarity depends on the sign of $\dfrac{de^*}{dE}$, which can be obtained by totally differentiating (5):

$$\frac{de^*}{dE} = -\frac{(1 + \gamma e)S_{eE}}{\gamma S_e + (1 + \gamma e)S_{ee}} \geq 0, \tag{6}$$

and this will be a strict inequality for $e > 0$.

Thus, under the reasonable assumptions made above, to wit $S_{eE} < 0$, $S_e > 0$, and $S_{ee} > 0$, strategic complementarity obtains. Expectations regarding what the aggregate level of child labor in the economy will be, i.e., what the others will do, affect each individual's decision and thus the outcome, opening the possibility of multiple equilibria. The response of the agents to the expected aggregate level of child labor derives in multiple rational expectations equilibria, shown as points A, B, and C in figure 3.2. The social effect is introduced by the norm, given that the adult's expectation of E determines

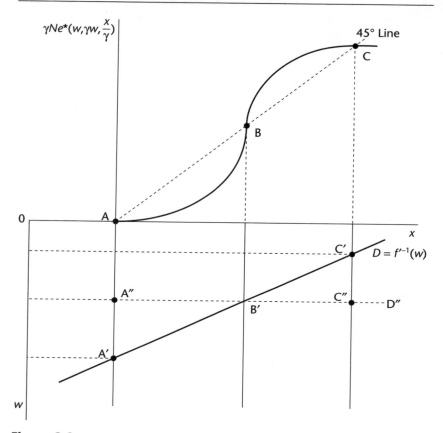

Figure 3.2 Rational expectations equilibria and the labor market

the expected stigma cost – "embarrassment" level – she will face at a given e.

The possibility of multiple equilibria in the labor market is shown in figure 3.2, for a given shape of the stigma cost.[3] The horizontal axis is in units of x, which is defined as aggregate child labor measured in adult equivalence, $x = \gamma E$. The distance 0A in the quadrant below is equal to N, and represents the fact that parents supply their labor inelastically. The main quadrant shows the points that satisfy the rational expectations property for E, points A, B, and C. The vertical axis represents the total amount of effective child labor supplied as a response of the expected aggregate level, E, for given wages. The total amount of effective child labor supplied as a response of the expected aggregate level is obtained by correcting for adult equivalence the optimal amount supplied by the individual household, and multiplying it by the number of households, N.

The lower quadrant in figure 3.2 is the one that depicts the market clearing in the labor market, showing the demand for effective units of labor, $L^* = f'^{-1}(w)$, as well as the supply. The supply is inelastic with respect to wages and determined by the expectations about E (see first order condition). The two stable rational expectations equilibria are A and C. These determine two stable equilibria in the labor market, A′ and C′, as shown in the quadrant below.

The main result thus obtains: (a) one equilibrium is at C′, where wages are low and children work; and (b) a second equilibrium is represented by A′, with high wages and no child labor. This result derives directly from the social stigma attached to parents who send their children to work, and the quite realistic assumption that such an "embarrassment" decreases as the proportion of children working in the economy increases. Thus, a social norm, sustained through social pressure, derives in a coordination problem.

The existence of multiple equilibria is robust to different specifications of the demand for labor. Suppose this is a small, open economy, which implies that the labor demand is perfectly elastic at a given wage level, D″. The two stable equilibria are then A″ and C″. The existence of multiple equilibria is robust to that specification, as opposed to the model in Basu and Van (1998). An extension where the wages affect the set of rational expectations equilibria is developed in López-Calva (2002).

But the discussion on whether such effects exist is an empirical question. As discussed in Brown et al., there are basically three econometric models in the literature for dealing with the work–school multiple choice problem: bivariate probit, multinomial logit and sequential probit. Tables 3.8 and 3.9 show the sequential probit and bivariate probit models analyzing child labor and schooling decisions in Mexico for the period 1994 to 1998. (The variables used in the bivariate, multinomial logit and sequential probit models are shown in table 3.10.) A more extensive discussion of similar results for Mexico and Venezuela is in Freije and López-Calva (2000).

The empirical test uses the National Urban Employment Survey (ENEU) for the period 1994 to 1998. This survey is representative of the 41 largest urban areas in Mexico since 1993. It includes microdata on household characteristics, work status, wages, and demographic characteristics of the household, with individual information for all family members 12 years old and above. A working child will be defined as a family member who is between 12 and 16 years old and worked positive hours, for a salary, during the week of reference. Compulsory schooling in Mexico goes up to secondary school, the equivalent, on average, to 15–16 years of age. Also, the law does not permit working until such age. The options given in the questionnaire of the survey, in addition to asking the number of hours worked

Table 3.8 Sequential probit results for 1994–98

Variable	First stage: Only school dF/dx	Robust Std. Err.	Second stage: School and work dF/dx	Robust Std. Err.	Third stage: Only work dF/dx	Robust Std. Err.
Child characteristics						
Age5	−0.0598**	0.0089	0.0079	0.0122	0.0640**	0.0160
Gender5	−0.0287	0.0229	0.0956**	0.0314	0.2038**	0.0408
Household head characteristics						
Headsex	0.0623**	0.0281			−0.0591	0.0510
Headage	0.0011	0.0014	−0.0024	0.0018	−0.0009	0.0023
Headedu	0.0153**	0.0022	−0.0007	0.0032	−0.0247**	0.0047
Hdemp1	−0.0144	0.0466	0.0137	0.0769	0.0451	0.0912
Hdemp2	−0.0022	0.0425	0.0045	0.0680	−0.0517	0.0740
Hdemp3	−0.1254**	0.0490	0.0272	0.0723	0.0227	0.0744
Headms			0.0696**	0.0287		
D_hdemp	0.0075	0.0692	−0.0610	0.0630	−0.1277	0.0683
Household characterisitcs						
boy04	−0.0272	0.0177	−0.0252	0.0247	0.0667**	0.0290
boy59	0.0156	0.0172	−0.0259	0.0249	0.0073	0.0320
boy1013	−0.0228	0.0151	0.0180	0.0195	−0.0538**	0.0253
boy1416	−0.0366**	0.0172	0.0317	0.0250	−0.0204	0.0327
girl04	−0.0534**	0.0210	−0.0282	0.0294	0.0316	0.0345
girl59	0.0016	0.0173	−0.0239	0.0244	0.0686**	0.0283
girl1013	−0.0227	0.0153	0.0204	0.0219	0.0364	0.0268
girl1416	−0.0239	0.0176	0.0709**	0.0237	0.0121	0.0331
adul1759	0.0070	0.0084	−0.0078	0.0119	−0.0006	0.0141
elder60	−0.0274*	0.0150	−0.0201	0.0217	0.0820**	0.0273
Nopov	0.0165	0.0315	0.0334	0.0408	0.1211**	0.0527
Staypov			0.0629	0.0667	0.0952	0.0873
Fallpov	0.0341	0.0369				
Escpov	−0.0090	0.0395	0.0115	0.0585	0.2328**	0.1005
wage1759	0.0000	0.0001	0.0001	0.0001	0.0000	0.0001
d_wg1759	0.0000	0.0001	−0.0001	0.0001	0.0000	0.0001
Ourate	−1.4806	0.9785	1.3664	1.3425	1.3516	1.8637
hrwg1216	0.0022	0.0140	−0.0073	0.0194	0.0191	0.0265
d_hrwage	0.0069	0.0164	0.0233	0.0224	−0.0070	0.0313
schenra5	0.6626**	0.1353	1.0830**	0.1943	0.4680*	0.2636
laborin5	−0.2087	0.2417	0.9598**	0.3605	2.9993**	0.4946
Log likelihood	−1744.1571		−368.4466		−331.8698	
Wald Chi2	281.36		79.84		188.67	
Pseudo R2	0.0836		0.0974		0.2395	

** Significant at 95%.
* Significant at 90%.

Table 3.9 Bivariate probit results for 1994–98

Variable	School5	Std. Err.	Work5	Std. Err.
Intercept	−0.7110	0.7272	−5.9313**	0.9176
Child characteristics				
Age5	−0.1129**	0.0321	0.2331**	0.0424
Gender5	0.0613	0.0845	0.4262**	0.1127
Household head characteristics				
Headsex	0.1292	0.0978	0.0016	0.1286
Headage	0.0020	0.0049	−0.0034	0.0062
Headedu	0.0389**	0.0079	−0.0688**	0.0110
Hdemp1	−0.0794	0.1766	0.1419	0.2203
Hdemp2	0.0085	0.1644	−0.0183	0.2001
Hdemp3	−0.2603	0.1692	0.3224	0.2032
Hdemp4	5.6576	23524.4100	−4.4122	30595.9100
D_hdemp	−0.4188*	0.2421	−0.6238	0.5305
Household characteristics				
Boy04	−0.1121*	0.0646	0.0618	0.0794
Boy59	0.0270	0.0612	−0.0648	0.0798
Boy1013	−0.0444	0.0541	0.0195	0.0679
Boy1416	−0.0455	0.0634	0.0309	0.0811
Girl04	−0.1977**	0.0747	0.2039**	0.0898
Girl59	−0.0066	0.0615	0.0513	0.0777
Girl1013	−0.0233	0.0557	0.1514**	0.0681
Girl1416	−0.0293	0.0636	0.1497*	0.0828
Adul1759	0.0362	0.0309	−0.0177	0.0368
Elder60	−0.0750	0.0539	0.1079	0.0696
Nopov	0.0584	0.1201	−0.1041	0.1496
Fallpov	0.1189	0.1437	0.3230*	0.1907
Escpov	−0.0031	0.1466	−0.0529	0.1825
Wage1759	0.0006*	0.0004	−0.0006	0.0005
D_wg1759	−0.0001	0.0002	0.0002	0.0003
Ourate	1.9286	3.8432	−2.6686	5.0799
Hrwg1216	−0.0566	0.0564	0.0791	0.0737
D_hrwage	−0.0316	0.0581	0.0929	0.0758
Schenra5	2.3934**	0.5450	−1.4433**	0.6727
Laborin5	1.2898	0.8683	5.6262**	1.1982
School	0.1684**	0.0728	−0.1702*	0.0909
Work	−0.3743**	0.1095	0.7178**	0.1162
Log likelihood	−1797.6323			
Wald Chi2	406.52			
Rho	−0.4154			
Likelihood ratio test of rho=0	Chi2(1)	69.693		

** Significant at 95%.

* Significant at 90%.

Table 3.10 Variables used in the bivariate probit, multinomial logit and sequential probit models

Variable	Definition
Child occupation	
School5	Child attends school (final period)
Work5	Child works in the labor market (final period)
Worksch5	Child only goes to school=1, child goes to school and works=2, Child only works=3, none of the others=4 (final period)
Onlysch5	Child only goes to school=1 (final period)
Wksch5	Child goes to school and works=1 (final period)
Onlywk5	Child only works (final period)
Child characteristics	
Age5	Age of child (final period)
Gender5	Gender of child, 1=male (final period)
Household head characteristics	
Headsex	Household head gender, 1=male (final period)
Headage	Household head age (initial period)
Headedu	Household head years of education (initial period)
Hdemp1	Household head employed in the government = 1 (initial period)
Hdemp2	Household head employed in the formal sector = 1 (initial period)
Hdemp3	Household head employed in the informal sector = 1 (initial period)
Hdemp4	Household head unemployed = 1 (initial period)
Headms	Household marital status, 1=couple, 0=single (initial period)
D_hdemp	Change in the household head employment status, 1= become unemployed, 0=no change (initial period)
D_hdms	Change in the household head marital status, 1=change, 0=no change (initial period)
Household characteristics	
Boy04	Number of boys age 0–4 in the household (initial period)
Boy59	Number of boys age 5–9 in the household (initial period)
Boy1013	Number of boys age 10–13 in the household (initial period)
Boy1416	Number of boys age 14–16 in the household (initial period)
Girl04	Number of girls age 0–4 in the household (initial period)
Girl59	Number of girls age 5–9 in the household (initial period)
Girl1013	Number of girls age 10–13 in the household (initial period)
Girl1416	Number of girls age 14–16 in the household (initial period)
Adul1759	Number of adults in the household (initial period)
Elder60	Number of elderly in the household (initial period)
Nopov	Household stays out of poverty
Staypov	Household stays in poverty
Fallpov	Household falls into poverty
Escpov	Household escapes from poverty
Wage1759	Median wage for adults, by state (initial period)
D_wg1759	Change in the median wage for adults
Ourate	Open unemployment rate, by state (initial period)
Hrwg1216	Mean hour wage for children, by state (initial period)
D_hrwage	Change in the mean hour wage for children
Schenra5	Child school enrolment rate, by basic sampling area (final period)
Laborin5	Child labor incidence, by basic sampling area (final period)
School	Child attends school (initial period)
Work	Child works in the labor market (initial period)

and salaries received, can be grouped into four categories: a) only going to school, b) going to school and working, c) only working, and d) neither studying nor working.

The results show a robust effect of what we hereby defined as the "social interaction." Child labor incidence is calculated at the lowest level of aggregation, called "basic sampling area" (AGEB). Higher incidence of child labor among the neighbors has positive and significant effect on a child's probability of participation, controlling for all possible economic and demographic variables. The opposite is true for the case of average school attendance. Manski (2000) has criticized this kind of analysis of social interactions arguing that it would be necessary to have "subjective data for subjective concepts." Also, we might think of other variables whose effect could be picked up by the variable being used here – for example, school quality in the neighborhood. However, given the available data, it is clear that the effect of social interactions is an issue that should be studied more carefully if one is to implement effective policies against child labor.

A Comment on Policy

Brown et al. discuss evidence on the effect of specific policies to eliminate child labor. One of these policy experiments is the case of the PROGRESA program in Mexico. It is very important to emphasize that such kind of direct interventions, in which the government gives transfers to the families to compensate for the economic loss of school attendance of their children, have proven quite succesful. By 2002, there are eight different countries in Latin America with PROGRESA-like interventions. One of the main advantages of PROGRESA is the fact that the evaluation of the program was conceived and designed as part of the program itself, which has allowed a statistically robust analysis of its effects. It is true as well that the effects have been measured in a static fashion, when some of the expected benefits are by definition long-run effects. More appropriate evaluation will be needed in the future to capture the long-run effects of the program, given that the elimination of child labor, though important, is not the main goal *per se.* The main point is to evaluate whether the elimination of child labor and a higher educational attainment would indeed result in higher individual welfare of the children involved. That long-run effect is yet to be assessed.

Concluding Remarks

The literature on the economic analysis of child labor is rich and insightful, as shown in Brown et al. There are, however, lines of research that should be encouraged. One of the main issues to be incorporated more seriously in the literature is the formal analysis of cultural and behavioral rules at the community level and their impact on household decisions, including child labor. A simple model has been shown in this chapter. Also, more empirical evidence on the effect of social interactions is needed to move forward in the thorough analysis of social norms and economic behavior. In order to do that, more data and a different quality of data are needed. Finally, in terms of the policy perspective, it is important to emphasize that reducing child labor is not the objective *per se*. The main objective is to relax some important constraints on household decision-making to improve household welfare and, more important, to increase income-generation capabilities of individuals in the future. That leads to the incorporation of other variables, which should not be neglected, in the analysis namely, economic growth, regional development, and quality of schooling. As it has been the case historically in development economics, the literature on child labor discussed in these chapters has taught us a good deal about the microeconomics of development.

NOTES

1. I would like to thank Kaushik Basu for helpful conversations on the subject and comments to earlier versions. Alan Krueger and Deborah Levinson provided very useful comments to the empirical section. Participants at the EGDI-Seminar on International Labor Standards in Stockholm, provided useful comments to improve the chapter. The usual disclaimer applies.
2. Such is the case of the Andean regions of Peru, as shown by anthropological work.
3. It is important to mention that a linear specification of the stigma cost, given that e is bounded both from above and below, would result in the same multiplicity.

REFERENCES

Akerlof, G. and R. Kranton (2000) "Economics and Identity," *Quarterly Journal of Economics.*

Basu, K. (1987) "Monopoly, Quality Uncertainty, and 'Status' Goods," *International Journal of Industrial Organization,* 5, pp. 435–46.

Basu, K. (1999) "Child Labor: Cause, Consequences, and Cure, with Remarks on International Labor Standards," *Journal of Economic Literature,* 37, pp. 1067–82.

Basu, K. (2000) *A Prelude to Political Economy: The Social and Political Foundations of Economics,* Oxford: Oxford University Press.

Basu, K. and P. Van (1998) "The Economics of Child Labor," *American Economic Review,* 88, pp. 412–27.

Basu, K., E. Jones, and E. Schlicht (1987) "The Growth and Decay of Custom: The Role of The New Institutional Economics in Economic History," *Explorations in Economic History,* 24, pp. 1–21.

Becker, G. (1991) "A Note on Restaurant Pricing and Other Examples of Social Influences on Price," *Journal of Political Economy*, 99, pp. 1109–16.

Brown, D., A. Deardoff, and R. Stern (2003) "Child Labor: Theory, Evidence, and Policy", (this volume).

Besley, T. and S. Coate (1992) "Understanding Welfare Stigma: Tax Payer Resentment and Statistical Discrimination," *Journal of Public Economics*, 48, pp. 165–83.

Coate, S. and M. Ravallion (1993) "Reciprocity Without Commitment: Characterization and Performance of Informal Insurance Arrangements," *Journal of Development Economics*, 40, pp. 1–24.

Elster, J. (1989) "Social Norms and Economic Theory," *Journal of Economic Perspectives*, 3, pp. 99–117.

Emerson, P. and A. Portela (2000) "Is There a Child Labor Trap?, Intergenerational Persistence of Child Labor in Brazil," Department of Economics, Cornell University, Working Paper.

Freije, S. and L. F. López-Calva (2000) "Child Labor, Poverty and School Attendance in Mexico and Venezuela," El Colegio de Mexico, Working Paper.

Lindbeck, A., S. Nyberg, and J. Weibull (1998) "Social Norms and Economic Incentives in the Welfare State," *The Quarterly Journal of Economics*, 114, pp. 1–35.

López-Calva, L. F. (2001) "Child Labor: Myths, Theories, and Facts," *Journal of International Affairs*, 55 (1, Fall) pp. 59–73.

López-Calva, L. F. (2002, forthcoming) "A Social Stigma Model of Child Labor," *Estudios Economicos* 17 (2, July–December).

López-Calva, L. F. and K. Miyamoto (2002, forthcoming) "Filial Obligations and Child Labor," *The Review of Development Economics*.

Manski, C. (2000) "Economic Analysis of Social Interactions," *Journal of Economic Perspectives*, 14 (3, Summer).

Rasmusen, E. (1996) "Stigma and Self-Fulfilling Expectations of Criminality," *Journal of Law and Economics*, 39, pp. 519–43.

PART V

The International Organization and Enforcement of Labor Standards

CHAPTER 4
A Role for the WTO

Robert W. Staiger

Introduction

What international action should be taken with regard to labor standards, how should this action be organized, and by what means should it be enforced? The purpose of this chapter is to provide answers to these three questions, and along the way to answer a more pointed question: What role should the World Trade Organization (WTO) play in determining the labor standards of its member governments?

Arguing from the perspective of economic theory, I suggest that progress can be made in answering these questions only after a basic distinction is drawn between the three kinds of problems that are typically associated with the setting of labor standards in a global economy. First, it is often argued that a choice of weak labor standards in one country may trigger "race-to-the-bottom" or "regulatory-chill" effects in other countries, who then face competitive pressures to weaken or refrain from strengthening their own labor standards. Second, it is sometimes argued that weak labor standards and poor labor conditions in one country may create social unrest, thereby inducing "political" concerns in other countries. And third, a country's choice of weak labor standards may induce "humanitarian" concerns in other countries, if those countries have a direct concern for the well-being of workers in this country. I accept that these three problems may each constitute legitimate bases for international action regarding labor standards, but I argue that the first of these problems is distinguished from the other two by the nature of the international externality that is associated with a country's choice of labor standards. And I argue as well that, once this distinction is appreciated, answers to the questions raised above follow readily.

Specifically, in the following section, I begin by observing that the international externality that drives race-to-the-bottom/regulatory-chill effects is a *pecuniary externality* that is transmitted via *market access* channels. By contrast, the international externality associated with humanitarian/political concerns is a *non-pecuniary externality* that does not travel via market interactions at all. With this basic distinction established, I then to consider the institutional features of the WTO (formerly GATT), and I briefly describe as well the institutional features of the International Labor Organization (ILO), the central international organization focused on labor issues. I argue as a general matter that the WTO is well-designed to address problems that arise as a result of international externalities that are transmitted via market access, and that the organizing principle of the GATT/WTO has been to remain focused on problems that can be cast as market-access issues. The WTO, however, has no particular expertise in the area of labor standards *per se*. The ILO, by contrast, possesses just this kind of expertise. Therefore, I suggest the following perspective: if a problem associated with labor standards is a market-access problem, then its solution should be sought in the WTO; otherwise, its solution should be sought in the ILO.

The fourth section adopts the perspective developed in the previous section to consider the assignment of problems to institutions. On the basis of the distinction drawn in earlier, this perspective leads to the conclusion that the WTO should be assigned the task of preventing race-to-the-bottom/regulatory-chill problems from arising in the context of labor standards choices, while the ILO should be assigned the task of addressing the humanitarian/political problems that are associated with the choice of labor standards. By assigning the problems associated with labor standards across institutions in this way, I suggest that the underlying goals of each institution can be better attained.

This assignment of problems to institutions raises two further questions with regard to the WTO's role in determining the labor standards of its member governments. First, exactly how should the WTO approach the race-to-the-bottom/regulatory-chill problem? And second, what role might the WTO play in helping to *enforce* labor agreements that are negotiated in the ILO?

I take up the first of these questions in the fifth section, where I consider and evaluate two distinct approaches to solving the race-to-the-bottom/regulatory-chill problem. Under a first approach, WTO member-governments would negotiate directly over their labor standards, and would, as a consequence of these negotiations, undertake new WTO commitments concerning their national labor standards. I describe how this approach could work, but in the process I identify key differences between this approach and existing proposals for direct WTO negotiations over labor standards, such as those embodied in the so-called social clause. More specifically, I explain why the proposed WTO social clause is poorly designed as a solution to the race-to-the-bottom/regulatory-chill problem.

I then consider more deeply the source of the race-to-the-bottom/regulatory-chill problem, and argue that this problem would not arise if property rights over negotiated market access levels were sufficiently complete. I observe that a number of GATT Articles can indeed be interpreted as helping to complete the system of property rights over negotiated market access levels in the WTO, a system that is built upon negotiated tariff commitments. And I describe a central role in this regard for the renegotiation and non-violation nullification-or-impairment provisions embodied in these articles.

From this perspective, I suggest a second approach to solving the race-to-the-bottom/regulatory-chill problem: strengthening the renegotiation and non-violation nullification-or-impairment provisions already present in existing GATT Articles. I argue that, like the first approach, this second approach could work to prevent race-to-the-bottom/regulatory-chill problems from arising in the context of labor standards choices. However, I argue that this second approach conforms more closely with existing GATT/WTO practice and principles. For example, a distinctive feature of this second approach is that direct negotiations over labor standards are not necessary to prevent race-to-the-bottom/regulatory-chill problems from arising, and so under this second approach the traditional line between national sovereignty and GATT/WTO commitments is not blurred. I therefore conclude that, of these two approaches, this second approach represents the more-promising avenue by which the WTO might solve the race-to-the-bottom/regulatory-chill problem.

I then consider the role that the WTO might play in helping to enforce labor agreements that are negotiated in the ILO. I observe that economic theory points to circumstances in which explicit "linkage" between the WTO and the ILO for enforcement purposes – whereby violation of ILO commitments would trigger retaliatory trade measures orchestrated by the WTO – may be beneficial, and also circumstances in which such linkage provides no benefits or might even be harmful. But I also observe that explicit linkage of this kind may not be necessary in order for the WTO to play an important role in the enforcement of ILO commitments. More specifically, I suggest that the non-violation nullification-or-impairment provisions and the renegotiation provisions contained in GATT Articles can play a significant role in enforcing ILO agreements. Hence, I conclude that strengthening these already-existing principles may be the most effective way to utilize WTO commitments as a means to help enforce labor agreements negotiated under the ILO.

Collecting the arguments of the previous sections, I propose, in the seventh section, an overall approach to the international organization and enforcement of labor standards, and I comment on some of the appealing and unappealing features of this approach relative to other approaches that have been proposed. This is followed by a brief summary and conclusion.

Identifying the Problems

Why is the United States concerned about the labor standards that India enforces within its own borders? A sensible place to find an answer to this question is to consult the Preamble of the ILO Constitution. After all, the ILO has been concerned with answers to questions of this kind for most of the twentieth century. An examination of the ILO Preamble suggests three possible answers. A first possibility is that the United States is concerned about India's choice of labor standards because of the implications of this choice for the *economic* well-being of US citizens (i.e., the effects that the trade and/or investment implied by India's choice would have on real incomes and working conditions in the United States). A second possibility is that the United States is concerned about India's choice of labor standards because of the possibility that weak labor standards and poor working conditions in India could lead, in the words of the ILO Preamble, to social "unrest so great that the peace and harmony of the world are imperiled," and thereby create *political* spill-over for the United States. A third possibility is *humanitarian*: the United States cares directly about the welfare of workers in India.

Under each of these possibilities, there arises an international externality associated with India's choice of labor standards. The existence of this international externality, in turn, suggests that India's choice of labor standards may be inefficient from an international perspective if this choice is made unilaterally (i.e., without the input of the United States and other affected countries). And the international inefficiency of unilateral choices of labor standards is what gives rise to the possibility of mutually beneficial international action with regard to the determination of labor standards (i.e., eliminate the inefficiencies, and all can potentially gain). Hence, at a basic level, identifying the problems that can be solved by international action over labor standards amounts to characterizing the international externalities imposed by unilateral choices of labor standards.

In standard economic terms, the distinction between the possibilities described above is simple: the first possibility describes a *pecuniary externality* of international dimensions, while the remaining two possibilities each describe a *non-pecuniary externality* of international dimensions. However, to make progress in characterizing these externalities more succinctly, it is convenient at this point to introduce a term that lies at the heart of much of what goes on in the WTO: the term is *market access*. Market access is interpreted in the WTO to reflect *the competitive relationship between imported and domestic products*. For example, all else equal, when the US government agrees to lower an import tariff on a particular product, it alters the competitive relationship between imported and domestic units of the product in favor of imported units, and it thereby provides greater market access to foreign producers. By agreeing to reduce its tariff, the United States is effectively agreeing to engineer an outward shift of its import demand curve – that is, a greater volume of imports will be demanded in the United States at any given price charged by foreign exporters – and as a result foreign exporters can expect to enjoy an increase in sales into the US market and to receive a higher price.[1]

The key observation about the first possibility described above is that the externality associated with India's unilateral choice of labor standards is in this case transmitted to the United States via its effect on market access. That is, a weakened labor standard in India can effect the *economic* well-being of US citizens if – and only if – it has the effect of altering *market access* in India, in the United States, or in a third-country market where the United States and India both trade or invest.

Several examples illustrate this fundamental point. Suppose first that India were to weaken a labor standard that it applies to its domestic import-competing producers. All else equal, such an action would reduce the market access that India affords to its trading partners – including the United States – to the potential detriment of workers and capital owners in US export industries, who would as a consequence face declining demand for their products (and hence for their factor services) at existing prices.[2] This impact could be attenuated for US capital owners and accentuated for US workers by the possibility of international capital mobility (if US production facilities then relocate to India to produce for the local market). But the essential point is that the externality associated with the weakened labor standard in India is transmitted to the US economy through changes in market access (in this case, access to the Indian market): if there were no change in market access stemming from India's weakened labor standard, there would be no effect on the economic well-being of US citizens.

As a second example, suppose that India were to weaken a labor standard that it applies to its export industries. All else equal, this would have the effect of increasing the access of Indian exporters to the markets of other countries, including the United States, to the potential detriment of US import-competing capital owners and workers. Again this impact could be attenuated for US capital owners and accentuated for US workers by the possibility of international capital mobility (if US production facilities then relocate to India to produce for export), but the essential point again is that the externality associated with the weakened labor standard in India is transmitted to the US economy through changes in market access (in this case, access to the US market).

In short, one country's choice of labor standards can alter the *economic* well-being of the citizens of another country if, and only if, it alters *market access*. As a consequence, if the United States is concerned about India's choice of labor standards because of the implications of this choice for the economic well-being of US citizens, then the United States is raising an issue that is, fundamentally, a market-access issue.

It is now immediate that fears of a "race to the bottom," in which countries attempt to gain a competitive edge in the international market place by lowering their labor standards, or of "regulatory chill," in which the push for stronger labor regulations in one country is stymied by the competitive consequences when other countries do not follow suit, are fueled by the market-access implications of each country's labor standards choices. That is, these fears reflect a concern that the market-access implications of one government's choice of weak labor standards could trigger other governments to respond in kind, by either weakening their own labor standards or postponing further strengthening of their labor standards, in the name of international "competitiveness."

Thus, in the first example above in which India weakens a labor standard that it applies to its domestic import-competing producers, the United States might be tempted to regain access to the Indian market by diluting the labor standards it applies to its own export industries. Likewise, in the second example above, where India weakens a labor standard that it applies to its export industries, the United States might seek to reduce the level of access that Indian exporters enjoy in its markets by diluting labor standards in its own import-competing industries. Alternatively, the United States might refrain from a planned strengthening of a labor standard in its import-competing sector, if it could not also convince India to apply stronger labor standards to the Indian export sector and thereby avoid unintended market-access consequences of the planned changes in US labor law. Simply put, *the race-to-the-bottom/regulatory-chill problem is driven by a pecuniary externality of international dimensions, and changes in market access are the manifestations of this pecuniary externality.*

Now consider the other two possibilities described above, namely, the political and humanitarian concerns. According to the political concern, the United States is concerned about India's choice of labor standards because of the possibility that weak labor standards and poor working conditions in India could lead to social unrest, and have political spill-over for the United States. And according to the humanitarian concern, the United States is concerned about India's choice of labor standards because it cares directly about the welfare of workers in India. The key distinction between these two possibilities and the first possibility described above is that these possibilities each describe a *non-pecuniary externality* of international dimensions, in which market interactions play no transmission role. In particular, under each of these remaining possibilities, changes in market access play no direct role in determining how the United States is affected by India's choice of labor standards.

To see this distinction, it suffices to return to the first example considered above, in which India weakens a labor standard that it applies to its domestic import-competing producers. As described above, all else equal, such an action would reduce the market access that India affords to its trading partners. But suppose now that, in addition to weakening its labor standard, India also reduces its import tariff in such a way that it preserves the original market access level (i.e., so as to preserve the original competitive relationship between imported and domestic products). While this combined policy action can have no effect on the economic well-being of US citizens, it could certainly alter the welfare of workers in India, and if the United States (a) suffers political effects from the resulting social unrest in India, or (b) cares directly about the welfare of Indian workers, then an international externality is nonetheless transmitted by India's policy choices. But this externality is not a pecuniary externality, and it is in this sense distinct from the first possibility described above.

In summary, the international externality that drives race-to-the-bottom/regulatory-chill effects is a *pecuniary externality* that is transmitted via *market access* channels. By contrast, the international externality that is associated with humanitarian/political concerns is a *non-pecuniary externality* that does not travel via market interactions at all. Of course, non-pecuniary externalities are no less "real" than pecuniary externalities, and each can be the source of important and costly inefficiencies. They are, however, distinct kinds of problems.

But why is this distinction important? Is it largely academic? I think not. Rather, I believe that this distinction has practical importance, because the solutions to each kind of problem described above may look quite different, and because different institutions may have developed specialized expertise for finding solutions to these distinct problems. Before turning in the next section to consider the institutional features of the WTO and the ILO, I close this section with a few additional examples in order to illustrate more concretely how this distinction can arise in practice.

Suppose India chooses to stop enforcing an existing minimum-wage policy in its import-competing sector. If the United States is concerned about India's change in policy because of the implications of this choice for the economic well-being of US citizens, and if this US concern leads India to make an inefficient unilateral choice, then a possible solution might entail India agreeing to mitigate the market-access implications of its decision to do away with its minimum-wage law, perhaps by accompanying this change in its labor standards with a reduction in its import tariff. By so doing, the economic well-being of US citizens is insulated from India's policy decisions, and the international externality that accounted for the inefficiency of India's unilateral labor standards choices is thereby eliminated, yet India retains a degree of sovereignty over its choice of national labor standards.

But such a solution, which focuses on the market-access implications of India's labor standards choices, would be ineffective if the United States is instead concerned about India's change in policy because of the implications of this choice for the welfare of workers in India, and the implied humanitarian/political ramifications. In this case, if international efficiency is to be achieved, a more invasive solution would have to be sought, whereby the United States was given a voice in India's decision about whether to scrap its minimum-wage laws. In particular, it would no longer do to simply provide the United States with assurances that the decision India made would have no important market-access implications. Finally, if both elements of US concern are present in this example, then it may still make sense to seek "targeted" solutions, which address the first concern with market-access agreements and the second concern with more invasive agreements.

Alternatively, suppose that India chooses to stop ensuring the right of workers to organize and form unions in its export sector. If the United States is concerned about India's change in policy because of the implications of this choice for the economic well-being of US citizens, and if this US concern leads India to make an inefficient unilateral choice, then a possible solution might entail India agreeing to mitigate the market access implications of its labor-law decision, perhaps by accompanying this change with an increase in the minimum wage it applies to its export sector. By so doing, the economic well-being of US citizens is once again insulated from India's policy decisions, and the international externality that accounted for the inefficiency of India's unilateral labor standards choices is eliminated, yet India retains a degree of sovereignty over its choice of national labor standards. But once again, such a solution, which focuses on the market access implications of India's labor standards choices, would be ineffective if the United States is instead concerned about India's change in policy because of the implications of this choice for the welfare of workers in India, and the implied humanitarian/political effects. In this case, as in the previous example, a more invasive solution would have to be sought, whereby the United States was given a voice in India's labor-law decisions. In particular, once again it would no longer do to simply provide the United States with assurances that the decision India made would have no important market-access implications. Finally, as in the previous example, if both elements of US concern are present in this example, then it may still make sense to seek "targeted" solutions, which address the first concern with market-access agreements and the second concern with more invasive agreements.

Finally, consider a third and more difficult example. Suppose that India allows the products of prison labor to be exported. This example differs from the first two examples in two potentially important ways. First, I am supposing that there is no *change* in Indian policy being contemplated here, but rather that this has always been Indian policy. And second, the example of prison labor may invoke strong concerns about "fairness" in the United States. But once again we may ask the question: Does the United States concern for the fairness of the Indian policy emanate from its concern for the economic well-being of US citizens, or rather from a direct concern for the welfare of Indian prison workers or a fear that the treatment of prisoners in India could fuel social unrest with international ramifications? If the United States believes that it is unfair for its citizens to have to compete in US markets with the products of prison labor from India, then this is a market-access issue, and a possible solution might entail the United States taking action to block imports from India if these imports have been produced using prison labor. On the other hand, if the United States is concerned directly about the welfare of prison workers in India or about possible social unrest in India, then a market-access solution is no solution at all, and instead the United States will need to acquire a voice in India's decision of how it treats its prisoners. And once again, if both elements of US concern are present in this example, then it may still make sense to seek "targeted" solutions, which address the first concern with market-access agreements and the second concern with more invasive agreements.

As each of these examples demonstrates, the distinction drawn in this section between the race-to-the-bottom/regulatory-chill problems and the humanitarian/political problems that can arise at an international level with unilateral choices of labor standards has practical importance, because the solutions to each kind of problem may look quite different, and because different institutions may have developed specialized expertise for finding solutions to these distinct problems. I now turn in the next section to consider the institutional features of the WTO and the ILO.

The Institutional Features of the WTO and the ILO

At one level, the WTO and the ILO are similar institutions: each serves as an international negotiating forum for its member governments.[3] At another level, these two institutions are quite distinct. The central purpose of ILO negotiations and agreements is to improve labor standards. The central purpose of WTO negotiations and agreements is to reduce trade barriers or, at its core, to increase market access. In this section, I describe some of the broad features of each institution. I begin with the WTO.

The WTO

My purpose in this subsection is two-fold. First, I describe how the WTO is an institution that is well designed to facilitate international negotiations over market-access problems, and I suggest that its central purpose is to sponsor tariff negotiations that increase market access in a reciprocal fashion. Second, I show that the race-to-the-bottom/regulatory-chill problems described in the previous section are most likely to arise only when governments have bound their tariffs in market-access negotiations such as those sponsored by the WTO. Consequently, in this subsection I lay the groundwork for two arguments why race-to-the-bottom/regulatory-chill problems associated with labor standards might sensibly be handled in the WTO: they are market access problems, which the WTO is experienced in handling, and they are problems that are likely to be exacerbated by other WTO commitments.

To accomplish my first purpose, I return to the issue of international externalities, and consider a basic question that lies at the heart of the WTO's existence (and the reason for the existence of GATT before it): What is the source of the international inefficiency associated with unilateral tariff choices? After all, if no international inefficiency associated with unilateral tariff choices can be identified, then no basis for mutually beneficial tariff negotiations can be articulated by the WTO member governments, and there would as a consequence be no reason for the WTO (and GATT before it) to exist.

The discussion above is suggestive of two possible sources of international inefficiency that might be associated with unilateral tariff choices. One possibility is that governments impose pecuniary externalities on their trading partners when they make their unilateral tariff choices. I will take up this possibility shortly. But a second possibility is that there are non-pecuniary externalities that extend internationally when governments make their unilateral tariff choices. For example, perhaps the domestic redistributive consequences of one government's tariff choices are of direct concern to other countries, and when the government makes these tariff choices unilaterally an international inefficiency is created. As a general matter, does the WTO appear well designed to solve this second kind of problem?

There is a simple reason why the design features of the WTO appear ill equipped to handle non-pecuniary externalities associated with tariff choices, at least as a general matter. The reason is that WTO tariff commitments ("bindings") are designed to work in one direction: WTO bindings prevent governments from unilaterally raising their tariffs above their bound levels, but these commitments place no constraints on the freedom of governments to set tariffs below their bound levels. Hence, the WTO is "hard-wired" to help governments make reciprocal commitments to *reduce* their tariffs. This is reflected in the Preamble of both the GATT and the WTO, where it is stated that the goals of the member governments will be served by "entering into reciprocal and mutually advantageous arrangements directed to the substantial reduction of tariffs and other barriers to trade . . ."

Yet if a government's tariff choices impose non-pecuniary externalities on other countries, there is no particular reason to expect that the problem involves tariffs that are generally too high from an international perspective. For example, depending on the impact of a country's tariff changes on the income distribution within its borders and on how other governments care about this impact, tariffs could just as easily be too low from an international perspective, implying that a mutually beneficial agreement would entail commitments to *raise* tariffs. The point is, the WTO is designed to promote negotiations that result in agreements that reduce tariffs and expand market access on a reciprocal basis, and the existence of non-pecuniary externalities associated with unilateral tariff choices does not provide a compelling reason why mutually beneficial negotiated outcomes should necessarily lead to agreements that take this form.

I now return to the first possibility mentioned above, namely, that governments impose pecuniary externalities on their trading partners when they make their unilateral tariff choices. I ask whether this could be a source of inefficiency that the WTO is well designed to solve. To answer this basic question, a promising line of attack begins with the observation that tariffs affect market access, and hence governments do indeed impose pecuniary externalities on one another when they raise tariffs against imports and thereby restrict market access. Now as a general matter, the existence of pecuniary externalities across decision makers is not enough to conclude that the decentralized choices of these decision makers will be inefficient: inefficiency requires the further condition that at least some of these decision makers are large enough to alter − with their unilateral decisions − the prices at which they trade. In the particular case of government tariff choices, this further condition amounts to the stipulation that the markets of some countries are large enough that, when access to these markets is denied to foreign exporters, the prices received by these foreign exporters fall. There is in fact ample evidence that this further condition is met for many countries and on many products.[4] Consequently, a natural source of inefficiency in unilateral tariff choices that could form the basis for mutually beneficial tariff negotiations between two member-governments of the WTO is the ability of each government to reduce the prices received by the other's exporters via market-access restrictions.

To be more concrete, let us consider further the international inefficiency that arises as a result of pecuniary externalities when a government makes its tariff choice unilaterally. Suppose that the government in question has made its preferred (unilateral) tariff choice, and consider now how this government would feel about setting its tariff slightly higher. The first thing to observe is that the government should be indifferent to making slight changes in its tariff (since otherwise it would not have achieved its preferred unilateral tariff to begin with). This means that the additional benefits that the government perceives from this slight tariff increase must just balance against the additional costs of this tariff increase, as the government perceives these costs. But the key point is *how* the government perceives these costs. Crucially, what the government is not taking into account in this unilateral calculation – and has no reason to take into account – is the additional cost of the slight tariff increase that is born by foreign exporters who, facing diminished access to the domestic market, receive a lower price for their product. *The ability to shift a portion of the costs of import protection on to foreign exporters is a source of international inefficiency associated with unilateral tariff choices.*

Several important observations may now be made. First, I have said very little about the underlying objectives of governments. In particular, I have said nothing about whether these governments see tariffs as a legitimate means of pursuing various national goals (such as production targets or distributional objectives). Evidently, the existence of the inefficiency associated with unilateral tariff choices described above does not depend upon the details of government preferences: international cost-shifting will lead governments to choices that are collectively inefficient, regardless of their individual trade-policy goals. Second, and again regardless of these details, the nature of the inefficiency associated with unilateral tariff choices will be *insufficient market access*. This follows from the fact that, on the margin, shifting costs on to foreign exporters is associated with *restricting* market access, and so unilateral tariff choices will imply too little market access from the perspective of international efficiency. Put differently, if the international externalities associated with unilateral tariff choices are of a pecuniary nature, then *the essential purpose of mutually beneficial tariff negotiations such as those sponsored in the WTO must be to increase market access*, since it is only by increasing market access that the collective inefficiency associated with unilateral choices can be reduced, and it is only by reducing this inefficiency that all governments can gain. And third, if two member-governments have a basis for engaging in mutually beneficial tariff negotiations, then they can each assuredly gain from the *reciprocal exchange* of (at least a small amount of) market access, provided that reciprocity is understood to imply tariff reductions that result in an equal expansion of exporter sales into each domestic market. This follows from the fact that linking their tariff movements in this reciprocal fashion eliminates the cost-shifting component associated with each government's unilateral tariff calculation, and thereby induces each government to desire a lower tariff (i.e., to offer greater market access).

Hence, if international inefficiencies arise as a result of pecuniary externalities when a government makes its tariff choice unilaterally, mutually advantageous agreements must involve a reciprocal exchange of market-access concessions between countries, much as the Preamble of the GATT and the WTO indicate. In this general way, the central purpose of the WTO may be seen as sponsoring negotiations to solve a fundamental problem related to the market-access implications of the unilateral tariff choices of member governments. I therefore conclude that the WTO is an institution that is well designed to facilitate international negotiations over market-access problems.[5]

I now turn to the second purpose of this subsection. Specifically, I argue that the race-to-the-bottom/regulatory-chill problems described in the previous section are most likely to arise only when governments have bound their tariffs in market-access negotiations such as those sponsored by the WTO. I accomplish this in two steps. I first make a *stronger* argument: in principle, the race-to-the-bottom/regulatory-chill problems described in the previous section can arise *only* when governments have bound their tariffs in market-access negotiations such as those sponsored by the WTO. I then suggest reasons why in practice this argument might be too strong, but that it nevertheless illustrates clearly why tariff negotiations are likely to exacerbate the race-to-the-bottom/regulatory-chill problem.

To begin, consider again the international cost-shifting motives that enter into a government's unilateral tariff choices. In the absence of market-access negotiations such as those sponsored by the WTO, these cost-shifting motives lead governments to place inefficiently high restrictions on market access, as I have just discussed. If, in addition to tariff choices, governments also make decisions about their labor standards, then these labor-standards choices too can have market-access implications, as I described earlier.[6] Nevertheless, even with this richer portfolio of policies, the point remains that international cost-shifting is achieved – and the international externality that leads to inefficiency at the international level is transmitted – through *changes in market access*. We may therefore conclude that, when a government contemplates adjustments to its *mix* of policies that preserve a *given* level of market access, there is no international cost-shifting occurring, and consequently the government confronts the *full costs and benefits* of these contemplated policy-mix adjustments.

From this conclusion, two important points follow concerning a world in which governments have both tariff and labor policies at their disposal (and when humanitarian/political concerns associated with the choice of labor standards do not arise). The first point is that, when governments choose *all* of their policies unilaterally, the level of market access they provide is inefficiently low, but the mix of policies with which they deliver this market access *is* efficient. Put differently, in a world without international tariff negotiations, levels of market access would be inefficiently low, but governments would have no incentive to distort their labor standards for competitive effect (i.e., there would be no race-to-the-bottom/regulatory-chill problem). This can be understood by noting that each government's unilateral policy decision – given the policy choices of its trading partners – may be broken into two components: a choice of the level of market access (i.e., the competitive relationship between imported and domestic products), and a choice of the mix of policies that deliver this level of market access (e.g., a low tariff and a weak labor standard, or a high tariff and a strong labor standard). As I have observed above, each government's unilateral choice of the level of market access will be inefficiently low, but having chosen a level of market access, each government faces all the costs and benefits of its policy mix decision, and so this second decision will be made in a globally (and nationally) efficient manner.

The second point is that, if governments attempt to negotiate an expansion of market access to more efficient levels by agreeing to bind their tariffs, these attempts will *create* incentives for each government to subsequently change its labor standards with an eye toward "withdrawing" market access it had previously granted through commitments to lower tariffs. This in turn means that the mix of policies by which each government chooses to deliver market access to the other is now inefficient, in the particular sense that each government now has an incentive to distort its choice of labor standards for competitive effect. And, quite possibly, the level of market access which governments attain with negotiations over tariff bindings will also be inefficient as a consequence. Put differently, *international tariff negotiations such as those sponsored by the WTO can help governments achieve a mutually beneficial expansion of market access, but these tariff negotiations also create the potential for race-to-the-bottom/regulatory-chill type problems.*[7]

I have just argued that, in principle, the race-to-the-bottom/regulatory-chill problems described in the previous section can arise *only* when governments have bound their tariffs in market-access negotiations such as those sponsored by the WTO. In practice, this argument might be too strong. For example, even absent the constraints on a country's tariffs that might be imposed by any formal international commitments, the government of this country might face informal constraints on its tariff choices, imposed perhaps by issues of policy transparency or other concerns.[8] And, like the formal constraints imposed by negotiated tariff commitments, these informal constraints could lead the government to distort its choice of labor standards for competitive effect. But my essential point is simply to illustrate why tariff negotiations are likely to *exacerbate* the race-to-the-bottom/regulatory-chill problem, and this point is likely to remain valid in the presence of these and other practical considerations.

In summary, I have now described two reasons why race-to-the-bottom/regulatory-chill problems associated with labor standards might sensibly be handled in the WTO: (a) they are market-access problems, which the WTO (and GATT before it) has had over 50 years of experience in handling; and (b) they are problems that are likely to be exacerbated by other WTO commitments (i.e., tariff bindings). I now turn to a brief description of the institutional features of the ILO.

The ILO

The creation of the ILO at the Peace Conference of April 11, 1919 predates the creation of GATT by almost 30 years. According to David A. Morse, who was elected to the post of Director-General of the ILO in 1948 and served in this position for over two decades, the basic reason for the ILO's existence is "to improve the working and living conditions of workers everywhere" (Morse, 1969, p. 96). On this there appears to be broad agreement. Indeed, as Johnston (1970, p. 13) observes, the two words "social justice," which are contained in the Preamble to the Constitution of the ILO, have come to symbolize the main objective of the ILO.

However, as Morse (1969, pp. 82–3) describes, there is considerable disagreement over the appropriate means for achieving this objective:

> In the view of some people, the ILO is primarily a standard-setting organization whose most important task is to defend the rights of workers and to protect them from exploitation in the drive for growth, development, and industrialization. In the view of others, the ILO is fundamentally an operational organization which needs to concentrate its efforts on promoting the economic development of the proper countries. Certain people see the ILO's main value as a forum for tripartite discussion; others see it as an organization providing assistance in the training of the labor force.
>
> The truth is that the actual situation of the ILO contains elements of each of these positions . . ."

According to Johnston (1970, p. 88), the functions of the ILO have in fact evolved over time, but it is now seen as serving three basic functions for its members relating to labor issues: standard setting, information dissemination, and technical assistance.

For my purposes here, the important features of the ILO are three: first, the ILO's involvement in international labor issues has been broadly defined, and from the beginning it has included race-to-the-bottom/regulatory-chill concerns as well as concerns of a humanitarian/political nature related to labor policies; second, the ILO does not appear to have any particular expertise in addressing market access issues *per se*; and third, the ILO does have considerable expertise in addressing the details of national labor law. Below I briefly elaborate on each feature in turn.

The humanitarian and political motivations that led to the founding of the ILO can hardly be in doubt. These motives are not surprising given the state of the world into which the ILO was born. And they are reflected most prominently in the Preamble to the ILO Constitution. The first two sentences of the Preamble read:

> Whereas universal and lasting peace can be established only if it is based upon social justice; And whereas conditions of labor exist involving such injustice, hardship and privation to large numbers of people as to produce unrest so great that the peace and harmony of the world are imperiled . . .

But while concerns of the founding members of the ILO were largely of a humanitarian/political nature, it would be incorrect to claim that the motivation behind the formation of the ILO in 1919 had nothing to do with the market-access concerns associated with weak labor standards that underlie fears of race-to-the-bottom/regulatory-chill type problems. Two observations support the position that the ILO was indeed expected to address such concerns. First, the third paragraph of the Preamble to the ILO Constitution says as much:

> Whereas also the failure of any nation to adopt humane conditions of labor is an obstacle in the way of other nations which desire to improve the conditions in their own countries . . .

This is a direct reference to the "regulatory chill" problem as I have described this problem above. And second, there is ample evidence in the drafting history of the ILO to support the position that the ILO was expected to play a role in addressing race-to-the-bottom/regulatory-chill concerns.

As one example, a memorandum prepared by the British Delegation to the Peace Conference of 1919 discusses (The Paris Peace Conference, Volume II, pp. 124–5) how conventions ratified in the ILO would be enforced, and makes the following observations, suggesting that the competitive effects of labor standards in the international market place were very much on the minds of the drafters of the ILO:

> *Complaints against inadequate enforcement.* If the enforcement of conventions is to be made fully effective, it will be necessary to provide some machinery for complaint against inadequate enforcement, otherwise countries might obtain unfair advantage in industrial competition through lax administration of the international standards. To meet this point, it is suggested that it should be open to any Government which considered that it was suffering from such unfair competition to lodge a complaint with the Bureau against the alleged offender . . .
>
> One of the fundamental objects of conventions as to labour conditions is to eliminate unfair competition based on oppressive conditions or working. Any State, therefore, which does not carry out a convention designed to prevent oppressive conditions, is guilty of manufacturing under conditions which create a state of unfair competition in the international market. The appropriate penalty accordingly appears to be that when a two-thirds majority of the

Conference is satisfied that the terms of the Convention have not been carried out, the signatory States should discriminate against the articles produced under the conditions of unfair competition proved to exist unless those conditions were remedied within one year or such longer period as the Conference might decide.

A second example illustrating that the competitive effects of labor standards in the international market place were very much on the minds of the drafters of the ILO can be found in a memorandum submitted by the National Committee on Prisons and Prison Labor in support of a provision proposed by the US delegation which stated, "No article of commodity shall be shipped or delivered in international commerce in the production of which convict labor has been employed or permitted." The memorandum (The Paris Peace Conference, Volume II, pp. 365–6) continues:

> This provision . . . will recognize on an international basis one of the few prohibitions to international commerce which is found in statutory law. The prohibition existing in the several countries became law because of the fact that convict made goods were being shipped into these countries and were under-selling home manufactures. It was found that the conditions under which the convict made goods were manufactured proved universally to be that of payment of little or no wages or remuneration in return for the labor and workshop facilities which entered into the cost of production . . . Furthermore, this provision will not interfere with the right of a State to conduct its prisons as it may so determine and provides only that the conditions under which they are conducted shall not prove a detriment to the citizens or interests of any other country.

As this memorandum makes clear, the international concern about prison labor was a simple market-access concern. It is therefore evident that market-access concerns associated with the choice of labor standards were part of what motivated the formation of the ILO, and this is the first feature of the ILO that I wish to emphasize. The second feature is simply that the ILO does not appear to have any particular expertise in addressing market-access issues *per se*. This is self-evident, at least when the ILO's expertise in this regard is assessed in relation to that of the WTO where, as I have described above, market-access concerns are *the* central preoccupation.

The third feature of the ILO that I wish to emphasize is that it has considerable expertise in addressing the details of national labor law. This detail is certainly what the business of the ILO was envisaged to be, as the second paragraph of the Preamble to the ILO Constitution indicates:

> And whereas conditions of labor exist involving such injustice, hardship and privation to large numbers of people as to produce unrest so great that the

peace and harmony of the world are imperiled; and an improvement of those conditions is urgently required; as, for example, by the regulation of the hours of work, including the establishment of a maximum working day and week, the regulation of the labor supply, the prevention of unemployment, the provision of an adequate living wage, the protection of the worker against sickness, disease and injury arising out of his employment, the protection of children, young persons and women, provision for old age and injury, protection of the interests of workers when employed in countries other than their own, recognition of the principle of equal remuneration for work of equal value, recognition of the principle of freedom of association, the organization of vocational and technical education and other measures . . .

And the ILO's expertise in addressing the details of national labor law are especially evident when compared to the WTO's (almost complete lack of) expertise in these matters.

Summarizing this section, I have considered the institutional features of the WTO, and I have briefly described as well the institutional features of the ILO. I have argued as a general matter that the WTO is well designed to address problems that arise as a result of international externalities that are transmitted via market access, and that the organizing principle of the GATT/WTO has been to remain focused on problems that can be cast as market-access issues. The WTO, however, has no particular expertise in the area of labor standards *per se*. The ILO, by contrast, possesses just this kind of expertise. Therefore, I suggest the following perspective: if a problem associated with labor standards is a market-access problem, then its solution should be sought in the WTO; otherwise, its solution should be sought in the ILO. In the next section, I combine this perspective with the characterization of problems associated with labor standards offered earlier to suggest an assignment of problems to institutions.

The Assignment of Problems to Institutions

I have now arrived at the first major policy question regarding the international organization and enforcement of labor standards: How should the international problems associated with the national choices of labor standards be assigned to international institutions? In the previous section I proposed a perspective from which to approach this question: if a problem associated with labor standards is a market-access problem, then its solution should be sought in the WTO; otherwise, its solution should be sought in the ILO. In the second section I offered a characterization of the central problems that arise at the international level when countries choose their national labor standards unilaterally, and I argued that the race-to-the-bottom/regulatory-chill problem associated with the choice of labor standards

is a market-access problem, while the humanitarian/political problem associated with the choice of labor standards is not. In this section I combine the
perspective of the previous section with this characterization to suggest an
assignment of problems to institutions

The suggested assignment is straightforward: the WTO should be assigned
the task of preventing race-to-the-bottom/regulatory-chill problems from
arising in the context of labor standards choices, while the ILO should be
assigned the task of addressing the humanitarian/political problems that
are associated with the choice of labor standards. From the perspective of
the current institutional arrangements of the WTO and ILO, this implies a
*re*assignment away from the ILO and toward the WTO. I now briefly consider the implications of this reassignment for each institution.

This implied reassignment would leave the ILO with what is in principle
a more narrowly defined labor agenda. In practice, however, the breadth of
the labor issues taken up by the ILO (e.g. the right to freedom of association
and the eight-hour work day) and the nature of the solutions it has attempted
(e.g. conventions and recommendations to alter the labor laws of its member
countries) might see little change under such a reassignment, as each seems
broadly consistent with international actions taken to solve humanitarian/
political problems relating to labor standards.[9] And a tighter overall focus
might even strengthen the ILO's ability to achieve its fundamental objective
"to improve the working and living conditions of workers everywhere." But
this reassignment does raise a number of important further questions for
the WTO.

One key question for the WTO, which is raised by this reassignment, has
to do with enforcement. As the memorandum prepared by the British
Delegation to the Peace Conference of 1919 and quoted earlier suggests,
effective prevention of race-to-the-bottom/regulatory-chill problems in the
context of labor standards requires that enforcement measures be put in
place and potentially utilized. Would it be wise for the WTO to utilize its
scarce enforcement power to prevent race-to-the-bottom/regulatory-chill
problems from occurring?

It turns out that, as long as the WTO's focus on labor issues is narrowly
confined to the issue of preventing race-to-the-bottom/regulatory-chill
problems, the answer is "Yes."[10] The essential reason is that, as discussed
earlier, the race-to-the-bottom/regulatory-chill problem is a market-access
issue, and, as noted earlier, the WTO exists to solve the basic problem of
insufficient market access. As the problem of enforcement of WTO commitments can be boiled down to the task of keeping each country's market-
access commitments at a manageable level – so that no country has an
incentive to break its market-access commitments[11] – it is never a good idea
for the WTO to focus on some ways by which countries could break their
market-access commitments (e.g., a unilateral increase in tariffs) to the

exclusion of others (e.g., a unilateral weakening of a labor standard). Therefore, preventing race-to-the-bottom/regulatory-chill problems from developing is exactly the sort of thing that the dispute settlement procedures of the WTO *should* be used for.

Two additional questions for the WTO are raised by this implied reassignment as well. First, exactly how might the WTO approach this new assignment? This question is the topic of the next section. And second, should the WTO's dispute settlement procedures be used to help enforce agreements reached in the ILO? This question is discussed later.

The Role of the WTO in Preventing Race-to-the-bottom/Regulatory-chill Problems

In this section, I consider and evaluate two distinct approaches to solving the race-to-the-bottom/regulatory-chill problem. Under a first approach, WTO member-governments would negotiate directly over their labor standards, and would, as a consequence of these negotiations, undertake new WTO commitments concerning their national labor standards. I describe how this approach could work, but in the process I identify key differences between this approach and existing proposals for direct WTO negotiations over labor standards, such as those embodied in the so-called social clause. More specifically, I explain why the proposed WTO social clause is poorly designed as a solution to the race-to-the-bottom/regulatory-chill problem.

I then consider more deeply the source of the race-to-the-bottom/regulatory-chill problem, and argue that this problem would not arise if property rights over negotiated market-access levels were sufficiently complete. I observe that a number of GATT Articles can indeed be interpreted as helping to complete the system of property rights over negotiated market-access levels in the WTO, a system that is built upon negotiated tariff commitments. And I describe a central role in this regard for the renegotiation and non-violation nullification-or-impairment provisions embodied in these articles.

From this perspective, I suggest a second approach to solving the race-to-the-bottom/ regulatory-chill problem: strengthening the renegotiation and non-violation nullification-or-impairment provisions already present in existing GATT Articles. I argue that, like the first approach, this second approach could work to prevent race-to-the-bottom/regulatory-chill problems from arising in the context of labor standards choices. However, I argue that this second approach conforms more closely to existing GATT/ WTO practice and principles. For example, a distinctive feature of this second approach is that direct negotiations over labor standards are not necessary to prevent race-to-the-bottom/regulatory-chill problems from arising, and so under this second approach the traditional line between national sovereignty and GATT/WTO commitments need not be blurred. I therefore conclude that, of these two approaches, this second approach represents the more-promising avenue by which the WTO might solve the race-to-the-bottom/regulatory-chill problem.[12]

A direct approach: WTO negotiations over labor standards

If the WTO is to be assigned the task of preventing race-to-the-bottom/regulatory-chill problems associated with the choice of national labor standards, how should it approach this task? One approach would be the following: when two or more member governments meet to engage in market access negotiations sponsored by the WTO, they negotiate over both tariffs *and* labor standards. How does this approach solve the race-to-the-bottom/regulatory-chill problem associated with national labor standards?

Consider first the race-to-the-bottom problem. Recall that this problem arises when countries attempt to gain a competitive edge in the international market place by lowering their labor standards, and that this problem leads to inefficiencies in market-access levels and/or the mix of policies with which market access is delivered. So suppose that, perhaps as a result of prior tariff commitments negotiated in the GATT/WTO, each of these sources of inefficiency exists. When governments are permitted to negotiate over both tariffs and labor standards, they can eliminate both sources of inefficiency (the inefficient market-access level and the inefficiencies in policy mix), solve the race-to-the-bottom problem, and each benefit as a result of the efficiency gains: they simply agree to tariff levels and labor standards that are collectively efficient in light of each government's individual policy goals.

Consider next the regulatory-chill problem. This problem arises when one government's push for stronger national labor regulations is frustrated by the international competitive (i.e., the market access) consequences when other countries do not follow suit. But again, when governments are permitted to negotiate over both tariffs and labor standards, this problem will not arise. Instead, the government who wishes to strengthen its national labor standard but is concerned about the competitive consequences of doing so alone can negotiate with its trading partners over tariffs and labor standards, and through these negotiations "de-link" its choice of national labor standards from market access issues (i.e., it can "agree" in these negotiations to any national labor standard it desires and then focus market access negotiations on its tariff level).

Hence, if governments negotiate over both tariffs and national labor standards in the WTO, they can achieve efficient levels of market access without triggering a damaging race to the bottom or regulatory chill with regard to labor standards. In a sense this is unsurprising: after all, if governments are permitted to negotiate over each of these policies, why should any inefficiencies remain in the way these policies are set?

But I now observe that, while this direct approach could work to solve the race-to-the-bottom/regulatory-chill problem, there are a number of key differences between it and the commonly heard proposals for a WTO social clause. A first key difference is that, in the direct approach to solving the race-to-the-bottom/regulatory-chill problem that I have just described, all negotiations between governments are *voluntary*, and as a result any commitments made by these governments are perceived by them as *mutually beneficial*. This feature is, of course, standard practice in WTO negotiations, and it was standard practice in negotiations under GATT as well. But it stands in sharp contrast to the proposed WTO social clause, under which the governments of the developing world would effectively be *forced* to accept a set of "core" labor standards, which they would then have to meet or see their access to the markets of the developed world curtailed. A second key difference between the direct approach outlined above and the proposed social clause is that there is no presumption under the former that labor standards need be harmonized across countries, while such harmonization is the stated goal of the social clause. That is, the proposed social clause envisions the international harmonization of labor standards as a key feature of the solution to the race-to-the-bottom/regulatory-chill problem, but the direct approach that I have described above solves this problem without the need for harmonization.

As I have just described, direct negotiations over labor standards in the WTO can solve the race-to-the-bottom/regulatory-chill problem, and this approach exhibits the features that it is structured on a completely voluntary and mutually beneficial basis and that labor standards need not be harmonized across countries. These features are not shared by the proposed WTO social clause. I therefore conclude that, whatever objectives the proposed WTO social clause might be designed to achieve, it is poorly designed as a solution to the race-to-the-bottom/regulatory-chill problem.

An indirect approach: reliance on renegotiation and non-violation nullification rights

While the direct approach described above can in principle work to solve the race-to-the-bottom/regulatory-chill problem associated with the choice of labor standards, it exhibits a number of troubling aspects. First, by making national labor standards the object of direct international negotiation, this approach crosses the traditional line between national sovereignty and

GATT/WTO commitments. And second, having crossed this line with labor standards, there would seem to be no end in sight: the same race-to-the-bottom/regulatory-chill forces are presumably at work in other national regulatory realms, such as environmental policies and even building codes. Is *everything* ultimately to be a matter for international negotiation?

I now describe an ingenious way around this problem. I can say ingenious, because the idea is not mine: it was a creation of the drafters of GATT. Hudec (1990, p. 24) describes the problem as it was perceived at the drafting sessions of the time:

> The standard trade policy rules could deal with the common types of trade policy measure governments usually employ to control trade. But trade can also be affected by other "domestic" measures, such as product safety standards, having nothing to do with trade policy. It would have been next to impossible to catalogue all such possibilities in advance. Moreover, governments would never have agreed to circumscribe their freedom in all these other areas for the sake of a mere tariff agreement.
>
> The shortcomings of the standard legal commitments were recognized in a report by a group of trade experts at the London Monetary and Economic Conference of 1933. The group concluded that trade agreements should have another more general provision which would address itself to any other government action that produced an adverse effect on the balance of commercial opportunity . . ."

Evidently, it was accepted that governments value tariff reductions from their trading partners for the increased access to foreign markets that these tariff cuts imply. And it was accepted as well that subsequent changes in domestic policies could undermine these implied market-access levels. The concern was that such changes could interfere with the maintenance of "reciprocity" – the balance of negotiated market access commitments. As Hudec documents, this concern eventually led to the inclusion of a catch-all "non-violation" nullification-or-impairment right in the articles of GATT.

There are three conditions that have been established by GATT (and now WTO) panels for a successful non-violation complaint (see Petersmann, 1997, p. 172). First, a reciprocal concession was negotiated between two trading partners. Second, a governmental measure, while not in direct violation of any GATT rules, had been introduced subsequently by one of the governments which adversely affected the market access afforded to its trading partner. And third, this measure could not have been reasonably anticipated by the trading partner at the time of the negotiation of the original tariff concession.

In principle, the non-violation nullification-or-impairment right is designed to prevent governments from altering policies that they have *not bound* in GATT/WTO negotiations in such a way as to unilaterally "withdraw" market-access levels that were implied by the tariffs they *did bind* in GATT/ WTO negotiations. To see that this right can in principle solve the race-to-the-bottom problem, it need only be recalled that it is precisely the incentive to alter labor standards in such a way as to unilaterally withdraw market-access levels (which were previously granted with commitments to lower tariffs) that gives rise to the race-to-the-bottom problem. By preventing such unilateral withdrawals, the non-violation nullification-or-impairment right in principle prevents the race-to-the-bottom problem from arising.

Now consider the regulatory-chill problem. As I have shown earlier in the chapter, this too is a market-access problem, and so it might be expected that the non-violation nullification-or-impairment right could prevent regulatory chill as well. But this is not quite correct. The reason is that the market-access forces that create the potential for regulatory chill work in the opposite direction to those that underlie the race to the bottom, and the non-violation nullification-or-impairment right only applies in one direction. To see the problem, recall that the potential for regulatory chill occurs when, as a result of previous commitments that bind its tariffs, a government confronts un-intended market access consequences – *increasing* access to its own markets – when it unilaterally strengthens its domestic standards. The non-violation nullification-or-impairment right cannot help in this circumstance, because this right does not apply to a circumstance in which a government takes a unilateral action that *increases* the market access that it affords its trading partners.

Nevertheless, the underlying reason why the non-violation nullification-or-impairment right works in principle to solve the race-to-the-bottom problem is instructive for thinking about an analogous solution to the regulatory-chill problem. The underlying reason why this right works to solve the race-to-the-bottom problem is that the race-to-the-bottom problem reflects a deeper problem: the problem of imperfect property rights over negotiated market-access levels. More specifically, *negotiated tariff bindings alone create imperfect property rights over market-access levels, and the race to the bottom is a manifestation of these property-rights imperfections.* The non-violation nullification-or-impairment right enhances the property rights over market access levels created by negotiated tariff bindings, and in principle it does so sufficiently (in combination with other GATT Articles that contribute to the same purpose) to prevent the race-to-the-bottom problem. But the non-violation nullification-or-impairment right does not complete the property rights over market-access levels created by negotiated tariff bindings sufficiently to prevent regulatory chill. A possible approach to solving the regulatory-chill problem, then, is to make changes to the rules of the WTO so that this right becomes symmetric.

One way to introduce this symmetric right is to work through the already-existing right of renegotiation contained within GATT/WTO rules. Under these rules of renegotiation, a government may modify or withdraw a tariff concession, but in return it must offer compensating tariff concessions on other products or else accept equivalent withdrawals of concessions by its affected trading partners. The purpose of these renegotiation rules is to permit governments the flexibility to alter their commitments over time without permitting them to upset unilaterally the balance between the rights and obligations that had been established by previous negotiations. In this way, each government is granted the flexibility to amend its negotiated market-access commitments when the need arises while at the same time its trading partners are granted the ability to defend their property rights over the balance of negotiated market-access commitments. In principle then, if a government wished to unilaterally strengthen its domestic standards, and if this action would by itself increase the market access this government affords to its trading partners, then the government might seek to renegotiate its tariff to a higher level and to offer as compensation for its higher tariff the strengthened domestic standards.

With the introduction into the WTO of this symmetric right, a government would be able to offset the market-access implications of a decision to strengthen its domestic standards with an adjustment to its negotiated GATT/WTO commitments (e.g., its tariff bindings). In principle, this change in WTO rules would serve to complete the property rights over market-access levels created by negotiated tariff bindings sufficiently to prevent regulatory chill. To see this, it need only be observed that, with this change, each government could "de-link" its choice of national labor standards from market-access issues.[13]

I will refer to this second, indirect, approach as one of *strengthening the renegotiation and non-violation nullification-or-impairment provisions already present in existing GATT Articles*, and I note that in addition to the introduction of a symmetric right into WTO rules as I have described above, this strengthening might also require other measures which ensured that the renegotiation and non-violation nullification-or-impairment provisions work in practice as I have argued they can work in principle. But like the direct approach described in the previous subsection, I have now argued that this indirect approach can in principle solve the race-to-the-bottom/regulatory-chill problem. I close this section by comparing the two approaches.

I have observed that both approaches entail changes in current WTO rules and/or practice. However, I now argue that, of these two approaches, strengthening the renegotiation and non-violation nullification-or-impairment provisions already present in existing GATT Articles conforms more closely to existing GATT/WTO practice and principles. There are two main components of my argument.

First, a distinctive feature of this approach is that direct international negotiations over labor standards are not necessary to prevent race-to-the-bottom/regulatory-chill problems from arising. Therefore, under this approach the traditional line between national sovereignty and GATT/WTO commitments is not blurred.

It is worth pausing here to consider how this feature could possibly be part of a solution to the race-to-the-bottom/regulatory-chill problem. After all, isn't the race-to-the-bottom/regulatory-chill problem fueled by the weak labor standards of the developing world, and therefore mustn't the solution to this problem involve finding a way to induce developing countries to accept commitments to strengthen their labor standards? In fact, the answer is "No" on both counts. The race-to-the-bottom/regulatory-chill problem is not fueled by the weak labor standards of the developing world but rather, as I have indicated above, by the weak property rights over market access associated with negotiated tariff bindings. The weakness of these property rights in turn, involves the relationship between each government's tariff bindings and its *own* labor standards. As a consequence, the key to solving the race-to-the-bottom/regulatory-chill problem is to forge the appropriate link between a government's negotiated tariff commitments and its own standards choices: there is no reason that governments need negotiate over their individual standards choices in order to accomplish this.

The second reason why I believe that, of these two approaches, strengthening the renegotiation and non-violation nullification-or-impairment provisions already present in existing GATT Articles conforms more closely with existing GATT/WTO practice and principles, is a more subtle reason. While I have observed above that direct negotiations over labor standards would raise the question, "Is *everything* ultimately to be a matter for international negotiation?," this indirect approach would raise the analogous question: Is *everything* ultimately to be a matter for renegotiating one's tariffs or lodging international complaints of non-violation nullification-or-impairment? Neither question is easy to answer. However, the GATT/WTO dispute settlement bodies have, over the past 50 years, developed some experience and expertise in answering the second question.

Therefore conclude that, of these two approaches, the approach of strengthening the renegotiation and non-violation nullification-or-impairment provisions already present in existing GATT Articles represents the more-promising avenue by which the WTO might solve the race-to-the-bottom/regulatory-chill problem.[14]

The Role of the WTO in Enforcing ILO Agreements

In this section, I consider the role that the WTO might play in helping to enforce labor agreements that are negotiated in the ILO. Difficulties in enforcing ILO agreements have plagued the ILO almost since its inception. For example, in discussions relating to procedures for ensuring the application

of ratified ILO "Conventions," the most substantive form of ILO agreements, the British delegate to the 1926 session of the Conference (as quoted
in Landy, 1966, p. 18) stated:

> There is hope that we shall render application more solid and more frequent
> . . . Not only should we achieve a greater mutual self-confidence as a result of
> this procedure, but we should be able to prove to the world at large that
> the common taunt which is so often leveled at our work, namely, that our
> Conventions are purely paper Conventions, would be finally and completely
> dissipated and we should be able to prove to the world by the best possible
> means, by actual fact, that when we pass Conventions and when they are
> ratified a definite measure of social progress has followed.

The ILO's early struggles with enforcement have continued to plague it into
the present, which in large part explains the widespread current interest in
exploring ways to bring the enforcement power of the WTO to bear on
countries that are not upholding their ILO commitments. However, before
considering ways to enhance the enforcement of ILO agreements by forging
links between it and the WTO, it is instructive to briefly consider further
the ILO's own early discussions of enforcement. Johnston (1970, p. 90)
describes some of these early discussions as follows:

> When the original Constitution was being drafted at the Paris Peace Confer-
> ence in 1919 proposals were made that the International Labour Conference
> should be given full legislative powers. The French and Italian delegations in
> particular supported the workers' claims that the Conference should be a
> legislative assembly in the fullest sense of the term, adopting laws which
> would be obligatory upon all the members of the Organization. Very wisely,
> as experience has proved, most of the delegations took the view that the
> attribution of such supra-national powers to the Conference would not be
> accepted by the majority of States as consistent with the exercise of their
> sovereignty. The Constitution therefore limited the basic obligation of mem-
> bers to the submission by them of Conventions and Recommendations to the
> national competent authority (in most cases the legislature) for the enactment
> of legislation or other action.
>
> Under the Constitution, therefore, none of the decisions of the Conference
> have compulsory effect, and no member is under any obligation to ratify them.
> Nevertheless, the special provisions relating to the procedure of the Confer-
> ence in the adoption of its decisions constitute an important step forward as
> compared with the procedure of former diplomatic conferences. The signific-
> ance of this advance is often overlooked.
>
> In the procedure of the Conference the concept of unanimity which had
> previously appeared to be the necessary corollary of the sovereign rights of
> States was definitely set aside. No member has a right of veto at any stage in
> the procedure leading to the adoption of a Convention or a Recommendation.

These discussions illustrate an important point. Key institutional features of the ILO, such as its non-unanimity voting rules (simple majority voting for some decisions, two-thirds majority voting for others), exist *because* it was decided early on *not* to endow the ILO with independent legislative authority to determine the labor laws of its member countries.

In this light, it would, therefore, be naive to conceive of the ILO as an organization that could dictate national labor standards if only it had the power to enforce its Conventions. If the ILO had been designed with such power, the voting rule acceptable to its members would surely have been unanimity, and with the consequent right of veto few if any ILO Conventions would have ever been adopted. Similarly, it would be unwise to assume that simply "bringing in" outside enforcement powers – such as those supplied by the WTO – would necessarily "fix" the ILO in such a way that it could become a greater force in determining the national labor laws of its member countries. Johnston (1970, p. 279) offers these words of caution:

> Arising out of the criticism that the ILO relies too much on compromise is the further criticism that it is constitutionally too weak; it has no teeth; should its machinery not be strengthened to enable it to put more pressure on governments? When the Constitution of the ILO was being drafted in Paris in 1919, some members of the Commission strongly urged that the Conventions adopted by the Conference should have immediate status and effect of national labor legislation in all member States. If that proposal had been adopted the ILO would inevitably have foundered. The world was not ready then for such a supranational power; it is not ready for it now. National sovereignty is a very tender plant; it has to be handled very carefully.

With this caution in mind, I now briefly consider the question of linkage. In particular, I focus on the specific question of whether the WTO might usefully become involved in helping to ensure that countries who ratify ILO Conventions in fact live up to these Conventions. I wish to emphasize two points.

First, economic theory points to circumstances in which explicit linkage between the WTO and the ILO for enforcement purposes – whereby violation of ILO commitments would trigger retaliatory trade measures authorized by the WTO (and possibly vice versa) – may be beneficial, and also circumstances in which such linkage provides no benefits or may even be harmful.[15] Moreover, explicit linkage of this kind could lead simply to a *reallocation* of enforcement power across WTO and ILO agreements, in which case the effectiveness with which WTO commitments are enforced might be diminished in order to enhance enforcement of ILO commitments, or explicit linkage could lead to the *creation* of additional enforcement power that could in principle enhance the performance of each agreement. The first point I wish to emphasize is simply that the impacts of explicit linkage will depend on circumstances.

The second point I wish to emphasize is this. *Some* linkage between the WTO and the ILO can occur even without the creation of any explicit links between these two organizations, and this "implicit" linkage can in principle *always* enhance the performance of both organizations. Like the explicit linkage described above, the implicit linkage I am referring to involves the possibility of trade measures authorized by the WTO in the circumstance where an ILO commitment is violated. But unlike explicit linkage, where the retaliatory trade measures would represent the use of new retaliation rights under augmented WTO rules, the trade measures under the implicit linkage I am describing simply represent an exercise of already existing non-violation nullification-or-impairment or renegotiation rights in the WTO.

Consider, for example, a country that has ratified an ILO Convention and must therefore ensure that its labor policies are in line with this Convention in order to be in conformance with its ILO obligations. Suppose now that this country binds its tariffs in WTO negotiations. If this country subsequently violates its ILO commitments by non-application of the ratified ILO Convention, and if this non-application has *market-access* implications – by for example reducing access to the country's markets from the level that its trading partners could have reasonably anticipated in light of its bound tariffs *and* ILO-conforming labor policies – then in principle its trading partners would have a right of redress under the WTO's non-violation nullification-or-impairment provisions. Under this right of redress, the country would either have to find a way to restore the original level of market access, or else its trading partners could be authorized under WTO rules to seek compensation for the nullification or impairment of their market-access rights (which could include reciprocal withdrawals of market access, i.e., tariff increases that affect this county's exports). While I have described here a role for use of the WTO's non-violation nullification-or-impairment provisions to help enforce ILO commitments, a similar role can in principle be played by the renegotiation provisions of the WTO.[16]

In this general way, "implicit" linkages between WTO and ILO commitments – implicit because there is no sense in which the violation of an ILO commitment would be considered a violation of WTO commitments – can in principle play a useful role in contributing toward the enforcement of ILO commitments. And at the same time, the legitimate exercise of these links is an important component of enforcing WTO commitments and maintaining the balance between rights and obligations for WTO member governments.[17]

In summary, in this section I have considered the role that the WTO might play in helping to enforce labor agreements that are negotiated in the ILO. I have observed that economic theory points to circumstances in which explicit "linkage" between the WTO and the ILO for enforcement purposes – whereby violation of ILO commitments would trigger retaliatory trade measures orchestrated by the WTO – may be beneficial, and also circumstances in which such linkage provides no benefit or may even be harmful. But I have also observed that explicit linkage of this kind may not be necessary in order for the WTO to play an important role in the enforcement of ILO commitments. More specifically, I have described how the non-violation nullification-or-impairment provisions and the renegotiation provisions contained in GATT Articles can play a significant role in enforcing ILO agreements. Indeed, in light of the uncertain impacts of developing explicit links between these two organizations, strengthening these already-existing principles of the WTO may be the most effective way to utilize WTO commitments as a means to help enforce labor agreements negotiated under the ILO.

Evaluating the Options

In this section, I collect the arguments of the previous sections and propose an overall approach to the international organization and enforcement of labor standards. I then briefly comment on some of the appealing and unappealing features of this approach relative to other approaches that have been proposed.

Together, the discussions of the previous sections suggest the following overall approach to the international organization and enforcement of labor standards. The ILO should tighten its focus to cover only labor issues that arise as a result of international humanitarian or political concerns, and should set aside race-to-the-bottom/regulatory-chill concerns associated with national labor standards choices. The WTO should take on labor standards issues as they relate to race-to-the-bottom/regulatory-chill concerns. However, the WTO should address these new responsibilities by strengthening the renegotiation and non-violation nullification-or-impairment provisions already present in existing GATT Articles, not by initiating direct negotiations over labor standards between its member governments. Finally, no explicit links between the WTO and the ILO should be established for enforcement purposes, but the enforcement links already implicit between these two organizations – as embodied in the non-violation nullification-or-impairment and renegotiation provisions of the WTO – should be encouraged.[18]

I now briefly comment on some of the appealing and unappealing features of this approach relative to other approaches that have been proposed. I consider in turn three alternative approaches. A first approach is to maintain the status quo operations of the WTO and the ILO. A second approach is to follow the example of the WTO TRIPs agreement in addressing the issue of labor standards in the WTO. A third approach is to expand the use of Article XX of the WTO to allow it to address in a more systematic fashion the labor standards concerns of WTO member governments.

According to the line of argument I have developed in the previous sections, the overall approach I have proposed above is in principle a sensible way to proceed. However, this line of argument is predicated on the view that the essential problem that the WTO is well designed to prevent is the problem of international cost-shifting through unilateral government policy decisions, and that this cost-shifting is fundamentally a market-access issue. If this view is wrong, and if the WTO is in fact acting to solve some other kind of international problem that I have not identified here, then it may be ill-advised to assign additional tasks to the WTO simply because these tasks address what are fundamentally market-access issues. Moreover, even if this view is right, what the WTO can sensibly be asked to do in principle may be very different from what it can competently do in practice. There are serious risks of overburdening the WTO legal system with intractable measurement problems, questions of a "slippery slope," and concerns that WTO could be "hijacked" for protectionist purposes. For these and other reasons, maintaining the status quo operations of the WTO and ILO is an option that should not be dismissed without considerable trepidation. And the arguments I have made in previous sections cannot really offer a convincing case against maintaining the status quo. Rather, they should be interpreted as arguments of the form, "*If* changes are to be made to the existing international organization and enforcement of labor standards, here is a sensible way to proceed."

A different approach to addressing concerns over the setting of national labor standards would be to follow the lead of the WTO TRIPs agreement – as that agreement approached intellectual property rights standards – and to attempt to negotiate an analogous WTO agreement over a set of minimum labor standards that all member governments must meet. Advocates of the proposed WTO social clause often point to the TRIPs agreement in support of their approach to labor standards. But as I have emphasized in the preceding sections, we must ask the question: What problem is such an agreement attempting to solve? I have argued above that when the different kinds of international problems associated with the unilateral choice of labor standards are distinguished, the social clause does not appear to offer a sensible solution to any of these problems. But in fairness, the TRIPs agreement should be held accountable to the same question. In principle, only if the TRIPs agreement can be understood to be a sensible solution to an international problem associated with the unilateral choice of national laws which protect intellectual property rights would the force of the analogy between the TRIPs agreement and the proposed WTO social clause be extinguished.[19]

A final approach that I comment on here is to expand the use of Article XX of the WTO to allow it to address in a more systematic fashion the labor standards concerns of WTO member governments. Already Article XX(e) permits member governments to take exception from their general MFN obligations and raise discriminatory barriers against imports of the products of prison labor. Accordingly, under this approach, the circumstances under which general exceptions to WTO obligations are granted might be expanded to permit, for example, discriminatory trade barriers to be raised by one member against the imports of another member if that member violates its ILO commitments.[20] This approach would represent a step toward forging explicit enforcement linkages between the WTO and the ILO. One distinctive feature of this approach relative to utilizing the enforcement links already implicit between these two organizations as I have proposed above is that this approach would allow for *discriminatory* trade barriers in response to violations of ILO commitments. A second distinctive feature of this approach relative to utilizing the enforcement links already implicit between these two organizations is that it would presumably be more straightforward for the WTO dispute settlement bodies to administer. These features could be appealing, by giving more "teeth" to the enforcement links between the WTO and the ILO, but they could also have unappealing consequences, if they ultimately led to a significant rise in discrimination in trade relations.

Summary and Conclusion

What international action should be taken with regard to labor standards, how should this action be organized, and by what means should it be enforced? In this chapter I have attempted to provide answers to these three questions, and along the way to answer a more pointed question: What role should the WTO play in determining the labor standards of its member governments?

Taking the perspective of economic theory, I have described here a line of argument that supports the following overall approach to the international organization and enforcement of labor standards. First, the ILO should tighten its focus to cover only labor issues that arise as a result of international humanitarian or political concerns, and should set aside race-to-the-bottom/regulatory-chill concerns associated with national labor standards choices. Second, the WTO should take on labor standards issues as they relate to race-to-the-bottom/regulatory-chill concerns, but should address these new responsibilities by strengthening the renegotiation and non-violation nullification-or-impairment provisions already present in existing GATT Articles, not by initiating direct negotiations over labor standards between its member governments. And third, no explicit links between the WTO and the ILO should be established for enforcement purposes, but the enforcement links already implicit between these two organizations – as embodied in the non-violation nullification-or-impairment and renegotiation provisions of the WTO – should be encouraged.

I do not advocate that this overall approach is necessarily better than maintaining the status quo operations of the WTO and ILO. But I suggest that *if* changes are to be made to the existing international organization and enforcement of labor standards, then this approach is a sensible way to proceed.

ACKNOWLEDGMENTS

I thank Robert Baldwin, Kaushik Basu, Francis Maupain, and Devashish Mitra for helpful comments. I am particularly indebted to Henrik Horn for many detailed comments on an earlier draft, and to my discussants, Petros Mavroidis and L. Alan Winters, for insightful discussion. This chapter is part of a larger project on international labor standards, initiated and funded by the EGDI, Sweden.

NOTES

1. These statements reflect the standard conditions of tariff analysis, under which the Metzler and Lerner paradoxes do not arise. More concisely, when I refer to a change in "market access" or a change in "the competitive relationship between imported and domestic products," I mean a change in the relationship between, on the one hand, the cost in the domestic market of the imported product when exporters receive their original exporter prices, and on the other hand, the cost in the domestic market of the domestic import-competing product when exporters receive prices that maintain either the volume of domestic import demand or the volume of foreign export supply at its original level. A more technical discussion of these points is contained in Bagwell and Staiger (2001a).
2. Of course, US consumers might gain from the ability to purchase US products at lower prices, and so not everyone in the United States need agree on whether the economic effect of India's supposed change in labor standards is good or bad. The important point is that such effects, however complex they may be, travel through changes in market access.
3. More accurately, while WTO negotiation are among the member governments, ILO negotiations have a "tripartite" structure, in which each member country is represented by a government official, a representative for workers and a representative for employers.
4. See, for example, the evidence reviewed in Bagwell and Staiger (2000a).
5. More detailed and formal arguments that various GATT Articles can be interpreted as helping to solve this basic problem may be found in Bagwell and Staiger (1999a, 2000b, 2001b, 2001c, and 2001e).

6. As I described in the second section, the choice of labor standards may also have humanitarian/political implications. However, in order to focus here on the possibility of race-to-the-bottom/regulatory-chill problems associated with the choice of labor standards, I temporarily ignore these humanitarian/political issues, and return to them when I discuss the ILO.

7. More detailed and formal arguments along these lines may be found in Bagwell and Staiger (1999b, 2001b, and 2001e).

8. Wilson (1996) considers a number of reasons that constraints on tax policies might give rise to race-to-the-bottom type problems.

9. Notice that this reassignment does not preclude the ILO from addressing labor issues that have important market access implications. Rather, it implies only that any market access implications of ILO decisions would be handled in the WTO.

10. See Ederington (2001b) for a formal demonstration of this general point.

11. On the general question of how international trade agreements are enforced, see for example Dixit (1987), Bagwell and Staiger (1990, 2000a), and Maggi (1999).

12. A more complete and formal treatment of these points may be found in Bagwell and Staiger (2001b).

13. These points are made formally in Bagwell and Staiger (2001b). It is also interesting to observe that, as compared to GATT, the WTO has already begun moving in this general direction. In particular, the amended rules on subsidies incorporated into the WTO go part way toward explicitly accommodating the granting of domestic subsidies that are intended to offset the financial burden of new environmental regulations on existing firms. Article 8 of the WTO Agreement on Subsidies and Countervailing Measures designates as "non-actionable" the granting of specific domestic subsidies which represent "assistance to promote adaptation of existing facilities to new environmental requirements imposed by law and/or regulations which result in greater constraints and financial burden on firms . . . ," and which also meet additional criteria specified in the article.

14. Of course, I am ignoring here an important set of practical measurement difficulties by implicitly assuming that tariff changes can be crafted so as to more-or-less offset the market-access implications of changes in labor standards. The subtle way in which labor standards can impact market access suggests that such practical issues could pose a formidable impediment, and these considerations must surely be weighed in assessing the advisability of any new approach to the issue of labor standards. I interpret such considerations mainly as suggesting the wisdom of maintaining the status quo operations of the WTO/ILO (I return to this point in the two final sections).

15. Recent papers on the topic of linkage and trade agreements include Conconi and Perroni (2001), Ederington (2000, 2001a), Limao (2000), and Spagnolo (2001).

16. The WTO's renegotiation provisions might come into play if a country's non-conformance with its ILO obligations were responsible for enhanced export volumes that its trading partners did not wish to accept.

17. It should also be noted that enforcement threats need not be limited to the withdrawal of market access. For example, direct foreign aid can be withheld from a country if it fails to meet its ILO commitments.

18. More generally, while I have presented the arguments above in the context of labor standards, the broader point is that the WTO should handle market access concerns associated with all unilateral policy choices, and that other international institutions should address the non-pecuniary aspects of each specific policy issue (e.g., labor, environment).

19. Some preliminary formal work along these lines can be found in Bagwell and Staiger (2001d, in process). An alternative interpretation would be that the TRIPs agreement was itself, in fact, ill-advised. A formal analysis that lends some support to this alternative interpretation can be found in Deardorff (1992).

20. Such an approach might build off an analogy with GATT Article XX(h), which allows general exceptions to WTO obligations to be taken "in pursuance of obligations under any intergovernmental commodity agreement which conforms to criteria submitted to the CONTRACTING PARTIES and not disapproved by them or which is itself so submitted and not so disapproved". This general line of approach has been discussed in the context of environmental concerns, for example, by Hudec (1996).

REFERENCES

Bagwell, Kyle and Robert W. Staiger (1990) "A Theory of Managed Trade," *American Economic Review*, 80 (September), pp. 779–95.

Bagwell, Kyle and Robert W. Staiger (1999a) "An Economic Theory of GATT," *American Economic Review*, 89 (1, March), pp. 215–48.

Bagwell, Kyle, and Robert W. Staiger (1999b) "The Simple Economics of Labor Standards and The GATT," in Alan V. Deardorff and Robert M. Stern (eds), *Social Dimensions of U.S. Trade Policies*, Ann Arbor: The University of Michigan Press.

Bagwell, Kyle and Robert W. Staiger (2000a) "GATT-Think," NBER Working Paper no. 8005, November.

Bagwell, Kyle and Robert W. Staiger (2000b) "Multilateral Trade Negotiations, Bilateral Opportunism and the Rules of GATT," mimeo, March.

Bagwell, Kyle and Robert W. Staiger (2001a) "Technical Notes on the Economics of Market Access," unpublished mimeo, March.

Bagwell, Kyle and Robert W. Staiger (2001b) "Domestic Policies, National Sovereignty and International Economic Institutions," *The Quarterly Journal of Economics*, 116 (2, May), pp. 519–62.

Bagwell, Kyle and Robert W. Staiger (2001c) "Shifting Comparative Advantage and Accession in the WTO," mimeo, February.

Bagwell, Kyle and Robert W. Staiger (2001d, in process) "Tariffs and Patent Protection in a Global Economy."

Bagwell, Kyle and Robert W. Staiger (2001e) "The WTO as a Mechanism for Securing Market Access Property Rights: Implications for Global Labor and Environmental Issues," *Journal of Economic Perspectives*, 15 (2, Summer), pp. 69–88.

Conconi, Paola and Carlo Perroni (2001) "Issue Linkage and Issue Tie-in in Multilateral Negotiations," mimeo, Warwick University, February.

Deardorff, Alan V. (1992) "Welfare Effects of Global Patent Protection," *Economica*, 59, pp. 35–51.

Dixit, Avinash (1987) "Strategic Aspects of Trade Policy," in Truman F. Bewley (ed.), *Advances in Economic Theory: Fifth World Congress*, New York: Cambridge University Press.

Ederington, Josh (2000) "Trade and Domestic Policy Linkage in International Agreements, manuscript, October.

Ederington, Josh (2001a) "Global Environmental Agreements and Trade Sanctions," manuscript, February.

Ederington, Josh (2001b) "International Coordination of Trade and Domestic Policies, *American Economic Review*, 91 (5), pp. 1580–93.

Hudec, Robert E. (1990) *The GATT Legal System and World Trade Diplomacy* (2nd edn), New York: Praeger.

Hudec, Robert E. (1996) "GATT Legal Restraints on the Use of Trade Measures against Foreign Environmental Practices," in Jagdish Bhagwati and Robert E. Hudec (eds), *Fair Trade and Harmonization*, vol. 2, pp. 120–42, Cambridge, MA: MIT Press.

Johnston, George A. (1970) *The International Labor Organization: Its Work for Social and Economic Progress*, London: Europa Publications.

Landy, E. A. (1966) *The Effectiveness of International Supervision: Thirty Years of I.L.O. Experience*, London: Stevens & Sons Limited.

Limao, Nuno (2000) "Trade Policy, Cross-Border Externalities and Lobbies: Do linked Agreements Enforce More Cooperative Outcomes?," mimeo, August.

Maggi, Giovanni (1999) "The Role of Multilateral Institutions in International Trade Cooperation," *American Economic Review*, March, pp. 190–214.

Morse, David A. (1969) *The Origin and Evolution of the ILO and its Role in the World Community*, Ithaca: New York State School of Industrial and Labor Relations, Cornell University.

Petersmann, Ernst-Ulrich (1997) *The GATT/WTO Dispute Settlement System: International Law, International Organizations and Dispute Settlement*, London: Kluwer Law International Ltd.

Spagnolo, Giancarlo (2001) "Issue Linkage, Delegation, and International Policy Cooperation," mimeo, February.

The Paris Peace Conference, James T. Shotwell (ed.) (1934) *The Origins of the International Labor Organization: vol. I – History*, New York: Columbia University Press.

The Paris Peace Conference, James T. Shotwell (ed.) (1934) *The Origins of the International Labor Organization: vol. II – Documents*, New York: Columbia University Press.

Wilson, John D. (1996) "Capital Mobility and Environmental Standards: Is There a Theoretical Basis for a Race to the Bottom?," in Jagdish Bhagwati and Robert E. Hudec (eds), *Fair Trade and Harmonization: Prerequisites for Free Trade?, vol. 1*, Cambridge MA: MIT Press.

COMMENTARY 4.1

Trade and Labor Standards: To Link or Not to Link?

L. Alan Winters[1]

This chapter is inspired by and complementary to Bob Staiger's excellent study in this volume. I find myself very largely in agreement with Staiger substantively and greatly esteem his methodological contribution as simplifying a complex and contentious debate.[2] He distinguishes between the natures of the various international externalities that figure in the trade and labour standards debate and uses that distinction as the basis for the assignment of policies and institutions to address the different externalities. I seek not to challenge Staiger's argument but to clarify it and place it in context.

Staiger is very cautious – he says "if you must link trade and labour standards together, do it as follows . . ." This is sensible and legitimate, for before we decide between two options (to link or not to link) we must know what each entails, and Staiger gives us his view of the best (dominant) outcome in the link scenario. However, policy-makers ultimately have to grapple with the main question and economists exist to help them, so we do need to consider seriously the question of "the Staiger plan" vs. the status quo. This chapter mainly pertains to this latter question in the sense that I argue that, while Staiger has correctly ranked the alternative ways of linking trade and labour standards, he has under-estimated the problems of his proposal absolutely.

Staiger identifies three externalities – the pecuniary one, which might cause a race to the bottom in standards, a political/civil unrest one and a moral one. The pecuniary externality operates via market access and is, *prima facie*, a candidate for solution via the WTO, since market access is the main business of the WTO. I am less sanguine than Staiger – let alone the enthusiasts for introducing a social clause into WTO – that this is desirable.

First, let me re-emphasize that the economic argument for intervention is not that low Indian standards reduce American exports and wages *per se*, but that they induce suboptimal standards in America (and that competition with America induces suboptimal standards in India). If standards were given or were optimal in each country, India's competitive advantage in "low-standard" industries would be no different from advantages stemming from technology or natural resources. And as such would provide, in economic terms, no case for intervention. In fact, the evidence that labour standards are affected by trade-related spillover is mixed, as Belser (2001) shows, but the exports/wages/jobs argument still has wide currency. This, I suspect, is because workers and politicians conceive of it in mercantilist terms and object to the implications of labour standards on exactly the same grounds as they object to those of trade liberalization and the falling relative price of manufactures (deindustrialization). Indeed, labour standards that reduce developed countries' import prices (and thus which raise the importing country's *economic* welfare if not that of its import-competing producers) attract just as much opposition as other standards issues. In short, much of the popular and political debate is instinctively protectionist in nature rather than "economistic." Consequently, one needs to worry about whether theoretically correct solutions to problems might get captured and abused. This is particularly important when it comes to writing laws or creating institutions, for these have, at best, a huge degree of inertia and, at worst, a capacity to devour their creators and their good intentions. The continuing expansion and spread of the antidumping business is proof enough of this.

Second, all the market-access concerns presume that lower labour standards confer a competitive advantage. If that were not the case there would be no threat to competing producers and hence no incentive for them to press for compensatory reductions in their own local standards. But industries that discriminate against workers typically *reduce* the supply of labour that they can draw on and so *cut* their production levels relative to those possible by paying a competitive wage (Martin and Maskus, 2001). Similarly, if labour is generally under-rewarded, effort and investments in human capital will suffer, again reducing productivity. Evidence that weak labour rights engender competitiveness is absent, and if this is the correct view of the world, there is no problem, and creating institutions to cure it will merely create new opportunities for mischief. Both arguments suggest that Staiger could be over-stating the importance of the pecuniary externality.

Staiger argues that it is *only* because tariff bindings constrain one instrument of market access that the other instrument (labour standards) is liable to be set at suboptimal values. If countries can manipulate both tariffs and labour standards, market access will be inefficiently low but the tariff/labour standards division will be efficient. This is an important insight, which is not restricted to importers' own markets. If low labour standards also confer competitive advantages in export markets – and if governments value these – then quite independent of tariffs, governments will compete in labour standards.[3]

Staiger's proposal to extend property rights in market access has an important limitation that means that it will be viewed as inadequate by most advocates of labour-standards activism. It pertains only to *changes* in labour standards *after* a trade deal has been struck. But most activists want to use it to address current inadequacies. A particular problem of using trade sanctions – in WTO, that means permitting the imposition of restrictions on imports of specific goods – is that even if it works, it will focus labour standards improvements in developing countries just on the tradable sectors. This will tend to worsen standards elsewhere in the economy as labour demand is reduced in the controlled sectors and labour flows out into the uncontrolled sectors. And since the non-tradable sectors are where the weakest members of society are already concentrated, such a development is likely to exacerbate overall poverty and hardship.

The political externality – the spread of civil strife – seems clear enough, but it is worth noting that there may be spillovers in both directions. In addition to the developed country wishing the developing country to raise its standards, the latter might have a legitimate interest in the former reducing its. Suppose that the USA raises its labour standards strongly and that this persuades Mexican workers that they too could ask for an increase. But suppose that Mexico's institutions for compromise and dispute settlement were not as robust as the USA's and that these demands precipitate civil strife. Is there not a case for Mexico asking the USA to desist from the initial improvement? By the logic of spillovers, the USA should be required to negotiate its standards as well.

Second, while the pursuit of peace is clearly a very high priority, it seems to me that the gross violations of labour rights that precipitate *contagious* civil strife are of a different order of magnitude from those that most people have in mind when discussing labour standards. Given the crossovers between objectives and instruments that Staiger identifies – viz. the commercial objectives that clearly pervade the political ILO – one needs, again, to protect carefully against the abuse in everyday life of measures designed to deal with extreme circumstances. If contagion is the problem, let us be very clear that it is rare and that "solutions" should be similarly rare. In fact, for extreme cases we already have access to trade sanctions – as used, for example, against apartheid in South Africa – and to other forms of embargo as ILO has now initiated against Burma (Myanmar). Thus it is not clear that the "peace agreement" really calls for any changes at all to the status quo.

The moral externality is also real – we are our brothers' keepers to some extent. But it too is a two way street. US citizens' concerns over labour rights elsewhere may be legitimate, but what about Indian concerns about family breakdown and drug use?

In the cases of both the non-commercial spillovers, I am less ready than Bob Staiger to consider the right of one nation to interfere in another.

Sovereignty is a dangerous thing – it can be used to justify non-intervention in the face of heinous crimes and it lies behind most armed conflict. However, it is also a useful way of allowing groups of people the self-determination that is politically so attractive in western politics. Economists preach the pre-eminence of individual objectives, so I believe that we should be very clear about the benefits before we sanction interference in other countries' affairs. We must recognise that there are trade-offs – that the solution of one problem may not be worth the possible creation of another. Excess interference (even advice) to weaker states is not ultimately a way of advancing peace and understanding. I do not rule it out, but I do urge caution.

I have similar reactions to Staiger's proof that the WTO *should* deal with the market-access spillover from labour standards. His argument presumes that any market-access issue can be as easily dealt with as any other (implicitly at zero cost), and thus that it is just plain inefficient to leave holes in WTO's coverage. But if the spillovers from labour standards are actually weak but they nonetheless still generate great political heat, and if WTO procedures are costly under these circumstances, then leaving holes – recognising that a small degree of market-access slippage may occur – may be rational. The cost of WTO procedures should not be underestimated. The actual cost of the skilled labour required for a dispute is significant, but the opportunity cost of diverting very scarce skills away from domestic or other trade policy-making could be very high. Worse, the WTO runs on rather a low stock of political capital. If countries fight over labour standards, they are likely to make less progress in other dimensions (Rollo and Winters, 2000). If labour standards contributed significantly to the crash at Seattle in December 1999, the dangers are plain enough.

A particular drain on the WTO's goodwill, legitimacy, and credibility would arise if it became the direct enforcement mechanism for ILO conventions that countries have already signed. Staiger admirably sets out the case that if the ILO had a legislative role and some 'teeth', very few conventions would have been agreed. But it does not seem to me overly cynical to argue that the same applies to individual conventions. To sign a convention as a means of signalling aspirations and objectives is one thing if the cost of failure is a "severe talking to." It is quite another if the cost is trade sanctions.

Two further issues arise if the WTO's dispute settlement procedure (DSP) is extended to cover labour standards. First, Staiger's proposal to make the property rights in market access more symmetric means that before long a country will simultaneously raise labour standards and raise tariffs and justify the latter in terms of maintaining market access at its original level. Suppose that this country is challenged in DSP and loses. Apart from the political fall-out of the "WTO undermines standards" variety, we must also ask how the plaintiff might enforce its "victory." The answer is ultimately by trade sanctions. Now suppose that it is the USA that raises standards and

Ecuador that complains. Effective enforcement is more or less absent: Ecuador will hurt itself much more deeply than it hurts the USA by curtailing their bilateral trade. This asymmetry in the DSP is well known, but it is nonetheless a good reason to avoid putting more strain on it by adding conflicts over labour standards to its coverage. Staiger's proposal offers just one more reason for raising tariffs, and by legitimizing such increases, it increases the probabilities that some domestic interest will eventually persuade a government to use it.

Finally, there is a problem of dimensionality. Labour standards are generally pretty broad in application, but tariffs and the DSP are narrow and specific. A government pursuing the "Staiger portfolio" of tariff and labour standards increases will very probably wish to raise many tariffs. Its trading partners will have to challenge every one separately.

In summary, I think Bob Staiger's chapter is very useful, but I also think that it is a potentially dangerous one. If ever there were a slippery slope in commercial policy, I fear that this is it.

NOTES

1. I thank Bob Staiger and T. N. Srinivasan and other participants for comments on the earlier draft of this chapter.
2. I also heartily commend Bagwell and Staiger's whole insightful research programme on the theory of GATT, of which this chapter is part.
3. Placing this argument in a general equilibrium framework reduces its force, but does not undermine it, for exactly the reasons alluded to Staiger's note 1.

REFERENCES

Belser, P. (2001) "Four Essays in Trade and Labour Standards," unpublished DPhil thesis, University of Sussex.

Martin, W. and Maskus, K. E. (2001) "Core Labor Standards and Competitiveness: Implications for Global Trade Policy", *Review of International Economics*, 4, pp. 317–28.

Rollo, J. and L. A. Winters (2000) "Subsidiarity and Governance Challenges for the WTO: The Examples of Environmental and Labour standards," *The World Economy*, 23 (4), pp. 561–76.

COMMENTARY 4.2

The Need to Micro-Manage Regulatory Diversity

Petros C. Mavroidis

The Argument in Staiger's Study

Staiger's chapter distinguishes between a pecuniary and a non-pecuniary externality that stem from weak labor standards in some parts of the world: the former stems from the fact that, as a result of weak labor standards (that must be the effect of a change in regulatory policy, see the discussion), a WTO Member is in a position to win more market access (either at home or away) than anticipated when the trade concession (in the form of tariff binding) was agreed; the latter stems from the fact that, as a result of weak labor standards, and independently of market-access concerns, citizens in parts of the world with higher labor standards suffer enough to persuade their governments to do something about it. The non-pecuniary externality can take the form of either social unrest in some societies or could even lead to some humanitarian activity.

Based on this diagnosis, the author goes ahead and proposes an institutional function for the WTO and a different institutional function for the ILO: he argues that the WTO should deal specifically with the pecuniary externality since it is anyway geared to deal with market access issues only and lacks the expertise to do anything else. Conversely, the ILO should deal with the non-pecuniary externality.

He finally advances arguments to ensure that both institutions will be in a position to honour their objective function, as defined by the author.

The Argument in this Commentary

In this brief commentary, I am essentially addressing two questions:

1. How much can be done with respect to labor standards within the existing WTO contract and the adjunct question how much is left out? ·
2. Where should whatever is left out be discussed?

The methodology I use to address the two questions could be described as instrumentalist, that is, my starting point is the legal instruments available in the WTO contract.

Following this methodology I conclude that the WTO law (that is, both the primary law – the WTO contract – and the secondary law – the WTO case-law) as it now stands, definitely allows WTO Members to address pecuniary externalities stemming from labor standards. It could be the case, although this point is not crystal-clear in case-law, that it also allows WTO Members to address non-pecuniary externalities by invoking their domestic legislation to this effect. It is even less clear to what extent they can do the same by invoking an international agreement concluded outside the WTO and which acknowledges their right to counteract non-pecuniary external-ities stemming from (weak) labor standards.

This is not a labor standards-specific conclusion: WTO Members can request from their partners that they respect their public order when trading with them. Because the extent and the shaping of public order differs across nations, there is a need to micro-manage regulatory diversity.

In principle, of course, it is legally possible that the WTO provides the forum for an agreement on labor standards. I do, however, raise a series of objections (complementary to those raised by Bob Staiger) against this thesis. First, remarkably, while there is a lot of talk about the potential form of an international agreement on trade and labor, no (or almost no) comprehensive discussion on whether there are gains from international cooperation when it comes to setting labor standards has taken place (the chapters by Brown et al., and Singh published in this volume being notable exceptions). Second – and assuming my first grounds or critique falls – the existing remedies in the WTO contract do not guarantee that an eventual trade and labor agreement will always be respected, especially if cases are brought against the relatively "big" players. The point here is that the effectiveness of the WTO legal system has probably been exaggerated; third, it would be quite odd to trust the issue of labor standards, which only tangentially has a trade component, to trade delegates.

I take each point in turn.

The Function of the WTO Contract in a Nutshell

Imagine that Oecedia (an OECD-type country) and Developia (a small de-veloping country) are WTO Members. They exchange concessions whereby

Developia binds its tariffs with respect to Oecedian computers and Oecedia binds its tariffs with respect to wheat from Developia and they start trading with each other.

Oecedia, for the purposes of this example, is the high-labor-standards country and Developia is its low-labor-standards counterpart. We further assume for the sake of the example, that Oecedia is hence the *demandeur* in the trade and labor discussion, that is the only party requesting from the other higher standards.

Oecedia and Developia might or might not have a bilateral (or even be part of a multilateral) agreement which obliges them to follow a particular benchmark with respect to labor standards. In case an agreement obliges them to respect an agreed benchmark, such agreement might or might not be reflected in the WTO contract. I take each point in turn.

The case of no bilateral agreement

The WTO: Predominantly negative integration

In this case, both countries are free to endogenously set their own standards. There is absolutely no legal compulsion at all imposed by the WTO contract *per se* with respect to labor standards. The WTO is, with respect to labor standards, a negative integration-type contract. The WTO case-law has by now developed a constant jurisprudence (first in *Shrimps—Turtles* but also more recently, during the *FSC* litigation) accepting this point.

Oecedia and Developia have each unilaterally defined their labor standards, and, as a result, for the sake of our example we are in the presence of regulatory diversity in this context. Now Oecedia, might or might not condition access of products originating in Developia upon the labor standards followed in the latter country. If it does not, we do not need to worry. If it does, it will have to comply with the WTO contract.

The matrix of possible legal actions

What does this mean in practice? Two considerations are important in this respect: on the one hand, as Staiger notes, it could very well be the case that Oecedia counteracts either pecuniary or non-pecuniary externalities. On the other, Oecedia can choose between two strategies: it can decide to take no regulatory action against products from Developia (and attack Developia's practices before the WTO) or do the exact opposite (that is ban, for example imports and expect to defend its measures before a WTO panel). If it chooses the former option, it will use a non-violation complaint (and argue that as a result of Developia's low labor standards, it has lost expected market access).

	Violation complaint (Developia attacks)	Non-violation complaint (Oecedia attacks)
Pecuniary externalities	Arts. III/XI/XX GATT TBT	Art. XXIII.1b GATT
Non-pecuniary externalities	Arts. III/XI/XX GATT TBT	

Figure 4.1 The Oecedia/Developia complaints matrix

If it chooses the latter, it will be prepared to face a violation complaint submitted by Developia against its import ban. The matrix is shown in figure 4.1.

Oecedia attacks

The non-violation complaint instrument is available only in case of pecuniary externalities. This instrument, as it has been interpreted in GATT/WTO case law, essentially allows WTO Members to attack domestic policies by their trading partners, which were not reasonably expected at the moment a concession was negotiated and which reduce the value of the negotiated concession. This latter element is what makes it clear that non-violation complaints cannot be used against non-pecuniary externalities.

Moreover, for a non-violation complaint to succeed, the domestic policy attacked must, as stated above, not have been reasonably anticipated at the moment the concession was negotiated. In its *Kodak–Fuji* jurisprudence, a WTO panel clarified that if the domestic policy attacked occurred after the negotiation was agreed, then there is a legal presumption that the policy at hand could not have been reasonably anticipated by the affected WTO Member (the burden of proof shifts to Developia, if it weakened its labor standards). Conversely, if the measure pre-dates (Developia maintains the same low labor standards pre- and post-conclusion of the concession) the conclusion of the concession, there is a legal presumption that it should have been reasonably anticipated. (In this case, Oecedia would have to show, for example, that, although the weak labor standards were known to it, it could not have anticipated the impact they would eventually have on trade.)

Although this has never so far been the case, existing WTO case-law makes it quite plausible that a non-violation complaint can be based on weak labor standards. In its *Asbestos* jurisprudence, the Appellate Body accepted that non-violation complaints can be submitted against unanticipated health-based trade-obstructing measures. *A fortiori* this should be the case with respect to labor standards.

In case the complaint succeeds, Oecedia and Developia will have to negotiate a mutually satisfactory adjustment (Art. 26.1a DSU). Developia, however, is under no legal obligation to withdraw its policy (and this is consonant to the fact that WTO with respect to labor standards is a contract respecting regulatory diversity).

Oecedia defends (a) an import ban

Now what if Oecedia bans imports of products originating in Developia? In this case it is simply irrelevant, from a legal perspective, if Oecedia wishes to address a pecuniary or a non-pecuniary externality. Or at least, so it seems to be the case following the *Shrimps–Turtles* jurisprudence.

Assume that Oecedia bans imports/sales of all goods produced through unfair (to its mind, defined as anything below its own) labor standards. To start with, Oecedia will have an incentive to ban sales and not imports: if it bans imports, it will almost immediately carry the burden of proof; Developia will have to assume the relatively easy task to demonstrate the existence of a quantitative restriction. By doing that it will have shown a violation of Art. XI GATT. Then Oecedia will have to show why its measures are justified through recourse to Art. XX GATT.

Two important hurdles are there for Oecedia to overcome: first, it will have to show that the list of Art. XX GATT covers this case. Charnovitz (1998) has taken the view that the term "public morals" appearing in Art. XXa GATT should be interpreted in this sense.

A contextual argument could be advanced to support this thesis: Art. XIV GATS (which has the same function as Art. XX GATT with respect to trade in services) refers to the wider notion of "public order". Since GATT and GATS are, in the Appellate Body's view, Annexes to the same (WTO) agreement, the argument would be that they would have to be co-extensive. It could also be argued that Art. XXd GATT is applicable. It should be noted however that so far there is no case law in the context of Art. XX GATT with respect to labor standards.

Assuming the *ratione materiae* coverage hurdle has been overcome, Oecedia will have to show, irrespective whether it invokes Art. XXa or Art. XXd GATT to justify its import ban, that the measure is necessary for it to achieve its goal: that is, it will have to show that an import ban is the least restrictive option to achieve its goal (which is, either protection of public morals in case Art. XXa GATT has been invoked, or Art. XXd GATT in case enforcement of its otherwise GATT-compatible legislation is sought). The term necessary in GATT/WTO case-law has been constantly interpreted as obliging WTO Members to choose the (reasonably available) least restrictive option to reach their goals.

Given the quasi-customary inability of WTO adjudicating bodies to work with the counterfactual, the burden of proof imposed by Art. XX GATT has proved so far to be insurmountable for WTO Members.

However, in its *Shrimps–Turtles* jurisprudence, the Appellate Body made it clear that policies addressing non-pecuniary externalities can very well be justified through recourse to Art. XX GATT (more on this below).

In a nutshell, the import ban route is not the most attractive option for Oecedia.

Oecedia defends (b) a sales ban

Were however, Oecedia to choose a sales ban, the initial burden of proof which Developia will have to assume is substantially higher. Two WTO Agreements are potentially relevant here: the GATT and the TBT. The latter is applicable in case Oecedia phrases its legislation as described by the Appellate Body in its *Asbestos* litigation (mandatory compliance with product characteristics; applicable to more than one particular transaction; no import ban). Let us turn to the GATT first.

Oecedia has enacted legislation, which bans sales of products produced with weak labor standards. Assume that Oecedia applies this law with respect to both domestic and foreign products. Since the measure is a domestic measure, Developia will have to show that Art. III.4 GATT (since the measure is not of a fiscal nature) has been violated. Moreover, since the measure is facially neutral, Developia will have to show *de facto* discrimination against its products.

In this vein, Developia will first have to show that goods (let us say Oecedian and Developian wheat) produced are the same irrespective whether they have been produced through high- or low-labor standards.

What does WTO case law have to say about that? The frank answer is that it is not at all clear what the law is in this respect: the *Japan–Alcohol* case made it clear that cross-price elasticity is the instrument to determine likeness. In this vein, Oecedian consumers would be asked whether, in the absence of regulatory intervention, they would purchase interchangeably Oecedian and Developian wheat. If Developia could submit persuasive evidence to this effect, then the burden of proof will have to shift to Oecedia to show that a policy reason (reflected in Art. XX GATT, as described above) allows it to intervene and justify the established violation of Art. III.4 GATT.

Recently however, in its *Asbestos* jurisprudence, the Appellate Body seems to deviate from this approach. The Appellate Body, at least in some paragraphs of its report, takes the view that regulatory objectives should be taken into account when defining likeness regardless of consumers' reactions. Independently of the soundness of this approach, if the *Asbestos*-standard prevails, it will be quite hard for Developia to meet its burden of proof.

Hence, the Appellate Body opened the door through its *Asbestos* case law for Oecedia to justify effective exclusion from its market of low-labor-standards-produced goods. To what extent the Oecedias of this world will use this opportunity (which has to be confirmed since, as stated above, the internal consistency of the *Asbestos* report should not be taken for granted) remains to be seen. At any rate, however, the better option for Oecedia is to impose the sales ban and choose to defend along the lines described above.

The likeness issue in *Asbestos* follows, to a large extent the logic of the TBT Agreement (which combines elements of Art. III.4 and Art. XX GATT). Hence, a similar outcome should be expected in case Oecedia chooses to adopt a technical regulation instead of a pure import ban.

A bilateral agreement is in place

It could of course very well be the case that Oecedia and Developia have agreed to a certain standard to be observed with respect to labor standards by signing an agreement to this effect. Theoretically, such agreement can either be or not be reflected in the WTO contract. I take each point in turn.

The agreement is reflected in the WTO contract

The recent second Art. 21.5 DSU panel report between Brazil and Canada on *Aircraft Subsidies* (WTO Doc. WT/DS46/RW/2) makes it clear that panels will take into account international agreements concluded outside the confines of the WTO to the extent that such agreements are explicitly referred to in the WTO contract.

The agreement is not reflected in the WTO contract

So far there is no precedent in WTO case-law where a panel, when interpreting the WTO contract, took into account an international agreement signed outside the confines of the WTO and not explicitly referred to in the WTO contract itself. The opinion (Palmeter and Mavroidis, 1998) has been expressed that, following customary rules of treaty interpretation, this should indeed be the case. This opinion has been criticized by authors (Trachtman, 1999) who believe that WTO panels should apply to WTO law only.

At this stage it is uncertain which way WTO case law will evolve on this issue.

The Limits of the Current WTO Contract

Where does this analysis leave me? Although the WTO contract contains no rules on labor standards, labor standards can be enforced before WTO panels. This can be the case when a WTO Member with high labor standards wishes to unilaterally apply its laws to all transactions in its territory. It is less clear that this can be the case if the Member at hand wishes to invoke an international agreement to this effect (unless, of course, the agreement is explicitly referred to in the WTO contract).

Staiger's chapter in a sense proposes a carve-out from the existing regime: only pecuniary externalities should be dealt with in the WTO context. An extension of the *Shrimps–Turtles/Asbestos* case law to labor standards is henceforth in his opinion unwarranted. Unwarranted yes, unavoidable though, maybe not. At the end of the day though the discussion on this issue seems to be how much of its public order Oecedia would like to request its partners to observe and for how much it is prepared to tolerate deviations.

In a nutshell, it seems plausible to argue that Oecedia can legitimately condition access of Developian products to its markets upon compliance with its public order, the latter extending to labor standards. What can be legally done and what is sound policy is not necessarily the same thing.

From can to should: *The need to micro-manage regulatory diversity: non-pecuniary externalities and the effects doctrine*

In a sense, *Shrimps–Turtles* stated the obvious: in the absence of transfer of sovereignty, the United States are free to choose and enforce their own environmental policy. This much is true. Problems start when the United States apply their legislation to their trading partners. Can they do it? The Appellate Body said yes without however discussing at all in a systematic way the permissible extent of a national legislation.

This is where we enter the discussion on extraterritoriality. The WTO contract does not at all address this issue. This however does not mean that the WTO contract provides its Members with a *carte blanche* to enforce their legislation in a manner inconsistent with public international law. Precisely because the WTO is an international contract, WTO adjudicating bodies will have to turn to public international law for inspiration when dealing with the concept of extraterritorial application of national laws.

This is a concept quite well defined in antitrust-jurisprudence on both sides of the Atlantic. In short, if an activity occurs outside national frontiers but its effects are felt within such frontiers, action following national laws of the affected state can legitimately (from a public international law perspective) occur.

To stick to the example of this chapter, if a Developian cartel practices monopoly prices in Oecedia, the latter can enforce its own antitrust laws although the addressees of its decision are Developian nationals and the activity was decided beyond Oecedian frontiers. The fact that the effects of the activity are felt within Oecedia suffices for the latter to exercise jurisdiction.

The next logical question is of course what effects? Do any effects, even if completely indirect, fit the bill? Customary international law answers in the negative: it has to be substantial, foreseeable, and direct effects. It is the latter condition that probably poses the most serious problems when discussing the application of the effects doctrine on non-pecuniary externalities.

It is quite clear that the directness criterion is satisfied when a cartel decides to price in a monopolistic manner when exporting to a foreign country: there is an uninterrupted link between the cause (decision to charge monopoly prices) and the effect (reduction of consumer welfare). Is it also the case when we discuss non-pecuniary externalities? We do not discuss here the case when Developia adopts weak labor standards in order to gain market access in Oecedia; we address the case when Developia's weak labor standards do not impose a pecuniary externality. Hence we must establish a link between Developia's revealed preference and the distress of Oecedia citizens. Is such link so obvious?

The argument here is that the effects doctrine as it currently stands is quite warranted when addressing pecuniary externalities. This is less so the case when addressing non-pecuniary externalities. It is difficult to predict however whether this will indeed be the case. Adjudicating bodies, and especially international ones have the tendency not to interfere too much with national sovereignty. If Oecedia defines its public order so as to include a particular benchmark of labor standards, it is not realistically to be expected that such a choice will be put into question by a WTO panel.

The *Shrimps–Turtles* report could avoid the issue of extraterritoriality since the US measure was designed to save exhaustible natural resources, which might or might not be confined within national frontiers (sea turtles). When the Appellate Body accepted that sea turtles are an exhaustible natural resource, it effectively by-passed the issue of extraterritoriality. This is of course not the case of labor standards.

Do we need an international agreement on labor standards?

In the absence of an international agreement, as mentioned above, Developia runs the risk of seeing its exports to Oecedia blocked because of its labor standards. Is this risk completely imaginary? Not at all. The EC and US GSP- (Generalized System of Preferences) lists now contain a reference to labor standards and provide developing countries with extra preferences in case they raise their standards (this is the attempt of the EC and the US to avoid regulatory chill by developing countries in this respect). The United States and Jordan agreed to include a labor standards–clause in their free-trade agreement. Belgium enacted a standard (in TBT-parlance), which makes it possible for companies to label fair labor standards-produced goods. There is certainly a growing voice linking trade to labor.

Should then Developia be better off if it is led to the table of negotiations to discuss an international framework for labor standards? This is definitely the case for Developia to decide. It is its sovereign right, as Benvenisti (1999) mentions, however, it belongs to its margin of appreciation to decide whether it should or it should not participate in such a negotiation.

As things stand now, an over-zealous enforcement of public-order-based exceptions to international trade by WTO Members mathematically increases transaction costs. And where does one draw the line? As Henrik Horn in his comments to a previous draft of this chapter suggested to me, what if tomorrow the EC decides not to accept any products from a country which accepts the death penalty and thus bans all US exports to the EC market?

At the same time, it puts into question the very essence of the WTO contract: by forcing trading partners to respect each and every facet of a nationally defined public order, trading partners show little tolerance to regulatory diversity and *de facto* force the internationalization of public order. Is this really the way to go especially when the most ambitious integration process (the European Union) more and more relies on divergence among its constituents?

There is a need for WTO Members to micro-manage their public order. Practice shows that so far there has been a certain self-policing by WTO Members of their respective public orders. The Belgian TBT, the US–Jordan FTA and the GSP lists of the two biggest trading partners show that the picture is changing.

On the other hand, the remedies system in the WTO does not put every WTO Member on the same footing when it comes to providing incentives to act upon their rights (assuming that conditioning market access upon compliance with labor-standards legislation is accepted by WTO case-law as a right) before the WTO adjudicating bodies. There is a gross exaggeration surrounding the effectiveness of the WTO legal system: yes, it is (along with the UNCLOS) the only truly multilateral compulsory third party adjudication-system. But this should not be understood to mean that the system, as it now stands, guarantees always and by all respect of the assumed obligations and effective exercise of rights. Recent discuss in Geneva on implementation of the Uruguay round showed the deplorable record of implementation of the Uruguay round commitments.

If the WTO is not respected, at the end of the day, the complaining party wins the right to take countermeasures. The effectiveness of countermeasures depends on the identity of the complaining party and that of the defendant. Factors such as the extent to which the defendant depends on international trade and/or the particular market, the capacity of the complaining party to cope, for some time at least, by raising costs for its consumers while awaiting a change in the defendants policies (Mavroidis, 2000) will heavily influence the ultimate decision. The point here is that the WTO system is probably effective when the Oecedias of this world take action against the Developias and not the other way round.

It would be quite Machiavellian to suggest that an agreement is needed because in the alternative, Developia will have to comply anyway with labor-standards-based demands. An agreement should come into place if there are good arguments that gains from cooperation exist in case an agreement is concluded. The chapters by Brown et al., and Singh published in this volume suggest that this is not necessarily the case. Staiger, in his chapter, does not address the issue. He assumes that the need for an agreement has been demonstrated and goes on to suggest that the WTO is probably not the appropriate forum for such an enterprise. Before I move to this discussion, there is one final comment that I would like to make. For the reason mentioned above (the effectiveness of the WTO dispute settlement system depends on the identity of the complainant and the defendant) it is probably not so obvious that one should entrust the WTO with the task of enforcing labor standards negotiated elsewhere.

First, trade sanctions, as economic theory suggests, are not the most appropriate instrument to address this externality (assuming an externality indeed exists). Second, proponents of such linkages should keep in mind that to a large extent, by linking trade to labor in this way, they proclaim the United States and the European Union to be policemen of this world. And the incentive structure of either the United States or the European Union does not necessarily coincide with that of a world-policeman. So even a minimal link (agreements are concluded in the ILO, they are enforced at the WTO) should be viewed with scepticism.

But if we are all for it, where should an agreement be negotiated?

Staiger suggests that if the political will to negotiate an agreement about labor standards is taken for granted, such agreement should not be negotiated within the WTO. Lack of institutional expertise in dealing with non-pecuniary externalities is in his view the decisive factor why this would be the case.

I would add that such an issue might lose its intellectual integrity if negotiated in the WTO. WTO negotiations are *quid pro quo*: Oecedia opens its textile trade as consideration for Developia's decision to buy more computers from it. The aim is to strike a deal that will keep two trading partners happy. Should the same logic apply to labor standards? I have my reservations.

First, the case must be made that labor standards should be discussed at the international plane: in plain language the issue will be why should Developia abandon child labor anyway when the alternatives for its children are horrifying, before even investing on establishing plausible alternatives. A case must be made to this effect and this case has not been made.

Can *quid pro quo* negotiations help? They might persuade Developia to abandon child labor faster than anticipated and create even more social unrest at home, or they might not. At any rate however, Developia will not be addressing the issue in its intellectual integrity. Its arm might be twisted towards one direction precisely because of the state of necessity that Developias of this world find themselves to be in.

Finally, there is something to be said about the administrative over-burdens of the WTO. By continuously adding new subjects (while steadily increasing the non-implementation/unfinished business docket), proponents of a new bigger WTO should also keep in mind the potential of the institution to maintain its credibility which could be undermined if the effectiveness of managing the WTO domain is undermined as well.

Acknowledgment

For useful discussion on the issue, I am, as usually, indebted to Henrik Horn af Rantzien.

References

Benvenisti, Eyal (1999) "Margin Of Appreciation, Consensus and Universal Standards," *New York University Journal of International Law and Politics*, 31, pp. 843–54.

Charnovitz, Steve (1998) "The Moral Exception in the GATT," *Virginia Journal of International Law*, 30, pp. 689–746.

Mavroidis, Petros C. (2000) "Remedies in the WTO Legal System: Between a Rock and a Hard Place," *European Journal of International Law*, 4, pp. 763–813.

Palmeter, David and Petros C. Mavroidis (1998) "The WTO Legal System: Sources of Law," *American Journal of International Law*, 92, pp. 398–413.

Trachtman, Joel (1999) "The Domain of WTO Dispute Settlement Resolution," *Harvard Journal of International Law*, 40, pp. 333–77.

Index